'They sought him here, they sought him there, until that damn'd elusive dog was caged in 1994 by French counter-espionage authorities. Carlos's usefulness as a pawn in the Cold War is emphasised in this chilling and briskly written account of the bloody career of a revolutionary finally betrayed by his own masters' *The Times*

'Absolutely brilliant, with a thrill on nearly every page. *Jackal* is probably the best book on international terrorism, with professional knowledge of the criminal underworld, intelligence and sabotage organisation from Moscow to Paris and from Baghdad to Havana. Follain gets the attitudes of the KGB absolutely right and his knowledge of the French scene is just stunning' Oleg Gordievsky, former senior KGB officer, and at the same time British secret agent

'Investigative journalist Follain details the life and philosophy of the Jackal ... Thoroughly researched, this is the first definitive biography of the man who was able to hold the world at bay for over two decades. Recommended' *Library Journal*

'Like a Frederick Forsyth novel, but with ... a more gripping plot: this is ex-Reuters correspondent Follain's exposé of international terrorist Carlos the Jackal, with access to "secret files" and all' *Guardian*

'Essential reading for anyone interested in the history of modern international terrorism. Its brilliant portrayal of the Jackal shows how he was driven by a mixture of dogmatism, hatred, cruelty, and absurd vanity. It is also a timely reminder of the dangers of tolerating and appeasing international terrorism in the post-Cold War era' Professor Paul Wilkinson, Chairman, Centre for the Study of Terrorism and Political Violence, University of St Andrews

'[Follain] admirably fills the gaps and provides Carlos fanciers with many insights ... Few stones remain unturned in his assessment of the rise and fall of the Jackal' Ronald Payne (co-author of *The Carlos Complex*), *Literary Review*

'For a man of Carlos's tastes in liquor, women, silk sheets, the high life and an ill-defined revolutionary zeal, [his arrest] was a bump into reality. The world can never be safe, but this is one less jackal to account for. And, until such time as East European and KGB files may reveal additional material, Follain's book must remain the definitive story' *Canberra Times*

John Follain, who was born in Paris in 1966, studied at Oxford University before starting his journalistic career at Reuters. Following a three-year posting as a foreign correspondent to Rome, he wrote *A Dishonoured Society: The Sicilian Mafia's Threat to Europe*, which received widespread critical acclaim: 'As a snapshot of organised crime in Italy and Southern Europe it has no peer' (*Daily Telegraph*); 'An excellent account of the Mafia's rise from small-time banditry to global power' (*New Statesman and Society*). John Follain was based in Paris for Reuters from 1993 to 1997, and is now the Rome correspondent for the *Sunday Times*.

By the same author

A Dishonoured Society: The Sicilian Mafia's Threat to Europe

Jackal

The Secret Wars of Carlos the Jackal

JOHN FOLLAIN

An Orion Paperback
First published in Great Britain by
Weidenfeld & Nicolson in 1998
This paperback edition published in 1999 by
Orion Books Ltd,
Orion House, 5 Upper St Martin's Lane,
London WC2H 9EA

Fifth impression 2004

A CIP catalogue record for this book
is available from the British Library.

ISBN: 0 75282 669 7

Typeset by Selwood Systems, Midsomer Norton

Printed and bound in Great Britain by
Clays Ltd, St Ives plc

www.orionbooks.co.uk

To my family

Jackal, wolflike carnivore of the dog genus *Canis*, family Canidae, sharing with the hyenas an exaggerated reputation for cowardice.

Jackals inhabit more or less open country. Nocturnal animals, they usually conceal themselves by day in brush or thickets and sally forth at dusk to hunt. They live alone, in pairs, or in packs and feed on whatever small animals, plant material or carrion is available. They follow lions and other large cats in order to finish a carcass when the larger animal has eaten its fill, and when hunting in packs they are able to bring down prey as large as antelopes and sheep.

Like other members of the genus, jackals sing at evening; their cry is more dismaying than that of the hyena.

The New Encyclopaedia Britannica

GREAT BRITAIN
DENMARK
North Sea
NETH.
The Hague
London
W. GER.
Berlin
E. GER.
POLAND
BELG
Bonn
Frankfurt
Prague
CZECH.
Saint Nom
la Bretêche
Paris
Munich
Vienna
Zurich
Bern
Gstaad
SWITZ
AUST.
Budapest
HUNGARY
ROMANIA
Trieste
Limoges
Lyon
Brioni Islands
Belgrade
Bucharest
FRANCE
YUGOSLAVIA
Marseille
Rome
BULGARIA
ITALY
ALBANIA
PORT
SPAIN
GREECE
Athens
Algiers
Tunis
Valletta
MALTA
TUNISIA
Mediterranean Sea
Tripoli
ALGERIA
LIBYA
Beirut
LEBANON
Damascus
SYRIA
ISRAEL
Ajlun
Jerash
Tel Aviv
Lod
Amman
Jerusalem
JORDAN
MALI
NIGER
CHAD

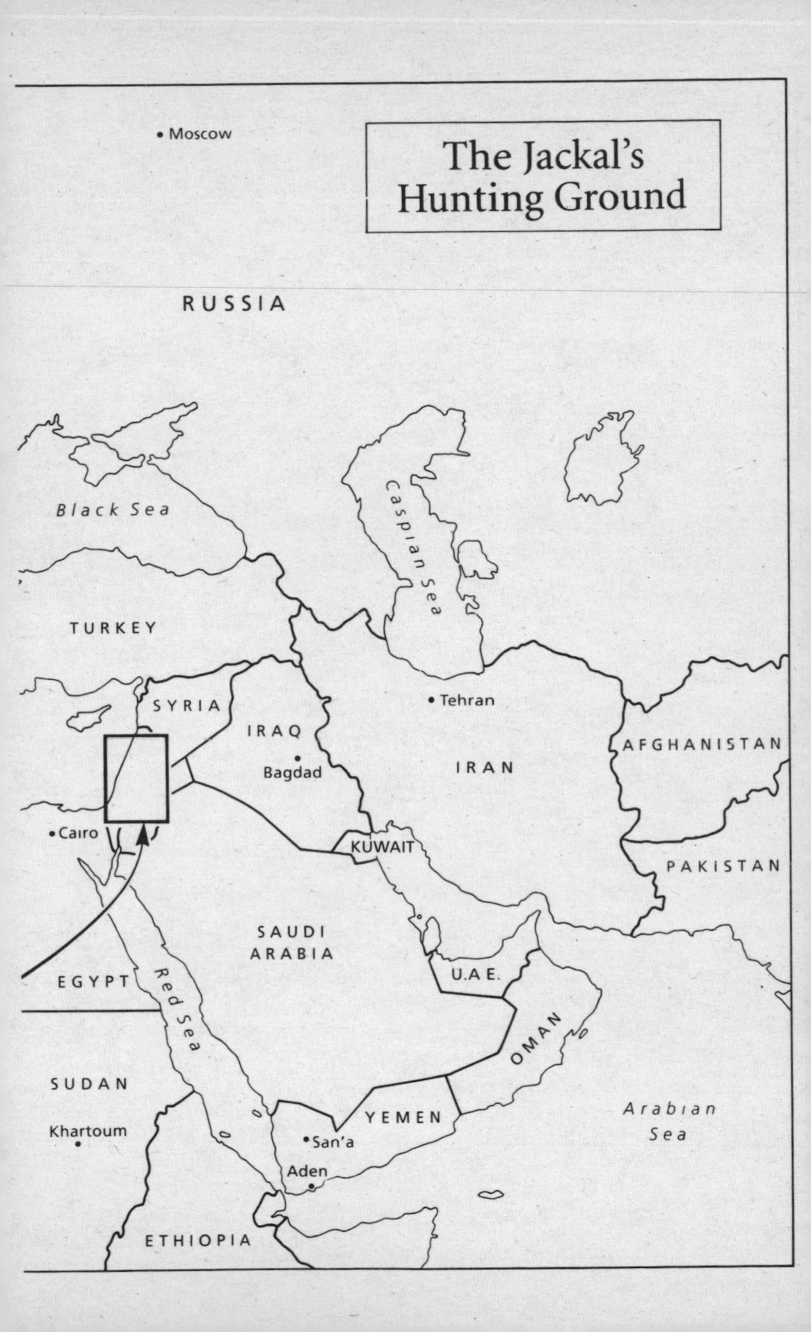
The Jackal's Hunting Ground
Moscow
RUSSIA
Black Sea
Caspian Sea
TURKEY
SYRIA
IRAQ
Tehran
Bagdad
IRAN
AFGHANISTAN
Cairo
KUWAIT
PAKISTAN
SAUDI ARABIA
EGYPT
Red Sea
U.A.E.
OMAN
SUDAN
YEMEN
Arabian Sea
Khartoum
San'a
Aden
ETHIOPIA

Contents

Principal Characters

The Carlos Organisation

Johannes Weinrich Carlos's right-hand man, Paris and East Berlin
Ali Al Issawe Syrian intelligence officer, also a key Carlos accomplice
Magdalena Kopp Carlos's first wife
Hans-Joachim Klein Member of West German Revolutionary Cells
Gabriele Kröcher-Tiedemann Member of West German Revolutionary Cells
Nydia Tobon Colombian lawyer, and Carlos's lover, London
Fouad Awad Alias Antonio Dagues-Bouvier, Lebanese former army officer
Bruno Bréguet Swiss militant
Christa-Margot Froelich West German teacher, former member of the Red Army Faction

The Palestinians

Dr George Habash Founder and leader of the Popular Front for the Liberation of Palestine (referred to as the Popular Front)
Dr Wadi Haddad Chief of foreign operations, Popular Front

Bassam Abu-Sharif Chief recruiting officer, Popular Front
Mohamed Boudia Chief European representative, Popular Front
Michel Moukharbal Boudia's successor

The French

Count Alexandre de Marenches Chief, Service de Documentation Extérieure et de Contre-Espionnage (SDECE, the foreign intelligence service)
Pierre Marion De Marenches's successor at the SDECE, which he renamed the Direction Générale de la Sécurité Extérieure (DGSE)
Yves Bonnet Chief, Direction de la Surveillance du Territoire (DST, the counter-intelligence service)
General Philippe Rondot Arabist, associated with the SDECE and then the DST
Commissaire Jean Herranz Chief, B-2 Middle East division, DST
Commissaire Pierre Ottavioli Chief, Brigade Criminelle (police criminal investigation unit)
Gaston Defferre Interior Minister
Charles Pasqua One of Defferre's successors as Interior Minister
Jean-Louis Bruguière Chief investigating magistrate, anti-terrorism section, Paris
Jacques Vergès Carlos's lawyer

The Americans

Duane R. Clarridge Deputy chief, Near East Division for Arab Operations, CIA, then Head of Counter-Terrorist Center, CIA
John Siddel Head of Paris station, CIA

Mark Palmer Deputy Assistant Secretary Responsible for Eastern Europe and the Soviet Union, State Department

The East Germans

General Erich Mielke Minister of State Security, or the Stasi secret police
General Markus Wolf Chief, Stasi foreign intelligence
Colonel Harry Dahl Chief, counter-terrorism, Stasi
Lieutenant-Colonel Helmut Voigt Chief, international counter-terrorism division, Stasi

The Hungarians

General Miklos Redei Chief, counter-intelligence, State Security
Colonel Andreas Petresevics Chief, counter-terrorism unit

The Syrians

Hafez al-Assad President
Rifaat al-Assad Hafez's brother, Chief of the Defence Brigades
General Mohamed Al-Khuli Chief, air force intelligence

The Sudanese

Sheik Hassan al-Turabi Speaker of Parliament
General Hachim Abou Zeid Chief, Sudanese secret service

Illustrations

[1] Frank Spooner Pictures
[2] SYGMA, Paris
[3] Camera Press Ltd

Prologue

The evening of Sunday, 30 December 1973 was so cold that the tall, heavily built man who strode through St John's Wood wore a woollen scarf over the lower part of his face, the fur-lined hood of his green army surplus parka over his head. In the pocket of his parka was an Italian-made, 9mm Beretta pistol.

As on many London streets, half the lights of Queen's Grove had been turned off because of the energy crisis caused by an Arab oil embargo, which had come on top of a coal miners' strike. The Heath government had appealed for people to use coal, electricity and petrol sparingly. Industry had slowed to a three-day week. That morning the Queen had set an example when she had dispensed with her usual cortège to travel to the parish church at Sandringham by mini-bus – only to find Prince Charles appearing alongside his friend Lady Jane Wellesley, and drawing a record postwar crowd of 10,000 people to the royal estate, virtually all of whom had come by car.

The man turned off the wide pavement of the leafy avenue, swung open the wrought-iron gate at number 48, and walked up the paved path to the porticoed entrance of a mock-Georgian mansion. Two imposing columns flanked the entrance, which was topped by a white frieze of a deer resting gracefully. The house was home to Joseph Edward Sieff, the president of Marks and Spencer. As honorary vice-president of the British Zionist Federation, Sieff had helped to raise millions of pounds for Israeli charities. Like all prominent Jewish businessmen in London, he had recently been warned by Scotland Yard to be on the look-out for booby-trapped mail sent by Palestinian terrorists.

Manuel Perloira, the young Portuguese butler who answered the doorbell, opened the door to a stranger with a dark complexion who appeared to be in his mid-twenties. The stranger was pointing a gun at him. 'Take me to Sieff.' The order was spoken quietly, in heavily accented English that the butler could not place. With the gun trained on the small of his back, Perloira led the way up the stairs to the master bedroom. The stranger showed no interest in the paintings by Gainsborough, Tiepolo and Warhol hanging on the walls. From the first-floor landing, Sieff's American-born second wife Lois saw the gunman pushing the butler up the stairs. She rushed into her bedroom, closed the door behind her and telephoned the police. Her call was logged at two minutes past seven.

It did not take long to find Sieff. The sixty-eight-year-old, whose stern expression was softened by glasses that gave him a slightly owlish look, was in the bathroom getting ready for dinner. He heard the butler calling him and pushed the door open. All he saw was a leather-gloved hand clutching a revolver, and he froze in disbelief. The gun jerked like a startled rodent. The bullet, fired from only a metre away, thudded into Sieff's face and he slumped to the floor. Standing in the doorway of the bathroom, the stranger brought his arm down and, aiming at the unconscious Sieff, tried again and again to squeeze off another shot, but his pistol had jammed. At four minutes past seven – two minutes after the anguished call by Sieff's wife – a police car drew up outside the house. The gunman fled, without knowing whether his mission had been accomplished. No one saw which way he went.

Sieff had come within a centimetre of death, but survived. The bullet bore a hole through his skin just above the upper lip but was deflected by exceptionally strong front teeth and bone away from his jugular vein, lodging in his jaw instead. He would have choked to death on his own blood had his wife not made him lie on his stomach. The surgeons who operated on him that night removed not only the bullet but also fragments of bone that had been embedded in his jaw. When he recovered sufficiently to speak, he told a visitor: 'The door of the bathroom opened and I saw a gun and that was it. The next thing I remembered I was here in hospital.'

For an apprentice assassin, it was a disappointing baptism. But the novice had shown daring, kept his nerve throughout, and managed to get away unharmed. The would-be murderer's name was Ilich Ramírez Sánchez. The Jackal had thrown down the first marker in his trail of terror.

1

Marx and the Holy Cross

> I acknowledge that my name is Ilich Ramírez Sánchez alias Carlos, born in 1949 in Caracas in Venezuela. I am an international revolutionary.
>
> – Carlos to French counter-intelligence

There was no argument over the surname of the boy born at the Razetti clinic in Caracas at five o'clock in the morning of 12 October 1949. He was given the surnames of both his Marxist father and his Catholic mother, Ramírez and Sánchez, as is common in Spanish-speaking nations. The sticking point was the first name.

Elba Maria Sánchez pleaded to be allowed to give her first child a Christian name, but her husband was adamant. 'The biggest man in all humanity,' he would often insist, 'is Vladimir Ilich Ulyanov, alias Lenin. Humanity before the bomb is divided into two periods. Before and after Lenin, not Christ who was an ordinary, run-of-the-mill man.'[1]

So José Altagracia Ramírez Navas rode roughshod over his wife's objections and, ignoring the registrar's raised eyebrows, paid his personal tribute to the father of the Bolshevik Revolution with a few strokes of his pen. Years later, the *nom de guerre* under which his son became notorious infuriated him: 'Why do they call him the Jackal? His name is Ilich. It is a proud name, the name of a revolutionary.'[2] Within hours of his birth, Ilich Ramírez

Sánchez embodied – if only by his name – the revolutionary ideals of his father.

A land both Caribbean and South American, Venezuela had been dubbed 'the land of grace' by Columbus who had discovered it on his third voyage to the New World in 1498. But his legacy failed to live up to that name, as Spanish conquerors massacred native Americans or traded them as slaves. In the early nineteenth century at least 150,000 Venezuelans died in the country's independence wars, and home-bred revolutionaries strayed further afield to spearhead liberation across much of South America. Devastated by the fighting, its economy in ruins, the young nation staggered through a mess of coups and civil wars. After years of bloody stagnation, the discovery of oil in the early twentieth century would in time transform the prospects of the country.

Like the four dictators who ruled Venezuela in the first half of the century, Ilich Ramírez Sánchez was born in the western state of Tachira. Aggressive pig-headedness, mixed with a strong religious streak, is popularly held to be common among its people. It is as if the Andes, piercing through the small province, serves as a rigid backbone to the local character. Natives of Tachira and other Andean provinces are also known for an odd physical characteristic: the tops of their heads slope rather than curve downwards at the back, something Venezuelans joke is due to mothers slapping their children across the head. The Tachira state capital San Cristobal nestles on a damp plateau 900 metres above sea level, a few hundred kilometres short of where the Andes sink into the Caribbean. The architecture of the cathedral and palaces bears witness to the Spanish colonialists who founded the city.

Ramírez Navas had the inflexible convictions of the disillusioned drawn to a new faith. In his youth he had felt a religious vocation and enrolled at the St Thomas Aquinas seminary run by the French Eudist order. But he abruptly turned his back on the Church to proclaim himself an atheist while still a teenager. 'I studied to be a priest for three years and I swallowed 1800 hosts before realising when I was sixteen or seventeen years old that it was a lie,' recalled the adult Ramírez Navas, a slight, dapper figure with deep-set eyes and wiry hair.[3] The seminary drop-out abandoned his theology textbooks, packed his bags and returned home to the small town of Michelena in Tachira in the early 1930s. Another clash with the powers that be awaited him, but this time with the secular authorities. He was expelled from Tachira for sheltering an outlaw in his study. The authorities labelled him a Communist, although he protests: 'I didn't even know what the word meant.'[4]

He found out soon enough. His spiritual vocation in shreds, the young Ramírez Navas crossed the nearby border into Colombia and started studying for a law degree at the Free University in Bogotá. His discovery of the works of Marx and Lenin, allied with his personal experience of the harshness of the regime governing Venezuela, fanned his spirit of rebellion. He drifted into the circles of two prominent left-wingers living in Bogotá, the Colombian Jorge Eliécer Gaitán who became his friend, and the exiled Gustavo Machado, a leading light of Venezuela's banned Communist Party. By the time he had completed his studies at the Central University in Caracas, and launched his career in Tachira where he had been allowed to return, the disoriented failed priest had become a diehard Marxist-Leninist.

The mid-1930s was a time of stimulating turmoil for the left in Venezuela. For the greater part of the previous three decades a suspicious cattle rancher who looked very much like Stalin, General Juan Vincente Gómez, had ruled like a tyrant. His dictatorship had nipped leftist and all other opposition in the bud with an efficient secret police and an ambitious programme to build new roads and improve communications. Both ensured that no rival, even those headstrong agitators from his native province of Tachira, could marshal a force large enough to challenge him without his finding out and quickly crushing any rebellion. A stereotypical Latin American despot with a splendid handlebar moustache, and the father of more than a hundred children (the general never married), Gómez trod so warily that he stopped the citizens of Caracas from creating a Rotary Club because he feared it might turn political. So efficient was his apparatus of repression that he lost power in 1935 only because he died a natural, peaceful death at the age of seventy-nine.

In the euphoria that followed the general's passing, Ramírez Navas was involved in the setting up of Democratic Action, a new party led by the outspoken idealist Romulo Betancourt. But the lawyer suffered yet further disillusionment: after the party wrested power in a broad-based revolution in 1945, he became convinced that as far as political honesty went there was little to choose between his friends now in power and their predecessors. He said so, and was detained for a brief period because of his outspokenness. On his release, he swung towards the pro-Soviet Communist Party, which, dogged by persecution under successive regimes, had operated underground until the early 1940s. For all his ideological commitment, Ramírez Navas disapproved of the party's apparatchiks. In his own view they were too conservative and he never signed up as a member – yet another example of the strong streak of independence in his character.

His chosen dogma did not stop him upholding a legal system that gave pride of place to private property and capitalism. He was successful in his profession, and became well established in the provincial capital San Cristobal. Opposites attract, it is said, and the woman ten years his junior with whom Ramírez Navas fell in love, and whom he married in 1948, was as determinedly Catholic as he was atheist. Born in San Cristobal, the attractive, dark-haired and sociable Elba had been more lastingly marked by the local religious streak and never did reconcile herself to her husband's intolerance of her faith, nor to his infidelity. She too was strong-minded, but she lost the battle over the name of her first-born.

From Ramírez Navas's own account, his eldest son also paid quite a price for his father's revolutionary fervour and for the Leninist incarnation imposed on him at birth, a year after another *coup d'état* ushered in a new period of military rule. There was no question of Ilich reliving his father's wasted years sitting on hard church benches or dissecting the Holy Bible. The Marxist doctrine that Ramírez Navas had discovered as an undergraduate was drummed into Ilich long before he reached puberty. The demolition of Stalin's personality cult by Khrushchev in 1956, when Ilich was seven years old, did nothing to sway his father. By the age of ten, the father trumpeted, Ilich had read Trotsky's *Life of Lenin* not once, but twice. (There is no such work: perhaps Ramírez Navas was referring to Trotsky's *Lenin: Notes for a Biographer*, or to the same author's *Stalin*.)

The boy met his parents' high expectations. 'Although the father was rigid, he was also loving and very worried about his family,' remembered Mireya Gonzalez de Ruiz, a childhood friend of Ilich and his two younger brothers, Lenin and Vladimir (they were born in Caracas in 1951 and 1958), who like several other children feared the strict disciplinarian. 'The one Ramírez Navas liked best was Ilich. Everything he did his father would praise. He was definitely the favourite.'[5] Neither Lenin nor Vladimir lived up to their names, and their father's hopes of spawning 'valiant Communists' proved forlorn, although Ramírez Navas once confusedly described his second son Lenin as 'a Marxist-Leninist but not interested in politics'.[6]

Ramírez Navas made sure that his first-born's childhood, although inevitably bourgeois by virtue of his own legal profession, included the legends of South American revolution. Again and again Ilich heard from his father that God does not exist and that a man must fight to be strong. There was no lack of gun-wielding, revolution-preaching ancestors for the young Ilich to live up to in what was, after all, the homeland of the most revered of all South American independence heroes, the great Libertador Simón Bolívar whose statue graces virtually every Venezuelan city, town and village.

An uncle of Ilich had taken part in the coup which overthrew President Isaias Medina in 1945. But the family hero was Elba's grandfather, a doctor who transformed a sixty-strong band of followers into an army big enough to help overthrow the government in Caracas in 1899, only to lose power a few years later. Unbowed, the doctor repeatedly tried to assassinate the Tachira state governor, resisting the forces sent after him in a courageous last and lone stand to give his comrades time to flee into the Andes. Ilich delighted in the tales of how the doctor, after he was caught, refused to betray his companions under torture. 'Physically, he was slender, powerful. A handsome man who emerged from torture with a stoop,' Ilich recalled. 'He revealed no names. He remained in jail for seven years, in heavy iron chains which were never removed, even during torture. His wife loved him for his virility and his good looks. He was released, but his family had lost everything.'[7]

The indoctrination of her eldest son rested to a significant extent on her own family tree, but Elba reacted to it with growing resentment. Physically, Ilich took after her rather than Ramírez Navas: the round face and full lips, the pale complexion that flushes easily and even the soft, high-pitched voice are all Elba's legacy. The aquiline nose, however, marked him out as his father's son. Frustrated that her resistance had proved so fruitless, she complained bitterly to her friends about the outlandish names given to her three children. Defying her dogmatic spouse and aided by a local priest, she managed, according to friends of the family, to have Ilich baptised in secret.When Ramírez Navas was busy receiving clients or away at the law courts, she would furtively shepherd the brothers to mass. This clandestine struggle waged by Elba did not, however, have a lasting result. Reminiscing about his childhood, Ilich dismisses the Roman Catholic faith much as his father had: 'Marxism was my religion for a long time, not Catholicism. For hereditary reasons really. It was in the atmosphere of my home, in my parents' blood.'[8]

Ilich is unwilling to talk about Elba. 'I have very strong ties with my mother. She is a very courageous and honest woman,' is all he would say in his judicial testimony.[9] He refuses to describe her or go into the disputes that rocked the household, but the courage he admires in his mother was as much a tribute to her refusal to be browbeaten by her domineering husband as to the way she came to terms with her eldest son's career. Ilich was more expansive with his friends, telling one that Elba was beautiful, gentle, sensitive and unpretentious, and that she loved nature and socialising.[10] According to one friend, Elba was 'the only thing he really loved'. He would have done anything for his cultured mother and always spoke of her with great tenderness.[11]

Ilich describes the father who spoon-fed him Communist ideology as 'a man of conviction, with an almost religious concept of his commitment'. Any suggestion that the lawyer was a millionaire angered Ilich: 'You know, there are a lot of fibs about that. There are people in our family who are much richer. My uncle, for example, who owns a coffee plantation. He lives in San Cristobal. As for my father, he's comfortably off. That's all.'[12] In fact, his father owns several agricultural properties, and Ilich labelled the family's social origins as '*petit bourgeois*'. However Ilich did not think much of the names that his father had dreamed up for his offspring: 'It was bloody stupid of my father to give his children such weird names. That kind of thing weighs on the children. In my case it was fortunate, but things were different for my brothers. They are not ashamed of their names, but it did cause them problems later in life.'[13]

Childhood friends of the family, who played with Ilich and his brothers in San Cristobal during the holidays, could not help noticing the uneasy nature of the parents' marriage, fuelled by the father's extra-marital affairs and the incompatible convictions of the two partners. Whenever the father was present the brothers would be stiff and cold as they did their best to live up to the instructions codified in a pamphlet on ethical behaviour which he wrote for them, *Social, Moral and Civic Formation.* 'I tell anybody the truth to his face,' was one of the father's mottoes.[14] In Elba's company, the brothers softened and became more gentle.

Ilich was tall for his age, handsome but heavily built. The nickname 'El Gordo' (Fatso) would bring him near to tears and prompt him to shout back furiously and shrilly, his face flushed scarlet: 'The whole world will hear of me.' But for a time Ilich was sheltered from such taunts. His father's successful career meant that he could afford to hire Communist teachers to give Ilich lessons in the privacy and comfort of the family home. Not that the son had sought out such seclusion; indeed he came to resent it because he had less opportunity to play with other children: 'We studied at home, we had a private instructor. That's not normal.'[15]

Ilich was a natural figure of authority for his playmates. 'When there was a game to be organised, Ilich was always the one who would do it. He was the leader. He would decide, but not in an authoritarian manner. He was the most organised, the one who took the initiative and made the rules,' according to Emir Ruiz, a boyhood friend. His favourite game was hide-and-seek, a pastime that loomed large later in life. 'Ilich liked to play at goodies and baddies with plastic weapons. In our group he was the strongest and the most aggressive.'[16] It was from Ilich that his friends learned how to tip their arrows with metal to avoid making a mess of the small birds they hunted. Whenever a game ended, he and Lenin would rush to the bathroom to clean up, Ilich emerging with his generous head of hair neatly combed and his nails scrubbed. Organising afternoon snacks for the children was also his domain.

Partly because the marriage was under particular strain, Elba took the three sons on an extended tour from late 1958 which disrupted Ilich's education and affected his academic record. The first school he attended was a Protestant establishment in Kingston, Jamaica, before moving on shortly afterwards to Mexico, then back to Jamaica and later to Caracas. When Elba went to live in Bogotá for a period with the sickly baby Vladimir, Ilich stayed on in Caracas with his father and Lenin. Ilich learned the hard way how to adjust to constantly changing countries, schools and classmates, although this was cushioned by his aptitude for languages, a skill inherited from his father.

The years of travel ended in early 1961, giving husband and wife pause for thought. For years Elba, faithful to her Catholic beliefs, had resisted the idea of divorce advocated relentlessly by her husband. She had agreed to marry a failed seminarist and a Marxist, but she drew the line at divorcing him. Elba finally relented, however, and the marriage ended when Ilich was barely a teenager, although the couple, unusually, decided to continue living together in Caracas. Ramírez Navas bluntly explained: 'I got divorced because in my house I thought that I was the only one who did anything right.'[17]

The divorce was a relief for Ilich. Years afterwards, he recalled: 'my father would bring his mistresses home. My mother suffered because of this. We lived together, but it was unbearable ... I was very pleased about the divorce. My brothers took it less well.'[18] In his judicial deposition, his single and brief reference to the painful episode is in sharp contrast to the rest of his testimony: 'My parents divorced in 1962 or 1963 but they continued to cohabit until 1966.'[19] He was always surprisingly precise about dates, but of his parents' separation he could not remember even the exact year. Rather than a failing of his prodigious memory, this was perhaps an unconscious attempt to avoid recalling a painful event.

In 1962, just as she had lost the battle over her children's first names, so Elba failed to stop her husband sending Ilich to the sprawling Fermin Toro lycée in Caracas, which was nursery to budding radicals at a time when the capital's streets often resounded with violent left-wing demonstrations. The more enterprising students skipped classes to march in protest at the liberal government's ban on the Communist Party. 'This school was renowned. All the revolutionaries had studied there,' Ilich recalled. 'It was my father's decision. As for my mother, she was hardly enthusiastic about the choice. Did my father choose this school on purpose to annoy my mother?'[20]

By his own testimony it was in January 1964, when he was fourteen, that Ilich defied authority for the first time. He joined an organisation banned by the authorities, the Venezuelan Communist Youth: 'That's where I made my début in the revolutionary movement. I was one of those in charge of the organisation in a lycée in Caracas.'[21] In 1965–6, that young flock counted some 200 members and Ilich claims that he helped to organise anti-government street marches which scared the President, Raul Leoni. The protests also taught Ilich how to make Molotov cocktails and set cars on fire, while visits to the shanty towns on the outskirts of Caracas, he later claimed, revealed to him the plight of the poor. But Ilich did not impress his contemporaries, and it is likely that he depicts his exploits in excessively glowing terms. The president of the Venezuelan Communist Party, Pedro Ortega Diaz, testified in a letter to judicial authorities in Caracas: 'His activity was normal and we can find no outstanding event.'[22]

'Revolution is my supreme euphoria,' Ilich once declared.[23] That his first taste of such euphoria came courtesy of both Cuba's Fidel Castro and the Soviet Union's State Security Committee, better known as the KGB, was for long considered an unassailable truth by the media.

His father is said to have sent Ilich to Cuba, probably late in 1966, to complete his education at a political indoctrination camp which also ran courses in sabotage techniques. Camp Mantanzas, not far from Havana, was run by Fidel Castro's secret service, the Direccion General de Inteligencia (DGI), and the local KGB boss, General Viktor Semenov. According to two writers, Ilich was the DGI's 'prize alumnus'.[24] His instructors are said to have included an Ecuadorian guerrilla expert and senior KGB official, Antonio Dagues-Bouvier, who reportedly took him in hand from then on. Ilich is also said to have met Father Camillo Torres, a Colombian priest turned guerrilla chief who fought alongside Che Guevara. Many years later a French Interior Minister gave credence to these reports, writing that Ilich underwent 'terrorist training in Cuba (automatic arms, explosives, bombs, mines, destruction of pipelines, cryptography, photography, falsification of documents, etc.)'.[25]

Rather than confirm or deny that he was given this guerrilla training, Ilich today prefers to hide behind the rules of the first revolutionary movement he joined. Asked during his judicial testimony whether he went to Cuba, perhaps in 1966, Ilich invokes his duty as a party member: 'There is a discipline in the Venezuelan Communist Youth to which I belonged at the time. I don't have the right to speak in its name. And you should ask the Venezuelan Communist Party which still exists whether I went to Cuba at that time. And the Cuban authorities too.'[26]

But when pressed, he dismissed what he called 'outrageous stories about this supposed Cuban episode which border on the soap opera. I read that I went to the Mantanzas camp and was trained in terrorist methods. All that is fable.'[27] He also denied ever meeting Father Torres. It is highly unlikely that Ilich did meet Father Torres in Cuba, as the priest was killed in action against the Colombian army in February 1966.[28] There is another date that does not tally. General Semenov was in fact appointed to head the KGB operation in Havana in 1968, two years after Ilich is said to have passed through.

The reports that Ilich's rite of passage took place in Fidel Castro's shadow are CIA propaganda. When the report was first circulated, the CIA let it be known that it was based on revelations from Orlando Castro Hidalgo, a DGI defector from the Cuban embassy in Paris who had supposedly told the agency that Ilich was among as many as 1500 Latin Americans trained in Cuba every year, adding that Venezuelans tended to focus on guerrilla operations and sabotage techniques. Today a former head of the counter-terrorism division at the CIA, who has consulted the agency's file on Ilich, admits that the CIA had no evidence whatsoever that he had trained in Cuba.

Western security forces had not waited to hear any such admissions to pour cold water over these reports. A profile drawn up by France's homicide squad, the Brigade Criminelle, struck a dubious note: 'US intelligence gives it to be understood that Ilich may have been sent to Cuba by his father in 1966.'[29] The recruitment of Ilich by the DGI, it concludes, is at best difficult and at worst impossible to establish.

Had Ilich studied at university in his homeland, perhaps he would have emerged in the same mould as his rebellious ancestors: a revolutionary in the best local Zapatista tradition, marching down from the heights of Tachira state to overthrow Venezuelan dictatorships. Venezuelans are notoriously reluctant to emigrate, loath to leave the white

Caribbean beaches, snowy Andean peaks and steamy jungles about which the tourist guidebooks enthuse. But his father Ramírez Navas was unhappy with Ilich's new activism, and worried that his eldest son might come to some harm in the violent street protests rocking Caracas. In 1966 Ramírez Navas resolved to send Ilich and his brothers to study an ocean away, in London, accompanied by Elba. Under their mother's protective wing, the boys stood to benefit from learning a new language and experiencing European culture at first hand.

The tail end of the swinging 1960s, London's nightlife and above all its liberated young women were a revelation to Ilich. Years later he recalled that he had no difficulty adapting to life on a different continent, nor did he feel homesick in London where he arrived in August 1966. Often sharing a bedroom, the three brothers lived with their mother in a series of rented flats in west London, the first of which was in Earls Court.

Ilich studied initially at Stafford House Tutorial College, a sixth-form crammer in Kensington where he took O-levels in English, physics, chemistry and mathematics. His teachers at the select institution did not take kindly to the seventeen-year-old, complaining of his laziness and irritating verbosity. 'He was a snide little blighter,' was his English teacher Hilary King's unflattering appraisal. 'He was quite convinced he was God's gift to everyone. He was podgy and pasty but he was always incredibly elegantly and expensively dressed. He was a cheat and would avoid doing work whenever he could.' Indolence did not prevent the clever Ilich, who had mastered English before he came to London, successfully passing his O-level exams, and he moved on to study A-levels at the Earls Court Tutorial College.

In the absence of Ramírez Navas, Ilich took on a paternal role in the eyes of the youngest of his two brothers, Vladimir. 'My brother was a father-figure to me,' Vladimir recalled. 'He told me how to behave, as a family member and as an exemplary citizen. He always seemed to me a very correct, very good and very moral person. He was not violent, he had an affable manner and he was an affectionate brother.'[30]

British newspapers have made much of one violent hobby in which the two older brothers Ilich and Lenin supposedly indulged. They are both said to have learned to handle firearms at the Royal Kensington Rifle and Pistol Club. Former members of the club have been quoted anonymously as remembering two smartly dressed young Venezuelans. The club's records, however, carry no trace of the two brothers, nor did they sign up for the three-month probationary period usual for prospective members. According to the results of an investigation by Scotland Yard's SO13 anti-terrorism branch, Ilich and Lenin never went near the club.

Rather than gunfire, it was the sound of champagne corks popping that interested Ilich during this period. Dressed to look older than his teenage years in a navy blue blazer or a smart suit complete with waistcoat, he escorted his gregarious mother to the receptions that Latin American embassies laid on for the expatriate community. Judging by a rare photograph of him at one cocktail party, filial duty was not his only motivation for attending such gatherings. Hair parted immaculately, eyes shining greedily and a crooked smile on his face, Ilich stands behind his bejewelled mother, his left hand clutching the arm of an attractive, dark-haired girl who stands stiffly beside him. 'The society life of a Latin American playboy,' scoffed French police years later.[31]

Ilich had no qualms about admitting his love of luxury, and professed his admiration for the way of life advocated by the Greek philosopher Epicurus based on simple pleasure and friendship. 'I like good food, I like to drink and I like good cigars,' Ilich confessed. 'I like to sleep in a comfortable bed which has just been made. I like to wear good shoes. I like to play cards, poker and blackjack. I also like parties and dances. But I am against "possessions". What I possess belongs to others as much as to me.'[32] The pleasures he was fond of, Ilich proclaimed, could all be renounced for 'life, duty, revolution'.

Shortly after arriving in London he met a group of young British activists who wanted to set up an international Communist students' organisation. Ilich has been widely credited with helping to create this, but in fact he dropped out after attending only one gathering 'because I realised that we had the police on our backs day and night'.[33] Ilich cut his political teeth in a more discreet fashion. A mission entrusted to him by an emissary of Lieutenant-Colonel Juan De Dios Moncada Vidal, leader of the revolutionary Armed Forces of National Liberation, the main Venezuelan guerrilla group active in the 1960s and 1970s, provided his first introduction to the Communist East bloc: 'I was asked to organise young Venezuelan Communists in Eastern Europe. I said that I was ready to carry out this mission.'[34]

Ilich's efforts were cut short when his father flew in from Venezuela in late 1967. Ramírez Navas's plan was for Ilich and Lenin to move on from London to take a university degree at the Sorbonne in Paris, and he took them across the Channel on an exploratory trip to find out about courses and student accommodation. It was the brothers' first taste of the French capital. Father and sons paced the ornate lecture halls and never-ending corridors of the venerable Sorbonne as the equally venerable French bureaucracy slowly revealed the secrets of the Byzantine entrance procedure.

But their efforts were wasted because of the May 1968 riots, when the Latin Quarter erupted with students manning barricades, hoisting the red flag and hurling stones at the hated CRS police. Despite the fact that the biggest student and worker revolt in recent French history was to a large extent inspired by kindred Marxists, Ilich's father had no intention of seeing his offspring take to the barricades – and perhaps be counted among the 800 people injured during that upheaval. France was judged too unsettled an environment, and the Sorbonne plan was abandoned.

Instead Ramírez Navas decided to send the brothers to Moscow, which only the previous year had celebrated the fiftieth anniversary of the Bolshevik Revolution. The father's lobbying of the cultural attaché at the Soviet embassy in London paid off, although the diplomat cannot have appreciated his theatrical assurance that 'we have not been, are not and never would be' members of Venezuela's Communist Party. Ilich and Lenin won places at the Patrice Lumumba University in Moscow, starting in September 1968.

Again the shadow of the KGB falls across Ilich's path. Did his university entrance mark his recruitment by the Soviet secret service, as many have speculated? Ilich is eager to fuel the mystery. 'Even before I arrived in Moscow, I got in touch with the KGB in London through the resident at the Soviet embassy. Thanks to this contact I was able to get a visa for Moscow and a plane ticket, despite the fact that I hadn't been granted a scholarship that year because it had gone to my brother Lenin. This gave me a certain weight in Moscow,' he said in his testimony to French investigators.[35]

But at his next deposition Ilich backtracked: 'During my previous questioning, I had told you that the KGB resident in London had offered me a plane ticket for Moscow. In fact, this is untrue. The ticket was offered to me, but I refused it. I paid it out of my own pocket with the money my father had given me. I had to take a British airline flight.'[36] And before another French judge some time later, he confessed that his contradictory statements were part of a plot to draw attention to his plight. 'I had to do something that would come out in the newspapers. "Carlos and the KGB" – I was sure that would come out. In the summer of 1968 I was eighteen and a half. Do you really think that a young man of that age would know the KGB resident in London? Come on, that's ridiculous!'[37]

Had he lied the first time, or was he worried that he had gone too far in speaking about a 'Kremlin connection'? The records of the Venezuelan Communist Party show that Ilich obtained a study grant from the Soviet-Venezuelan House of Friendship, a fact confirmed by the party's president in a letter to investigators and which reflected some form of Soviet endorsement.[38]

The Patrice Lumumba University, which was also known as the University of Friendship Between Peoples, served as a training ground for the ruling classes of the Soviet Union's Third World client states. The very name was a denunciation of its Cold War foe: in the autumn of 1960 it was with the CIA's blessing that a young colonel in the Congolese army, Joseph Mobutu, had arrested Prime Minister Lumumba. A vital asset for Moscow's African ambitions, Lumumba was then tortured and assassinated. Mobutu had had no need of the dozen or so poisons concocted by the CIA, ready to mix with the Prime Minister's food or toothpaste.

'Going to Moscow was a dream for us,' Ilich said years later.[39] He and his younger brother started the course within weeks of Soviet tanks rolling into Czechoslovakia to crush the heady 'Prague Spring'. But they soon found that discipline at the cosmopolitan university, whose 6000 students were all selected through the Communist Party of their country of origin, was as stifling as its modernist architecture. Drab grey concrete blocks squatted around a charmless artificial pond. The only dash of colour was a map of the world painted on to the façade of one block in a valiant attempt to symbolise the ideals of the university:

from an open book, symbol of learning, a torch emerges, issuing multicoloured flames that spread like waves across the planisphere. Perhaps Ilich drew some comfort from glancing up at the mural as, huddled against the rigours of the Russian winter and wearing a black beret in tribute to Che Guevara who had died riddled by bullets in October of the previous year, he trudged across the bleak square on his way to lectures. Coincidentally, the base of the flame is very close to Venezuela.

Rules and regulations governed virtually every aspect of Ilich's life from the moment he started the first year's induction course, which was designed to flesh out his knowledge of the Russian language and introduce him to the delights of Marxist society before he launched into his chosen subjects, languages and chemistry. Like father, like son. Ilich rebelled against the rules, preferring to spend his time chasing girls. He would often crawl back to his room drunk. His professors at the university, some of them children of Spanish Civil War veterans who had sought refuge in Moscow, were unimpressed by his academic performance.

'His name alone, Ilich Ramírez Sánchez, was so strange that people were curious about him,' relates Kirill Privalov, a journalist on the newspaper *Druzhba* (Friendship) which was printed at the small university press, and an acquaintance of Ilich. The Venezuelan's escapades, wildly excessive by the standards of the university, only fanned people's interest. 'Ilich was not at all the typical student sent by his country's Communist Party, nothing to do with the good little soldier of Mao who laboured in the fields every summer. He was a handsome young man although his cheeks looked swollen, and he was a great bon viveur.'[40] Flush with cash sent by his parents, Ilich could afford to spend lavishly on whisky and champagne in the special stores that only accepted payment in hard currencies and which were off-limits to most people. More Russian than the Russians, the privileged student and his friends would throw over their shoulders not only empty glasses but bottles as well.

The university authorities, frustrated in their attempts to impose discipline on Ilich, reasoned that his freedom of action would be drastically limited if the allowance that his father sent him were reduced. But when they asked Ramírez Navas to be less generous, the father, piqued, retorted that his son had never wanted for anything. 'The university had a sort of vice squad, and at night students were supposed either to study or sleep,' recounts Privalov.

> One night the patrol entered Ilich's room and saw empty bottles of alcohol and glasses on the table, but he was apparently alone. The squad opened the cupboard door and a girl who was completely drunk fell out. She was naked and was clutching her clothes in her hands. They asked her what she was doing there and she answered: 'I feel pity for the oppressed.' She was obviously a prostitute. Another time, and with another girl, Ilich didn't bother to hide her in the cupboard. He threw her out of the window. This one was fully dressed and landed in two metres of snow a floor or two below. She got up unhurt and shouted abuse at him.[41]

These were not just the high jinks of a turbulent student but symptomatic of what Ilich himself considered his inability, at least until his late twenties, to forge a lasting love affair: 'I love women, I mean the good life! But not only sex. In the end, I love friendship a great deal ... I haven't lived many love stories in my life. At the same time, I can fall in love easily, like any old schoolboy. I can love several women at the same time.'[42]

Sonia Marine Oriola was an early exception. A Cuban woman whose marriage had failed, she was the young Ilich's only 'great love story ... I like girls very much, but I like to be "in control". With Sonia, I wasn't a ruler. We were one.'[43]

Two Latin Americans unhappy with Moscow, they had much in common. Years later Ilich recounted that she had taught him to smoke cigars. But the relationship came to an end and Sonia returned to Havana where she gave birth to his daughter in 1970, when Ilich was twenty years old. Ilich wrote to Sonia several times, asking that at the very least she let him know his daughter's name – he had suggested 'Sonia', like her mother – but his letters went unanswered. When a French judge asked him, fifteen years and two weddings later, whether he had married Sonia, Ilich would not be drawn. But the judge had got the woman's name wrong, asking him whether he knew someone called Sonia Maria Oriola (Maria instead of Marine), and Ilich's answer sounds more than a little tongue in cheek: 'I know no one of that name. I know several Sonias including my cousin. From my point of view this person does not exist.'[44]

Ilich's academic syllabus motivated him much less than far-left politics, as he readily recognised: 'I acquired a personal culture by travelling in Russia and other countries. I learned to use Marx's dialectic method. It's an experience which is useful to all revolutionaries.'[45] Fellow students describe him as passionate about Marxism, but as a romantic rather than an ideologue. An envoy of the Venezuelan Communist Party came to the conclusion that this young man had potential. But the offer of a post as its representative in Bucharest which Dr Eduardo Gallegos Mancera, a member of the party's politburo, made to Ilich when they met in Moscow did not tempt him. As his father had done, Ilich decided to keep the party at arm's length and turned Mancera down.

His snubbing of the appointment did not endear him to the Venezuelan Communist Party, and he further blackened his name by supporting a rebel faction. Since 1964 a storm had been brewing back home following the refusal of the young Commander Douglas Bravo, in charge of the party's military affairs and loyal to Che Guevara's doctrine, to toe the official line. Party policy dictated that armed struggle as a means to revolution should be abandoned in favour of a 'broad popular movement for progressive democratic change'. The storm broke in the late 1960s when Bravo left the party. Ilich, still at Lumumba University, wholeheartedly supported him as a true revolutionary, and this led to his expulsion in the early summer of 1969 from the Venezuelan Communist Youth, the first political movement he had joined.

Robbed of the backing of a Soviet-endorsed party, Ilich was an easy target for the university authorities, whom he had again angered earlier in 1969 when he joined a demonstration by Arab students. Moscow had no time for Bravo's followers: one *Pravda* editorial condemned Cuban-backed revolutionary movements in Latin America like Bravo's as 'anti-Marxist' and declared that only orthodox parties held the key to the future. When he recalls this period, Ilich blames Gustavo Machado, one of the leaders of the Venezuelan Communist Party, for his troubles. It was Machado who had helped Ilich get into Lumumba University in the first place, an indispensable prop given the fact that neither Ilich nor his father were card-carrying party members. 'I saw Ilich in Moscow and he was not studying,' said a disheartened Machado. 'There was no control over him. He received a lot of money, he played the guitar, and he ran after young women. He was a ladies' man.'[46] The rector of the university, Machado added, did not take kindly to Ilich posing for a photograph in Russian folkloric costume while strumming a balalaika.

Ilich gave Machado as short shrift as he had given the university authorities, who determined to rid themselves of this turbulent student on the grounds of 'antisoviet provocation and indiscipline', and to expel his brother at the same time. Ilich was among thirteen members of the Venezuelan Communist Youth, and seven other Venezuelan students whose studies had not been satisfactory, expelled in 1970. Ilich himself insists that the university had nothing against his academic performance, but this is flatly contradicted by those who knew him as a student.[47] Few missed him. Most people thought that he had returned to his apparently rich mother in London, and quickly forgot about him.

Countless newspaper stories have reported that this expulsion was a cover dreamed up by the KGB to hide the fact that it had recruited Ilich. Such smokescreens were standard practice in Soviet intelligence, and the KGB did use the university as a talent pool for Third World agents, as it did a host of other institutions where students could be easily observed and approached. With a Slavic first name that the Soviets could not have bettered, a Marxist upbringing and early membership of a Communist youth movement, Ilich may have appeared a potential candidate on paper. But no evidence has ever been published to back the idea that Ilich joined the KGB payroll at university. Officers of both the CIA and MI6 admit they have no such proof. According to one MI6 spy: 'The Eastern European secret services were interested in dealing with known quantities and people who could be kept under control. They would have been wary of someone who was a loose cannon. But that doesn't mean they couldn't use him as a pawn.'

There were plenty of reasons for the KGB to avoid any dealings with Ilich: he was a heavy drinker, a braggart who had become a notorious figure on campus because of a string of scandals, and, as his behaviour amply demonstrated, he had no liking for the Soviet way of life. As his later cool relationship with Moscow was to show, he was far too independent-minded to take orders from the doctrinaire Soviets. Even if they did try to recruit him, the attempt was doomed to fail. 'They are full of self-importance and convinced that only they hold the truth. There is no truth other than theirs,' he fumed bitterly in front of one of his lawyers years later. To the same lawyer he also said that he hated the Russian Communists. He made a point of reaffirming his independence from Moscow, a matter of national pride in his eyes. 'Unlike other parties, the Venezuelan Communist Party is not pledged to Moscow, although it does have privileged relations with the Soviet Union. Venezuelans are a proud people. There is a strong libertarian tradition in the country.'[48]

Hans-Joachim Klein, Ilich's fellow traveller for almost six months in the mid-1970s, recalled his antipathy towards the Russian Communists: 'He didn't like them. He thought they were corrupt. He did not define himself as a Marxist, but rather as an international revolutionary, a bit like Che Guevara.' Klein dismissed out of hand the story that Ilich was a KGB agent: 'That's a joke. He was expelled from Lumumba University after he took part in a demonstration. They don't really like that over there.'[49]

Ilich's banner was not the hammer and sickle. Before his expulsion from Lumumba University the bright, high-spirited and well-travelled Venezuelan who once described himself as 'an orthodox in politics, and an adventurer in life' had started looking for adventure beyond its uninspiring campus.[50]

2

Training for Terror

> 'Round here, we all use a *nom de guerre.* What about the name Carlos?' I asked. He flashed his even teeth at me. 'Carlos will do just fine,' he said.
>
> – Bassam Abu-Sharif of the Popular Front for the Liberation of Palestine

A would-be revolutionary from Latin America has at first sight few reasons to plunge into the labyrinth of the Arab-Israeli struggle. As Ilich's ancestors had demonstrated to him by example, albeit with varying degrees of success, fighting dictatorships back home was a noble enough cause. One option for the expelled student who dreamed of emulating the slain Che Guevara was to return home and sign up to fight with the guerrilla leader whose cause he had espoused, Douglas Bravo. Years later, any suggestion that he shunned his homeland's battlefields rankled. Asked whether he had ever considered fighting a guerrilla campaign in Venezuela, he proclaimed: 'As a member of the Venezuelan Communist Youth since January 1964, I have never stopped my militancy for the Venezuelan Revolution.'[1]

Ilich's university years were a time of extraordinary ferment for the Palestinians. The humiliation of the Arab defeat in the Six Day War of June 1967, when unstoppable Israeli units occupied the Sinai peninsula, the Golan Heights, East Jerusalem and the West Bank of the Jordan, had fostered a wave of resentment among Palestinian refugees whose numbers swelled in neighbouring Arab states. Convinced that they must take matters into their own hands if they were ever to win land from Israel, Palestinian guerrillas then based in Jordan, the fedayeen, staged hit-and-run raids on Israeli targets. With his privileged upbringing, and hailing from another continent, Ilich had little in common with these guerrillas, nor with the 800,000 Palestinians who had fled Israel at its creation in 1948. But the struggle to give them the land they demanded was a leading revolutionary rallying cry for tens of thousands of left-wing students the world over.

Early discussions with his father may well have played a part in shaping Ilich's outlook. Ramírez Navas made no secret of where his own sympathies lay: 'Do you think that if the Jews, the Israelis and the Zionists did not have the support of the United States, they'd be committing the crimes that they are committing in the Middle East? Are the Jews people who can't be killed?'[2] In Moscow, Ilich grilled his Palestinian fellow students and learned about the man twenty years his senior whom he would later come to call 'Master', Wadi Haddad.

Like Ilich, Haddad was born to a bourgeois family, in Galilee, the son of a renowned professor of Arabic and mathematics. On the day the Israeli army destroyed his family home Haddad swore he would pursue the Israelis all his life.[3] As a medical student at Beirut's American University, he started discussing with friends just how this could be achieved. The closest of those friends was another medical student, George Habash. The pair opened a clinic to give free treatment to Palestinian refugees in Jordan, and then helped to found in the early 1950s the Arab Nationalist Movement dedicated to wresting back Palestine. The bitterness they felt at the fiasco of the Six Day War turned that movement into the Popular Front for the Liberation of Palestine, founded within weeks of the defeat and led by Habash. From the outset, the Popular Front's one-line manifesto sought the liberation of Palestine by means of armed struggle. Its ideology was Marxist, and its tactic was terror.

The idea of resorting to terrorism was Haddad's. Convinced that raids by the fedayeen against Israeli military targets were futile, he launched the first Palestinian hijacking in July 1968: two guerrillas forced an El Al Boeing 707 flying from Rome to Tel Aviv to land in Algiers, and renamed it for the occasion 'Palestinian Liberation 007'.

Israel publicly proclaimed that it did not negotiate with terrorists, but it did just that in the long month that followed. In exchange for releasing the passengers unharmed, the hijackers won freedom for sixteen Palestinians serving prison terms in Israel. The mighty victor of the Six Day War had been brought, albeit briefly, to its knees. 'To kill a Jew far from the battlefield,' Habash concluded, 'has more effect than killing hundreds of Jews in battle.'

From then on, hijackings and other outrages grabbed world headlines and forced Western governments to acknowledge Palestinian grievances. That same year the Palestinian Liberation Organisation, which as an umbrella group included the Popular Front and other factions, issued a charter which decreed that 'Armed struggle is the only way to liberate Palestine' and that 'Commando action constitutes the nucleus of the Palestinian popular liberation war'.

Haddad's promises of world revolution struck a chord with the Venezuelan student in Moscow brought up on Marxist doctrine. For Haddad, the annihilation of Israel and the birth of a revolutionary Palestine was only the first step in a struggle inspired by teachers like Che Guevara and Mao Tse-tung. 'After that,' he promised, 'we will overthrow the feudal Arab thrones and then we will spread our revolution to the whole world.' In the years to come, revolutionaries and guerrillas the world over were welcome to join Haddad, including West Germany's Baader-Meinhof gang, Italy's Red Brigades, Japan's Red Army and South America's Tupamaros. A few years later, however, and after long, enforced conversations with him, Saudi Arabia's Sheikh Yamani concluded that Ilich had never believed in the Palestinian cause or in Arab nationalism, and that if he showed support for these it was because they were stepping-stones on the way to world revolution.

Attracted by Haddad's ideology, and fascinated by his violent propaganda coups, Ilich was eager to find out about the guerrilla training camps run by the Popular Front, at which its most promising pupils were taught how to shoot in aircraft cabins. Companions relate that it was in Moscow that Ilich first established contact with the Palestinians.[4] The Soviet authorities looked favourably on the Popular Front, and the KGB was at the time making its first approaches to Haddad. The contacts were described as 'secret active relations' in a letter from the service's chief Yuri Andropov to Soviet leader Leonid Brezhnev.[5] Ilich names his first Popular Front contact in Moscow as Rifaat Abul Aoun, then the organisation's representative in the city. The Palestinian emissary took a liking to Ilich, and invited him and several of his Latin American fellow students to attend a military training camp for foreigners in Jordan.

'The idea was appealing and my comrades and I had thought of doing it while continuing our course in Moscow. But we had a new problem when we were expelled from the Patrice Lumumba University. We would not have been allowed back into the Soviet Union if we left the country,' Ilich explained.[6] By his own account, the original plan of the would-be combatants had been to sample a short training course before returning to Moscow. They would then place their skills at Douglas Bravo's disposal in Venezuela. Ilich was elected to serve as advance scout for the young radicals and in July 1970 at the age of twenty, he set out alone for the Middle East, 'because I had more experience than the others and, having lived in Europe, I spoke several languages. I had also been the first to contact the Palestinians.'[7]

That same month, on the eleventh, Haddad narrowly survived an attempt on his life when six Soviet-made Katyushka rockets smashed into his flat in Beirut as he sat talking late at night with Leila Khaled, who had hijacked a TWA plane to Damascus in August 1969 at the age of twenty-three. An electronic timer had been programmed to fire the rockets from a rented flat across the street. Two of the missiles failed to explode but the other four did their job. Incredibly, Khaled and Haddad were only slightly injured, but his wife Samia and their eight-year-old son suffered cuts and burns. The Palestinians were unanimous in seeing the attack as Mossad handiwork.

After an overnight flight from Moscow to Beirut, Ilich appeared unexpectedly at the office of Bassam Abu-Sharif, dubbed 'the public face of terrorism' because of his role as spokesman for the Popular Front. A Palestinian barred from his family home in Jerusalem by the creation of the Israeli state, Abu-Sharif had met Habash while studying at the American University of Beirut. He was a de facto recruiting officer for many of the idealistic young foreigners who knocked at his door, including two Germans who soon became notorious partners in crime, Andreas Baader and former television journalist Ulrike Meinhof.

From his vantage point, Abu-Sharif painted a sanguine tableau of his recruits' motivations: 'Haddad's spectaculars proved that a relatively small number of committed and well-organised people could kick the West up the backside and get away with it. This was like a magnet to these fledgling Che Guevaras. Many of them really hated the machinery of capitalism: the power of big business and big government, which crushed the spirit of the individual. They wanted freedom and power. And they hung their revolutionary aspirations on the peg of Palestine.'[8]

Ilich was no exception. As he sat waiting in Abu-Sharif's offices on West Beirut's Corniche Mazraa, the Palestinian was struck by the earnest expression of his baby-faced, round-eyed visitor. A shy but determined Ilich launched into a prepared speech.

'I come from Venezuela. I have been studying in Moscow at Patrice Lumumba University. I've been following your struggle. I want to join the Popular Front because I'm an internationalist and a revolutionary.'

Abu-Sharif scrutinised him, noting his well-tailored suit, silk tie and hand-stitched leather shoes, and could not help a condescending smile. 'It is a tough thing to be a fighter,' he told the young stranger.

'I can take it. I don't wish to be a student any longer. I wish to fight for the cause,' Ilich retorted, snapping to attention like a cavalry officer of the old school, Abu-Sharif thought. Ilich told the Palestinian about his father, and the two men talked books for a while, Ilich displaying his knowledge of South American literature.

Abu-Sharif thought it worth taking another look at this newcomer who was only four years his junior. There is something underneath the babyish charm: some steel that we might be able to use, he thought, and told him to come back the next day. Ilich paused to kiss gracefully the hand of the secretary on his way out.

There was little reason to discourage such volunteers. For Haddad, foreign blood was a precious asset because it demonstrated that the Palestinian cause had universal appeal, and he liked to pool talent from different nations when selecting teams for his missions. Within twenty-four hours of Ilich's arrival, Abu-Sharif told him that he could start training, and gave him his *nom de guerre*, suggesting Carlos because it was a Spanish corruption of the Arabic name Khalil, which refers to Abraham and was brought to Spain by the Moors. 'I thought it might suit a South

American who wanted passionately to fight for an Arab cause. It was just my own little joke,' recalled Abu-Sharif.[9]

To show his gratitude, the new recruit gave Abu-Sharif an expensive present which he had brought from Moscow. Abu-Sharif thought at first that the box contained a complicated gun, but the gift was a Russian-made camera with a selection of different lenses. A few years later Abu-Sharif lost an eye and several fingers when he opened another present, this time a parcel containing a book about Che Guevara which turned out to be a bomb sent by Mossad.

Having accepted his *nom de guerre*, Carlos flew in to the Jordanian capital, Amman. For all his worldliness and linguistic skills, he was unprepared for the confusion that he found on his arrival. There could not have been a greater contrast with the Soviet drabness he had endured: 'It was anarchy. There were organisations everywhere, and many foreigners. French, Scandinavians, Italians, people of all nationalities. When I first contacted the Popular Front, people thought that I was a representative of the Komsomol [the Soviet youth organisation] because I had a red passport and they thought it was Soviet. I explained to them that I was Venezuelan and that we were Communist militants experienced in revolutionary practice.'[10]

Carlos was despatched to Jerash in the Galaad hills north of Amman. Once a jewel in the crown of the Roman empire, where Jesus is said to have exorcised demons from a local man and unleashed them on a herd of pigs, the town was in 1970 home to a Palestinian training camp where Carlos enlisted along with some ninety others. Most of his companions were French, Belgian or from elsewhere in Europe. Displaying more concentration than at school or university, Carlos worked his way through a heavy diet of lectures and seminars on politics, and practical courses on handling light arms and explosives. One popular test of the trainees' courage was to make them stand in the open air a metre away from an exploding plastic bomb. Barring accidents, the examinee would emerge unscathed as the charges were powerful only in confined spaces. Carlos's chief instructor, a major who had deserted the Iraqi army, was impressed by him and praised his speedy learning ability, his command in debates, and his courage. The new recruit, however, was far from bowled over. 'We followed military training but it wasn't very serious. The course was essentially about propaganda,' Carlos complained.[11]

The course was nearly over when, before dawn one morning, a fake attack on the camp was staged to test the apprentice guerrillas. Live mortar exploded close at hand, machine-gun fire flashed overhead. The class had been ordered to pull out across the nearby river and regroup on the other bank in the event of an attack. When Abu-Sharif and the Iraqi major toured the camp they found everyone except Carlos had obeyed instructions. He was stretched out on his kit, coolly smoking a cigarette. 'What the hell are you doing here? You're supposed to be under attack. Jump to it!' Abu-Sharif ordered. 'That's rubbish,' answered Carlos, by no means flustered. 'If it was real, I'd be dead by now.'[12]

The 'seriousness' for which Carlos had been hungering came suddenly that summer when the Israeli air force strafed a nearby camp used by the Palestinian commandos who guarded the new recruits. One member of PLO chairman Yasser Arafat's personal guerrilla faction, the Fatah, was killed in the attack, and another was wounded. The raid was Carlos's first brush with both death and war. He talks of it dispassionately: 'The camp was bombed by the Israelis in July 1970. There was one wounded and one dead among the Fatah members who were just above the river, not far away.'[13]

Within a week of the air-raid, tired of the never-ending course, he was back in Amman trying to meet a Popular Front leader. 'No one was taking me seriously. I was there to fight a war,' he recalls.[14] Abou Semir, a member of the party's politburo and in charge of Jordanian affairs, heard him out and he was sent to an élite camp training commandos where, Carlos noted, the recruits were all Arabs, chiefly Palestinians. This was the start of what was to be a life spent on the run: 'We were never in the same place for security reasons,' he said of the camp.[15] Yet again he earned top marks from his superiors. But he failed in the mission entrusted to him by the students back in Moscow: none of his Venezuelan comrades ever followed him to the Middle East because he was unable to contact them. 'I know that they returned to Venezuela,' he explained later. 'Half of them were imprisoned.'[16] Had Carlos not been picked to lead the way in the Middle East he might have suffered a similar fate.

Carlos may have been entrusted with some form of 'diplomatic' mission even before he completed his training. He said in his testimony to French investigators that during 1970 he made several visits to France, using a Venezuelan passport. Asked why he refused to reveal the purpose of these journeys, Carlos answered elliptically: 'I am not refusing. I simply want to show you that the questions you are asking me are not in France's interest and that you are trying to squeeze information out of me.'[17]

The war that Carlos was so impatient to fight was, when it came, not against the Popular Front's sworn foe but against the Arab nation that had, with increasing reluctance, granted safe haven both to it and to myriad separate Palestinian factions. In one census, the Jordanian government counted fifty-two different Palestinian groups on its territory, with leftists proselytising not Islam but Marxism from the minarets of mosques. The lightning raids by Palestinian guerrillas on Israel, and more insidiously the PLO's forging of a power base on the east bank of the River Jordan, undermined King Hussein's authority and left his country vulnerable to military retaliation by the Israelis. In February 1970 Palestinian fedayeen clashed with Jordanian troops in the streets of Amman for three days. They forced the monarch to withdraw a decree barring them from openly carrying arms in towns, and ordering them to turn in their weapons and explosives.

A few months later the most spectacular of the Popular Front's attacks cast all its previous propaganda coups in the shade. On 6 September 1970 Haddad's team tried to hijack four airliners bound for New York and several hundred passengers virtually simultaneously.

Leila Khaled had been assigned the hardest objective: hijacking an El Al Boeing 707 flying from Tel Aviv via Amsterdam. On Interpol's wanted list since her hijacking of a TWA plane to Damascus a year earlier, the good-looking Khaled had had her face reshaped by a German plastic surgeon so that she would not be recognised by El Al security. Still attractive, she posed as a buxom Mexican newly wed, complete with sombrero and bolero waistcoat. High above eastern England Khaled and her supposed husband, Nicaraguan-American Patrick Arguello, got up from their seats. But as they made for the cockpit, guns drawn, the pilot threw his plane into a nosedive. The sudden manoeuvre sent the two hijackers tumbling, and in the pandemonium that followed an El Al sky marshal shot Arguello dead – the first of Haddad's foreign volunteers to die in action – but not before he had managed to pull the pin from a grenade and hurl it down the passenger aisle. Fortunately, it failed to explode. Khaled tried to free the grenades she had stuffed into her bra but she was bitten, kicked and punched by male passengers who jumped on top of her. She had to endure more discomfort when the plane made an emergency landing at Heathrow airport: British police and El Al security fought over who should take her into custody, pulling at her feet and shoulders in a tug-of-war until the Israelis gave up on their attempt to take Khaled back to Israel with them.

One other hijacking did not go quite to plan. A Pan Am

Boeing 747 which had taken off from Amsterdam was found to be too big to land safely at the desert airstrip near Zarqa in Jordan that Haddad had selected. The jumbo was instead ordered to land in Cairo. Passengers and crew were given minutes to tumble out before the hijackers blew it up. But the other two jets – a TWA Boeing 707 flying out of Frankfurt, and a Swissair DC8 from Zurich – were directed as planned to the remote base. To the RAF, which had abandoned it, the base was known as Dawson's Field. The Palestinians renamed it Revolution Airstrip.

Abu-Sharif was prominent among the guerrillas shepherding the passengers. 'Look,' he apologised, 'I'm sorry, we have just hijacked you to a desert in Jordan. This is a country in the Middle East, next to Israel and Syria. We are fighting a just war, a war for the liberation of our country from Israeli occupation . . . You relax tonight; there is food and drink here for you.'[18] The hijackers announced that this episode of their war, which had picked off American airliners because of 'the American plot to liquidate the Palestinian cause by supplying arms to Israel', would come to a swift close if the governments of Switzerland and West Germany released several of their jailed comrades.

Israel put its army on alert and President Nixon ordered the Sixth Fleet to bomb Palestinian bases, a raid aborted by Defense Secretary Melvin Laird who gave bad weather as a pretext. In an unplanned addition to the desert party, which put Britain on the spot, a freelance sympathiser impressed by Khaled's exploits hijacked a BOAC VC10 bound from Bombay to London, and brought it and its 150 passengers to the airstrip in an attempt to prise her out of jail. The guerrillas blew up the planes (worth $30 million) but none of the 360 passengers, whose passports were stamped with the words 'liberated zone', was harmed. The last of the hostages were freed in exchange for Khaled and six convicted terrorists after a twenty-four-day ordeal. By no means dispirited by her failure, Khaled told a news conference after her release that hijacking was 'a perfectly normal thing to do, the sort of thing all freedom fighters have to tackle'.

Relegated to the sidelines, Carlos was furious that he had not been called to participate in what he called Operation Revolutionary Airstrip. The slain hijacker, Arguello, shared with Carlos both Latin American roots and a bourgeois family background, and like Carlos he had been attracted to the Palestinian cause while at university. 'Instead of selecting me for the operation, they used the most experienced troops and they let me guard a munitions depot with young recruits,' Carlos protested.[19] 'I was furious and I even complained to the officer in charge of the camp. Nevertheless, I stayed and went on guard around the small Jordanian village of Oum-Jerzy.'

Dawson's Field was the straw that broke the Jordanian camel's back, and brought down the wrath of the army not only on the Popular Front but on all other fedayeen. Jordanian troops had encircled the airstrip with tanks and armoured cars but had been powerless to intervene because the planes had been wired up with gelignite. 'The Popular Front has gone too far,' raged a humiliated King Hussein. 'Not only do they establish a pirate aerodrome on my territory, they also manufacture official seals, deliver visas, govern traffic on the main roads, hold hostages and launch negotiations with foreign powers.' Desperate to rid his kingdom of their open challenge, Hussein donned his marshal's uniform, decreed martial law and threw his faithful Bedu army into battle. The ensuing clash, Black September, drove Yasser Arafat together with those fighters who survived to Lebanon.

With the Palestinians in increasingly dire straits, Carlos was finally drafted in to meet enemy fire. 'A sheer massacre,' Carlos recalled. 'Thousands of dead. I fought until 1971. I was on the front line, in the mountains. The enemy was trying to force us down to the banks of the River Jordan.'[20]

Abu-Sharif fought alongside him in the mountains of Ajlun where the Palestinians, supported by Syrian forces, had been obliged to withdraw. From a village overshadowed by an ancient fortress which had slowed the progress of crusaders, Carlos and his companions dominated the valley of the River Jordan, and could see as far as the hills of Judea and, to the east, the wooded hills above Jerash where he had first trained and which was now encircled by the Jordanian army. Republic of Palestine, the beleaguered fedayeen defiantly named their precarious fiefdom.

The long and often dull months of training had turned the baby-faced stranger into a ruthless soldier. 'Not only was he nerveless under fire, but he could take life without blinking,' gauged Abu-Sharif approvingly. 'The Jordanians shelled and mortared us daily; under this intense fire, Carlos stood out again and again for his sheer *sang-froid*, joining in several successful counter-attacks on Jordanian army positions. He was blooded.'[21] The Palestinians whom Carlos fought alongside were armed with little more than their trademark Kalashnikovs, hand grenades and a few mortars, and were often without even so much as a tent to shelter from the blizzards that lashed the mountains. Pitted against the British-trained Jordanian army and air force, about three thousand Palestinian fighters died. Carlos was wounded along with the leader of his unit, an officer roughly his age, but his injury cannot have been very serious because he remained attached to his section.[22]

According to Carlos it was this experience of the battlefield that shaped his future commitment: 'I was a supporter of the Palestinian cause even before Moscow. It was being there in the September 1970 massacres in Jordan that made me decide to be a front-line fighter in the continuous struggle for the Palestinian cause.'[23] Couched in warrior-like terms, this was the rationale that he professed to stick to in the career that followed. In this he echoed many Palestinians including Abu Iyad, eventually appointed to head Arafat's intelligence agency, who justified the recourse to terrorism as a reaction to 'the state of despair' which engulfed them all after they were defeated by the Jordanian army.

The war ended for Carlos in the winter of 1970, long before the Jordanian army finally threw out the last of the outgunned guerrillas from the Jerash-Aljun stronghold in July 1971. In the last months of battle the Jordanians massacred many of those whom they captured, with the result that ninety Palestinians chose to flee to Israel rather than fall prisoner to Hussein's Bedu soldiers. Carlos's orders came from the very top: 'George Habash, who was secretary-general of the movement, had just come back from North Korea and China. He sent for me to tell me the cause was in jeopardy and that I must leave the struggle in Jordan because he needed me abroad.' Carlos told how a thoughtful Habash enquired after his parents and his Cuban lover Sonia and daughter. Obviously flattered by such attention, Carlos added in his account of the meeting: 'I was already a member of the Popular Front, of the political organisation, and I was a combatant and the only foreigner until the October 1973 war.'[24]

Habash's order, on his return from an Asian fund-raising tour during which he had spoken with leaders of the Japanese Red Army, signposted a shift of emphasis in the movement's strategy. Like the Six Day War, Black September stirred deep anger among the Palestinians, for whom the massacres perpetrated by the Jordanian troops showed that, despite all the rhetoric, Arab states would always put their own selfish interests first. This was justification for more terror. Habash's eye fell on Carlos because he was young, committed, and had proved his courage in the face of enemy fire. Carlos's travels, and the languages he spoke (the latest was Arabic) also made him stand out among his peers.

Before he could set out, however, there was one more

course for him to take. Carlos followed Abu-Sharif to Beirut, where over the next few months Haddad put him through a 'special training programme in the black arts of terrorism at the feet of "the Master"'.[25] Yet again, Carlos passed with flying colours, meeting the exacting standards set by Haddad who, according to Abu-Sharif, looked for intelligence, persistence, strength of character, resourcefulness and physical toughness. But beyond his academic achievement, that training set the seal on a relationship that guided Carlos through his first years in the terror business. The pupil had boundless admiration for Haddad, far more than he had for Che Guevara.

Carlos, who had cut his teeth in war, was deemed ready for a more secretive battle: 'In February 1971 I left Amman for London. I was obeying orders from Dr Habash who had asked me to go to Europe for the sake of the revolution. He felt that this new post was more interesting than the one I had in the Jordanian scrub.'[26] The way Carlos describes his appointment makes it sound like a promotion to middle management which he dutifully accepted.

Carlos finally went home to his family, or at least the maternal half of it, in early 1971. Elba and his brothers had had no communication with him for months, apart from a single letter he wrote to them which they answered through the offices of the Popular Front's newspaper *Al Hadaf*. Carlos now played the dutiful son, despite the fact that since he last saw his mother he had trained as a guerrilla, killed Jordanian soldiers during Black September, and had been sent to London by an extremist Palestinian organisation.

He returned to the cocktail-party circuit and attended economics lectures at the University of London, although he never took a degree, and Russian language courses at the Central London Polytechnic. He moved in with his mother, in Walpole Street, Chelsea. But the flat shared with his family, the cocktail parties and the Russian classes were all a façade.

The 'more interesting post' that brought Carlos back to London put him under the orders of a handsome, thin-faced Algerian, Mohamed Boudia, who was Haddad's man in Europe, based in Paris. During the Algerian war of independence, Boudia had been jailed for his part in a spectacular sabotage raid on petrol depots in Mourepiane in southern France, which started a fire fed by 16 million litres of petrol. The end of French colonial rule led to his release after only three years and, as a respected playwright, he shone in the reinvigorated arts establishment as director of Algeria's new national theatre. He fled to Paris after a *coup d'état* by Colonel Boumedienne and managed a theatre in Boulogne-Billancourt, a western suburb of the French capital. Theatre was just a front, however, and Boudia's true life was led off-stage directing a cast that from now on included Carlos.

It was under the supervision of Boudia, who occasionally sent him money from Paris, that Carlos started to draw up a list of people to be kidnapped or murdered. Rich Saudi Arabians were considered possible targets for kidnappings in a plan to raise funds for the cash-starved Popular Front, which was struggling to recover from its expulsion from Jordan. As an emissary of the despised and 'reactionary' King Hussein, the Jordanian ambassador to London was also a candidate.

Carlos pored over newspapers for inspiration. The names that caught his attention were those of public figures from various walks of life, above all ones with a Jewish background. The London cocktail circuit was another good source of information, and Carlos's combination of handsome looks, three-piece suits and good manners was popular at diplomatic receptions. Captain Porras, Venezuela's naval attaché, was among those favourably impressed: 'He was a very pleasant, well-balanced young man. His suits came from the best tailors. I don't think his mother knew what he was doing. I'm sure he told her lies.' When the young man started describing his years as a student in Moscow, the attaché diplomatically steered the conversation away from politics.

Carlos accumulated so much material he could have qualified as a Fleet Street diary columnist. Writing in red ink in a childlike scrawl inherited from his mother,[27] he filled page after page of lined paper with some five hundred names plucked from the worlds of politics, the arts and business. His detective work, which included thorough reading of the *Jewish Chronicle*, yielded a treasure-trove of private addresses and ex-directory telephone numbers, and in some cases nicknames known only to close friends.

He found out Vera Lynn's married name, and the address and telephone number of her home in Sussex. He trawled through the arts world and picked directors Richard Attenborough and Sam Wanamaker, playwright John Osborne and the virtuoso Yehudi Menuhin as possible targets. Retailers such as Lord and Lady Sainsbury and publishers such as Lord Weidenfeld were also deemed worthy of attention. British politicians interested him less, although former Prime Minister Edward Heath did rate a mention. For some strange reason he also listed the National Council for Civil Liberties. Carlos supplemented his list of names with a cuttings library which included articles about Israeli politicians, many of whom were pictured visiting Britain and meeting the local Jewish community. Advertisements for trips to Israel placed by travel companies, and for fund-raising campaigns for Jewish organisations were also filed away.

The list he had compiled so diligently and Carlos's career were almost nipped in the bud by the Special Branch three days before Christmas 1971. Acting on a tip-off which Carlos believed came from militants of a rival Palestinian faction, seven carloads of officers raided a friend's house where one of Carlos's brothers was staying. The officers, who were following up the discovery of an arms cache to which Carlos had been tenuously linked, held everyone present at gunpoint. The squad then called at the flat he shared with his mother at Walpole Street, bursting through a basement window at around ten o'clock in the evening. He and Elba were watching television. Carlos had no power to stop the police carrying out their search warrant, but the raid yielded nothing to justify his arrest. A false Italian passport bearing his photograph was, surprisingly, not deemed of great interest, and the only aggravation that Carlos suffered was to have to endure police surveillance for the next few days. Two months later the family moved to a two-bedroom flat in Phillimore Court on Kensington High Street, where Carlos was forced to share one of the rooms with his two brothers.

Finding it necessary to supplement the cheques his father still sent him, he taught Spanish from September 1972 to July 1973 at the Langham Secretarial College. The well-bred young ladies at this smart Mayfair establishment off Park Lane turned up their noses at the advances of the smooth Latin American who smelled so strongly of aftershave.

One girl who had previously lived in Caracas, Lynn Cracknell, swapped anecdotes with Carlos about its night-clubs and noted that he was always smartly turned out although his dress sense – the ubiquitous blazer and grey flannel trousers – was old-fashioned for a young man. She was even more damning in her assessment of his professional skills. 'He spent most of the time chatting in English and maybe the last ten minutes in Spanish,' she told Scotland Yard years later. 'He constantly chatted me up which I found quite annoying ... He mentioned his brother Lenin who was a swimmer [and] said to me that I could go out with Lenin if I didn't want to go out with him.'[28]

Rebuffed by Lynn, in whose exercise book Carlos had written his home address in case she fancied 'extra tuition' at any time of the day or night, Carlos tried his luck with another of his charges, nineteen-year-old Hilary Slade: 'He always suggested that if we were in the area where he lived then we should come and see him. He did at some stage write his address details on a scrap of paper and gave it to me. I probably threw it away after he gave it to me.'[29] But she still has the copy of *A Hundred Years of Solitude* by Gabriel García Márquez that Carlos gave her as a present. The younger of Carlos's brothers, Vladimir, had far better luck with local girls and to Carlos's envy went out with Irish and English girls whom he met at St Marylebone Grammar School.

Carlos's attempts at mixing with the opposite sex were more successful with a mature Colombian emigrée whom he met barely a month after starting his relaxed classes at the secretarial college. Like Carlos, the thirty-seven-year-old Maria Nydia Romero de Tobon could be proud of her lineage: her grandfather had helped to found the Colombian Liberal Party, and her father was a wealthy businessman in Bogotá. A graduate in law and politics, she had set up her own practice there and gained respect for her dogged determination in fighting any case relating to justice in the workplace. However, she had wanted to come to London to relaunch her university career after the collapse of her marriage to a Colombian university law professor.

Carlos's mother introduced them at a reception marking the *Día de la Raza*, the anniversary of Columbus's discovery of Venezuela, at the Colombian cultural centre in London where Nydia occasionally worked. Nydia was struck by the forceful personality of her new acquaintance, whose birthday was that same day. She liked his smile, his 'magnetism which was true charisma', and his convincing manner.[30] 'We talked, and talked, and talked. We immediately talked politics: the situation in our two countries, and Che Guevara. He was a young man, full of enthusiasm. He said that one day we should go back to Latin America to start a revolution and change everything.'[31] Nydia felt a political kinship with Carlos, believing that like her he was a Maoist, convinced that Russia was too bourgeois. Carlos told her that his short time at Lumumba University had made him dislike the Soviet model.

The two quickly became close, partly because Nydia came to appreciate the fatherly advice that Carlos gave her eldest son Alphonso, whom she had brought with her to live in London. The trip had turned out badly for the son, who was in trouble with the police for drugs and theft offences, bringing his mother close to a nervous breakdown as she feared he might be expelled if he appeared in court.

A few months after their first meeting, Carlos made a stirring appeal to his friend in an attempt to recruit her: 'Nydia, I need you. If we make a commitment, we must accomplish revolution everywhere. We must not be ashamed of being alive,' he told her. He promised her a long and bloody battle ahead until socialism triumphed across the globe, before blending modesty and arrogance in the same breath: 'You know, I have committed myself to a struggle without glory, a struggle in which I have invested all my ability, everything that I am, everything that belongs to me. I am not ready to give up my weapons, and nor do I believe I am close to death. On the contrary! I am almost certain that people are going to talk about me for a long time.'[32]

Carlos's tasks involved setting up a network of safe houses for himself and any other envoys sent to the city, and Nydia was the first to help him achieve this. His attempts at seducing English trainee secretaries had failed, but it was in London that Carlos perfected the art of manipulating his female conquests as tools of the trade. As one of his instructors had taught him: 'To succeed in missions, you must have the support of girls. You must strike up friendships with these apparently inoffensive creatures, because they are very useful in supplying havens and warding off suspicion.'[33]

Carlos gave Nydia a stolen blank Italian identity card and told her to get Alphonso out of the country and never see her son again as, he argued, the boy was past saving. It was cynical advice, given that Carlos wanted to use Nydia, while her son was a liability because of his record. At Carlos's request, she posed as the wife of a man with an Ecuadorian passport in the name of Antonio Dagues-Bouvier. She helped Dagues-Bouvier in his house-hunting in the West End, looking after documents for both men, and banked money for Carlos. Estate agents saw nothing odd about the Latin American couple who rented a flat in Comeragh Mews. Two other flats were rented by Carlos as safe houses, in Chester Road and in Coleherne Road.

Dagues-Bouvier has for many years proved an enigma in Carlos's story. He has been widely described as a senior KGB officer who reportedly trained Carlos in Cuba, then ran him for Soviet intelligence, finally playing a pivotal role alongside Carlos in both London and Paris. His identity has baffled investigators in several countries. For a period, Scotland Yard laboured under the mistaken belief that Dagues-Bouvier and Carlos were the same man, fuelled by the fact that in his passport photograph Dagues-Bouvier looks like a more old-fashioned, older version of Carlos.

British investigators have only recently prised the mask off Dagues-Bouvier. Behind the Hispanic- and French-sounding names hides a former officer of the Lebanese army by the name of Fouad Awad, who at the age of thirty-two helped to launch a *coup d'état* in his homeland. In 1961 a derisorily small force of forty men rolled towards Beirut from Tyre in a column of eight armoured cars, while in the Lebanese capital two officers rallied the Syrian Popular Party. The regular army swiftly brought the column to a halt and quashed the takeover attempt. His dreams of seizing power shattered, Awad switched causes to fight alongside the fedayeen.

Asked during his deposition precisely what mission he had been sent on to Britain in 1971, Carlos gives a confused answer: 'We got down to business. We started hitting the Israelis and the Jordanians. We were killing each other everywhere, it was war ... [I] carried out commissioned work because I had become an officer of the Popular Front and I carried out the missions which were demanded of me everywhere in the world and not only in Great Britain.'[34]

This is bluster. It is Carlos trying to dress up a period of relative inactivity and frustration at the lack of stimulating missions while others were being more gainfully employed by Haddad. In February 1972 one team hijacked a Lufthansa jumbo jet to Aden with 172 passengers aboard, including Joseph Kennedy, son of the late Senator Robert Kennedy. The West German government paid a ransom of $5 million to get the plane back. In May Haddad used three extremists of the Japanese Red Army to carry out a massacre at Tel Aviv's Lod airport. Walking into the passenger lounge, they heaved two suitcases off the conveyor belt, opened them and whipped out machine-guns and grenades. The Japanese killed twenty-six travellers, most of them Catholic Puerto Rican pilgrims, and wounded seventy-six others. One of the three Japanese was shot dead by a stray bullet from one of his partners and another was killed by his own grenade.

Not to be outdone, a group calling itself Black September, set up by Arafat's Fatah faction to avenge the Jordanian defeat, broke into the Israeli dormitory at the Munich Olympic Games before dawn on 5 September. They killed a weight-lifter and the Israeli wrestling coach, who had held a door against them while shouting at the athletes to flee. The attackers demanded the release of 200 Palestinian guerrillas held in Israel. After negotiations that lasted the whole day, the West Germans agreed to supply a jet that would fly the commandos and their hostages to Cairo. But at the airport German snipers opened fire and in the chaos that followed the hostage-takers shot both at police and at their captives. Nine Israeli athletes were killed, as well as five of the Black September members.

Carlos watched these raids unfold with mounting impatience. So far, his clandestine activities were hardly the stuff of which legends, let alone a revolutionary's reputation, were made.

3

The Drugstore Saint-Germain

> I don't understand why the Japanese didn't kill their hostages one by one.
>
> – Carlos after Japanese guerrillas seized the French embassy in The Hague

The private life of Carlos's master in Paris, the theatre director Mohamed Boudia, was so rumbustious that Israeli intelligence, who had him under surveillance, nicknamed him 'Bluebeard'. One of his first conquests on his return to France was his theatre's box-office assistant Evelyne Barge, a blonde, wide-eyed German with the looks of a young Brigitte Bardot. Seduced by the man as well as his ideals, she accompanied him on a trip to Rotterdam to blow up an Israeli goods depot. Although pyrotechnics were Boudia's speciality, the explosives were laid in the wrong place and destroyed a Gulf Oil refinery instead.

Unbowed, Boudia's lover volunteered to make a new attempt. He despatched her along with two beautiful Moroccan sisters to Jerusalem during the Easter 1971 holiday. Their mission was to destroy several hotels. Boudia had turned the trio into walking bombs, their bras, girdles and lipsticks stuffed with explosives and timers, their underwear impregnated with inflammable liquid. Their boxes of sanitary towels contained other vital equipment. But Israeli police detained them at Lod airport. After quizzing them on their background, politics and Boudia, the investigators concluded that all three had been motivated by love.

The theatre director quickly adjusted to the loss. He started a romance with Thérèse Lefebvre, a French physiotherapist in her mid-forties, but once more the attempt to harness love to subversion yielded disappointing results. The couple tried unsuccessfully to attack Schonau Castle in Austria, which served as a transit camp for Russian Jews on their way to Israel. But in a more effective partnership Boudia and Thérèse used twenty kilos of explosives in August 1972 to blow up a refinery in the port-city of Trieste in northern Italy, which fed the Transalpine pipeline to Vienna, Bavaria and central Europe. The fire lasted two days, burned 250,000 tonnes of crude oil, and sent $2.5 billion up in smoke.

Shortly before lunchtime on 28 June 1973 Boudia left the Paris home of one of his mistresses on the Rue des Fossés-Saint-Bernard, near the River Seine and opposite the university science department. As usual, the security-conscious explosives expert glanced down at the exhaust pipe of his grey Renault 16 and checked the starter before getting in. Satisfied that they had not been tampered with, he opened the car door and, ignition key in hand, slipped into the driver's seat.

His left foot was not yet off the ground when an explosion whipped nuts and bolts through his body, lacerating his shirt as they exited his chest. The force of the blast snapped his head back and showered shreds of flesh on to the boot of the car parked in front. As if struck by lightning, Boudia's body sat frozen, his hand shrivelled up on the dashboard and his left foot still resting on the pavement. A French policeman found the ignition key in his lap.

'We have no choice but to strike at the terrorist organisations wherever our long arm can reach,' Golda Meir, the Israeli Prime Minister, had warned Palestinian guerrillas in the wake of the massacre of the Munich Olympics athletes. Boudia was one of the last victims of the Wrath of God teams of assassins, set up by Israeli authorities to avenge that butchery.

Boudia's killers knew that fixing a booby-trap to the underside of his car would have failed as he would have spotted it when he carried out his routine checks. Instead, the Israelis had simply hidden a pressure mine under the driver's seat while the Renault was parked in the street. With none of the wiring needed for more conventional booby-traps, which are set to explode when the engine starts, the bomb had taken less than a minute to put in place. To defuse any suspicion of its involvement, the Wrath of God team had made the device a rudimentary one. But the Wrath of God's responsibility for the assassination was established by the Direction de la Surveillance du Territoire (DST, the counter-intelligence service) when it tracked down the surveillance team which had rented several flats in Paris.[1] It was pure chance no one else was hurt.

Within a month of the assassination, Carlos flew to Beirut to report back to the Popular Front's headquarters. The Palestinians were satisfied with his work in London, and ordered him to extend his efforts to Paris to help fill Boudia's shoes. But Carlos's credentials were not impressive enough to warrant his appointment as Boudia's replacement, and on his return to Europe in September he remained based in London. A short, spruce Lebanese with a supercilious stare and a drooping moustache, Michel Moukharbal, was appointed as Boudia's successor in Paris, and graced with the sonorous title 'leader of the committee for external relations in Europe'. To his chagrin, Carlos was made his lieutenant.

The impetuous, twenty-three-year-old Carlos resented having to take orders from Moukharbal, who was an unlikely freedom fighter. A graduate of Beirut's fine arts school and an interior decorator by profession, he was not even a member of the Popular Front, although he had been a militant in parties very close to it. The thirty-two-year-old Moukharbal had settled in France in the 1960s and by 1973 he had a wife and a mistress, neither of whom was aware of his clandestine activities, which included ferrying money to build up a stock of weapons and explosives, and supplying false passports to Black September.

'He was a skilful, intelligent and hard-working man but physically he was not very courageous,' is Carlos's tempered assessment of his boss.[2] To his friends he complained continuously about Moukharbal. Carlos's girlfriend Nydia found the atmosphere tense when the three met for drinks. 'I'm the one who must tell you what to do, or what not to do,' Carlos admonished her. 'Beware of [Moukharbal], keep him at a distance. Remember that, for security reasons, you must consult me about any suggestion he makes.'[3]

Despite their obvious differences, Carlos and Moukharbal saw eye to eye on the need to avenge Boudia's death by striking against Zionist targets. Carlos put his death list to good use, and fired the first shot – at Joseph Edward Sieff, the president of Marks and Spencer, in his St John's Wood home in December. 'Strangely, Sieff was not dead,' Carlos related a few years later. 'Despite his serious injuries, people managed to save him at the hospital. When I wanted to try again, once I had the necessary weapons two weeks later, he had left London for Bermuda.'[4] The Popular Front belatedly claimed responsibility a day later on New Year's Eve at a news conference in Beirut.

Carlos so embellished his deed in his own mind that he got his facts wrong. 'I fired three times,' he recounted. 'A single bullet hit Sieff on the upper lip. Usually, I fire three bullets in the nose which kills immediately. The servant saw nothing at all. I left with my flick-knife in my pocket and my gun still loaded with two bullets.'[5] In fact, he shot at Sieff only once and not three times. A single cartridge was found at the scene.

Carlos acknowledged that his preparation had been poor.

'When you try to eliminate someone, you need two weapons. The first has a silencer; the second is very powerful. That way you can defend yourself if you're taken by surprise. You also need two grenades and a driver. That's what you need to pull off an operation. But I did nothing like that. I only had this old gun with five bullets, which I wasn't even able to try out.' Yet at last, he was fulfilling what he felt was his vocation as a revolutionary. 'My existence as a dissident student with revolutionary ideals had been transformed. I had become really active. It was at this time that the real Carlos was born.'[6]

Carlos attempted a less daring foray less than a month later. The target was again Israeli, this time the Hapoalim Bank in Cheapside in the City of London: 'I made two bombs of plastic explosive explode: 200 grammes of explosives in each of them. I threw them through the main door towards the tills. But one of them landed in front of an employee before sliding over the parquet floor and exploding. He wasn't killed because he had pulled back in time. That said, the bomb destroyed the entire façade of the bank. The operation created a big stir in the media although there were no victims.'[7]

Yet again Carlos had dressed up his achievement in glowing colours. He had simply walked up to the entrance of the bank in mid-morning on 24 January, held open the door with one hand, and with the other tried to throw a bomb packed into a shoebox and wrapped in brown paper over the counter. But the door swung back towards him, hitting the package as he hurled it. It slid across the floor and burst short of the counter, making a small crater in the floor, shattering a window, and wounding a nineteen-year-old secretary. Only the detonator went off. Police recovered a Russian-made hand grenade and some 600 grammes of orange-coloured high explosives. The explosives were of a type that had been used by the Popular Front in previous attacks.

In his judicial testimony Carlos refuses to confirm or deny that he shot Sieff and bombed the bank. He prefers to invoke his 'moral' duties as a newly appointed officer of his movement: 'In the Popular Front there is a discipline, a moral code and a division of labour. As far as I am concerned, I am not in a position to speak in the name of this organisation to claim responsibility for its actions . . . At the time I had become a professional revolutionary and all my actions, without exception, were part of the war for the liberation of Palestine. I was paid by the organisation.'[8]

But he was in a position to speak about his actions to his family. For months his parents had been kept in the dark about their son's new-found commitment, and the revelation was a shock. During one of his father's rare visits to London, Carlos took the opportunity to come clean. 'Ilich got us together once in London to tell us that he had become a guerrilla,' Ramírez Navas recalled. 'That is, to prepare me because, if not, I would have had a heart attack.'[9]

The veteran Marxist's first reaction on hearing what his son had to say was to burst into tears and weep for a quarter of an hour. The son, no longer daunted by his father, sternly told him: 'Okay. The best dad in the world has just reacted. Now I am waiting for the comrade's reaction because you set me on that road, and every day, from the moment I get up until I go to sleep at night, I am tormented by only one thought: to make myself more worthy of my father.'[10] Ramírez Navas wiped away his tears, and the two men embraced. 'At home, my father was a very tender man. To outsiders he was the opposite, he appeared hard and strong,' Carlos once said of Ramírez Navas.[11]

Over the years, father and son were to cross swords often because of their political differences, but in public Ramírez Navas identified with the stand his heir had adopted: 'The change from the capitalist system to the socialist system is possible only through armed struggle. So philosophically and politically I am in total agreement with my son Ilich, although we may diverge a little on strategic matters.'[12] On another occasion, Carlos explained to his father: 'Do you think that we are going to sort this world out ourselves? No. There are lots of generations to come but one must leave a mark on life.'[13]

With or without their knowledge, Carlos was increasingly using the girlfriends he bedded in both London and Paris to help him leave that mark. A few weeks before shooting Sieff he had met a Spanish waitress, Maria Angeles Otaola Baranca (Angela to her friends), at the Bayswater pub The Ducks and Drakes. As he lunched in the grill room, Carlos chatted to Angela in Spanish about his many trips and the languages he had mastered. He returned three days later to ask the dark, impish twenty-one-year-old to go out with him. She noticed how his small, dainty hands contrasted with his thickset build, and the way his slightly wavy hair curled in the nape of the neck.

Angela accepted the invitation, and found him amusing and cultured. They talked politics, Basque separatism and Palestine, with Carlos showing no particular militancy about the last subject. He posed as Carlos Martinez Torres, claiming to be a Peruvian economist whose employer was based in Lima; Angela was one of the first women with whom he adopted the *nom de guerre* bestowed upon him by the Palestinians. The pair became lovers, but to explain his frequent absences he told her that his job meant he had to travel widely, chiefly to France, Germany and Switzerland. The flat where he stayed with his mother and brothers was out of bounds for their affair, and so he would meet her at the Queens Hotel in Inverness Terrace, or at the seedy top-floor flat she rented above a launderette in Bayswater at 24B Hereford Road.

Partly because of his frequent trips abroad, Carlos eventually lost Angela to Barry Woodhams, a scientist who had worked at the chemical warfare research centre at Porton Down in Wiltshire. She introduced them to each other at her flat, and the two men became drinking partners. 'I quite liked him, it's as simple as that,' Woodhams recalled. 'I'd drink with him and talk; he wasn't unpleasant in any way. We'd chat about life in general.'[14]

With both Angela and Woodhams, Carlos cultivated an air of mystery, hinting that he travelled illegally and boasting about the sums he won at poker. He was sensitive about his weight. He and Woodhams had to stand on the scales in the kitchen to settle one dispute after Carlos took offence at his friend's request for space on the couch, 'Move over, fatty.' Discussing a murder case in France in which two criminals had been guillotined, Carlos said that men who killed for money and not for political reasons deserved to die.

Woodhams, who told Carlos of the African safaris he had been on as a child, found that his friend shared an interest in guns. Carlos often said he was keen on pistol shooting, implying that he shot at cardboard targets indoors. During one of their late-night chats Carlos bragged to Woodhams that he was a very good shot and could hit a target from twenty-five metres with a 22-calibre gun. He also insisted that despite all the security precautions taken at airports, citing the example of Paris's Charles de Gaulle airport, any determined commando could seize control of a plane.

Carlos was still going out with both Angela and the Colombian lawyer Nydia Tobon in London when, in June 1974, he met a young and pretty brunette in Paris who soon joined his circle of lovers. Carlos first came across the twenty-eight-year-old Colombian Amparo Silva Masmela at the Candelaria, a South American cabaret on Rue Monsieur-le-Prince in the Latin Quarter. A shy girl, Amparo was staying in a hostel with the Sisters of the Assumption in the sixteenth arrondissement. She was in Paris to study French at the Alliance Française, and cleaned the houses of wealthy Parisians to earn her keep.

With his talk of revolution, and his frequent gifts of

flowers, Carlos swept her off her feet. Dropping his usual cover, Carlos had confided to her that he was a member of the Popular Front – he was in charge of operations, he said, with André (alias Moukharbal) officiating as the political leader – and planned to commit attacks across Europe to exterminate all the Jews responsible for Boudia's death.[15]

But Nydia was the girlfriend to whom Carlos felt closest, and he turned to her for help as he slowly built up a stock of arms for operations in Europe. One evening in July 1974 he called Nydia from Paris and asked her to join him as soon as possible. She flew over, and Carlos handed her a heavy black suitcase. All her boyfriend told her was: 'Keep this with you until I come and join you, or until somebody calls at your flat and gives you a precise date, the date of my birthday.'[16]

According to Nydia, who took the suitcase back with her to London, it was only some time later that she found out what it contained. 'Look, my love, this beauty is a Czech pistol, a high-speed M52 automatic. It's marvellous,' Carlos told her as he guided her through the suitcase's contents with childish delight when they met again. 'Carlos brought the barrel to his mouth and blew on it with a tender gesture, as if it had been a first kiss of love. Then he seized a grenade ... and put it in my hands, showing me how I should remove the primer and throw it. "Forget that you are a woman," he added with a certain arrogance. "Don't close your eyes!" '[17]

In the summer of 1974 the anti-Zionist campaign plotted by Moukharbal and Carlos, who was spending more and more of his time in Paris, was aimed at three French newspapers. For good measure, they threw in the Maison de la Radio, a huge round building by the River Seine, home to French state-owned radio broadcasters. The papers, which were bombed in August with help from the French left-wing group Action Directe, were the daily *L'Aurore*, reputed to be pro-Israeli, the right-wing weekly *Minute* and the monthly *L'Arche*, whose premises harboured the Unified

Jewish National Front. Humanitarian considerations apparently prevailed: 'It was around two o'clock in the morning when we started the operation. In fact, we waited until there was no one left in the offices. We didn't want any victims. You can imagine the difficulty of this vast operation against three Zionist companies and one owned by the state, all at the same time and in the very centre of Paris.'[18]

Carlos gave the newspapers advance notice of the blasts. Rented cars packed with explosives blew up outside the newspaper offices but the timer on the bomb planted at the Maison de la Radio was not set properly and it failed to explode. Carlos, however, was satisfied with his most effective operation to date and, as planned, there were no casualties. An organisation calling itself the Mohamed Boudia Commando claimed responsibility for the blasts and branded the three newspapers 'tools of the criminal machinations of the Israeli secret services in Europe'.

Carlos's attacks in London and Paris had so far claimed no loss of life, although in Sieff's case at least it had not been for want of trying. His next move drastically raised the stakes. Haddad dictated with whom Moukharbal and Carlos should ally themselves, and their objectives. The new accomplices were members of the Japanese Red Army, a small but strident movement born out of opposition to the Vietnam War, and committed to the annihilation of capitalism. It was notorious for its habit of burying alive members whom it judged to be wanting in revolutionary commitment. For its first hijacking, in March 1970, the Japanese Red Army had used ritual Samurai swords and pipe bombs to force a Japanese plane to land in North Korea. Switching to the Palestinian cause after the United States started pulling out of Vietnam, the Japanese Red Army had carried out the Lod airport massacre for Haddad in May 1972. It was in the company of such zealots that Moukharbal and Carlos were ordered to repay the debt.

A month before Carlos bombed the three newspapers in Paris, French police arrested a Japanese Red Army member by chance. The athletic-looking, twenty-five-year-old Yutaka Furuya had been stopped by border guards at Paris's Orly airport as he stepped off a flight from Beirut. Furuya, whose real name police eventually concluded was Yamada Yoshiaki, refused to answer questions about the three false passports all bearing his picture which were found in his black and chrome executive briefcase. Nor was he helpful about $10,000 in counterfeit money and sheafs of coded notes. 'I am a Marxist-Leninist. I act out of ideology for the Palestinians, as a sympathiser, as well as for the Japanese Red Army,' he told the airport police, adding that he was unemployed.

The jobless traveller was passed on to the DST, France's counter-intelligence service, and Commissaire Jean Herranz, a newcomer to anti-terrorism. The DST, France's closest equivalent to MI5 or the FBI, had only two years previously created a bureau, code-named B, to specialise in counter-terrorism alongside the long-established counter-espionage (A), and technical and telecommunications (C) sections. All three were crammed into the DST head-quarters near the Champs-Elysées, a drab warren of offices which the Gestapo had occupied during the war. The cling-ing Nazi legacy irritated the chief of the B-2 Middle East division, Herranz, who had landed in Normandy on D-Day as a commando with General de Gaulle's Free French.

Before he confronted Furuya, Herranz ordered a trawl through the files. The search showed that Furuya was no menial courier but a fully fledged member of the Japanese Red Army who, in another joint operation with the Popular Front, had blown up a Shell oil refinery in Singapore in January of that year. With the help of the Japanese ambassa-dor to Paris, cryptographers cracked the code in his docu-ments and found that they detailed plans for attacks on Japanese embassies and various companies in seven

European cities. One of the messages written on rice paper was, to all appearances, innocuous enough: 'Little Miss Full Moon. I am ill with desire for you. Let me embrace your beautiful body again. Your love slave, Suzuki.' The object of Furuya's passion was Mariko Yamamoto, a Japanese Red Army member who worked as a sales girl at one of the luxury boutiques that line the Avenue de l'Opéra and cater to Japanese tourists.

Under a barrage of questions from Herranz, Furuya remained tight-lipped. But his address book spoke for him. It enabled the DST to arrest thirty Japanese Red Army members or supporters. The French Interior Ministry crowed that all Japanese Red Army backers based in Paris had been arrested, making no mention of the fact that one of them, a French national, was a card-carrying member of the French Communist Party and forged passports for the Japanese. To the DST's resentment the right-wing Interior Minister, Prince Michel Poniatowski – a descendant of Poland's last elected king – ordered the man's release. Furuya was also treated with leniency: he was charged only with carrying three false passports and counterfeit money, and sent to jail for just a few months.

Poniatowski, known for his regular '*coup de poing*' (literally, punch) raids in which police swept the Paris Métro clean of drug dealers, failed to live up to his hardline image and ordered eight of the Japanese Red Army prisoners to be expelled, to neutral but friendly Switzerland. Playing pass the parcel, the Swiss then expelled the Japanese Red Army members to West Germany, which in turn pushed them across the Dutch border.

A few days later, the French embassy in The Hague was attacked by Japanese Red Army guerrillas. 'You know who did it?' a Dutch colleague asked a senior DST official within hours of the start of the assault. 'The guys you threw out!'

The embassy raid had been planned several weeks

earlier and, before launching their attack, the Japanese who carried it out had teamed up with Moukharbal and Carlos. The pair helped to organise the attack and provided the funds, machine-guns and grenades. On 3 September Carlos had travelled to Zurich to discuss the plan with three of the Japanese Red Army members expelled from France. A week later he had returned to Zurich with Moukharbal to hand the Japanese 4000 francs to cover their living expenses.

The plan was for the Japanese to seize the French ambassador on his arrival at the embassy in The Hague on the following day, and then force their way into the building. But they were late in arriving and Carlos had to leave the area because guards at the nearby American embassy were becoming suspicious of him. Half an hour later, he heard the wail of police sirens, and saw people running towards the French embassy: 'I got closer to see what was happening. I heard shots in the embassy compound. At the same time I saw a policewoman leave the embassy. She was wounded. I waited a few minutes like the bystanders who were there. Until the police intervened. I called the office of the ambassador from a phone box but the police had already cut the telephone wires. What had happened?'[19]

The three-man commando who arrived at the French embassy, too late to meet Carlos, did spot the ambassador's car, which was empty save for its driver. At gunpoint, they ordered him to take them to the ambassador's office. When a police patrol which chanced on the scene intervened, a shoot-out ensued. The leader of the commando was shot in the arm. Two police officers were also wounded. But the Japanese managed to shake off the police and took the ambassador – the former Resistance fighter Count Jacques Senard – together with ten other people hostage in Senard's office. In a letter dropped from a window they demanded that Furuya be released from his Paris jail and that a Boeing 707 airliner and crew be made available to them. The Japanese insisted on their hostages staying in the office, and for some reason rejected offers from the Dutch authorities to supply a chemical toilet. As everyone was forced to share a wastepaper basket that stayed in the room, unemptied, the stench that developed helped to make life a misery.

As Carlos flew back to Paris later on Friday, a handcuffed Furuya was already setting out in the opposite direction. 'The decision was taken almost immediately,' admits Pierre Ottavioli of the élite Brigade Criminelle, the French police's criminal investigation unit, who took part in the negotiations. 'The counterpart for the release of the hostages was the release of one prisoner. And there were many people in the embassy.'[20] Prime Minister Jacques Chirac ordered Furuya taken from the maximum-security jail of La Santé in Paris. Under the escort of the garrulous Commissaire Broussard and his counter-insurgency unit, the Brigade Anti-Commando, the prisoner was flown to Amsterdam's Schipol airport where he awaited the outcome of the negotiations.

Furuya took it all with good-humoured self-assurance. Before boarding the Mystère 20 jet of the French ministerial fleet, he had exasperated the chief of police, Jean Paolini, with his levity. 'He doesn't talk, he laughs!' Paolini complained to Prime Minister Jacques Chirac.

In his memoirs Broussard writes that the orders he received from Paolini were that he should take part in the negotiations but also prepare for a possible raid on the embassy, with or without the cooperation of the Dutch authorities, because the diplomatic compound counted as French national territory. 'On the other hand, contrary to what a few journalists reported later, I did not receive the order to shoot Furuya if the terrorists were to kill a hostage! In favouring the "leak" of such information, perhaps the French authorities wanted to impress the enemy ...'[21]

In fact there was just such an order. That weekend a DST official who had ineffectually argued against the expulsion of the Japanese Red Army guerrillas filed a report on the embassy siege for Poniatowski's attention. The unfortunate official was summoned from a restaurant opposite the Interior Ministry before he could start on his already late lunch. He found the minister in his office, cigar in one hand and brandy in the other, digesting a roast chicken whose remains had not yet been cleared from his imposing desk. The DST, Poniatowski informed him, had been taken off the case. 'If anything happens to the ambassador, Commissaire Broussard will kill Furuya,' the minister said. Poniatowski was all for giving up the prisoner, especially as he had only three months of his sentence to serve. Rejecting the Japanese demands, he argued, would mean terrorist attacks on French soil. Having expelled all the other Japanese Red Army members, there was little reason not to rid France of Furuya too.

Unknown to the DST official, the minister's murderous musings reflected the Prime Minister's thinking. When Chirac was asked a few days later to confirm reports that he had warned the ambassador's captors that their comrade would die if a hostage was killed, he did so unequivocally: 'When such primitive violence surfaces, I am in favour of the elimination of troublemakers who are tied to no philosophy nor to any school of political thought.'

Out on the tarmac at Amsterdam's Schipol airport, deserted save for the French plane, Dutch army tanks and troops, Broussard had not expected to be stranded guarding the taciturn Furuya for hours on end. Anxious that the Japanese Red Army should leave with a good opinion of their country, Dutch officials plied Furuya with newspapers, hot food and drink. The French were given only cold food. At his guard's request, Furuya obligingly agreed to order more than he could eat so as to supplement their rations. They did not show much gratitude. On Broussard's initiative, the French decided to intimidate Furuya, who was in touch with the embassy by radio. An inspector approached and held a 375 Magnum to the captive's temple.

'If your friends kill even one hostage, we kill you. Understood?' Furuya showed no reaction.[22]

The negotiations dragged on for more than two days, with the hostage-takers refusing any food for fear of poison or sleeping drugs. The foul-smelling air in Ambassador Senard's office was made even worse by the arm wound one of the Japanese had suffered turning septic. Senard bravely kept his fellow hostages amused by devising card games, and bore stoically the distractions that the kidnappers invented for themselves, which included shooting between his feet when they got tired of taking pot-shots at the official photograph of the French President hanging above his desk.

In Paris, Carlos mulled over how he could show some support. Had he known that Chirac's government was about to give in to the guerrillas' blackmail, he would perhaps have refrained from an act that harked back to the tactics of French anarchists. But he feared that France, after failing to send the Boeing plane requested by the Japanese for their escape, would stand firm and refuse to free Furuya. And he believed their determination was wilting. 'I don't understand why the Japanese didn't kill their hostages one by one,' he said later.[23]

On the Sunday afternoon, carrying a gun and two US-M26 fragmentation grenades, Carlos made his way to Saint-Germain-des-Prés, a Left Bank neighbourhood patronised by Parisian intellectuals and artists. In the heart of the area, dwarfed by the massive, rustic bell-tower of the Saint-Germain church was the Deux-Magots café, a rendezvous of the intellectual élite which had attracted the likes of Oscar Wilde, Ernest Hemingway and Jean-Paul Sartre. On the other side of the boulevard was the Drugstore Saint-Germain', an all-in-one café, restaurant and boutiques complex of chrome and glass, doing a brisk trade as most local shops were closed. A chic French adaptation of American drugstores, it drew a young and trendy crowd and was owned by a Jew, Marcel Bleustein-Blanchet, the head of the Publicis advertising empire.

Carlos walked in to the Drugstore Saint-Germain and climbed the stairs to the restaurant on the first floor. He leaned over the brass balustrade and gazed down at the crowd milling in and out of the boutiques in the mall below. Slowly, deliberately, he drew the pin from one of his grenades and tossed it into the throng outside the tobacconist's kiosk. The grenade bounced on the marble floor, rolled along the ground, and came to a stop at the feet of a young couple who had come to look at records. Carlos was outside before the particularly vicious fragmentation grenade burst into a hundred shards of metal and pierced the bodies of the young man and his wife. Although seriously wounded with two fingers ripped off her hand the woman, Yarouchka Benzo, survived. Her husband lost so much blood that he died of his wounds.

Jean-Jacques Debout, a popular singer, narrowly escaped injury when he decided not to join the long queue at the tobacconist's. He was just about to walk out into the street when the blast happened: 'An eerie stampede of living dead trampled over each other. I saw a little boy, he was perhaps twelve years old, staring at his left arm with overwhelming incredulity: there was no hand.' Waiters from the neighbouring Brasserie Lipp applied rough tourniquets with napkins and tablecloths to try and stop the flow of blood. The blast killed two people and wounded another thirty-four.

That Sunday evening the Japanese holed up in the French embassy in The Hague cheered when they heard of the attack, but did not immediately attribute it to a supporter. The bombing, recorded in Moukharbal's notebook with the words 'Japanese Operation', was a particularly futile act. But Carlos, who flew to London and one of his safe houses four days later, travelling on a Peruvian passport under the name Carlos Andres Martinez Torres, always refused to recognise the fact. He was convinced his intervention made France give in: 'The French government feared that public opinion would turn against it.'[24]

French intelligence and police had no idea that the grenade attack was linked to the embassy siege, and the negotiations lasted for another two days. The French not only released Furuya but also supplied the Japanese with the Boeing jet and a $300,000 ransom, because they feared for the lives of the hostages. Carlos's attack had no relevance. A tearful Ambassador Senard could not hide his shame at the 'capitulation' which ended his 101-hour ordeal. At the next Cabinet meeting President Valéry Giscard d'Estaing strove to put a braver face on an outcome that he claimed had allowed France 'to behave like a great country and to protect the lives of our nationals'.

Only when three grenades abandoned by the Japanese at Schipol airport just before they left for Damascus were analysed did police establish a definite link between the Drugstore bombing and the embassy siege. The grenade thrown into the café was of the same type, and all four were traced to a consignment of seventy-five stolen from an American military base in Niesau in West Germany in June 1972.

Weeks later, the Drugstore café and restaurant reopened after painstaking refurbishment which had removed all trace of shattered glass, twisted metal and blood. Among the regulars who flocked back was Carlos: police later found tabs recording credit-card payments that he made for odds and ends purchased there in January 1975, four months later.[25]

'After the "Japanese operation", it became difficult to work,' Carlos explained. 'From that time on the task necessitated more courage, care and great know-how.'[26] Carlos was however still a complete stranger to the French police, and all Britain's Special Branch knew about him was that he had owned a false passport. For Haddad and the Popular Front, Carlos was a valuable asset and he was soon given a chance to wreak greater havoc.

The original scheme devised by Haddad and Moukharbal was to seize an El Al jet at Orly airport in December 1974, but a wildcat strike by El Al staff foiled the plot as it meant that Israeli planes no longer flew into the airport. Carlos, reduced to scouring airline timetables and a map of the airport, was forced to wait several weeks for the strike to end. Finally on 13 January he and a West German accomplice recommended to him by Haddad were sent into action.

The new assistant was the twenty-seven-year-old Johannes Weinrich, a man of slight build and cocksure expression who was the co-owner of a radical Frankfurt bookshop, the Red Star. While a student at Frankfurt University seven years earlier Weinrich and another young radical, Wilfried Böse, had ridden a wave of left-wing militancy that drew tens of thousands of students and young people into the streets to protest against the Vietnam War. The two friends created the Revolutionary Cells, an umbrella organisation for a host of small, independent groups which denounced world governments as being in the pay of American multinationals, and firebombed American companies' offices in West German cities. Carlos is believed to have first met Weinrich when the two trained in Palestinian guerrilla camps.

Shortly after midday on 13 January Carlos and Weinrich parked a rented white Peugeot 504 saloon car at the side of a road linking the Orly airport terminals, from where they had a clear view of the tarmac at the western complex. They sat waiting for the flight Carlos had chosen to take off, an El Al Boeing 707 which had stopped in Paris on its way from Tel Aviv to New York. Aboard were 136 passengers, most of them American tourists, and seven crew. The plane was just over a hundred metres away when both men got out of the car. They pulled out a long tube-shaped weapon from beneath an orange canvas cover on the back seat.

The weapon was a bazooka, a Russian-made RPG-7 (Rocket Propelled Grenade). Designed to bore its way through armour thirty centimetres thick, yet neither bulky nor heavy, the Russian-made anti-tank launcher was one of the few weapons with which the Palestinian forces had resisted the Jordanian onslaught in the winter of 1970. At a spot that was spectacularly indiscreet, Weinrich leaned the launcher on his shoulder, standing by the white, waist-high railing that separated the road from the airport tarmac. His antics as he tried to steady the long bazooka and squint down the optical sight intrigued several bystanders. An employee at the Lufthansa ticket desk some twenty metres away thought Weinrich's behaviour strange, as did an El Al security guard on a nearby roof who focused his binoculars on him. A French police officer on the tarmac noticed the bazooka's tube.

The El Al plane was 130 metres away when Weinrich fired, well within the weapon's maximum range of 300 metres. But the missile soared wide of the nose of the plane. Without waiting to see the rocket's final impact, Weinrich hurriedly consulted Carlos before reloading and taking aim a second time. The first rocket hit a parked car and then smashed into an empty workshop, where the black boxes recording flight-data were manufactured. It failed to explode. A moment later the radio in the cockpit of the El Al jet crackled with an urgent order from the control tower for all planes on the tarmac to come to an immediate halt. The Israeli captain, a former fighter pilot with combat experience, had no intention of obeying the order which would have offered his attackers an easy target. He accelerated sharply and made straight for the runway.

In his haste to fire a second rocket, Weinrich failed to brace himself for the recoil which punched him backwards and the bazooka's steel tube shattered the Peugeot's windscreen. The rocket pierced the fuselage of a parked and virtually empty Yugoslav JAT DC9 before exiting on the other side. Flying metal slightly injured a steward, a policeman and a baggage-handler but the rocket, like the first, failed to explode and burrowed its way into empty kitchens. The only damage caused was a few broken plates.

Weinrich and Carlos jumped into the car and sped away leaving behind a Soviet-made automatic pistol on the edge of the road. Outside the Thiais cemetery a few miles away they abandoned the Peugeot and paused only long enough to throw a cover over the launcher, a third unused rocket, two grenades and another Soviet-made pistol lying on the back seat before switching to another rented car. Carlos blamed his team-mate for the fiasco: Weinrich he explained, 'was courageous and experienced, but at the last minute he broke down.'[27] Shortly afterwards, someone called the Reuters news agency in Paris to claim responsibility for the attack in the name of the Mohamed Boudia Commando. The message ended with the promise: 'Next time we will hit our target.'

Within hours of the rocket attacks reinforcements of police, gendarmes and Corps Républicain de Sécurité (CRS) riot police had thrown a ring of steel around Orly. Police patrol cars escorted all El Al aircraft to and from the runway. This did nothing to deter Haddad's soldiers. 'We must try again,' decreed Moukharbal, and the others – including Waddi Fares Raghdan, a Lebanese who later confirmed that Carlos and Moukharbal were behind the new attempt[28] – agreed on a new vantage point. They chose an observation terrace that was open to the public. Carlos objected to carrying out the repeat attack on a Sunday, because the terrace would undoubtedly be crowded with families. He was overruled.

On the Friday, four days after the first attack, Carlos was at the airport to help three Palestinian guerrillas selected by Moukharbal carry out what Carlos called 'a dress-rehearsal'. The unarmed team established that only a short distance would separate them from their target, an El Al jumbo. 'We had three problems to solve,' Carlos related. 'To escape, we had to take hostages. Such an operation might cost the lives of several innocent people and this was not something we wanted to see happen. And in addition, the operation was very dangerous for our own men.'[29] Two days later, on the Sunday, Carlos and his team returned to the airport. It was a sunny afternoon and, as he had predicted, the terrace was indeed packed with sightseers and excited children on a weekend outing.

Because Carlos and Weinrich had abandoned their weapons in the Peugeot a week earlier, all Moukharbal could come up with at such short notice was a less powerful bazooka, an RPG-2. Before the new attack it had been hidden in the toilets closest to the observation terrace. As there were so many people milling about, it took the group longer than expected to retrieve the rocket-launcher. Anxious not to miss their target, they then raced out on to the terrace. A CRS officer on another higher terrace saw them, and promptly opened fire with his machine-gun. His act risked causing a bloodbath as the commando had already mingled with the sightseers. Amazingly the bullets harmed no one and only shattered the glass partition that lined the terrace. As the crowd ran for cover, one of the Palestinians added to the panic by firing into the air and throwing a grenade. Another Palestinian pulled out the bazooka which he had hidden under his coat and pointed it at the El Al plane.

The Tel Aviv-bound aircraft with 222 passengers aboard had left its berth and was by then 400 metres away, more than twice the effective range of the RPG-2 bazooka. The Palestinian stood for several seconds, launcher in hand and surrounded by panic, as he tried to decide whether to try a shot. An amateur photographer, who moments earlier had been taking pictures of planes, snapped the hesitant guerrilla. 'The terrorist walked up to me and pointed his bazooka at me. I was three metres away,' the photographer recounted. 'My heart was in my boots. Then he raced past me.'[30]

The commandos (Carlos had quietly slipped away by this stage) charged into the building, firing guns and throwing grenades as they cleared a way through the passenger lounge. They ran straight into a CRS patrol, which opened fire. Travellers dived for cover. Eight people were seriously injured in the shoot-out, including a CRS officer who received a bullet in the stomach. The Palestinians managed to hold the police at bay as they grabbed several hostages whom they ordered to crawl into nearby toilets. One brave, burly man swung punches at the Palestinians and saved his wife from being dragged away. An elderly woman who did not obey orders fast enough received a bullet in her shoe but was unharmed.

The guerrillas succeeded in taking ten hostages, including a pregnant woman, a four-year-old girl and a priest. The first ultimatum slipped to police under a door demanded safe conduct and an airliner to fly the Palestinians out of France. It was signed with a name increasingly familiar to police, the Mohamed Boudia Commando. In the agonising wait that followed, the priest gave the other hostages absolution. 'The gunmen were, as a whole, very correct but I think that if the negotiations had failed they would have killed us just as correctly,' was his ironic comment.[31]

The French government was in no mood for a firm stand. After seventeen hours of negotiations, during which the hostages were forced to stay standing, it caved in and supplied a Boeing 707 which flew the Palestinians unharmed to Baghdad.[32] Commissaire Ottavioli from the Brigade Criminelle, who was among those called to Orly, was furious at this new surrender: 'I was in favour of doing everything to neutralise the guerrillas. I had called in the élite GIGN commando unit of the gendarmerie. I still don't understand why we yielded. There were plenty of things we could have done to gain time.'[33]

Their plans foiled yet again, Moukharbal and Carlos fled to London, bringing with them a new addition to their movement, Hans-Joachim Klein. A Frankfurt bailiff's clerk who had joined the Revolutionary Cells, whose members knew him as Schnitzel (Escalope) because of his favourite food, the long-haired Klein had met Carlos in Paris a few months earlier. 'I saw a guy whom I thought was a Mafioso. That's what he looked like. He wore an Italian silk suit, he stank of perfume, he was affected in the extreme,' Klein said of his new acquaintance.[34]

But Klein was soon impressed by the way the sophisticated, self-assured and multilingual Carlos steered him through his armoury – which Klein likened to 'a James Bond-type accessories shop' – as calmly as if it were a stamp collection. 'I was told how he had studied in Moscow, and had been the only foreigner to fight with the Palestinians in Jordan. At that time I was crazy about arms, and hearing all this man had done, for me he was a little Guevara. And above all I was told that Carlos was not obliged to lead this life, that he was from a rich family.'[35]

In London, Moukharbal hoped to kidnap the United Arab Emirates ambassador and hold him for a ransom of $40 million. But the plot was ditched when two weeks of surveillance of the embassy from Kensington Gardens, much of it spent standing in the rain, showed that he had no fixed routine. 'After all these events, we decided to review all our plans. Given the fact that these operations were quite frankly not successes,' Carlos conceded.

At this time the French security services still had no idea who Carlos was, let alone that he had been involved in the newspaper and Drugstore bombings and the Orly airport attacks. 'For us, Carlos didn't even exist. It was only in June

1975 that we formally identified him and tried to follow his tracks,' admitted a former head of the DST counter-espionage service.

4

Secrets and Lies

> I'm not a professional killer. It's not easy to shoot in the eyes of a human being who is looking at you.
>
> – Carlos to the magazine *Al Watan al Arabi*

Even after the hostage-taking at the French embassy at The Hague, and the grenade attack on the Drugstore Saint-Germain in Paris, anti-terrorism was a low priority for the DST, the French counter-espionage service. It did not merit more than a 'sub-directorship' of the DST, which was staffed by only twenty employees. Marcel Chalet, appointed to head the DST in 1975, spoke for many when he dismissed counter-terrorism as 'a relatively marginal activity compared to the DST's initial mission' of counter-intelligence.[1]

It was therefore unsurprising that DST headquarters took little notice of an arrest that took place in Beirut on Saturday, 7 June 1975. The catch was the neatly dressed, sharp-eyed Moukharbal who had just made one of his regular visits to the headquarters of the Popular Front. The Lebanese criminal investigation department, perhaps acting on a tip-off, arrested him as he prepared to board a plane to return to Paris. Bemused by the notes, almost certainly plans for bombings and shootings, that they found in his attaché case alongside false passports and cash, the police turned to the French for help. The man they called was Jean-Paul Mauriat, a former DST officer who had been sent to Beirut to train Lebanese counter-espionage officials. Mauriat's first concern was to ask about Moukharbal's health after his night of questioning. He had led the DST's counter-terrorism section and was familiar with the heavy-handed tactics of Lebanese interrogators. 'We haven't touched him,' was the answer.[2]

All the Beirut police knew about Moukharbal was that he was a Lebanese Christian from a good family, a wealthy interior decorator, and a member of the Syrian Popular Party which advocated a 'Greater Syria' that would include Lebanon. His notes were intriguing. They were full of detail about the routines of personalities in Paris and London, including Interior Minister Poniatowski, the Israeli ambassador to Paris, and the chairman of Marks and Spencer. With advice from Mauriat, the police drew up a new interrogation plan.

The grilling lasted the best part of two days. Moukharbal's questioners – and Mauriat who was briefed about the outcome – learned that he headed a Paris-based group and that he worked for George Habash. But it was the name of a Popular Front contact he said he was due to meet in Paris, a certain Nourredine, which puzzled the interrogators. What is his full name? they asked. Moukharbal said he didn't know. What can you tell us about him? He is my hitman. That's all he is, a killer.

Moukharbal's disclosures were clearly worth passing on to Paris. At the French embassy, Mauriat and the local SDECE station chief began coding up and sending via radio all Moukharbal had revealed, the addresses in his diary, together with details of the notes and passports that had been seized from him at the airport. Under strict security guidelines, the report had to be sent in a series of short messages, with long pauses to await confirmation that Paris had received each one. The two men drank a bottle of whisky to alleviate the tedium.

It was obvious to the Lebanese interrogators that they

would get nothing more out of Moukharbal, and after consulting Mauriat they decided to release him and put him on a plane to Paris. Unfortunately for French counter-intelligence, the Lebanese police's willingness to cooperate did not stop at Western security services. In the name of the united Arab struggle for Palestinian rights, it also had discreet relations with guerrilla groups fighting Israel. The Popular Front, which quickly got wind of Moukharbal's arrest, asked the head of the criminal investigation department, Colonel Antoine Dahdah, for a few details of what had happened. The information the colonel released explains how Carlos had found out by Thursday, 12 June that Moukharbal was in Lebanese custody.

That Thursday evening Carlos called his pretty Colombian friend Amparo from a Paris café. Their affair had ended in December when, only too aware that he was chasing other women, Amparo had thrown him out of her flat. Now, in his telephone call, Carlos asked her to do him a small favour. He had been waiting, he told her, for his leader to return to Paris so that he could continue his revolutionary struggle. But the man had been arrested in Beirut, and Carlos was afraid that police would find out about the address of a flat in Rue Toullier in the Latin Quarter where some weapons had been hidden. Would Amparo agree to his moving the weapons to her home in Rue Amélie near the Eiffel Tower? As her address was known to no one it would be completely safe. She rashly accepted: 'I sincerely believed that I was simply doing a favour to someone I liked.'[3]

When she got back from work the next day – she had found a job at the Lloyds Bank branch near the opera house – she discovered that Carlos, who had kept his key to her home, had already dropped off some bags at the second-floor flat. He returned later that evening with more heavy bags that gave a clang when he accidentally knocked them together. Without showing her what was inside, he stored all the bags out of sight in a space above the ceiling.

On Friday, 13 June Moukharbal boarded the Middle East Airlines flight to Paris, a free man. But on arrival at the Orly airport terminal a plainclothed Lebanese officer who had tailed Moukharbal quietly pointed him out to a waiting DST team. The French believed Moukharbal would lie low for a while, but sooner or later he would make a mistake, and perhaps lead them to his accomplices.

Moukharbal collected his suitcase and then took a taxi to the Latin Quarter. The Lebanese walked into a dirty grey house at number 9 Rue Toullier, and emerged a quarter of an hour later with a tall, heavily built man with a pale complexion and dark wavy hair who was carrying his suitcase for him.

Using a telephoto lens, the DST watchers snapped two pictures of the pair, and one of the unknown companion alone as, deep in conversation, they turned into the Rue Soufflot and walked towards the Luxembourg Gardens. One photograph showed Moukharbal, still dapper despite his Beirut ordeal, waving a cigarette as he makes a point. Moukharbal's acquaintance listens intently, his lower lip set in a pout, and his open jacket flapping in the breeze.

The DST men tailing Moukharbal recorded his encounters with a French secretary, Catherine Bonnefoy, but the watch yielded little else. Budgets were tight at the DST, and surveillance was costly. DST chiefs, convinced from the outset that they were wasting their time with Moukharbal, needed little excuse to scale down the operation. A few days after his return to France the coded surveillance reports that had been sent to Mauriat via the French embassy in Beirut stopped arriving.

So episodic did the surveillance become that Moukharbal was able to give the DST the slip and cross the Channel to Britain on 20 June. With help from the French, the Special Branch found him and expelled him the following day. At Calais he was handed over to the regional branch of the Renseignements Généraux, a security service responsible for domestic intelligence and best known to the French for the hundreds of thousands of files it keeps on them. In what must have been a humiliating request, the DST was forced to demand that Moukharbal be handed back to it, with the pretext that it wanted to question him.

Face to face in the DST headquarters close to the Elysée Palace, Commissaire Herranz and Moukharbal played cat and mouse. 'I have three brothers and three sisters. I do painting and decorating work,' was all Moukharbal would say at his first interrogation.[4] But at the second session he admitted that one of the men he had met in Paris over the past few days was Nourredine. Moukharbal added that he had given Nourredine 10,000 francs and a letter from someone in Beirut, but refused to say anything more.

Finally on the fifth day of detention, Friday, 27 June, Herranz threatened to put Moukharbal on a flight to Beirut the next day. The exhausted prisoner cracked. Moukharbal knew that his revelations to the Lebanese police would soon reach the ears of his Palestinian masters and that returning to Beirut would mean certain execution. He blurted out that he was scared of dying, and he sold Nourredine. The man was the Popular Front's chief contact in Paris, he lied. Maria-Teresa Lara, a young Venezuelan woman whom Moukharbal claimed (equally untruthfully) was his lover, might have some more information on Nourredine. She lived in the Latin Quarter, in a studio flat at number 9 Rue Toullier. Moukharbal did not, however, tell the DST that so might the woman sharing the flat with Maria-Teresa, Nancy Sánchez Falcon. An anthropology student, Nancy had fallen in love with Carlos that winter, and her flat had for a time served as his weapons cache.

On the other side of the Seine from the DST, the two windows of a small flat on the Rue Toullier, a short, sloping street behind the Sorbonne University, gaped open as Paris languished in the worst heatwave in more than a dozen years. Green curtains hung motionless in the muggy evening air. The sound of laughter and South American music from a party echoed around the courtyard below, much to the chagrin of neighbours exasperated by the raucous fiestas that they frequently had to endure.

Carlos and three young Venezuelan students – Leyma Palomares, Edgar Marino Muller and Luis Urdaneta Urbina – had crammed into the flat at five o'clock that afternoon to drink Nancy's health before she left to spend her summer holidays in Venezuela. After a few drinks Carlos escorted Nancy to the taxi rank around the corner in the Rue Soufflot. Not bothering to accompany his girlfriend to the airport, he waved her goodbye and then walked up the street to buy a bottle of J&B whisky which he took back to the party.

With both flatmates away (Maria-Teresa was in Marseille on her way to a holiday in Algeria), Carlos played host. Socialising with Latin Americans might allow him to broaden his support network beyond current and ex-girlfriends to like-minded male acquaintances. To Urdaneta, Carlos had introduced himself when they first met at the beginning of the year as a Peruvian, and on a later occasion as an Argentinian, hastily adding that he had dual nationality. The sociology student thought him intelligent and an apparently keen cinema-goer.[5]

The flat on the Rue Toullier, decorated with posters including a blown-up photograph of Fidel Castro, and a skull and crossed swords above the slogan *Una pelea cubana contro los demonios* (A Cuban fight against the devil), was a less than ideal set-up for Carlos. The only, flimsy guarantee of privacy in the main room, in which both girls slept, were the curtains that could be drawn around Nancy's bed. But the flat was in the centre of Paris and it was cheap, with a monthly rent of only 650 francs. Carlos, who had by then settled in the French capital, had been nagging Nancy to let him move in. But her flatmate was so set against the idea that the two women were no longer on speaking terms. There was a camp-bed for him to sleep on when he did spend a night there, and he had so far been allowed some cupboard space where he kept clothes that were for the most part so expensive that they looked out of place in such humble accommodation: a raincoat with a Savile Row label, Nina Ricci ties, Italian leather shoes, a pair of Christian Dior glasses with neutral lenses, and cotton vests from Marks and Spencer.

Carlos's clothes were one of the first things that young people noticed about him. Angela Armstrong, a blonde British secretary who worked for the Collège de France science institute, and a friend of Nancy's, caught her first glimpse of Carlos at Rue Toullier: 'I came into the room, and they'd got only one big chair and he was sitting on it. He's fairly sort of well-built and they called him El Gordo, which means the fat one. He seemed very much at home, very sure of himself, better dressed than most of the students, you know, classic clothes, not blue jeans, not long hair. And I thought he was oversure of himself.'[6] Angela Armstrong knew him as Nancy's lover and a Peruvian carpet dealer.

There was one niggling drawback to the flat: the women could not afford to have a telephone line installed. So Carlos was reduced to conducting his business from nearby cafés, his pockets weighed down by coins needed for long-distance calls. Until Carlos became a regular fixture at the flat, friends had strolled in without bothering to knock. But he had a spyhole fitted into the door and people now had to wait before they were allowed in.

His pale complexion flushed with alcohol, Carlos joined in when the students at the party belted out a spirited song from Venezuela as one of them strummed a *cuatro*, a traditional four-stringed instrument similar to a ukelele.

But his bonhomie was a pretence. He knew that Moukharbal had been arrested by the DST several days earlier and he was worried that the Lebanese might inform against him.

Commissaire Herranz was due to join his family in Toulouse that evening, and he was in a hurry to wrap up the case ahead of Moukharbal's probable expulsion the following day, Saturday. Moukharbal's revelations left him with little alternative but to pay a quick visit to Rue Toullier.

It was late, and all the drivers had gone home. Herranz took the wheel of an unmarked car, and set off with the prisoner and two inspectors – Raymond Dous, an Algerian war veteran labelled a pacifist intellectual by his colleagues, and the good-looking Jean Donatini, a young recruit from the Champagne region who had just been at a colleague's retirement party. None of the men carried their Manhurin service guns, as they did not want to have to return later in the evening to sign them in for the weekend. Herranz had returned his two hours earlier, before dropping in on the retirement party.

As Herranz drove to the Latin Quarter, a decidedly talkative Moukharbal gave a detailed description of Nourredine's appearance. At around half past eight they neared Rue Toullier, but it took them some time to find a parking space. Herranz ended up parking the car some way from the flat. As he got out of the car he told Dous to follow him, and ordered Donatini to wait in the car and keep watch on Moukharbal.

There was no concierge at number 9, a confusing tangle of stairs and passageways. Clutching the brass railing, the men trudged up the steep red-carpeted stairs to the first floor, and then out over the little iron footbridge leading to a second house set back from the street, a more run-down version built originally for servants. The staircase up to the second-floor flat was even steeper, and very dark. Herranz, looking for the light switch, pressed the doorbell of another flat by mistake. A young Spanish woman, Incarnacion Carrasco, abandoned her dinner guests to open the door. 'I'm sorry, I made a mistake,' Herranz apologised before starting upstairs, in no mood to listen to Carrasco's complaints about her noisy neighbours.

Privacy was a rare commodity in the flat, so Carlos and the twenty-one-year-old Leyma Palomares had retreated to the tiny bathroom to talk about Leyma's worsening relations with her husband. She had first met Carlos a year earlier and although she saw him regularly she knew little about him.[7] As Carlos perched uncomfortably on the toilet seat, Leyma tried to make more room for herself. She bent down to move a brown briefcase resting on the floor. 'Be careful!' Carlos shouted. She froze, and then glanced at him quizzically. Carlos asked whether she would like to see what was inside the briefcase. He opened it and pulled out a pistol with a long barrel. Guns meant little to the young woman, but Carlos fondly cradled the Czech-made, CZ Vzor 52 automatic. It was a powerful 7.62-calibre gun capable of firing eight bullets a second.

A few minutes into their conversation, a friend glanced in and told them that police were at the front door. Leyma strode out of the bathroom ahead of Carlos. Herranz spoke to her in an aggressive tone and she lost her temper and tried to rip his pass card out of his hand. Her friends calmed them both down.

When Herranz asked to see everyone's identity papers, Carlos showed his passport.

'Do you know any Arabs?' Herranz asked Carlos.

'No, I don't because I hate Arabs.'

'What about the Beirut stamp in your passport?'

'Anyone can go there as a tourist,' Carlos replied. As he

looked edgy, and had been drinking, Herranz searched him but found no weapon.

Dous pulled three photographs from his jacket pocket, and turned to Carlos. On the back of one of the pictures someone had written 'Moukharbal', but he made sure that Carlos did not see this.

'What were you doing on 13 June?' Dous asked Carlos. Carlos protested that he did not look at all like the tall man in the picture. And no, he did not know the other man and had not carried his suitcase. As Herranz and Dous persisted, raising their voices in exasperation, Carlos threatened to appeal to his ambassador and shouted out: 'You don't know who my father is!'

The pair were difficult to shake off. Carlos offered them whisky. Only Herranz accepted, but the tension eased. Leyma took Marino by the hand and made him sit down next to her on the bed. She announced that she would play a tune on the *cuatro*. She started to sing. Carlos excused himself and went into the bathroom. He closed the door behind him and, out of sight of the others, reached down to his briefcase. When he emerged a few moments later, the Czech-made automatic nestled down the back of his trousers.

Herranz had not been convinced by Carlos's protestations, and he asked Dous to fetch the two men waiting in the car outside. In an attempt to ease the tension as he waited for their return, Herranz asked the students about their politics. They replied that they were leftists, but not violent.

'If you're not into politics what do you do?' Carlos asked him.

'I stand for the security of citizens,' Herranz answered.

'DST,' Carlos hissed, pointing at him.

Donatini, who had long been fed up with waiting, was relieved to see Dous. His only distraction had been watching the Friday night crowds stroll past the stuffy car. It was just after ten o'clock as the three crossed the footbridge that ran above the courtyard. They were greeted by the Venezuelan song 'Barlovento' bursting through the flat's open windows: 'Barlovento, Barlovento, ardent land of the drum, my slender Negress is on her way to the fiesta...' The three men started up the narrow flight of steps.

When he arrived at the flat Donatini was surprised to see Commissaire Herranz holding a glass of whisky as a young woman sitting on the bed strummed her instrument and sang at the top of her voice. Only Carlos had not joined in the party atmosphere, standing away from the others. He had been passing his hand through his hair when Moukharbal walked in and was surprised at the change in his friend's appearance: 'Michel had changed a great deal. It was as if he had fallen into a state of lethargy, no doubt the result of the psychological and physical torture which had been inflicted on him.'[8]

Confused by the sight of Herranz having a drink with Carlos in such rowdy surroundings, Moukharbal asked for silence. Dous enquired whether he knew anyone in the room. The Lebanese raised his arm – he was so weak that he could not stop it trembling – to point at Carlos. In a voice broken by exhaustion, he identified the man he had until then called Nourredine: 'It's him. He's the man who carried my suitcase.'

Carlos stopped stroking his hair. Suddenly his right hand came out from behind his back grasping a gun with a long barrel. All Leyma saw were 'flames, or rather flashes of light which blinded me'.[9] She heard the dry crack of the gun firing before she hid her head in her arms and threw herself sideways on the bed.

Moukharbal collapsed. His neck had been pierced by a bullet which entered below his right ear, sliced through his spinal cord, and exited beneath his left ear. Carlos, according to one of those present, was firing 'like a lunatic'.[10] But there was method in his madness. He had worked out who was the most senior of the three DST officers, and had swung his gun towards Herranz, who was standing to his right. The Second World War veteran dived to the ground as Carlos squeezed the trigger. A bullet carved a wide gash through the commissaire's bull-like neck.

Herranz, who broke two teeth when his face struck the parquet floor, was still conscious, and heard more firing. Donatini, the nearest to Carlos, was hit in the upper lip, with a bullet fired from such close range that much of his face was speckled with gunpowder. Dous almost managed to dodge Carlos's next shot, which blew a hole through his right hand. As the force of the impact spun Dous round, Carlos fired again, grazing the man's cheek, leaving a blackish mark five centimetres long. But the next shot buried itself into the base of his neck. Dous and Donatini fell close to each other, and their blood mingled as it soaked into a rug. Carlos had acted so fast and with such icy precision that none of his victims had time to seek refuge in the corridor only a few feet away. Their bodies all lay within a few feet of each other.

In the flat below, Incarnacion Carrasco's dinner party was over. She was standing by her front door, saying goodbye to one of her guests when two bullets whistled through the ceiling, bounced off the dining table and buried themselves in the floor. Carrasco watched a man hurtle down the steep stairs, taking them four at a time.

In the ground-floor flat, Olivier Martel, a photographer who had also had his evening spoilt by the noise of the party, leaped to the window when he heard shots. He saw the silhouette of a man gripping a gun with a long barrel in his right hand. The man ran across the footbridge, the wooden slats creaking under his weight, and jumped down into the courtyard before clambering up some scaffolding to scale a four-metre wall which separated the courtyard from that of the house next door.[11] Like the shots fired moments earlier, a woman's anguished cry echoed in the darkness: '*Dios mio*, what is going on?'

Carlos cleared the wall and, opening a door that led off the courtyard and was always left unlocked, rushed through the hallway of number 11, thrusting his gun once more into the back of his trousers. Out in the street, he forced himself to slow down and silently gave thanks for a sudden power failure which plunged Rue Toullier into darkness as he walked past an armed police patrol.

In the small flat, where the acrid smell of gunsmoke hung heavy in the warm night air, the students panicked. Marino, who had thrown himself off the bed and on to the floor when the shots rang out, picked himself up and ran outside, shouting at Leyma to follow him. She yelled after him to come back and get her bag. Together with their friend Urdaneta, they fled out on to the street and ran on down Rue Soufflot.

They had almost reached the Luxembourg Gardens when Urdaneta stopped abruptly, and convinced the others that they had done nothing wrong and should return to try to help the wounded men. Outside Nancy's house they came across Herranz, chest and shoulders spattered with the blood from his neck wound, who was on the verge of fainting. The students helped him into a taxi which took him to Cochin hospital. Of the four men hit by Carlos's bullets, he was the only one still alive.

Ambulancemen called by Carrasco turned the bodies on to their backs to find out if anything could be done. Minutes later, Commissaire Daniel Marcout stepped gingerly around the red puddles seeping into the rug and parquet. He felt the dead men's clothes and found they carried no guns.[12] Moukharbal lay across the legs of the two counter-intelligence officers, his cheeks and neck streaked with the blood that had gushed from his mouth. His eyes were wide open as was his mouth. He was only identified later, as all that was found on him was a pen and eighty francs.[13] Dous and Donatini lay side by side.

'I've seen many things in my time, but three bodies in one room is rather a lot,' mused Pierre Ottavioli of the Brigade Criminelle.[14] While forensic police dusted for fingerprints, Ottavioli tried to make some sense of the statements his men were taking down from the three shocked Venezuelans. They had little information on a man they referred to as 'Carlos', and none at all on the identity of one of the dead men (Moukharbal).[15]

Accompanied by a deputy of the Paris public prosecutor, Ottavioli left the flat to question Herranz at Cochin hospital. He found the commissaire in intensive care, on the point of being wheeled into an operating theatre. Herranz managed to give a few rough leads to his visitors. He named the fourth victim as Moukharbal, explained that he had been in custody for the past few days, and that he had pointed to the gunman when he entered the flat.[16]

In the Rue Toullier neighbourhood hundreds of police and gendarmes sealed off streets and ordered locals not to leave their homes. The concierges grouched that they hadn't seen so many excited *flics* since those Sorbonne students had torn up the pavements in May 1968.

The insistent ring of the telephone late that same night in another Paris flat a little more than a mile away woke Amparo. It was Carlos, who asked her if he could come and see her as soon as possible – not to rekindle a dormant passion, but to pick up some papers. Unhappy at being disturbed so late, Amparo told him to come round later because she wanted to go back to sleep. She hung up and glanced at her watch. It was midnight.

In the small hours of the morning, Carlos woke up one of his girlfriends, Nydia, in London. 'Hello, my love, it's me,' he said, calling from a phone booth. 'I had to do it. Moukharbal was a coward, the police took him and he sold us. I had to make a way for myself by shooting. There was no way of avoiding him ... It was him or me. I think that if I had fallen into their hands I would have been killed.'[17]

In fact, Carlos had shot dead three men and wounded a fourth at a time when police had nothing against him. He had left a string of witnesses and clues behind. Had he simply given himself up to the DST, he might only have been charged with illegal possession of a gun. If he had wanted to flee, threatening the officers with his pistol would have been enough. Even his escape route, involving a leap from the footbridge into the courtyard, had been clumsy. A more discreet alternative would have been to run up to the fifth floor where one of those rambling, communicating corridors which are so common in old Parisian houses would have allowed him to slip unseen into the neighbouring building.

Carlos allowed Amparo only five hours' sleep. At about five o'clock in the morning, his gun still stuffed into his belt, he used the key she had once given him to barge into her flat. He had no guarantee that Moukharbal had not passed on the Rue Amélie address to the DST, just as he had disclosed the Rue Toullier address. But Carlos was past caring. Without even greeting Amparo, he flicked the light on, went up to a chest of drawers next to her bed, opened the bottom drawer and grabbed a paper bag. Emptying the bag on the table, he selected and pocketed a red Chilean passport. He then pulled another bag from a cupboard and rummaged inside it. In his haste, he mistakenly rang the Gare de l'Est instead of the Gare du Nord to ask when the next Trans-Europe-Express to Brussels was due to leave.

After getting the information he wanted, the man whom Amparo had loved for his gallantry finally acknowledged her. What he then told her forced her fully awake. Constantly glancing at his watch, he explained that he had killed his chief because he had betrayed him, that he had also shot and killed three policemen (Carlos had left the three officers for dead), and that he was leaving for Brussels. He cautioned Amparo, telling her to be careful. The menacing way Carlos gave her that advice made her feel afraid of him for the first time.

After pulling the pistol out of his belt, slipping the magazine out, reloading and then snapping it back, he settled at a table with pen and paper and started writing. It was a hurriedly phrased letter, in Spanish, to another of his London girlfriends, the Spanish waitress Angela Otaola. He addressed it to the bar where she worked, Bistro 17 in Queensway. He signed it, underlining his name twice.

> Dear Angela,
>
> As you know, things are very serious here. I had a narrow escape. I will cross the border. I'm not telephoning you, because I must have torn up the postcard. I'm sending you this letter twice, to the bistro and to the house, in case my memory fails me and I get the address wrong, so that one of them reaches you. Don't ring my girlfriend, I'm going on a journey, I don't know how long for but I hope that I won't be long in returning. As for the 'Chiquitin' [little baby], I have sent him to a better world, because he was a traitor.
>
> Kisses,
>
> Carlos[18]

He then made another phone call, to Linda Escobari, an air stewardess in London who was a family friend. He asked her husband to take down a message in Spanish for his mother in Venezuela: 'I am leaving for Asia.'[19] Again Carlos glanced at his watch. At six o'clock he said a cursory goodbye to Amparo and strode out of the flat.

He did not make straight for the Gare du Nord, but hung around the neighbourhood before once again taking a big risk. Inexplicably, he strolled into a building that police were very likely to make a priority in their hunt for a fugitive: the Air France bus terminal at the Invalides. At around eight o'clock that morning, he bumped into the British secretary, Angela Armstrong, who was buying a plane ticket at the terminal. Her five-year-old daughter, Nina, was with her. Carlos looked relaxed when he greeted Angela, but took her by the shoulder and steered her and Nina towards a quiet corner of the bus terminal.

'Have you heard the news?' he asked her in English.

'No.'

Carlos suddenly switched to Spanish, speaking urgently in hushed tones as he launched into a short disjointed monologue.

'I've killed three policemen and a dirty Arab who betrayed me. I'm not in the habit of killing. I kill all those who betray me. Write to Nancy, tell her to stay in Venezuela, nothing will happen to her. It's annoying, I'm leaving for the Middle East to fetch some papers and then I'll come back.'

And he was gone.

He's gone mad, or he's drunk, Armstrong thought. But as she walked past the newspaper kiosk outside the terminal, her eye caught the front-page headlines. 'TWO POLICEMEN KILLED, ANOTHER WOUNDED. The two murderers were reportedly Venezuelan. One of them was killed,' the popular daily *L'Aurore* (which Carlos had bombed the previous summer) inaccurately informed its readers in its first version. Slowly the truth sank in. The words 'I kill all those who betray me' began to sound more like a threat than a confidence.[20]

For a week the DST had neglected a clue that might have prevented the murders. In Moukharbal's flat on Avenue Claude-Vellefaux in eastern Paris investigators had found a cheque for 2500 francs bearing Amparo's name. The cheque was signed by a jeweller who said she had asked him to lend her money, and he revealed her address. But it was only on

Monday, 30 June, three days after the bloodbath, that the manhunt reached the Rue Amélie flat.

The woman's home was a cavern worthy of Ali Baba and the Forty Thieves, marvelled *L'Aurore*. Amparo had not asked to look inside Carlos's bags. Nor had he offered to show her the unsettling collection which had turned her flat into a high-risk incendiary zone. Among the most valuable items were Czech-made Skorpion machine-pistols, lightweight technical wonders that boasted a greater range than conventional pistols. Besides these the bags contained ten pistols also mostly of Czech origin, thirty three chargers, twenty-eight grenades, fifteen sticks of dynamite, six kilos of plastic explosives, detonators and some thirty electric igniters, as well as three home-made bombs ready for use.

Among the grenades from Eastern Europe were two igniting caps marked 'UZRGM 08–73354' – the same inscription as had been found on part of a grenade discovered at Orly airport after the second failed rocket attack on an El Al plane. The markings on an M26 fragmentation hand grenade showed that it was similar to the one thrown in the Drugstore, and to the three that had been abandoned by the Japanese Red Army after the siege of the French embassy in The Hague.[21]

As well as weapons, explosives and ammunition, Carlos had stored in Amparo's flat a forger's kit and a list of leading French Jews or figures linked to Jewish circles, including the popular politician Simone Veil, an Auschwitz survivor who was then Health Minister. Other names listed by Carlos included that of Saudi Arabia's Oil Minister, Sheikh Ahmed Zaki Yamani. There were also files containing plans of the offices of the three Paris newspapers bombed the previous summer, and Moukharbal's little green notebook detailing operations and accounts over the past year – down to the two-franc charge for access to the Orly airport observation terrace on the day of the second attack.

As the DST men who raided the flat at gunpoint picked

their way through Carlos's belongings, they found four passports bearing his picture. The DST had no idea which if any of the four identities matched that of the real Carlos: Cenon Clark, an American, born in New York on 20 June 1945; Glenn H. Gebhard, also an American, born in New York on 1 August 1950; Carlos Andres Martinez Torres, a Peruvian, born in Soltero on 4 May 1947; and Ilich Ramírez Sánchez, a Venezuelan, born in Caracas on 12 October 1949. It was only much later that five of the fingerprints that had been discovered in the flat on Rue Toullier were matched to a set of prints sent by the Venezuelan authorities.[22]

'I am in love with him,' Amparo told the state security court after she was charged with possession of arms and explosives, and with collusion with the agents of a foreign power, a catch-all charge often used in counter-terrorism investigations. But she readily described to investigators the dawn visit to her flat by a distraught Carlos.[23]

It was Carlos's reliance on young women that led police one step closer to him. In London in mid-June when Angela Otaola and her boyfriend Barry Woodhams were moving a chest of drawers in her flat he had discovered two envelopes containing an out-of-date Chilean passport bearing Carlos's photograph but with the name Adolfo José Müller Bernal, and a Kuwaiti international driving licence also with his photograph but made out in yet another name. There was also a list of prominent British figures, many of them Jewish. Intrigued, Woodhams had then picked the cheap lock on the black Antler holdall that Carlos had asked Angela to store behind a bookcase several months earlier. The neatly wrapped parcels on top in the holdall contained a Czech automatic pistol, a silencer and ammunition. Woodhams had gone no further, worried that Carlos would guess that he had opened the bag.

On 1 July, a day after the DST discovered the arms cache at Amparo's flat in Paris, Woodhams read about the

Toullier case in the *Guardian.* Woodhams began to wonder whether Carlos the killer and the Carlos he knew were the same man. Like Paris, London was suffering a heatwave and the flat was stifling when he went home that evening. It also smelled sickly sweet. Woodhams took another look inside the black bag. He found three guns whose serial numbers had been filed down – a Browning and two Czech-made pistols, one of which had been fitted with a silencer. There were also rubber coshes, ammunition, and rubber stamps for forging entry visas into various countries. The strange sweet smell was coming from packs of sweating gelignite, so unstable it could have been detonated by the flick of a light switch.

Woodhams's leftist sympathies meant that he had little confidence in the police, so he decided instead 'to go to a part of the press I could trust'. But when he telephoned the *Guardian*, the newsdesk worried that he might be one of the dozens of eccentrics who call up newspapers every day. Bring the bag in, Woodhams was told. He turned up in the newsroom with a gun and the list of names taken from the bag.

One of the *Guardian* reporters who accompanied Woodhams back to the flat spotted a paperback copy of a thriller which he had recently finished reading, Frederick Forsyth's *The Day of the Jackal*, in the bookcase. A new *nom de guerre*, Carlos the Jackal, was born. No matter that the novel's hero was a tall, blond Englishman with a lean build and grey eyes 'as bleak as a Channel fog', or that he had little to do with Palestinian extremists.

Had Carlos been modelling himself on the English assassin? Years later, Woodhams wrote in to the newspaper to set the record straight: 'Which is true? Was the Jackal a Frederick Forsyth fan? Or, even more insidious, had he planned his own nickname? I am afraid the second version is wrong. The book was in the bookcase and belongs to me – a Frederick Forsyth fan.'[24]

As Scotland Yard, called in by the *Guardian*, turned the flat upside down, Angela Otaola smoked a cigarette and clowned around with a police helmet several sizes too large for her. Asked about her relationship with Carlos, she described him as 'a friend – well, a former friend now'. The black bag was sent to the Home Office's forensic explosives laboratory, which analysed its contents. They found detonators; grenade-igniter sets; three live Mills hand grenades, the standard issue for the British army, wrapped in paper marked '3 British hand grenades' in Carlos's handwriting; a half-kilo slab of orange, claylike Semtex plastic explosive of Czechoslovak origin; three slabs of another, probably Swedish explosive, again wrapped in brown paper and marked '6 cartridges of dinamyte' (*sic*); two lengths of safety fuse; and a Russian-type F1 fragmentation hand grenade.

Both Barry Woodhams and Angela Otaola were arrested. He was freed after three days. But she was jailed for a year on charges of possessing arms and then deported. Woodhams's revelations ruined their relationship: 'She never spoke to me again after we were arrested.'[25]

Angela Otaola was not the only woman to suffer for Carlos's sake. Even those who had not sought out his company paid a price. After their sudden encounter at the bus terminal in Paris, Angela Armstrong had felt too afraid to write to her friend Nancy as Carlos had requested. She tried to persuade her boyfriend in London to send a message but he too had read the newspapers and refused. Fearing that she was in danger, Angela Armstrong flew to London but decided only a day later that she should talk to the police. She was arrested on her return to Paris. The police abandoned her in her cell during the day, and questioned her at night. When her nerve snapped under the strain and she turned hysterical, one of the interrogators hit her across the face. She was freed after twenty-five days. Nydia Tobon paid a heavier price. Investigators found that she had acted as Carlos's banker and had helped him use a false identity. Although no evidence was discovered at the time to suggest that she knew or suspected anything about his guerrilla activities, she was jailed by an Old Bailey court for a year.[26]

The revelation by the *Guardian* that Carlos had lived in London sparked a flood of supposed sightings across Britain. A frightened Dahlia Fuentes, an employee at the Venezuelan consulate who knew Carlos, testified that she saw him knocking at the door of her home late one evening but that she did not let him in because he seemed very dirty, which struck her as unusual given his customary neatness. Carlos retorted years later that this had been a feminine ruse, a ploy by Fuentes to have herself recalled home where she could pursue a former Venezuelan ambassador with whom she was in love.[27] What is now clear is that after the shooting in Paris, Carlos passed through Brussels and then flew to Beirut to give Haddad his version of events.[28]

There, on the day after the three murders, the chief of the criminal investigation unit, Colonel Dahdah, summoned the former DST serviceman who had helped question Moukharbal, Jean-Paul Mauriat. With the top brass of the department assembled in their parade uniforms in his office, the colonel told him in grave tones what had happened in Paris. The department, the colonel assured him, expressed its sorrow and stood by the French on this day of all days.

The political party of which Moukharbal was a member, the Syrian Popular Party, lost no time in avenging its deceased member. Mauriat had only just returned home when a barrage of 12.7-calibre bullets hit his apartment, sending him and his wife diving for cover. The Syrian Popular Party was not the only one after Mauriat. Carlos was also seeking revenge. 'Colonel Dahdah told me that Carlos wanted to shoot me dead on his return to Beirut,'

Mauriat later recalled in a matter-of-fact tone. He was lucky: 'The Palestinians warned Carlos that if he did so the French secret services would turn venomous and many people would die. One of the PLO leaders, Abu Iyad, sent him off to the Libyan capital Tripoli.'[29]

With no progress in the French investigation since the finding of the arsenal at Amparo's home, the Interior Ministry announced on 10 July that it had ordered the expulsion of three Cuban diplomats it linked to Carlos and his friends at the Rue Toullier flat. The ministry said the three – the embassy's first secretary and two cultural attachés – were all members of the Cuban DGI secret service, an organisation that worked closely with the KGB.

The ministry dropped heavy hints that Carlos might have sought and obtained refuge at the Cuban embassy after the shootings. Officials under Interior Minister Poniatowski spread the word that the DGI had helped Carlos to flee from Marseille to Algiers on a fruit cargo boat or, in what would have been a much more comfortable journey, by car to East Germany with a Cuban diplomatic passport, and then by air to the Middle East. The expulsions for terrorist links were a first for France, which until then had only thrown out diplomats for spying. 'Certain foreign intelligence services,' thundered Poniatowski, 'are giving aid to international terrorist organisations.' The press had a field day speculating on Carlos's Moscow ties.

More discreetly, Havana urgently recalled Pedro Lara Zamora, a second secretary at the Paris embassy who had been due to go on leave the following month. DGI officer Zamora had been a regular caller at Nancy Sánchez Falcon's flat on Rue Toullier where he discussed politics with her friends, and had often accompanied her to events at the Maison de Cuba cultural centre.

The Rue Toullier shootings humiliated the DST. The counter-intelligence service had blundered because it did not believe in the vitally important coded messages sent from Beirut. There was enough in Moukharbal's testimony to show that he was dangerous, and that there might be an accomplice in the Rue Toullier flat. The failure to understand Moukharbal's importance, the casual way in which the visit to the flat was handled – three unarmed officers, no back-up, an informer in tow, drinks before setting out and at the flat – all contributed to the bloodbath. Herranz owned up to part of this when he admitted in public that he had thought Carlos was small fry. For years afterwards, Herranz would start every time he saw Carlos mentioned on television. 'He would have liked to track him down, and he never gave up. Following Carlos, knowing where he was, was his life's work,' according to Herranz's son Jean-Noël.[30]

In one of its earliest disinformation campaigns after the murders, the DST encouraged newspapers to speculate on whether the three officers had been carrying their guns. One article referred to the DST refusing to confirm or deny that the victims were armed, at a time when it was known they were not, since this had been established within hours of the crime. In his report, the first police officer at the scene, Commissaire Marcout, said that no weapons were found on or near any of the dead men.[31] Senior DST officer Philippe Parant confirmed shortly afterwards at the flat that their weapons were at headquarters.[32] 'It was a technical error. The DST officers did not imagine that Carlos would defend himself in that way, and so they weren't armed,' former President Valéry Giscard d'Estaing admitted.[33] Salt was rubbed in to the wound later when, in their indictment of Carlos for the Rue Toullier shootings, public prosecutors criticised the DST officers for calling on the flat unarmed.

Fresh humiliation was avoided when the DST suppressed further evidence of the cavalier way the visit to Rue Toullier had been handled. Donatini's autopsy revealed that his body had a blood-alcohol content of 1.45 grammes per litre, officially defined as 'a light alcoholic condition' but enough to affect his vision, lower his guard, and slow his reflexes.[34] The DST kept the results of the autopsy secret. Donatini should never have gone to Rue Toullier.

In the DST's clumsy attempt to hide its tracks, it even doctored one of the photographs showing Moukharbal and Carlos. Officially, the DST maintained that it knew nothing of the Rue Toullier address until Moukharbal revealed it a few hours before the bloodbath. In fact, the files of the judicial investigation contain two versions of the picture which are identical save that in one the name of the street, Rue Soufflot, and the street number (number 20) have been blanked out – a clear attempt to conceal the fact that the DST had come so close to Carlos a few days earlier. A coded report on Moukharbal's visit to Rue Toullier on the day of his arrival in Paris was sent to Mauriat in Beirut at the time.

The DST was not alone in twisting events. 'I am not a professional killer,' Carlos modestly observed in his account of the shootings four years later. He fired first at the DST officers, he explained, and then pointed his gun at Moukharbal who was walking towards him with his hands over his face. 'The fatal moment had arrived. It was the rule of the game: a traitor is condemned to die. When he was in front of me, I shot him between the eyes. When he hit the ground, I shot him again in his left temple.'[35] The autopsy however showed that only one bullet had hit Moukharbal, piercing his neck from left to right.[36]

When Carlos was shown the surveillance photographs by French investigators two decades after the DST officers had asked him about them in the flat, he again denied that he was one of those portrayed. 'It looks like a Libyan man but it can't be him because the photograph dates from twenty years ago and at that time he was a child. It's not me. That's obvious. Look at the face, it's not human. It looks like a mask,' he bluffed.[37]

But he was now much more talkative about the other man in the picture, Michel Moukharbal, who he said was in charge of the Popular Front's military operations in Europe. In the same breath he branded him as 'a traitor, a triple agent working simultaneously for the Israeli Mossad and the French secret services, probably the DST. He died when under French police protection.' Asked whether he was in Paris on the night of the shootings, Carlos answered, 'It's difficult to know after twenty years where I was on that day since I've been to most of the countries in the world.'[38]

Within hours of Moukharbal's death his Palestinian masters hailed him as 'a fighting comrade who took part in the planning and execution of numerous, heroic and audacious actions' with the conclusion: 'The death of Comrade Moukharbal is not the end but just a new incentive to future struggle.' According to Carlos however, 'Comrade Moukharbal' had given the Popular Front cause for concern before his death: 'In Paris, the security service of our organisation had noticed that Moukharbal was being followed everywhere he went, which worried it greatly because it didn't know who was interested in him. The organisation mentioned this to Moukharbal and asked him to carry a gun and agree to have bodyguards. His response was evasive and he refused all protection measures. The organisation then considered pulling him out, and again he refused ... The situation was critical and the warning signs were flashing. His behaviour was illogical, it even became suspect.'[39]

It was only some time after Moukharbal's death that the Popular Front found an explanation for his puzzling behaviour. According to Carlos, Mossad awarded Moukharbal the princely salary of around 40,000 francs a month. 'Obviously, the Popular Front wasn't able to obtain material proof of this but we reached this conclusion by cross-checking,' Carlos testified later.[40] A former Mossad *katsa*, or intelligence case officer, Victor Ostrovsky, writes that

Moukharbal was recruited as far back as June 1973, and supplied information on the routine of his predecessor, Boudia, which was used by the Wrath of God commando that blew Boudia up later the same month.

Ostrovsky, a former weapons-testing expert, decided to write a book on his four years inside Mossad because he wanted to expose the 'twisted ideals, self-centred pragmatism ... greed, lust and total lack of respect for human life' which he claimed permeated the organisation.[41] He tells how the Paris-based spy Oren Riff, who later served as a Mossad course commander, turned Moukharbal around in a London hotel. After reciting all he knew about the Lebanese, Riff reportedly challenged him bluntly: 'I'm from Israeli intelligence and we're willing to pay you a pretty penny. We want you to work with us.' With a big grin, Moukharbal shot back: 'What took you so long?' According to Ostrovsky, Moukharbal agreed to collaborate not so much for the money as to ensure that he was protected by both sides.

The Popular Front was happy to accept Carlos's version of events. After his escape from Paris he earned a vote of confidence from his recruiting officer Bassam Abu-Sharif, who publicly described Carlos as 'the most brilliant agent and our chief international operative. Carlos is outside of the grasp of the police forces which are after him. We can tell all that Carlos will make his presence felt in the months to come. He will prove our point.'

5

An Awful Party

Tell them I'm from Venezuela and my name is Carlos.
Tell them I'm the famous Carlos. They know me.
– Carlos to the mediator at the OPEC raid

In the eyes of his Palestinian masters, Carlos had shown his mettle in Paris. He had also murdered the Popular Front's chief European envoy. But in Beirut he had managed to persuade Haddad that Moukharbal had died a traitor's death. Carlos's arguments, and his notoriety as France and Britain launched a worldwide manhunt for him, ensured advancement rather than a reprimand.

At meetings in Beirut and Aden through the late summer and early autumn of 1975 Haddad discussed a new plan with Carlos. Until then Carlos's task had required little more than the personal networks he had set up in London and Paris, which were answerable only to him and inextricably entwined with his private life. Haddad's new mission meant that Carlos needed more than girlfriends, in or out of love with him, ready to run an errand or hide his weapons in their flats. With Haddad's encouragement, Carlos looked further afield.

Among European guerrilla movements, West Germany's Revolutionary Cells was the group that Carlos knew best. It had helped him to carry out the first rocket attack at Orly airport, and it agreed to form the backbone of the new team. Carlos approached his friend Wilfried Böse, the co-founder of the Revolutionary Cells. They agreed that Böse should brief the long-haired Hans-Joachim Klein, the former bailiff's clerk who had mistaken Carlos for a Mafioso when the two had met for the first time. Klein had sought refuge in the Revolutionary Cells partly to escape his past: he laboured for most of his life under the illusion that his drunken father who beat him as a child was a former SS member, and his mother a Jewish survivor of the Ravensbrück concentration camp. In fact, his father had served with the Wehrmacht on the dreaded Russian front, and his mother was not Jewish. Carlos trusted Klein after the failed attempt to kidnap the United Arab Emirates ambassador in London a few months earlier.

In November, in woods outside Frankfurt well away from any eavesdroppers, Böse briefed Klein. Now was Klein's chance, Böse told him, to strike a resounding blow for the Palestinian resistance. The fedayeen based in Beirut were in jeopardy, and the oil-rich Arab states were refusing to get involved. The Popular Front must jolt the Arab oil producers, most of whom advocated peace between Egypt and Israel, into standing up for their Palestinian brothers.

When Klein asked how this would be done, the answer startled him. Kidnap all the government ministers at the next conference of the Organisation of Petroleum-Exporting Countries (OPEC) in Vienna the following month. Surely the OPEC headquarters in the Austrian capital were too well protected, Klein objected. He was told that the commando which would carry out the raid could count on help from one of the OPEC member states – advance information that had been lacking when Carlos helped the Japanese Red Army seize the French embassy in The Hague. The plan was simple: Carlos would lead the guerrilla group into the building, kidnap the Oil Ministers, and demand a ransom which would help fund the Palestinian resistance movement. However, two of the ministers would not be released. They would be executed: Saudi Arabia's

Sheikh Yamani and Iran's Jamshid Amouzegar.

Klein accepted. The Revolutionary Cells also supplied Carlos with an activist who could claim 'combat' experience, the twenty-three-year-old Gabriele Kröcher-Tiedemann. Two years earlier West German police had discovered Kröcher-Tiedemann, then a sociology student, unscrewing number plates in a car park. She pulled out a gun and managed to wound one of the policemen before she was forced to give herself up. She was described by Interpol as having 'a flat chest, brown hair sometimes tinted a dark reddish colour, a pale face, grey-blue eyes, a big pointed nose, a small mouth, and big teeth'. The 'distinguishing features' section carried the entry: 'submissive, and a heavy smoker'.[1] Three other recruits – a Palestinian and two Lebanese known only by their code-names (Khalid, Yussef and Joseph) – completed Carlos's team.

In early December, after a final briefing from Haddad in Aden, Carlos returned to Europe. He took the scenic Alpine route from Switzerland into Austria, aboard the same train as Böse and Klein but without their knowledge. Carlos took a room at the Hilton east of Vienna's city centre, the first modern hotel to be built there since the war. Not for him the old-world splendour of the Habsburgian palaces that had been converted into hotels.

Böse and Klein stayed in a less luxurious hotel near the cathedral, and begrudged Carlos his expensive tastes: 'When Carlos spoke of his lifestyle, he would willingly admit that he had remained a bourgeois,' Klein explained. 'And I have to admit that this way of life did not displease us, even if we criticised him. He would always be richly dressed and stay in luxury hotels. He would say that it was better for his security. I have to say that for these operations we were not short of money, something like a hundred dollars per day and per guy. With that you can live well.'[2]

Over the past few weeks the twenty-six-year-old Carlos had grown a goatee beard and sideburns. He wore his hair long, and needed one last item to complete his attempt to look like his hero Che Guevara. After a few days strolling unarmed through the Austrian capital, he finally found what he needed in a chic boutique: a black beret.

Böse and Klein, who met Carlos as he emerged from the shop wearing thc brand-new beret at a rakish angle, were anxious for details of the planned assault. Carlos, as ever enjoying the good life, imparted only a little information as they lunched in an elegant restaurant. Carlos did not speak German, so Böse translated from English for Klein's benefit. The raid was set for 19 or 20 December. Kröcher-Tiedemann was due to arrive soon. The three other members of the team, together with the weapons and explosives, would follow soon after. Four other members of the Revolutionary Cells had arrived, renting two flats on Vienna's outskirts, to help prepare the attack. They were carrying out surveillance of the OPEC head-quarters, and scanning the archives of local newspapers in search of photographs and articles about previous OPEC conferences. Böse would not be part of the commando.

Klein had nothing to do but wait. He soon became bored with walking around the city and going to the cinema. A week went by before Carlos arranged another meeting with him and Böse, in the latter's hotel room. This time, Carlos was more talkative. He revealed that once the commando had kidnapped the Oil Ministers, they would demand a plane to fly the hostages out of Vienna. The plane would make for an unnamed destination where it would be swapped for a long-haul aircraft. The ministers would be released one at a time in their respective countries, but only after the government concerned broadcast a pro-Palestinian statement. If not, the minister would be killed immediately. Save for Sheikh Yamani and Amouzegar, whom Carlos pledged, according to Klein, to execute 'on the way, not in Vienna. We didn't talk much about it. Carlos was supposed to do it alone, to kill both. That's how it's done normally, it's the boss who does it.'[3]

Carlos's next set of instructions angered Klein. 'Whoever resists will be immediately executed,' Carlos warned. 'Whoever does not obey orders without delay will be executed; whoever tries to flee will be executed; if someone turns hysterical, starts to yell and goes round the bend, he or she will be executed. If a member of the commando does not obey my orders or does not conform with the instructions agreed in advance and thus jeopardises the success of the operation, he will be executed.'[4]

Klein pointed out that if someone was fleeing or having a nervous breakdown there was little point in mowing them down. Carlos would not budge. Killing anyone who resisted would make the other hostages think twice about trying anything, and any hysterical secretary should be shot dead on the spot because she might cause a mass panic. Carlos and Klein argued the point for two hours, with Böse translating back and forth. The three suddenly realised they were shouting so loudly that someone in the next room or in the corridor might overhear. They abruptly ended their meeting. Klein was convinced that his objections had been watered down by Böse. Otherwise Carlos, Klein felt sure, would have dropped him from the team.

But Carlos could not afford to lose anyone, partly because his preparations were not going to schedule. Kröcher-Tiedemann had not yet reached Vienna and this threatened to wreck the whole operation. Carlos was also still waiting for the inside information he had been promised (including the layout of the OPEC offices), and for the weapons and explosives. He had no alternative but to postpone everything for a few days.

Carlos turned to Böse for help. Would the comrades of the Revolutionary Cells let him have all the arms, explosives and accessories they had in reserve? According to Klein, Carlos also urgently requested weapons from an intelligence contact, a secret serviceman from an OPEC member country whose name has not been disclosed. While he waited for an answer, Carlos moved out of the Hilton Hotel and rented a flat for himself and the rest of the commando. Kröcher-Tiedemann shortly thereafter made contact. The team was finally complete.

On Friday, 19 December, after meeting his intelligence source, a triumphant Carlos returned to the flat. He carried two bags heavy with Italian-made Beretta machine-guns and pistols, rapid-fire M-16 rifles, Skorpion machine-pistols, P38 revolvers, and some fifteen kilos of explosives. A few hours later, a member of the Revolutionary Cells appeared at the flat door with more weapons which she had smuggled into Austria in a large suitcase. That night and the following day the commando greased and oiled the new weapons they had selected, most of which were brand-new and still in their wrapping.

On the morning of Sunday, 21 December Carlos trimmed his goatee, moustache and sideburns. He dressed in khaki trousers, a light grey pullover, and a brown Pierre Cardin leather jacket. He wore his beret at a not-too-jaunty angle. Weapons, as well as ammunition, explosives, fuses and detonators, were stuffed into Adidas sports bags which Carlos, Klein, Kröcher-Tiedemann and the three Arab members of the group slung over their shoulders.

The six left the flat and took a tramway along the Dr Karl Lueger Ring west of the city centre and got off close to the Christkindlmarkt, the traditional Christmas market which the previous night had done a brisk trade in grilled Austrian sausages and festive knick-knacks as seasonal carols blared out over loudspeakers. The market was quiet as the team stepped on to the slippery, snow-packed pavement. Clad in raincoats or light coats, they caught the blast of an icy wind. Weighed down by their heavy bags, they slowly made for the OPEC headquarters further down the avenue. They reached the seven-storey building, which also housed the Canadian embassy and a branch office of the Texaco company, just after half past eleven.

Klein breezily greeted the young policeman guarding the entrance of the glass and concrete building who barely nodded in reply. All through the morning ministers and their retinues had been arriving and leaving, and there was no reason to check this particular group, or so the policeman thought. The start of the session and the possibility of catching ministers on their way in had drawn some thirty journalists. Although no dramatic announcement was expected, the oil-producers' lobby had been news ever since it had jacked up prices in recent years. But after the talks resumed behind closed doors at half past ten, only a handful of reporters had stayed. When Carlos walked in, three news agency correspondents to whom stoic door-stepping 'on the offchance' was second nature were sheltering in the hallway from the cold outside.

Carlos asked them in English if the OPEC meeting was still on. The answer was yes, and his unremarkable party started up the stairs to the first floor. They looked a little shabby, as if they were junior members of some unimportant delegation. No one thought the short girl wearing a long skirt and a woollen hat worth a second look. Several of them looked swarthy, and Barthélemy Healey of Associated Press quipped as they went on their way, 'There goes the Angolan delegation.'[5] Out of sight at the top of the stairs, Carlos and his team unzipped their sports bags, drew their guns out and then broke into a run. Klein donned a balaclava.

The ministerial session was still under way, but a few delegates were milling around the first-floor reception area and the corridor that led to the conference room. Only two plainclothed police officers were on duty on the first floor, Austrian Inspectors Anton Tichler and Josef Janda. They were among the first to see Carlos and his commando, clutching guns and grenades, burst through the red steel doors that led off the building's main stairway. Carlos's team started shooting.

Klein's orders were to take control of the telephone switchboard, and to search people in the reception area to make sure they were unarmed. The plan made no allowance for the no-nonsense temperament of the young blonde and bespectacled receptionist, Edith Heller. Squatting behind the reception desk which faced the stairway doors and the lifts, she managed to dial the police immediately and report, 'This is OPEC. They're shooting all over the place.' Klein realised what Heller was doing, ran up to her and aimed his pistol at the young woman's head. Heller felt as if her head had exploded when, after shifting his pistol very slightly, he fired a bullet through the telephone handset she was holding.

'I tried to signal to the operator that she must stop telephoning,' Klein related later. 'As she didn't react, I started shooting at the phones. But she was a hell of a woman, it was incredible. Each time I shot at a phone with my Beretta, a big automatic pistol, it made a huge racket. As for her, she would pick up another phone, so I tried to put a stop to it. I emptied my charger on the switchboard.'[6]

On reaching the reception area, Carlos had immediately turned to his right and run towards the corridor that led to the conference chamber. Inspector Tichler, with a dexterity that belied his sixty years – he was due to retire in two months – lunged forward and managed to grab the barrel of Carlos's machine-pistol. But Carlos broke free. It was left to Kröcher-Tiedemann to deal with Tichler. Kröcher-Tiedemann paused only long enough to ask him, 'Are you a policeman?' The inspector had his hands up and was in no position to risk reaching for the Walther PPK automatic nestling in its holster on his belt. He started to turn away from the girl who was standing very close, just over a metre away. His answer that yes, he was a police officer, earned him a bullet which entered the back of his neck and ripped through his throat. Kröcher-Tiedemann shoved the fatally injured Tichler into one of the three lifts that opened on the reception area and pressed the button for the ground floor.

Moments later, Kröcher-Tiedemann spotted a broad-shouldered man who was walking backwards away from her, his hands in the air, and making for the steel doorway that led to the stairs. Klein saw him too – 'a great hulking brute' – and thought, 'So much the better, one less to look after.' But Kröcher-Tiedemann strode up to the escapee, an Iraqi security guard called Hassan Saeed Al Khafari, and, undaunted by the fact that he dwarfed her, shoved her pistol into his chest. The Iraqi instantly threw his arms around her, and clasped her in a tight embrace. He began dragging her towards the doorway, the gun pressed tightly between them. The struggling couple disappeared out of Klein's view.

When Klein next saw the security guard, his brain lay spattered across the floor. Kröcher-Tiedemann had managed to draw another pistol. She later apologised to an Iraqi diplomat for the murder. The killing had been necessary, she explained, because the man had tried to take her weapon from her. She showed the diplomat her torn jacket. 'She behaved the way Carlos had ordered,' Klein observed.[7]

After shaking off Inspector Tichler, Carlos seized hold of the brawny Inspector Josef Janda and dragged him down the corridor towards the conference hall. Janda, a Second World War veteran, had sized up the attackers, and realised it would be suicidal for him to draw his Walther PPK automatic. He offered little resistance to Carlos, who did not know he was a police officer. Moments later, Carlos threw the unharmed inspector into one of the side offices that lined the corridor. The recording of Janda's telephone call to Vienna's police headquarters, which he made at

11.44 following the set formula he had been trained to use, caught not only his voice – 'Criminal Officer Janda, Department One. OPEC attack. Shooting with machine-pistols' – but also more shots, the sound of an execution carried out by Carlos.

A one-man offensive by a Libyan economist, Yousef Ismirli, had almost proved Carlos's undoing. Carlos was still in the corridor, which by then stank of gunsmoke and was half darkened as several lights had been shot to pieces, when the unarmed Ismirli – by all accounts a placid character – seized Carlos's weapon. The Libyan however did not know how to work the Beretta and fumbled with it ineffectually. Meanwhile Carlos drew an automatic pistol from underneath his leather jacket. A single shot would have been enough to put Ismirli out of action. But Carlos shot him first in the hand, making him drop the Beretta, then in a leg and in the stomach, before squeezing off a final shot into the back of the neck. 'I was furious, and what's more, I had to set an example,' Carlos coldly explained later. This was in line with one of his favourite mottoes: 'To achieve things, you have to walk on bodies.'[8] Klein thought otherwise. 'It was a massacre,' he concluded, 'pure showing off, a gratuitous act, because the man was out of the fight.'[9]

In the wood-panelled conference room an argument with millions of dollars at stake was in progress when Carlos's group walked into the building. Patience among the eleven Oil Ministers was running low, with everyone feeling put out by the failure to sign an agreement on oil prices two days earlier on Friday, as originally planned.

Shortly after the sixty or so people in the conference room heard the first shots being fired, two masked gunmen strode in and fired a volley of shots into the ceiling. With little regard for protocol or ministerial dignity, one of them ordered everyone to lie on the carpet and stay there. Sheikh Yamani's first thought was that he was the victim of an attack by Europeans seeking revenge for the oil price rises for which OPEC had been responsible. Convinced he was going to die, the forty-five-year-old Yamani began reciting to himself a verse from the Koran: 'To the righteous soul will be said: O thou soul, in complete rest and satisfaction. Come back to thy lord, well content thyself and well-pleasing unto him. Enter thou, then, among thy devotees. Yea, enter thou my Heaven.'[10]

From their low vantage point, the Oil Ministers and officials stared at the tall man with a pale round face and an aquiline nose who ordered, 'Yussef! Put down your explosives!' speaking Arabic with a heavy foreign accent. Carlos then asked in English 'Have you found Yamani?' There was nowhere to hide. 'I'm here,' said the minister. He later recalled how 'the gunman scanned our faces and as his eyes met mine he greeted me sarcastically and identified me to his colleagues.'[11]

It was soon afterwards, when Carlos sought out the Venezuelan Oil Minister, Valentin Hernandez Acosta, that the penny dropped – chillingly so for Yamani: 'The leader began talking to the Venezuelan minister in kindly fashion. That convinced us that the leader was the well-known terrorist, Carlos. This came as an unpleasant shock to me, for when the French government had raided his apartment last summer and he escaped, papers and documents were found there – and among them a plan to assassinate me.'[12]

Klein had stationed himself in the corridor leading to the conference room with Joseph, who according to Klein had until that moment been hiding somewhere, probably to avoid getting hurt. As far as Klein could tell the team was now in control of the first floor and of everyone on it. 'That must have been clear even to people outside,' he reflected. 'You could have heard a pin drop in OPEC headquarters.'[13] Unknown to Carlos's team, and within seconds of receiving Inspector Janda's telephone call, the duty officer at police headquarters had called out Vienna's

Special Command unit. Minutes later, by which time Carlos was in the conference room, three of the squad's steel-helmeted men stormed into the foyer on the ground floor, brandishing Uzi submachine-guns and wearing bullet-proof vests. They halted only long enough to make sure it was too late to save Inspector Tichler, whose body sprawled half in, half out of the lift, before charging up the stairs. A barrage of gunfire greeted them when they reached the reception area on the first floor.

Klein and Joseph were covering the corridor and reception area. The squad's commander Kurt Leopolder managed to make them out down the poorly lit corridor and returned fire. A bullet bounced off the wall and hit Klein in the stomach, while another grazed his thigh and a third hit his pistol. Leopolder was stopped from pressing his advantage when he was shot in the backside. Klein, who felt little pain from his stomach wound, threw a grenade, but clumsily. It exploded only four metres or so away from him, and six metres away from its target, Leopolder. Klein had dived to the floor in time and most of the shrapnel embedded itself in the walls.

The grenade, together with Klein's repeated shouts – 'Get out or everybody will be killed!' – convinced the Austrians that retreat was the best option. Klein walked into a kitchen next to the corridor, lit a cigarette and rolled up his sweater to examine his injury. He was surprised to see no blood flowing from the neat hole in his stomach. When Klein entered the conference room to show Carlos his wound and tell him about the injured Austrian in the reception area, Carlos gave him a comforting pat on the head and told him to sit down and help guard the hostages. Kröcher-Tiedemann also reported back to Carlos, sauntering up to him with a smirk: 'I've killed two,' she said. Carlos smiled and answered, 'Good. I've killed one myself.'[14] She asked him about Yamani, and Carlos pointed the minister out to her.

There was plenty for Carlos to smile about. By midday, after an attack that lasted less than half an hour, he had pulled off the first part of his mission. His group had seized control of the OPEC offices, and taken sixty-two hostages. From the windows of the conference chamber, Carlos could see Special Command units, equipped with machine-guns and tear gas, who had massed around the building. The units made no move to attack.

Carlos ordered his hostages to get up. As they dusted down their suits, the ministers and their delegations were told to stand in three separate groups: 'liberals and semi-liberals', 'criminals', and 'neutrals'. Algeria, Iraq, Libya and Kuwait counted as liberals and their representatives were shepherded to the far side of the oval conference table by the windows, uncomfortably close to where Yussef was stacking the gelignite explosive and connecting it to electronic detonators. Officials from the neutral camp – Ecuador, Gabon, Indonesia, Nigeria and Venezuela – were placed on the other side of the table. Saudi Arabia, Iran, Qatar and the United Arab Emirates, whose ambassador Carlos had planned to kidnap in London, were criminals. Turning to Yamani, Carlos said; 'I am Carlos. You know me.'

'Very well,' Yamani answered evenly.[15]

Carlos felt he owed his hostages an explanation. In less than fluent Arabic, he announced he was at the head of a Palestinian commando and that its main targets were Saudi Arabia and Iran. If everyone cooperated, he promised, no one would be killed. Carlos then made a young British secretary, Griselda Carey, copy out a note written in approximate English. Carlos's message was terse and to the point:

> To the Austrian Authorities
>
> We are holding hostage the delegations to the OPEC Conference. We demand the lecture of our communiqué

on the Austrian radio and television network every two hours, starting two hours from now.

A large bus with windows covered by curtains must be prepared to carry us to the airport of Vienna tomorrow at 7.00, where a full-tanked DC9 with a crew of three must be ready to take us and our hostages to our destination.

Any delay, provocation or unauthorised approach under any guise will endanger the life of our hostages.

The Arm of the Arab Revolution
Vienna 21/XII/75

Carlos also made Carey copy, this time in French, a rambling, seven-page communiqué which carried Haddad's stamp. The Arab people, the manifesto proclaimed, were under threat from a violent plot which would culminate in a victory for Zionism. The plotters were American imperialism, Zionist aggressors and several Arab governments, and they aimed to break the resistance of the Palestinian revolutionaries and to sow disunity in the Arab world. The communiqué also demanded that there should be no negotiation, no treaty and no recognition for Israel; no capitulation, tacit or otherwise, in the face of Israeli occupation of 'Palestinian Arab land'. It insisted there must be an Egyptian army offensive on Israel, with Syria, Iraq and the Palestinians forming a common front north-east of Israel. It also demanded the relaunch of Arab unification and, finally, that oil resources be handled 'for the benefit of the Arab people and other peoples of the Third World'.

When Carey had finished writing, Carlos told her to take the letter and the manifesto to the Austrian authorities. On her way, she should help out of the building the wounded policeman in the reception area. It was a daunting task for Carey. Clutching Carlos's messages, she had to make her way down the darkened corridor, managing to locate the injured Leopolder despite the lack of light. The terrorists, she told him, had agreed to his leaving the building but only on condition that his unit cease firing. Leopolder, whose men had retreated down the stairway, had no choice but to accept. Her job accomplished, Carey emerged at last into the cold air, trembling and shouting, 'Don't shoot! Don't shoot!'

As Carlos waited for an answer to his letter, he felt confident enough to ignore the rules he had tried to drum into Klein and allowed an Austrian secretary in hysterics to walk free. Moments later, Carlos casually left a loaded Beretta on a table close to several ministers and walked away, carrying only his machine-pistol. Had anyone been so foolish as to try to grab it, Carlos would have shot him and probably wounded others as well. 'I wanted to find out who the security guards were,' Carlos justified himself later. It was typical of the games Carlos liked to play, as he blew hot and cold on his hostages' fate. 'At times we believed our lives would be spared and at other times we thought our execution was a certainty,' recalled the Venezuelan minister Hernandez Acosta, who asked Carlos to pick up the gun he had left behind. Another delegate compared their plight to 'some awful party which you couldn't leave'.

With the hostages held at gunpoint, and the conference room wired with explosives, the Austrians had little choice but to start negotiating. Belaïd Abdessalam, the Algerian Oil Minister who was also a doctor, relayed to the officials waiting on the ground floor Carlos's demand that Klein should be taken to hospital for urgent treatment. Carlos emptied Klein's pockets so the police would have no clue as to his identity. The Algerian minister then escorted Klein down the staircase, holding Klein's hands up in the air as they walked.

As Klein was carried to a waiting ambulance on a stretcher, right hand clutching his wound and left hand masking his face, a policeman asked him in German: 'Are you a hostage?' Klein answered in the best English he could muster: 'My fight-name is Angie.' It was only then that he lost consciousness. He had been extraordinarily resilient. On the operating table, surgeons found that the bullet, which had broken up inside him, had pierced not only his colon, but also his pancreas and duodenal artery.

Carlos requested that the Libyan ambassador to Vienna act as mediator, but he was away in Hungary. The Iraqi chargé d'affaires in the city, Riyadh Al-Azzawi, volunteered his services and he proved acceptable to both the Austrians and Carlos. The diplomat was greeted with bravado. 'Tell them I'm from Venezuela and my name is Carlos. Tell them I'm the famous Carlos. They know me.' From then on, negotiations were conducted through Al-Azzawi who relayed the kidnappers' demands to Austrian officials on the ground floor of the OPEC building. The only telephone available there was in the porter's lodge. The negotiators were reduced to making long-distance calls to the organisation's various members one at a time.

Carlos hammered home his demands: a plane and crew; the return of the injured Klein who would travel with them; a radio; and twenty-five metres of rope and five pairs of scissors. If the demands were not met, or if government forces were foolish enough to storm the building, he would start shooting the hostages.[16] The mediator reported to Carlos that doctors at the Allgemeines Krankenhaus hospital, where Klein had had his fingerprints taken and was photographed by police, estimated that he needed a month to recover. He added that Klein was being kept alive with a breathing apparatus. Carlos turned to consult his companions. They were unanimous. 'I don't care if he dies on the flight,' Carlos said. 'We came together and we will leave together.'[17]

Carlos's demands were passed on to the Austrian Chancellor, socialist Bruno Kreisky, who had been plucked by an air force helicopter from his Christmas holiday in the mountain resort of Lech some six hundred kilometres away to confront what he later laconically termed 'a particularly difficult situation'.

At three o'clock in the afternoon, more than three hours after the first shots had rung out, Carlos motioned Yamani outside the conference chamber and into a smaller room. Of all the hostages, Yamani was the most famous. As a chief architect of the oil embargo that had led to crippling fuel price rises, he was for many years a bogey-man for the West. But the decision to lift the embargo in the spring of 1974 brought down on him the wrath of Palestinian extremists. The Popular Front had hoped the embargo would be used to isolate Israel from allies such as Washington. Notoriety in the West and Haddad's hatred for Yamani combined to make him an ideal target.

Yamani believed his execution was about to take place, out of sight of the other officials. So he was surprised to hear Carlos talking to him in a reassuring tone, even singing his praises. But the mask soon dropped. Carlos said he planned to make an example of Yamani in protest against the policies of Saudi Arabia. Much as he personally respected the sheikh, he insisted he had no alternative than to kill him. If the Austrian government failed to have the communiqué read on the radio and to supply the plane, his execution would take place at six o'clock that evening, and his body would be thrown into the street. A man of Yamani's intelligence and courage, Carlos concluded with a flourish, would bear no resentment against his executioners, and would understand the nobility of their objectives and intentions.

'How can it be that you tell me that you will kill me and then ask me not to feel bitterness towards you?' the sheikh asked. 'You must be trying to force me to do something.'

'You! Why should I put pressure on you?' Carlos exclaimed. 'I am putting pressure on the Austrian government to get out of this place. So far as you are concerned I am just making you aware of the facts.'[18]

As the Sunday afternoon wore on, Carlos relaxed. The ministers and officials were free to walk from the conference room to the toilets across the corridor without having to seek permission. The rope supplied by the Austrians was abandoned in a corner of the room. A radio which the Iraqi mediator had fetched from his home played in another corner, as Carlos's team took turns at listening to news reports about their coup and to find out whether Kreisky would broadcast their statement. Carlos chatted amicably, switching between Arabic, French and Spanish. He understood German, but the only time he spoke in that language was when he politely asked one of the officials, 'Would you like some more cigarettes?'

Carlos told his hostages that he was at war with capitalist society, styling himself a leader who must marshal his troops to final victory. 'Me, I'm a soldier and I live under the tent,' Carlos proclaimed. When a Gabonese delegate told him his nationality, Carlos reassured him: 'Don't worry, we have nothing against you. You are the defenders of the Third World.' Carlos also told the Iranian Oil Minister that the OPEC raid would not be his last, and boasted that he had forty trained commandos ready to launch attacks across the world.

At five o'clock the communiqué had still not been read out. Carlos walked up to Yamani and, with a smile, reminded him of their chat. 'My feelings had changed and there was less terror in my heart,' Yamani recalled. 'I began to think, not of myself but of my family, my children, my relatives and those for whom I had responsibility. I wrote a farewell letter to them, explaining what I wanted done.'[19]

The Austrian Chancellor agreed to have the statement broadcast for the first time at 6.22 p.m. It cannot have made a great impression upon its Austrian audience, although it expressed 'regrets for the predicament in which our operation has placed the peace-loving Austrian people'. The statement was read by a solemn Austrian announcer in laughable French every two hours until four o'clock the following morning.

Chancellor Kreisky had made one concession, but now he insisted on consulting the hostages before going any further. At Kreisky's request, a total of thirteen ministers and senior officials wrote letters addressed to him, and Carlos made a great show of respecting their confidentiality. All appealed to Kreisky to grant Carlos's demands, and wrote that they were willing to leave Austria under his guard. Yamani's letter urged Austria to accept Carlos's requests to spare any unnecessary bloodshed.

To feed his team and the hostages, none of whom had eaten since that morning, Carlos requested a hundred sandwiches and fruit. The Austrians promptly supplied these, but many of the sandwiches contained ham. As most of those held in the conference room were Moslem, Carlos rejected the delivery. He requested chicken and chips instead. The Hilton solved the problem. The hotel had planned to serve a banquet on its premises in OPEC's honour that evening. Although the reception was unavoidably cancelled the food was sent to the OPEC building at ten o'clock. As many of the conference room's lights had been shot at, the ministers and officials picked at the food by candlelight. Carlos showed no regret for the blood shed that morning. Perhaps the Libyan economist whom he had slain had taken him for a Mossad agent. 'It's not my fault if I look Jewish,' Carlos joked loudly.

After a midnight Cabinet meeting at the Chancellery, a strained-looking Kreisky announced that an agreement with Carlos had been reached by his government and OPEC officials. Austria caved in, hoping to prevent any more bloodshed, in return for a pledge that the hostages would be freed on arrival at their destination. To one reporter who challenged his decision, Kreisky snapped: 'What kind of alternative do you want? A storm attack on the building? That's no alternative ... We can't be generous with the lives of others.'

Later, the Chancellor cited the killings at the outset of the raid, the explosives laid around the conference room, and Carlos's insistence on taking the badly wounded Klein with him even though he might die on the flight as evidence that the gang had no regard for human life.[20] Algeria, one of the countries that Carlos had accepted as a possible destination, was willing to receive the planeload of hostages and their kidnappers. Kreisky saw no reason not to take up the offer, but insisted that Carlos should release all OPEC employees before leaving Vienna.

The Chancellor's condition infuriated Carlos. He shouted at the Iraqi intermediary: 'I command Kreisky and everybody else here. I decide who shall go and who shall stay.' But he then calmed down and added petulantly: 'I don't intend to take them. But I don't want people to tell me who to take and who not to take.' As for where to take them, Carlos had apparently not yet decided. In the small hours of Monday morning he asked the Iraqi mediator which Arab states were prepared to receive him.

The hostages had an uncomfortable night, settling down as best they could in the chairs around the conference table, or on the floor. The body of the Libyan economist who had made his one-man stand against Carlos was left close to where he had fallen.

At twenty to seven the following morning, a yellow Austrian post office bus – the only bus equipped with curtains that the authorities had been able to find at short notice – drew up outside the rear entrance of the OPEC building. 'We could have made Kreisky dance on the table,' Carlos bragged. Standing in the snow by the bus, like a schoolteacher on an outing cheerfully directing his flock, Carlos gave those whom he had agreed to free a hearty handshake or a playful tap on the shoulder. In full view of television crews, he even made to embrace one hostage, but the

Beretta slung across his chest got in the way. Carlos complied with Kreisky's request, but this still left forty-two hostages.

Wary of triggering a massacre similar to that which had claimed the lives of the Israeli athletes at the Munich Olympics three years earlier, the Austrians made no attempt to shoot at Carlos or his accomplices during the hour or so that they spent out in the open. As the bus, its curtains drawn, started down the Dr Karl Lueger Ring, an ambulance and two police cars with flashing blue warning lights led it slowly through the Monday morning traffic. Standing by the driver at the front of the bus, Carlos waved to people in the streets. '*Sonderfahrt*' (Special trip) read the sign behind the windscreen. Earlier, another ambulance had ferried Klein, and a doctor who had volunteered to accompany him on the flight, to the getaway Austrian Airlines DC9 at Vienna's airport.

The plane was ready to leave when Austrian Interior Minister Otto Roesch, a former member of the Hitler Youth who had helped the ministers abroad, made to shake hands with Carlos. Carlos caught his own hand in the shoulder strap of his machine-pistol but still managed to give the Austrian a clumsy handshake. 'Handshake of Shame', headlined the newspapers the next day as Roesch was castigated for his gesture towards a man whose accomplice had shot dead an Austrian police inspector. (More than twenty years later, Austrian police officers questioning Carlos refused to shake his hand, saying that they did not want to attract the same criticism as Roesch had.)

As he organised the hostages in the plane's cabin, Carlos segregated Amouzegar, Yamani and his deputy. Explosives were placed under their seats. According to Klein, Amouzegar was on the blacklist because he had headed the shah's internal security and secret police, the Savak – a role which Amouzegar denies having played. Created with a helping hand from the CIA and Mossad, the Savak rooted out dissent at home and abroad with its army of 30,000, and a vast number of collaborators. For Haddad, the fact that the shah had granted Israel diplomatic recognition was enough to justify Amouzegar's elimination.

Carlos began to relax once the plane took off just after nine o'clock on Monday, 22 December, its destination unknown to the hostages. Machine-pistol resting in his lap, he talked calmly and courteously with Amouzegar and Yamani. He even gave Yamani his mother's telephone number in Venezuela, asking him to ring her and tell her that her son was fine. 'We talked about everything, including his private life, his youth, his studies in London,' Yamani recalled. 'He was a man who loved life, running after girls and having fun. He was also very well dressed in luxury clothes. He chatted and joked, but I couldn't stop myself thinking that he had promised me he would kill me in cold blood.'

Sheikh Yamani took advantage of Carlos's bonhomie to seek some clues about their fate. The plane would fly to Algiers, spend a couple of hours there, and then move on to Tripoli. Yamani asked if he expected any problems in Libya. Carlos looked surprised: 'On the contrary, the Prime Minister will be there to receive us, and a Boeing plane will be ready to take us to Baghdad.' When Yamani asked if a stop in Damascus was on the cards, Carlos replied: 'They have become deviationists and dangerous, and I will not set foot on their soil.'[21]

On the flight Carlos handed out autographs, 'like a film-star', recalled the Venezuelan minister Hernandez Acosta. The one Carlos gave a Nigerian official read simply, 'On flight Vienna–Algiers. Carlos. 22/XII/75', with his name underlined. Carlos boasted to Hernandez Acosta that he was the man who, in his phrase, had 'liquidated' the French counter-intelligence officers and Moukharbal in Paris that June. When it was suggested to Amouzegar some time later that the autographs, and the way Carlos had previously waved to people from the bus, smacked a little of Robin Hood, the Iranian agreed. Carlos wanted to be loved, and felt that he was fighting for the poor, Amouzegar remarked.[22]

During the flight to Algiers Kröcher-Tiedemann squatted by Klein's side at the back of the plane, wiped the sweat off his brow, moistened his cracked lips with water and whispered words of comfort in his ear. She broke off looking after Klein to regale the hostages with an account punctuated by laughter of how she had shot dead 'the old man' (Inspector Tichler). Then she broke down and wept.

The red and white twin-engined plane touched down at the Dar El Beida airport outside Algiers after a two-and-a-half-hour flight. Carlos, still clad in his beret but now sporting sunglasses, emerged from the plane unarmed. A smiling Abdel Aziz Bouteflika, Algeria's long-serving Foreign Minister, embraced Carlos and patted him on the back as they walked to the VIP lounge.[23] A Red Crescent ambulance took Klein away, and when he regained consciousness he found himself back in hospital.

With the jet's engines still running, a cigar-smoking Carlos negotiated with Bouteflika and the Algerian Oil Minister, Belaïd Abdessalam, for the better part of five hours. In the aircraft, his hostages sat with the blinds pulled down. The atmosphere, as Yamani described it, was one of 'silent horror, caused by the alertness and anxiety of the terrorists' while everyone awaited the outcome.

Carlos agreed at the airport to release most of the non-Arab hostages, some thirty ministers and delegation officials. Carlos's countryman Hernandez Acosta, who was among those freed, asked before leaving: 'Tell me, Carlos, would you really have shot us?'

'Oh we wouldn't have shot you until the very last,' was the comforting retort.

Yamani and Amouzegar, together with senior officials from the other Arab delegations – a total of fifteen hostages – were told to remain on the plane. 'I am going to kill you,' Carlos told Yamani. 'I may not get you now, but I am going to kill you. You are a criminal, it won't be long before you are killed.'[24]

Despite the initial warmth of his hosts, the talks with the Algerian authorities did not go as well as Carlos had hoped: 'We demanded another plane but they refused, saying there were none available. We were in a DC9, which is worth nothing for long distances.'[25] On Monday afternoon Carlos decided to try his luck in another Arab state. The plane was refuelled and then flew from Algiers to Tripoli. But the reception did not live up to Carlos's expectations. The Libyan authorities ordered the plane to stop close to the runway and refused to give Carlos a red-carpet welcome. Frustrated and dismayed, Carlos protested that he had spent a month preparing the OPEC attack and that he could not work with the undisciplined Libyans.

Fanned by Carlos's nervousness, the atmosphere on board turned ominously tense. One of the exhausted guerrillas was taken ill and began vomiting in a corner. After talks with the Austrian ambassador to Libya who was acting as a go-between, Carlos set free the Libyan and Algerian ministers and five other delegates in the early hours of Tuesday, 23 December. One of the two Saudi officials released, who had tried to stay with his minister, said to Carlos as he left: 'For God's sake, do not harm Yamani.' Carlos replied: 'I have received instructions here in Libya from my bosses not to do any harm to him or to the Iranian minister, and I can now promise you that they will be safe. I could not make that promise to the Algerians.' Yamani, who overheard the remark, was unsure whether to believe him.[26]

The second stage of Carlos's mission, as planned by Haddad, was unravelling. Libya refused to supply a longer-range plane. Saudi Arabia, with Yamani's safety a key concern, also refused to oblige. Only Austria had broadcast the commando's political statement. The city-hopping tour of Middle East capitals – to drop ministers off on their front doorstep or to blow their brains out, whichever the governments decided – was on the verge of being abandoned.

The plane took off from Tripoli at one o'clock in the morning, bound again for Algiers. But as it flew over Tunis the radio crackled and air traffic control there refused them permission to land. Carlos had sought no such authorisation, and the veto provoked him into defiance. He ordered the captain to descend towards the airport, but the runway lights were promptly turned off. 'We knew that a battle would probably break out on our arrival [in Tunis],' a still embittered Carlos recounted. 'It was a stupid gesture on the part of the Tunisians ... The pilot was tired, and so we told him to go back to Algiers. We too were tired. We hadn't slept in four days, our nerves were stretched, rest was imperative.'[27]

At 3.40 a.m. the DC9 landed once more at Dar El Beida airport outside Algiers. Carlos again isolated himself with the Algerian Foreign Minister Bouteflika, who was less than pleased at his return. Shortly afterwards Carlos walked back to the plane. He sat next to the hostages he despised the most, Yamani and Amouzegar: 'I do not know what I should do. I am a democrat and you do not know the meaning of democracy. I shall have a meeting now with my colleagues and consult them on what to do about your case. I shall inform you later about the decision taken.'

The ministers were unable to follow Carlos's discussion with his accomplices at the front of the cabin, but they could see that Kröcher-Tiedemann and Khalid were angry about something. The ministers sat in silence. Eventually Carlos returned: 'We have finally decided to release you by midday and with that decision your life is completely out of danger.'

'Why wait till then?' Yamani asked. 'It is late at night and if you release us now both you and ourselves can have some rest which we badly need.' Carlos replied that he wanted the excitement to last until noon. 'We shall turn off the lights and pull down the blinds,' he proposed. 'You will sleep peacefully knowing that your lives are no longer in danger.' Carlos's solicitude enraged Kröcher-Tiedemann, who it seems was against sparing the lives of the two ministers. 'Fuck you!' she yelled at Carlos.

The Algerians then recontacted Carlos and asked him to return to the VIP lounge for more talks. Two hours later Carlos came back to the plane and strode up to Yamani and Amouzegar. Yamani noted that Carlos's attitude had changed a great deal – possibly under pressure from the Algerians. 'I am leaving the plane now, and you can come out in five minutes,' Carlos announced. Carlos's team followed him out of the plane. Yamani wondered whether the jet was about to blow up. After waiting for the five minutes to elapse, he decided to leave, but his deputy volunteered to go first: 'I will go, they may be waiting at the bottom of the steps aiming to shoot you.'

When the last of the remaining hostages finally found the courage to abandon the plane and walk to the VIP lounge to which police directed them, they found themselves sharing it with the guerrillas who had seized them forty-four hours earlier. Suddenly, Haddad's orders came very close to being carried out. As Yamani and Amouzegar sat down to talk over their ordeal with the Algerian minister Bouteflika, a distraught-looking Khalid approached and began threatening them, his right hand scratching nervously at his chest. Bouteflika thrust a glass of fruit juice into Khalid's hand, giving Algerian policemen time to approach and frisk him. They found that Khalid, apparently reluctant to follow Carlos's orders, had hidden a gun under his arm. 'I came here to carry out the agreed execution of these criminals. But you have prevented me,' Khalid told the policemen.[28]

Carlos stage-managed a lingering curtain-call. On the way out of the airport a black official car drove up to where a few journalists were standing and stopped while Carlos, lounging in the passenger seat, stared fixedly at them for a full minute or so. The three-car convoy bearing him and his team then swept away.[29]

It was Hernandez Acosta who confirmed to the waiting world that the leader of the Vienna hostage-taking and the Venezuelan guerrilla known as Carlos the Jackal were one and the same man. Passing through Charles de Gaulle airport near Paris after flying in from Algiers, he quoted Carlos's boast about the shooting of the DST officers, and showed French police a letter that Carlos had handed him. It was addressed to 'Sra Elba Sánchez, Apt 2B, Residencia Las Americas, Av Las Americas, Caracas'.

The French Interior Ministry, embarrassed that positive identification of the letter's author would force Paris to put pressure on the friendly Algerian government and seek Carlos's extradition, hurriedly denied that any such document existed. 'There is no positive proof,' an Interior Ministry statement insisted, 'that the letter really exists, and certainly there is no copy in the possession of the police chiefs in the French capital.' A few hours later the Interior Ministry admitted it had lied, saying that Hernandez Acosta had allowed police to photocopy the letter. This too was untrue. Hernandez Acosta believed that his integrity demanded that he respect the privacy of the letter's author, whom he described as 'young, spontaneous and talking a lot'. He refused to let the police photocopy the letter, as the police report drawn up at the time which only contains a copy of the envelope shows.[30]

According to the Interior Ministry, a graphology expert failed to establish a definite link with the notes found in Carlos's arms cache in Paris. But within hours, Scotland Yard brushed aside the reservations of its French colleagues and insisted that the writing on the envelope was identical to that on papers found in the London flat of Angela Otaola. The writer, and the master of the Vienna coup, was definitely Ilich Ramírez Sánchez, alias Carlos the Jackal.

Handing the letter to the Venezuelan minister was a typically flamboyant, but ultimately foolish act by Carlos. There was no need to ask Hernandez Acosta to act as a courier. Carlos could simply have stuck a stamp on the envelope and sent the letter from the nearest post office, and the police forces hunting him would have been none the wiser. But, as he had shown in handing out his autographs, Carlos felt the need, literally, to sign the OPEC raid.

'With hindsight,' said Klein, 'I think that what motivated Carlos was adventure, followed by money.'[31] Vienna supplied plenty of both as sparing the lives of Yamani and Amouzegar made Carlos a rich man. Twenty million dollars richer according to Western intelligence estimates. And once again, Carlos got away with murder.

6

The Renegade Revolutionary

> Stars are very bad at following instructions. You have not followed my instructions. There is no room for stars in my operational teams. You can go.
>
> – Wadi Haddad to Carlos

In January 1976 Duane R. Clarridge, CIA deputy director of the Near East Division for Arab Operations, flew into Athens. The Central Intelligence Agency, concerned that the Lebanese civil war meant the wives and children of officers stationed in Beirut were at risk, had moved the dependants out of Lebanon to live in hotels in the Greek capital. The wives, all in their early thirties, refused to believe they had been in any danger, and bitterly resented the agency's decision. The official purpose of Clarridge's trip was to try to placate them. Clarridge heard the women out but, much as he sympathised with them, his thoughts kept turning to the other reason for his journey out of Langley.

The CIA had begun to take an interest in Carlos in 1974, when its newly reinforced station in Beirut heard of his reputation as a promising recruit of the extremist Popular Front based in the Lebanese capital. Vague reports had also reached the CIA's Beirut station that the Soviet Union supported Haddad's Popular Front. Indeed, in May 1975, KGB chief Yuri Andropov had described Haddad as an 'authorised correspondent of the espionage services of the KGB'.[1]

Although it had no record of an attack by Carlos on American interests, the CIA decided 'to operate against him', in Clarridge's euphemistic phrase, as he was perceived to be a terrorist threat.[2] After the Rue Toullier killings, the Americans consulted the DST. Relations between the two secret services, however, were cool and the French made it clear that they were uninterested in cooperation.

'After the Vienna business, Carlos put people's teeth on edge,' Clarridge commented years later. 'Carlos made the secret services of the democratic world look inept and ridiculous. Even though the prestige of the agency was not on the line, Carlos's activities were still of concern because they involved issues that were of interest to the agency such as the Palestinian question. So we began to look at what was possible.'[3] The card that the agency held was an acquaintance of Carlos. The real purpose of Clarridge's journey to Athens was to play that card.

The view of the Acropolis bathed in moonlight was small compensation for the winter chill which Clarridge had chosen to endure in the rooftop bar of his Athens hotel. But Clarridge was anxious to ensure complete privacy for this particular encounter, and the cold guaranteed that no one would join him and his guest. The potential agent, recruited by a CIA Beirut case officer and whose name has not been revealed, soon arrived. Clarridge knew little about his guest – a good-looking. well-educated and left-wing European who spoke fluent English – but he knew that he had the potential to reach, and deliver Carlos. 'If Carlos is killed in the process, so be it,' a senior clandestine service officer at CIA headquarters had told Clarridge before he set out.

As Clarridge gently probed, the agent spoke about Carlos, describing him as a mercurial and charismatic character. The agent slowly explained what had made him offer to work for the CIA. 'He claimed to be fed up with the terrorists, their unpredictability and their paranoia, but I rather thought his real motivation was money,' Clarridge recalled. 'I liked that better; ideological conversions can be temporary. His access was promising, but hardly sure. All in all, the situation looked like a go, so I got down to it. When I finished, the agent said he understood perfectly and would do his best.'[4] The following month President Ford banned US government agencies from carrying out assassinations in Executive Order 11905. In his autobiography, which was published after being approved by the CIA's Publications Review Board, Clarridge wrote that what he asked of the agent was not in violation of Executive Order 11905.

In fact, the agent was told that the CIA's preference was for an advance tip-off when the Venezuelan next travelled to France, Britain or West Germany. But he was also promised that if he could arrange for Carlos to be killed, or do it himself, he would be paid $10,000. 'I suspect that the agent didn't have the courage to pull the trigger himself,' Clarridge explained. 'What's more, he had no back-up, he was alone. His opportunity to get at Carlos was very limited and if it had happened, it would have been a stroke of luck. We thought Carlos was in Beirut or a neighbouring country at the time, and we saw no evidence that he was roaming around Europe. After Vienna he stayed very close to his Palestinian colleagues. The agent could never arrange to see him again.'[5]

Vienna had made Carlos. Or rather, it had made the 'Carlos the Jackal' myth. Carlos himself played no small part in the myth's crafting. In a career where discretion is often the better part of valour, Carlos went to inordinate lengths to write his name all over the OPEC saga. Again and again he made his identity clear, and it was of course the letter to his mother given to Hernandez Acosta which, although ignored by the French, gave Scotland Yard proof that the hostage-taker was indeed Carlos.

Overnight Carlos turned into an icon of terrorism. The OPEC raid spawned hours of television and thousands of newspaper articles across the globe. The media coverage which Carlos's shooting of the DST officers had prompted paled in comparison. *L'Aurore*, whose offices he had bombed, marvelled at this 'mocking, shrewd, and exhibitionist character who scoffs at borders and Western police forces with insulting cynicism'.

From then on the name 'Carlos the Jackal' became a label which the world's press slapped on to the latest outrage, however poorly it stuck. In March 1976, just two months after Vienna, the Egyptian weekly *Al Mussawar* reported that Libya now had a new leader, Carlos. In May newspapers speculated that it was Carlos who had assassinated the Bolivian ambassador on a busy Paris street. Again in May 1976 he was rumoured to have blown himself up at Tel Aviv's Ben Gurion airport, together with a woman security officer. Carlos was reported arrested, almost arrested and dead several times.

In the aftermath of Vienna, Carlos started to believe in the image forged by the newspapers. He demanded that friends translate the articles about him that he did not understand. Whether or not he had read Forsyth's *The Day of the Jackal* before it was found near his London arms cache, he had done so by this time and would often compare himself to its assassin.

Worldwide notoriety was not all Carlos achieved in Vienna. He later assured Klein that he had decided not to kill the ministers, and to halt the operation, after the Algerian government promised him money and protection: 'The Popular Front couldn't protect me if the Saudis and the Iranians went after me.'[6] Years later, Carlos put the ransom at $50 million and explained that it was paid by the Saudis in their name and on Iran's behalf. But he denied pocketing the sum: it was 'diverted en route and lost by the Revolution'.[7] Had he taken one cent, he insisted to one of his lawyers, he would have signed his own death warrant.

Bassam Abu-Sharif confirmed that Carlos received a very large amount of money, and Klein quoted Carlos as admitting as much almost openly: 'And he put all this money in a safe place in Algeria. For him, not for the group. In the world of terrorism, manipulation was permanent. You never knew who was pulling the strings. Manipulation was there all right, you could feel it, if only with those huge sums of money which were spent on such operations. It meant hundreds of thousands of dollars.'[8]

Who had manipulated Carlos? Klein indicated that the commission for the Vienna raid came from 'an Arab President', but he would not say which one. 'All our information on the conference and the security measures came from that country which was part of OPEC and which was present at the conference,' Klein revealed.[9] Western intelligence services are convinced that Libya, possibly aided by Iraq, sponsored the OPEC raid. Libya wanted to impose its policy towards Israel on the Arab world, and Iraq had been angered by Saudi Arabian opposition to oil price increases. Of all the organisation's members, the two countries – both patrons of the Popular Front – were the most implacable foes of Saudi Arabia and Iran. Carlos himself has refused to point the finger, but he was still castigating Libya some time afterwards for failing to supply at Tripoli airport the long-haul airliner with which to fly on to Baghdad, a decision which he said showed that Libya was ready for a bloodbath as the lives of the hostages were at stake.[10] Years later, an accomplice of Carlos confirmed the view that Colonel Hu'ammar Qathafi had commissioned the attack, promising Carlos an annual payment of $1 million as a reward.[11]

While the world wondered where Carlos had vanished to after his theatrical exit from the Algiers airport, Austria assumed that he was still in Algeria and filed a request for his extradition. But the Austrian ambassador to Algiers was courteously informed that there was no extradition treaty between the two countries and that therefore, for legal reasons, the request could not be granted. Austria's demand was a move which France conspicuously failed to imitate although it had material proof (Carlos's letter to his mother) that he had led the OPEC raid. Seeking Carlos's arrest, France reasoned, would only offend its former North African colony, and rake up embarrassing memories of the Rue Toullier carnage. Better to let sleeping dogs – and jackals – lie.

Algerian President Houari Boumedienne was thus free to take Carlos under his wing. 'When the Algerians offered us political asylum in exchange for the hostages, we accepted,' Carlos explained. 'The attitude of Algeria was loyal and honourable.'[12] The head of state treated Carlos to pampered hospitality in a sprawling villa with a superb view of Algiers which had once welcomed the Viet-Minh commander-in-chief General Giap. Boumedienne also provided Carlos with bodyguards.

Carlos stayed at least a dozen days in the villa to give Klein, whom he visited in hospital, time to recover. During his stay his social agenda included several lunches with Bouteflika, the Foreign Minister who had embraced Carlos as he got off the plane, as well as dinners with the head of the secret service and the chief of police. When Klein was well enough to leave hospital, the chief of police surprised the left-wing guerrilla by singing the praises of his late countryman, Adolf Hitler.

Three weeks after Vienna, Carlos and the recovered Klein flew to Libya. As they stepped off the plane the pair were greeted by a television camera crew sent by the state broadcasting network to record their arrival.

According to French intelligence, Colonel Qathafi footed the bill for Carlos's stay in Algiers. After a round of official encounters, par for the course in a country that funded and trained a host of Arab and non-Arab guerrilla groups, the colonel put a private plane at the disposal of Carlos and Klein to fly them to a Popular Front meeting in the South Yemen capital of Aden on 10 February.[13] Qathafi's failure to arrest Carlos helped to earn Libya a place on Washington's blacklist of states that sponsor terrorism. Qathafi responded to the blacklisting by blithely allowing Carlos to make at least two other visits to Libya later in the year.

The Aden meeting in mid-February, a post-mortem on the Vienna operation, was a sobering experience for Carlos. The protagonists assembled before Wadi Haddad, Carlos's mentor, who had settled in South Yemen, a Marxist-Leninist oasis, two years earlier. Haddad's presence throughout the debriefing, which dragged on over several days, was an unsettling one. He remained icily silent virtually throughout, taking copious notes. The review turned into recrimination and bickering as the participants in the Vienna operation fought to justify themselves in the eyes of their master.

Carlos and Kröcher-Tiedemann sharply rebuked Klein for doing nothing to stop the Iraqi security guard fleeing. They accused him of taking too long to neutralise the switchboard, and of not being aggressive enough in repelling the Austrian Special Command unit. Klein protested that the Iraqi had been on his way out and that his hands were in the air. There had been plenty of other things to do, and having one fewer person to look after was fine by him. But none of this satisfied Carlos and Kröcher-Tiedemann, who returned to the attack. Klein had put them in danger, because Kröcher-Tiedemann was forced to catch up with the Iraqi herself when he neglected to do so. But despite his efforts to single out Klein for censure Carlos did not escape Haddad's inquisition. Again and again he was ordered to relive the events that led to the cancellation of the planned tour of Middle Eastern capitals, and the failure to kill Yamani and Amouzegar.

Carlos's unit waited nervously for Haddad's judgement. In the days that followed the stormy post-mortem, Carlos and Klein were assigned to a Popular Front training camp near what had once been the palatial home of the former British governor in Aden. There the Vienna veterans sat in on courses in military theory. Target and explosives practice was carried out in the desert.

Like the subject matter, the pupils from various radical groups were a potentially fiery mixture: they included Marxists and Christian Phalange militiamen from opposite ends of the political spectrum. Prudently, Haddad had ordered that guerrillas needed permission to speak to classmates from other movements. The atmosphere was hardly improved by the test imposed on candidates for the suicide squad. They had to go about their daily business with a grenade in one hand and a machine-gun in the other, both of which they were forbidden to put down for up to three weeks at a stretch.

Not surprisingly, after the excitement of Vienna, Carlos and Klein found the training camp boring. To while away the time as much as to keep fit, Klein went jogging in the desert. After courses, the pair drank and danced in Aden's nightclubs where Carlos spent lavishly. The 'jet-set terrorist', as the cash-strapped Klein called him, became friendly with officers of the Stasi (the East German secret police) who were stationed in Aden. Late at night, to refresh themselves after their carousing, the pair would go for a swim in Diplomats' Bay, one of Aden's few beaches that sharks did not visit.

Klein's six months with Carlos gave him plenty of opportunity to study the man at close quarters. Vanity, Klein concluded, was one of Carlos's chief characteristics. A wanted poster in West Germany hurt Carlos's pride so much that he considered writing to the authorities to lodge a protest: the price on his head was the same as that for other guerrillas, and Carlos considered this a personal affront.[14] The Venezuelan frequently treated himself to pedicures and manicures, and flushed crimson when Klein pulled his leg about his ceaseless washing and showering. For Klein, he was 'incredibly anal':

> Carlos was very interested in his appearance. When he went into the bathroom he stayed there an hour and a half at the very least. He always put talcum powder on from head to foot, like babies. He literally drenched himself with perfume. When he came out of the bathroom, there was enough of a smell to make the flies fall off the wall. There was a discussion once. As his face was becoming too well known, the idea of plastic surgery in Switzerland was suggested. But his only concern was that he had breasts which were rather developed, like a fourteen-year-old girl, and the only thing that interested him was to know whether they could be operated on. When we went bathing, he always kept his T-shirt on.[15]

Haddad's verdict was that Carlos had disobeyed orders by failing to shoot any of the Oil Ministers, and by negotiating their release in exchange for a ransom (which was shared with Haddad) and safe passage. The political rationale for the kidnappings had been sacrificed on the altar of Mammon, with an incomprehensible Austrian radio broadcast in French the only public justification. Haddad excommunicated his pupil with the words: 'Stars are very bad at following instructions. You have not followed my instructions. There is no room for stars in my operational teams. You can go.'[16]

In later years Carlos related that he had resigned from the Popular Front of his own free will and that his Palestinian comrades had wept at the prospect of losing him.[17] The truth was he was sacked. Greed and indiscipline were to blame.

Haddad allowed Carlos to keep his expulsion secret, giving him time to reflect on what to do now that he no longer had an organisation to support him. An embittered Carlos railed at the incompetence of the Popular Front. 'I won't go on with them, my brand image suffers from it too much,' Carlos burst out to Klein.

For Klein, Carlos's only purpose was to forge a brand image that would be tied to his name, like the Jackal. He was in the business of selling not soapsuds, however, but terror. 'Carlos would say: "The more they write about me, the more they say that I am dangerous, the less difficulty I will have the day I have a real problem,"' Klein recalled. 'He had a theory of massacre. He would say: "The more the acts of violence I commit are terrible, the more I will be respected and people will lay off me. For example, if I get caught in France, they will expel me discreetly, out of fear of reprisals." This reputation, it was his security.'[18]

Carlos's favourite topic of conversation was not politics but his future career. He shunned political discussions even with Palestinians. The ideological legacy of his father had been watered down: 'Carlos inspires himself from what Ho Chi Minh says: "Bring revolution to each country." So he goes from one country to another trying to start things up ... He did not like [Communists], he thought they were corrupt. He did not define himself as a Marxist, but rather as an international revolutionary, a bit like Che Guevara.'[19]

It took time for Carlos to decide what path to take. Still smarting from Haddad's sharp words, he left the Aden camp briefly to call without warning at Abu-Sharif's home in Beirut. 'He looked terrible. I had never seen him looking so devastated,' Abu-Sharif related. 'He told me he was going to strike out on his own, set up his own direct action group, maybe in South America where there were plenty of fascists who needed sorting out, but I knew it would never work. It takes a mastermind to run that kind of operation and the man before me was no mastermind, he was an executioner. And for once he had failed to execute.'[20]

Carlos's dismissal remained a secret for several months, which partly explains why press reports placed him in Uganda in July 1976 when an Air France Airbus was hijacked to the East African country's Entebbe airport. Carlos was in fact still at the camp in Aden. He was reduced to following events on the radio, knowing that his failure to play any part in them was a testimony to his cool relations with Haddad. Within hours of the hijack, newspapers speculated that Carlos was leading the operation. But the passengers were in the hands of his friend Wilfried Böse, and what the latter named the Che Guevara Force of the Commando of the Palestine Liberation Forces.

News that Böse, who had chosen the Airbus because 'Air France is easier than El Al',[21] had segregated Israeli passport-holders from the other passengers made Carlos angry. Carlos's fury was a rare display of solidarity with Jews. In fact Haddad's orders to Böse, overheard by Israelis bugging his telephone, had been to kill the Jewish hostages whether or not the hijackers' demands were met.

A few days later paratroopers of the Israeli Defence Forces shot their way into the Entebbe airport building where the 106 Jewish hostages were held. As the troops burst in, Böse made to throw a grenade at the hostages but then changed his mind. He barely had time to urge the hostages to duck and fire a few shots at his attackers before he was cut down in a hail of bullets. Böse died within forty-five seconds of the start of Operation Thunderbolt during which the Israelis, incensed by President Idi Amin's welcome to the hijackers, destroyed eleven Soviet-made MiG jets parked on the tarmac. The leader of the Israeli forces, Lieutenant-Colonel Yonatan Netanyahu (the elder brother of Israeli Prime Minister Benjamin Netanyahu), was killed by a Ugandan soldier who shot him in the back.

Carlos expressed admiration at the Israeli coup. He's a kind of Jekyll and Hyde, thought Klein.[22]

Since Palestinian movements had excellent relations with Belgrade, a holiday in Yugoslavia seemed a good idea. Carlos, accompanied by Klein, spent a pleasant three weeks in Yugoslavia, enjoying the late summer weather as they toured the country in September 1976. Carlos particularly appreciated the Brioni Islands, probably unaware that he was following in the footsteps of the European aristocracy and, in more recent times, of Marshal Tito who had ordered a luxurious villa to be built on the small Adriatic archipelago where he used to entertain visiting dignitaries in style.

West German intelligence found out about Carlos's visit to Yugoslavia, and notified its Belgrade counterpart, the National Security Council. The West Germans insisted that he be arrested and extradited to Bonn forthwith. Carlos, who had been travelling under a false name on an Algerian diplomatic passport, was arrested and taken to a hurriedly prepared prison that consisted of an entire floor of the federal police barracks at 34 Sarajevska Street in Belgrade.

Carlos's jailer was the commander of the federal police corps, Slovenian Pavle Celik, a tall, fresh-faced sociology graduate in his mid-thirties, who had been given only a day to prepare the prison: 'I did not know who was due to arrive. I was only told that the person would be held until his trial, that he was a very wanted individual and very dangerous, an enemy of the state.'[23] It was only through friends that Celik found out that the moustachioed foreigner who was ushered under heavy escort into the makeshift prison was Carlos. He was accompanied by Klein and another bodyguard. Carlos did not appear to be particularly flustered. Celik found him 'extremely calm, which is not surprising given his line of work'.[24]

After four days, during which Carlos was honoured with a visit from Interior Minister Franjo Herljevic, Marshal Tito ordered his release. The presence of Carlos in Belgrade during an impending visit by the French President, Valéry Giscard d'Estaing, was a potential embarrassment for the Yugoslavs. Belgrade fended off strong rebukes from both Bonn and Washington, replying ingenuously that its checks had thrown up no indication that Carlos had passed through Yugoslavia. 'It was a political decision, taken at the apex of the Yugoslav leadership,' Celik related. 'As a policeman, I obeyed ... It was the time of the Cold War. It was logical that the socialist countries gave asylum to the terrorists who were, in a way, undermining capitalist regimes. Yugoslavia wanted to stay neutral ... We benefited from his release because there were no terrorist actions against Yugoslavia.'[25]

Carlos and Klein were told that they would be put on the next plane for the Iraqi capital Baghdad which would first, for an unexplained reason, stop at Damascus. They were bundled into a car, and Carlos broke into a cold sweat as, rifling through the directory of international flights that he had with him, he could find no such flight. His fears that he and Klein might be bound for another destination proved unfounded. But at Damascus airport the Syrians refused the plane permission to take off again. Neither Carlos nor Klein was armed. 'When we go out, they will shoot us,' Carlos told his companion. A group of men describing themselves as cleaning staff, but whose bulging pockets betrayed them as members of the security forces, tried to enter the plane. However, the pilot insisted that they respect the principle of the cabin's extra-territoriality. 'Carlos armed himself with an axe, the kind you find in planes,' Klein recalled. 'He was more and more overcome by fear; it was the first time I saw him scared. I was scared too.'[26]

After some five hours of negotiations, during which the

'cleaners' unscrewed the wheels of the plane to prevent it taking off, Yugoslav diplomats to whom Carlos had appealed put pressure on the Syrians and the plane was allowed to leave. Carlos and Klein finally arrived in Baghdad where they were put up free of charge, and provided with bodyguards and a chauffeured American limousine.[27]

The two Vienna veterans spent only a few weeks in Iraq. The fact that Saudi Arabia had put a million-dollar price on Carlos's head, and the incident at Damascus airport, highlighted his precarious situation. He chose to settle in a country he knew would not betray him, South Yemen. In a further guarantee of his security, Carlos enjoyed the protection of Libyan Colonel Qathafi, who supplied South Yemen's rulers with the money to meet Carlos's expenses. Inevitably, given his experience and notoriety, Carlos soon found himself acting as an instructor to several of the myriad radical groups training in Aden.[28]

But Carlos's ambitions stretched far beyond teaching would-be guerrillas. As he had revealed to a sceptical Bassam Abu-Sharif of the Popular Front in Beirut, he was intent on setting up his own organisation. But Carlos was unsure where to do so: in South America, the Middle East or elsewhere. And while he had recently established some influential contacts in Algeria, Libya and Iraq, he presently lacked both the recruits and the steady source of funding that were necessary for such an organisation.

Carlos, however, was quick to pick his right-hand man. Unashamedly rekindling links established by Haddad, Carlos again looked to West Germany's Revolutionary Cells. As Böse had been shot dead during the Entebbe hijack, the man whom Carlos sent for was Johannes Weinrich, who had helped him carry out the first rocket attack on the El Al plane at Orly airport. Some two months after the Orly operation Weinrich had been arrested in Frankfurt and charged with hiring the cars used at the time. After eight months in custody he had jumped bail, which he had obtained on health grounds, and was now on the run. Weinrich accepted Carlos's offer, and was assigned the job of recruiting Hans-Joachim Klein.

During the months that he had spent at Carlos's side Klein had concealed his growing misgivings about the use of violence. Klein's doubts had caused a furious argument with Carlos on the eve of the Vienna raid, and Klein was wary of provoking another outburst. When Weinrich arrived at the chalet in the Italian Alps where Klein had sought refuge, the discussion was rowdy. Klein realised that his days were numbered. He defected from the Popular Front, rejected guerrilla violence in general, and fled to Milan. He sent a letter and his gun to the magazine *Der Spiegel* in April 1977, at the same time revealing plans for the murder by the Revolutionary Cells of two members of Germany's Jewish community. He then went into hiding: 'If my people get me, they'll kill me. If police get to me, I go to jail. Who knows, maybe for ever.'[29] Whatever Carlos's feelings towards Klein, he kept them to himself. Years later he refused to answer questions from German investigators on Klein's role in the Vienna raid.[30]

Klein's defection was a blow for Carlos. A close associate had not only declined to join his new organisation, but had actually switched sides. At this point Carlos appears to have taken a rest from the complexities of Middle Eastern politics, and the searing summer heat of the Arabian Peninsula, to visit Latin America. He travelled to Colombia to explore the possibility of following in his ancestors' revolutionary footsteps across Latin America. But Carlos decided this was not fertile territory for him, and he returned to the Middle East. As he continued to search for a new role, Haddad and the Popular Front struggled with a confused strategy. Neither the Vienna hostage-taking nor the Entebbe hijack could be viewed as successful operations. Haddad, however, refused to believe that he was losing his touch and began to plan for a repeat hijack. Carlos, who had by then returned to Aden, was again sidelined.

Instead, Souhalia Andrawes was among the four selected to erase the Entebbe humiliation by hijacking, on 13 October 1977, a day after Carlos's twenty-eighth birthday, a Lufthansa Boeing 737 bound for Somalia. Eighty-six passengers were taken hostage, their hijackers demanding the release of Palestinian and Baader-Meinhof guerrillas, and a ransom of $15 million.

For five days the plane's Captain Juergen Schumann was forced to follow the hijacker's orders, touching down in Italy, Cyprus, Bahrain, Dubai and South Yemen. The passengers were told to sit strapped into their seats, and were doused with kerosene, perfume and spirits from the bar as their captors threatened to set them alight. The hostages remember Andrawes as a fury, screaming at them continuously, with grenades held ready in her hands, the pins linked to rings on her fingers by a thin cord.

In South Yemen, the crazed leader of the hijackers, Mahmoud, castigated Captain Schumann for talking to officials at the airport outside Aden. With the pilot forced to his knees in front of him in the central aisle, Mahmoud insisted despite Schumann's denials that he had tried to flee. 'Guilty or not guilty?' the hijacker shrieked. Moments later, he pushed his gun into Schumann's mouth and pulled the trigger. Andrawes burst out laughing. 'Most mothers had just enough time to cover their children's eyes, then the captain toppled over, dead,' recounted one passenger. 'They left him lying there in front of us. We had to climb over his body to get water or go to the lavatory.' Captain Schumann's body was eventually thrown out of the plane on to the tarmac below.[31]

After the co-pilot had flown the plane to Mogadishu in Somalia, and ninety minutes short of a deadline set by the hijackers, an attack was launched by Green Berets of the

West German GSG-9, a commando unit set up in the wake of the 1972 Munich Olympic Games fiasco. Blinded like everyone else in the plane by magnesium-based stun grenades supplied by two British SAS officers, Andrawes barely had time to seek refuge in the toilet. She fired through the door at her pursuers. The shots fired in retaliation turned the door into a colander. Seven bullets hit Andrawes in the shoulder and legs before she fell to the floor. Blood covered the portrait of Che Guevara on her T-shirt. As she was carried away on a stretcher moaning in pain, Andrawes still found the strength to make a victory sign and to shout: 'The Arabs will win!' and 'Palestine!' She was the only hijacker to survive.

Haddad's new failure made it clearer than ever to Carlos that it was time to press ahead with his own plans. The violent response of Israeli and West German authorities to the Entebbe and Mogadishu hijacks suggested that Haddad's tactics needed refining. Escorted by Libyan intelligence officers, Carlos travelled to Baghdad in December 1977. According to French intelligence, Carlos met President Saddam Hussein during this visit.[32] Iraq was among the first Arab countries to offer Carlos support, with the blessing of the KGB-trained members of Iraq's most powerful secret service, the Al Mukharabat.

Mogadishu was Haddad's last hijack. Carlos's erstwhile mentor, aged only forty-nine, died an enigmatic death in March 1978 – officially of leukaemia in an East Berlin clinic, but rumours abounded that he was poisoned, perhaps by the Iraqis. His partner Habash mourned him as a martyr: 'Wadi was far from being a terrorist. He was a sensitive person, from whom the sight of suffering children would wring tears ... Wadi was a revolutionary and a humanist who hated evil. His role, among us, is equal to that of a Che Guevara.'[33]

Carlos would no doubt also have agreed with the tribute paid by another former student of Haddad's, Japanese Red

Army leader Shigenobu Fusako: 'He gave extreme care to each detail. He was a maniac for the most absolute secrecy. With him, the least risk of error was eliminated. He duped many secret services, especially the Mossad. He still remains today, even after his death, our master and our model.'[34]

Haddad's death acted as a catalyst for Carlos. It rid him of a powerful competitor for the favours of Middle Eastern states, released several combatants whose first loyalty had been to Haddad, and triggered Carlos's emergence as the leader of a private army for hire which broke free of Palestinian shackles. With the master safely dead and buried, Carlos borrowed the name for his new group – Organisation of Arab Armed Struggle – from the man he had slain in Paris three years earlier, Michel Moukharbal. The Popular Front newspaper *Al Hadaf*, in an article following Moukharbal's death, had made the first public mention of the name.

In order to attract patrons who would be ready to pay for violent acts to be committed on their behalf, Carlos needed to build a professional force capable of carrying out bombings, assassinations and kidnappings. His ambition was to serve more than one master at any one time, and for that reason his organisation must also be capable of carrying out simultaneous operations in the same or different countries. Each mission would involve careful planning based on detailed surveillance of the objective, to be carried out by a large number of associates boasting a variety of different skills.

Carlos needed not only a core of close subordinates dedicated to the cause but also an international network of 'sleeper' agents who could be activated at short notice to carry out specific missions: watching selected targets for weeks on end, transporting explosives and weapons across borders, or providing safe houses. Carlos's organisation would also have to rely on associates who were not fully fledged members, but who would keep the group supplied with false identity papers, intelligence on its enemies, and help transfer funds when necessary.

The men and women who swore allegiance to Carlos in the wake of Haddad's death made up a cosmopolitan group. They included Syrian, Lebanese, West German and Swiss radicals. The core of Carlos's organisation, which was permanently under his orders, was drawn from West Germany's Revolutionary Cells, whose members he had already recruited for several of his earlier attacks. Carlos also secured the allegiance of Ali Al Issawe alias Abu Hakam, a Syrian intelligence officer.

One contribution Weinrich made was the girlfriend he had fallen in love with when his attempt at married life with an American ended. Weinrich met Magdalena Kopp, the daughter of a post-office worker, when she worked in his Red Star bookshop after studying photography in West Berlin had failed to get her a job. Kopp was married at the time, and she had a young daughter who was being raised by her parents. But Kopp's relationship with Weinrich led her to divorce her husband and she joined the Revolutionary Cells in the early 1970s, where she soon earned a reputation as an expert forger.

After Weinrich told him about Kopp, Carlos asked to meet her and she flew out to Algiers where Carlos was staying at the time. He was entranced by the fragile-looking redhead with moist eyes and a finely chiselled face, who was just a year younger than him. Carlos felt no scruples in pursuing Kopp despite her relationship with Weinrich.[35] Kopp found Carlos smarmy at first. But when he later turned up outside her hotel room with a bottle of wine, Carlos's advances were successful and the two spent the night together. Carlos rose in her esteem: 'He was a real seducer. Very charming. He knew just how to woo a woman.'[36] Carlos's partnership with Weinrich did not suffer, however. As Kopp drily observed, 'What else could

Weinrich have done? Where could he have gone?'[37] In the years to come, Carlos had no qualms about entrusting Kopp to Weinrich's care whenever he travelled abroad.

The core of his team established within months of Haddad's dying, and with the backing of several Arab states, Carlos began to seek support across Eastern Europe. In this he was, yet again, following the example set by his deceased guardian.

At about the same time that the CIA commissioned an agent to do its dirty work, the French secret service also set out on Carlos's trail. The manhunt by the SDECE's Action Service, France's clandestine operations unit, was initiated in the late 1970s by President Giscard d'Estaing who ordered the unit to intercept Carlos when he next passed through France or Europe.

At the SDECE headquarters in a grimy neighbourhood of north-east Paris beyond the Père Lachaise cemetery, the brief was handed to a young and brilliant graduate of the Saint-Cyr military academy thirteen years Carlos's senior, Philippe Rondot. The Action Service chief, Count Alain de Gaigneron de Marolles, thought of Rondot as a French Lawrence of Arabia because of his impressive contacts across the Arab world. With impeccable Cartesian logic, Rondot began at the beginning: his quarry's origins in Latin America. His team, with some cooperation from friendly intelligence agencies, focused on Carlos's family, and on his parents in particular.

The letter to his mother, Elba, that Carlos had entrusted to the Venezuelan Oil Minister during the Vienna epic had signposted as publicly as possible the warmth of his filial affection. The SDECE also had reports that Carlos occasionally visited his parents. The French opted to exploit his love for his parents, and especially for Elba, as a potential flaw in his security.

An Action Service colonel settled in Colombia, and succeeded in befriending Elba who lived there, separated from her divorced husband Ramírez Navas and ill. In 1977 Carlos was spotted in a Colombian hotel restaurant, but the officer made the crass mistake of speaking in French with his companion. Carlos, who had been sitting at a nearby table, left the restaurant immediately. 'Carlos was a very cautious guy. He had a feel for war, like warriors and hunters,' acknowledged Count de Marolles, who had served with the battle-thirsty 11ème Choc parachute commandos in both Indochina and Algeria. 'When you go underground, only the anxious survive.'[38]

Across the border in Venezuela, another Action Service officer struck up an acquaintance with Ramírez Navas in San Cristobal, winning the father's confidence by pretending to share his passion for cycling. According to a widely published report, Rondot travelled to the border ready, green light from Paris permitting, to have Ramírez Navas drink a concentrate of hepatitis A virus, to be topped up if necessary with an inoculation of the hepatitis B virus.[39] With the father sick, Carlos would, according to this unlikely plan, rush to his bedside, be seized by the Action Service and flown to French Guiana or the West Indies in a small private plane. The go-ahead, the story concludes, was never granted and all the French intelligence officers were recalled.

There would be nothing extraordinary about an intelligence service using poison to eliminate a target, even though that tactic was more commonly associated with the KGB than Western services. For men of France's clandestine operations unit, one senior SDECE officer observed, 'assassination is part of the daily routine. They dutifully carry out their orders and are proud of their skill, confident that it is equal to that of the Gestapo or the KGB.'[40] As Rondot himself once observed in an essay on the secret services: 'Special operations prolong diplomacy by other means. Certainly, one could allege that any special operation conducted by a Western democracy is illegal, anti-constitutional, immoral and unseemly.'[41]

However, had there been an order to assassinate Carlos, it would have had to come from the French President. Asked whether he granted the intelligence agency a licence to kill Carlos in what would have amounted to a 'non-judicial execution', Giscard's eyebrows shot up into his high domed forehead: 'There was no question of shooting him down. The order was never given. The order was to identify him, to follow him, to become intimate with his family and thus to find out his movements and to intercept him when he came to Europe ... There was no plan for an operation over there. The officers did not suggest one to me. We respected international law and justice, we wanted to try him.' But the former President confided: 'If there had been an attack, if Carlos had been armed, things would have been different.'[42]

Count de Marolles, who later headed SDECE intelligence but resigned from the service after fostering a failed coup against Colonel Qathafi in August 1980, ridiculed the idea that he or his men could have considered resorting to a virus: 'It's literature. It was ethically unallowable for the service. The plan was to be present in all the places where the quarry might turn up, and we were.'[43] The Colombian hotel restaurant was the closest the French secret service got to Carlos in a very long time.

Giscard's order became a dead letter. According to the mistaken reports sent to the President by the secret service, Carlos had not returned to Europe by the time Giscard was voted out of office in May 1981. When Giscard handed over the presidency to François Mitterrand, he briefed the socialist victor about the mission to track Carlos down in Latin America:[44] 'I told Mitterrand that this operation was under way when I was informing him about matters of presidential responsibility on which there were no documents and he said nothing, he expressed no interest. After the spring of 1981 the mission was ended. I don't know why.'[45] Rondot however did not give up. In the words of former SDECE head Alexandre de Marenches, from then on 'Rondot turned this into a personal matter'.

7

A Match Made in Hell

> Carlos was a big mouth, an uncontrollable adventurer. He spent his nights in bars, with a gun hanging at his belt, surrounded by girls and drinking like a fish.
>
> – East German spymaster General Markus Wolf

From inauspicious beginnings, Carlos's affair with Magdalena Kopp blossomed. She was as meek and shy as he was assertive and extrovert, but the aura he had acquired as a notorious 'revolutionary' helped to bring the like-minded Kopp under his spell. In January 1979 Carlos, who was twenty-nine years old, married the slightly younger Kopp in Lebanon.[1] Carlos apparently wanted to set his private life on a stable footing at a time that coincided with a turning point in his career. Vienna had taught him about the high rewards, the cash and fame, that could be earned from state-commissioned terrorism. His expulsion from the Popular Front had prompted him to set out anew, no longer merely a member of an organisation but now the leader of his own private army.

As he attempted to sound out the intelligence services of the Soviet Union's Communist satellites, Carlos surfaced in the spring of 1979 in the spy capital of Cold War Europe – East Berlin. The Carlos group had inevitably come to the attention of the Ministerium für Staatssicherheit (Ministry for State Security), or Stasi for short, a reviled mainstay of the German Democratic Republic. The KGB had presided over its birth, dictating its structure, objectives and methods, which included a time-consuming filing system copied from the Czar's secret police. Part secret service, counter-intelligence arm, undercover police and even parallel judicial system, the Stasi kept such a close watch over 17 million East Germans that they have been described as the most spied-upon people in history. Like the KGB, the Stasi considered itself to be the shield and sword of the Communist Party. At the Stasi's disposal were some 400,000 employees and agents.

As Minister for State Security since 1957, General Erich Mielke was a feared Big Brother to the people of East Germany. The son of a cart-maker, Mielke had left school at the age of sixteen to start work as a dispatch clerk. He joined the Communist Party newspaper *Rote Fahne* (Red Flag) as a journalist in 1925, but he soon turned street-fighter for the Communist Party's paramilitary force confronting Nazi gangs in Berlin. After he and a comrade shot two police officers dead in a city square in 1931, Mielke fled to Moscow. A diehard Stalinist, he would brook no opposition to his habit of toasting his hero at official dinners and demanding 'three cheers for our model and inspiration'. Mielke was, in the words of his foreign intelligence chief, General Markus Wolf, 'a warped personality even by the peculiar standards of morality that apply in the espionage world'.[2]

The East Germans first took notice of pro-Palestinian terrorism when the Israeli athletes were gunned down at the Munich Olympics in August 1972. On the orders of the East German leader Erich Honecker, the Stasi established relations with Palestinian guerrillas. The delicate task was entrusted to Wolf, known in the West as 'the man without a face', precisely because until 1979 it had no idea what he looked like.

'Honecker received Yasser Arafat in late 1972,' Wolf

explained, 'and later on in Moscow my deputy responsible for Arab countries spoke to Arafat and told him that our condition for support was that the German Democratic Republic should not be used as a base for guerrilla attacks. Of course, to think that such a condition could be fulfilled was naïve. We also told Arafat that we had been very disappointed that the Munich attack had been carried out.'[3] For Wolf, both parties benefited from the ensuing collaboration. Palestinian officers were sent to East Germany for training in espionage as well as arms, explosives and guerrilla warfare. And the Stasi received much information on Israel and on Arab countries which it would otherwise have been unable to obtain, and which Wolf proudly passed on to Moscow.

In 1975 Mielke set up a new department inside the Ministry for State Security, Section XXII, nominally in charge of countering and monitoring foreign terrorists in East Germany, to deal with Palestinian and other guerrilla movements. This was a counter-terrorist unit in name only. The emphasis was on monitoring rather than countering. The only foreign guerrillas it interfered with were those thought to be planning attacks against East Germany and the rest of the Soviet bloc. Fighters passing through or staying in East Germany were contacted by Stasi officers and offered asylum and support in exchange for a pledge of non-aggression. Members of West Germany's far-left guerrilla organisation, the Red Army Faction, found permanent refuge on East German soil. Palestinians were also welcome, since theirs was classified as an 'international liberation movement'.

The ink was hardly dry on the 1979 Egyptian-Israeli peace treaty when the Stasi heard from an Arab informer, in late March, of Carlos's exploratory mission to East Berlin.[4] Stasi officers were despatched to the Stadt Berlin (now the Hotel Forum), a luxury hotel which towers charmlessly above the Alexanderplatz. Carlos had booked in to the hotel, one of the few in East Berlin open to foreigners, masquerading as a Yemeni diplomat, Ahmed Ali Fawaz. In one of its first reports on Carlos, the Stasi made a cautious evaluation of his political desirability and noted the rumours spread by the CIA that Carlos was a KGB agent: 'Western press reports have already contributed on several occasions to slander the Palestinian liberation movement, as well as to intensify anti-Communist hatred, notably in affirming that Carlos operated at the demand of "eastern European secret services".'[5]

Wary of approaching Carlos directly, Stasi officers contented themselves with making it obvious to him that he was being watched. Surveillance and meetings with Carlos's lieutenant Johannes Weinrich, who had also travelled to East Berlin, soon fleshed out the earlier press review with a precise outline of the visitor's plans. Drawn up by General Irmler, a close aide to Mielke, the report marked '*Ultrasecret: to be returned after reading*' was circulated to the minister, his number two Gerhard Neiber and Wolf before it was discussed at a politburo meeting chaired by Honecker. Weinrich had made no secret of Carlos's agenda:

> Create bases in the capital of the Federal Republic of Germany, with the collaboration of East German citizens ... send agents of the Carlos group on missions to West Germany and West Berlin; establish permanent contacts with the Yemeni, Iraqi and Libyan republics as well as the PLO in the East German capital; obtain arms, explosives, money and information ... inspire violent armed actions, including personal attacks against the imperialist policy of the United States and the Zionists; and reactivate contacts with anarcho-terrorist forces in West Germany and West Berlin. Finally, the group plans to ensure that the embassies of East Germany and the Soviet Union in Damascus help to set up bases for it in Syria.[6]

'Fundamental ideological orientations', as the Stasi

called them, played a key role in its assessment of Carlos, and the East Germans noted that he aimed 'to fight against imperialism, racism, colonialism and all other reactionary forces ... Armed revolutionary combat is the priority for the Carlos group. Socialist countries are themselves seen as zones of deployment.'[7]

There was no hint of disapproval from an institution which, like the rest of the East German state apparatus, was monolithic in its ideological outlook and firmly believed that 'the enemy of my enemy is my friend'. Somewhat confused by the long list of targets and objectives, the Stasi did not have an easy time understanding what exactly the Carlos group professed to be fighting. But in the eyes of the watchful Stasi there was no doubt who was in charge. Its reports describe Carlos as the force behind the new group's creation, its unchallenged leader. It also saw Carlos as the chief schemer in the group's relations with other states and their secret services.

In April 1979 Carlos was on the agenda at a meeting in Prague of deputy Interior Ministers of the Warsaw Pact. In the run-up to the Moscow Olympic Games the Russians were obsessed by security and the memory of the Munich Olympics massacre. The Russians pressed their allies for precise information on the activities of guerrillas and of Carlos in particular. The attempt to thrash out a common stand to adopt towards such groups came to nothing. Conceived by the Soviets as a ploy to gather as much information as possible from their allies without revealing anything themselves, the gathering broke up with a wooden communiqué warning against 'reactionary forces' pushing terrorists into exporting their activities to Communist soil.

'I have never met East German leaders or intelligence [Stasi] officers,' Carlos has insisted. 'If General Mielke was in charge "of manipulating me", I know nothing of this, and I ask myself how and with what effect!'[8] But the East German files tell a different story. To function, Carlos needed state sponsors willing to shelter him and to provide a steady supply of the tools of his trade: funds, weapons, safe houses, intelligence and commissions. Of all those who agreed to this unholy alliance, none was more generous than East Germany. Carlos was told to consider the country's rulers as 'allies in the struggle against the imperialists'. And Mielke issued instructions that the authorities should support Carlos's and similar groups 'during the transport of arms destined for combatants in the zone of operations'. The zone in question was Western Europe, and West Germany in particular.[9]

According to Wolf, who for three decades ruled the Foreign Intelligence Directorate, Carlos was accepted by the Stasi because it wanted to shield the East bloc: 'I can only imagine Mielke's way of thinking: he wanted to find a way to neutralise the terrorists as far as actions against socialist countries and the German Democratic Republic were concerned. We wanted to protect ourselves. The ministry tried to have very close control over terrorist movements across our borders, and this was a sign that it was trying not to support but to control them.'[10]

Another reason for treating Carlos cautiously were the diplomatic passports which he and his group used, and which were provided by several Arab patrons including South Yemen. The Stasi did not want to risk harming East German relations with these countries. Carlos had left Aden on good terms with the South Yemeni authorities. His East Berlin hotel bills were paid by the embassy of the People's Democratic Republic, courtesy of the South Yemeni taxpayer. The passports not only flagged the high-level protection Carlos enjoyed. They also made it unlikely that Carlos and his accomplices would be searched when entering a country. And even if the weapons, explosives and ammunition that they often carried were discovered, border guards had no power to arrest them. Under the

Vienna Convention on diplomatic privilege, the most the border guards could do was to send those holding diplomatic passports back to the country from which they had travelled.

The bureaucratic need for prudence dictated a constant stream of reports, often stamped *Streng Geheim!* (Very Secret!), and sometimes sent to the East German politburo. The arrivals and departures of Carlos's companions were monitored, and they were followed from a respectful distance. Hotel rooms at the Stadt Berlin, Metropol (now the Maritim), and Palast Hotel (now the Radisson SAS), and flats were bugged. Belongings were searched. Letters written to each other by Carlos and Weinrich, and the latter's notebooks, were photocopied surreptitiously. The records kept by Weinrich were especially informative given his habit of writing down all activities, contacts and expenses.

Initially at least, Carlos did not resent the Stasi's scrutiny. An early report noted that he considered the employees of the Ministry for State Security to be 'international terrorists', not a pejorative phrase in Carlos's eyes, and 'open, modest, communicative and sociable individuals'. As could be expected in a Soviet satellite state, they were also deemed to have acquired 'a solid Marxist education and clear opinions'. The Stasi noted respectfully that a suite used by Carlos at the Palast Hotel, a mausoleum-like edifice a stone's throw away from Honecker's glass status symbol, the Palace of the Republic, had been turned into 'an intelligence exchange. Telexes sent to the Carlos group were immediately sent on to other countries if its members were away.'[11]

Over the following months, Stasi officers – including Colonel Harry Dahl, head of the counter-terrorism Section XXII, and Major Helmut Voigt, in charge of its international subdivision Section XXII/8 – met Weinrich in East Berlin several times. Weinrich was the Stasi's main point of contact because he was based in East Berlin, while Carlos was almost constantly on the move. His visits to the city were short, and on these trips he met Arab diplomats, went shopping and spent much time in bars chatting up women.

From its observations the Stasi concluded that Carlos was the ideas man and Weinrich the quartermaster. It was Weinrich who supplied the private army's members with real and false passports, driving licences, vaccination certificates and other documents. The organisation's notes show that its members could count on an impressive stock of blank passports from a host of countries (including the United Kingdom, France, several Latin American countries, and even Israel). Drawing on his previous experience of running a bookshop, the thirty-two-year-old Weinrich kept meticulous record of accounts.[12] He took charge of the group's travel arrangements which included hotel bookings and visas negotiated with the Stasi. He managed relations with the Spanish Basque ETA, the Greek ELA and the Revolutionary Cells he had co-founded. He also helped to look after relations with envoys of the Syrian, Libyan and Yemeni secret services in East Berlin. Weinrich became increasingly wary of the Stasi and regularly drafted new lists of aliases for the members of the group. A wasted effort, because the lists were promptly photocopied by his guardians.

Carlos had won the Stasi's support, but he had greater ambitions. Just as he had sounded out the East Germans, so he made a first trip to the Hungarian capital Budapest on 2 May 1979. He could not have been more indiscreet. Asked for a credit card when he registered at the Hotel Intercontinental with Weinrich, an irate Carlos threw his briefcase on the counter and flung it open. The first thing the concierge saw was a large revolver, the second was wads of hundred-dollar bills on which the gun rested. Both men were travelling on Yemeni diplomatic passports: Carlos under the name of Ahmed Ali Fawaz, and Weinrich as Mohamed Hussaien.

Alerted by the hotel, the counter-espionage section at Hungarian state security investigated the strangers and soon established their real identities. But, like the Stasi when it first discovered the pair, the Hungarians held off making a direct approach. It was only on Carlos's third visit to Budapest that the counter-intelligence service, which had in the meantime sought advice from Moscow, decided to keep watch over him.

Carlos had by then rented a villa in Vend Street on Budapest's Hill of Roses, an exclusive neighbourhood on the right bank of the Danube popular with the politburo, diplomats and rich businessmen. On the evening of 29 August Carlos was seen leaving the villa in a taxi with his wife and Weinrich. A counter-espionage officer took advantage of their absence to break into the villa, where he discovered weapons and ammunition. A short while afterwards, spies sent by counter-intelligence chief General Miklos Redei spotted Carlos, Weinrich and Kopp at the airport, apparently waiting to welcome someone. Carlos soon realised he was under surveillance, and left the airport in a taxi with Weinrich. Kopp left in a different taxi. Several cars followed Carlos and Weinrich as they returned to their villa. Egged on by Carlos who promised a huge reward, their driver tried but failed to shake off the pursuers. Shortly after midnight, and minutes after reaching his villa, Carlos walked out into the road, and turned to see one of the cars that the Hungarian counter-espionage officers had used to follow him. He pulled his gun, a Parabellum 38, out of his belt, slowly took aim, and from thirty metres shot five bullets through the door of the car. Two of the bullets buried themselves in the front passenger seat, centimetres below an officer's buttocks. The number plate of the car, Carlos explained later, was not Hungarian and he had presumed that a Western intelligence service was following him.

Carlos's relations with the Hungarians were hardly placed on a firmer footing when the following day, with a shout of '*Hände Hoch!*' (Hands Up!), he pounced on another officer who had been tailing him. Carlos held the barrel of his gun to the man's temple as he marched him into the nearby police headquarters. A few days later Carlos accepted that he needed at least the tacit consent of the Hungarians if he were to stay in Budapest, and humbly asked them to assure his protection. The job of minding Carlos fell to Colonel Jozsef Varga of the counter-espionage unit.

When Varga, accompanied by two officers, called at his villa, Carlos showed them in, sat them down, and placed a big-calibre revolver on the table. Carlos soon realised that none of the Hungarians was armed, and asked a submissive Kopp to remove the gun, adding that she should take it by the barrel to avoid giving the wrong impression to their visitors. Varga told Carlos that a prolonged stay was out of the question, and the indignant Venezuelan launched into a long monologue on world revolution. 'How is it possible,' Carlos asked, 'that a socialist country refuses help to a combatant of imperialism, of America and of the countries and organisations which oppress the people?' Varga retorted that he was free to fight as he wished, but not from Hungarian soil, and set him a deadline for leaving the country along with his associates.[13]

Hungarian intelligence tried to prise some guidance out of Moscow. But the KGB station chief in Budapest, General Alexander Alexandrovich Kosov, had no advice for his comrades. When the Hungarians then appealed directly to the Foreign Intelligence Branch of the KGB, Moscow replied that it was familiar with Carlos as he had been dismissed from Patrice Lumumba University for bad behaviour. But Hungary was a sovereign country and should deal with him as it saw fit. 'If the Soviets had reached a deal with him, they would have told us,' said Colonel Varga. 'They gave us nothing, and they asked nothing of us. It was as if they were telling us: "It's your affair." '[14]

Colonel Varga may have hoped that his first meeting with Carlos would also be his last. But the two were to meet more than twenty times. Carlos made Budapest his main base for the better part of the next five years. Initially he and Kopp rented their own villa, but later the politburo allocated them several safe houses in the city. Carlos lived, in the words of an intelligence officer, like a 'man of the world',[15] enjoying the women supplied by the secret service behind Kopp's back, and downing the finest whisky. When drunk, he would draw his gun and shoot into the ceiling.

Hungary's generosity was tempered by tight surveillance and prudent searches of his group's homes.[16] Moreover, the Hungarians refused Carlos's constant requests for arms and explosives, turning Varga's job into a nightmare: 'I was a little scared of Carlos. So I had men ready to intervene. One day they nearly burst in because Carlos was hitting the table with his fist. Sometimes this guy foamed with rage, he was beside himself. I don't mean to say that he was mad, but he had a fiery temperament, he was capable of violent, brutal acts.'[17] But there was no question of arresting Carlos. General Redei considered him an untouchable: 'We knew that if something happened to Carlos here the whole terrorist group would have declared Allah's revenge on Hungary. All our embassies abroad would have been exposed to their revenge.'[18]

Despite his more administrative role, Weinrich was also quite capable of aggressive behaviour, as he showed at the Hungarian consulate in Prague in November 1979. In a hurry to get to Budapest, Weinrich demanded that an official give him a visa for later the same day. But the official was sceptical of the South Yemeni passport made out in the name of Tabet Ali Ben Ali, and refused to grant it. Weinrich pulled out an automatic pistol, and laid it on the desk as he told the official to contact the Yemeni embassy. A phone call later, the official apologised. The Yemeni embassy had informed the consular official that not only was the passport valid, but also that it had been provided by a highly placed authority. Failure to treat its bearer appropriately would be taken as an insult.

However, not all the Soviet bloc countries where Carlos tried to set up bases received him with open arms. Travelling incessantly through the East bloc, Carlos noted that some governments barely tolerated his passage, while others provided safe houses or allowed him to store weapons. Yugoslavia turned a blind eye to the arms trafficking from East to West, and put a villa in Belgrade at his disposal. Czechoslovakia allowed him and his accomplices to use its training camps. Bulgaria served as little more than an occasional place to stay, although members of his organisation were free to swagger around Sofia with their guns on public display.

War is the continuation of diplomacy by other means, Clausewitz wrote. And after establishing links with the secret services of much of the Soviet bloc, Carlos had done enough diplomacy and was more than ready for war.

Ever since his dismissal from the Popular Front Carlos had been careful to maintain contact with several Palestinian groups, including the PLO which – in public at least – had regularly and loudly condemned Haddad's outrages. As in his dealings with East bloc countries, Carlos approached an intelligence officer, Amine El Hindi, in charge of security for Yasser Arafat's Fatah faction. The Palestinians decided to take matters further and El Hindi served as Carlos's intermediary in talks with Abu Iyad, the head of the PLO's intelligence agency. In 1979 Carlos and the PLO considered a jointly organised assassination of King Hussein, the 'traitor' whose army had thrown the

Palestinian fighters out of Jordan eight years earlier. But Carlos demanded too high a fee and the plan was dropped.[19]

Frustrated in his attempt to murder King Hussein, Carlos decided to polish his public image. During a short stay in West Beirut in late 1979 he gave a long interview to a friend, Lebanese journalist and poet Assam El Jundi. Carlos had shown Jundi his own attempts at poetry and had asked him to write his biography. When Jundi chose a photograph of Carlos to go with the article, Carlos signed the picture: 'For a wonderful poet from an apprentice poet – Carlos.' The interview was published in *Al Watan al Arabi* (The Arab Nation), an Arab-language magazine based in Paris, in a three-part series in November and December. According to the Stasi files and to a member of the magazine's staff, the interview was carried out with the cooperation of the Palestinian who had recruited Carlos for the Popular Front, Bassam Abu-Sharif.

It cannot have been an easy interview. Carlos's idea of friendship and his sense of humour, as a close acquaintance during this period recalled, could set your teeth on edge. One night the two men argued over cards or some other minor topic and Carlos suddenly turned menacing.

'If you talk to me like that again in front of other people, you'll see what will happen.'

The friend left in the small hours to go to bed. But at eight o'clock in the morning there was a knock at the front door. It was Carlos, and he was holding a gun.

'Do you remember the movie where the cowboy says, "I kill you for money, I kill you for a woman and I kill you for nothing because you are my friend"?' Carlos asked, and with that he put the pistol to his friend's head – who remembers noting that it was big and Soviet-made – without even bothering to cross the threshold into the house.

'I kill you for nothing because you are my friend,' Carlos said. Then he hugged his friend. It had all been Carlos's idea of a joke.[20]

The interview brought French police to the Paris offices of *Al Watan al Arabi* in an attempt to track down the Rue Toullier murderer. But the weekly's Lebanese editor, Walid Abou Zahr, declined to help. A few weeks later in Baghdad Abou Zahr was introduced to a stranger by Bassam Abu-Sharif. 'Do you know this man? You publish him,' Abu-Sharif said. 'Carlos,' the editor replied. 'We shook hands and we talked politics,' Abou Zahr related. 'Carlos spoke of his ideals – that freedom could be brought to the Middle East and Europe, that Israel and American imperialism could be destroyed. Things that could happen only on another planet. Carlos was still idealistic then.'[21] Unknown to the editor, Carlos was displeased by the magazine's scoop. He believed that the way the interview had been published did him more harm than good and resolved, literally, to shoot the messenger. The Stasi files quote him as denouncing the interview as part of a plot by the Iraqi secret services to discredit him following his refusal to work for them.[22]

Walid Abou Zahr was no stranger to living dangerously. The rotund, bespectacled editor had a long history of upsetting the Syrian regime. When the newspaper he had previously run, *Al Moharrer*, criticised the entry of Syrian troops into Beirut, its offices in the Lebanese capital were surrounded by soldiers and a tank of the invading army. Shells and machine-gun fire hit the building in a two-hour battle with security guards and four people including the newspaper's manager were killed. The daily was eventually banned, and Abou Zahr moved to Paris to start *Al Watan al Arabi* which took a strong line against the Syrian government, giving plenty of space to Syrian opposition leaders. The editor collected death threats. In 1979 he narrowly escaped being stabbed to death when a gang of assassins armed with knives mistook a neighbour for Abou Zahr and attacked him. The neighbour survived.[23]

Publication of the interview with Carlos made a new enemy for Abou Zahr. Notes made by Carlos in the spring of 1980, which were copied by Hungarian intelligence in Budapest, detail surveillance of the *Al Watan* building. The movements of staff, including Abou Zahr, were recorded, down to the minute, and photographs were taken of several journalists.[24] One note, possibly written by Weinrich, made no attempt at discretion: 'It is possible that these two photographs may serve to illustrate the possibilities of an assassination just in front of the offices.' Carlos planned to murder the editor and simultaneously wreck the offices. A remote-controlled car bomb in front of the offices was to explode when the editor walked past. Another bomb was to go off inside the building at the same time.[25]

Shortly after the interview's publication Carlos had set the murder of the article's author, Assam El Jundi, as an initiation test for a candidate who wanted to join his organisation, twenty-two-year-old Kurdish refugee Jamal al-Kurdi. The would-be recruit, however, bravely refused to carry out the murder, but was spared Carlos's anger because one of his lieutenants, most likely Issawe, volunteered for the job. An unidentified gunman shot the journalist Jundi in the head with a pistol fitted with a silencer in the Lebanese town of Bourj el Brajneh on 19 June 1980. The bullet bored a large hole behind Jundi's ear, but he survived.

Issawe, who like Carlos was previously a follower of Haddad, was, according to the Stasi, the only associate who could talk to Carlos as an equal.[26] The fact that Carlos had chosen Issawe, a Syrian secret service officer, as one of his key subordinates was a sure sign of his new alliance strategy. Carlos's relations with Iraq had broken down early in 1979, because he resented what he perceived to be the domineering nature of the Iraqi secret service, and feared that it would punish him for refusing to carry out the missions it requested in exchange for support. Carlos badly needed a new sponsor, and Issawe played a vital role in mending relations with the Syrians, who in the autumn of 1976 had tried to seize Carlos and Hans-Joachim Klein at Damascus airport.

No longer attached to the Popular Front and now at the head of his own organisation, Carlos convinced the Syrians with Issawe's help that he could be of use to them. From 1979 onwards the Syrians welcomed Carlos every time he visited Damascus, where safe houses, arms depots and training camps were placed at his disposal. There was no limit to Issawe's reach. He was Carlos's link to the Syrian President's brother Rifaat al-Assad,[27] chief of the Defence Brigades whose nickname the Pink Panthers, due to the colour of their combat uniform, belied a ruthless fighting force. In early March 1981 Carlos met President al-Assad himself when he intervened in negotiations on the landing in Syria of a hijacked Pakistani plane.

Syria's support for Carlos held true within Eastern Europe. When Stasi officers questioned the Syrian ambassador to East Berlin on the validity of Issawe's diplomatic passport, the ambassador answered that such documents were provided to members of Palestinian groups on the personal orders of President al-Assad. Carlos used his Syrian diplomatic passport, in the name of Michel Khouri, and Kopp hers, in the name of Maryam Touma, to ferry weapons and ammunition from East Berlin to Hungary in July 1980. The Syrian ambassador to East Berlin was only one of many Syrian diplomats ordered to support Carlos. Other Syrian embassies in the Soviet bloc, in Hungary, Czechoslovakia and Bulgaria, received similar instructions from Damascus.

In mid-1980 Carlos flew from Aden via Moscow to East Berlin, again using his Syrian diplomatic passport. Part of the luggage that he checked in on the Aeroflot flight was a large metal case addressed to the Syrian embassy in East Berlin.[28] A short time later Weinrich also brought a heavy-duty suitcase into East Germany, passing himself off as Abdul Nabi Mohamed Hussaien, supposedly a diplomat at the Yemeni embassy. Between them, the two cases contained ten hand grenades, five Beretta submachine-guns, twelve Browning 9mm pistols, five detonators, a hundred detonating caps, four Russian-made RPG75 rocket-launchers, and ammunition. The consignment was destined for the Spanish Basque ETA.

Despite the diplomatic cover the project suffered a hitch when the Stasi, alerted by border guards, confiscated the arsenal. 'At the time, everyone was scared that in putting too much pressure on the Carlos group we would become a victim,' admits Colonel Günter Jäckel, a former Stasi adviser to Nasser and Mengistu. 'The Russians had given us no warning. Obviously, that gave us food for thought. Despite that we seized the weapons.'[29] Carlos sent Weinrich to negotiate with the Stasi, and his vigorous protests – he accused the East Germans of wrecking an arms transit agreement with the Soviets – were referred up the hierarchy to Deputy Minister Neiber. As Weinrich guaranteed that the weapons would not stay in East Berlin, but were destined for the Basque separatists, Neiber ordered that they should be handed back.

After the delay, two ETA members set out that October to fetch the consignment. Patrick Chabrol and Edith Keresbars drove to East Berlin in a Toyota minibus with French registration plates. A junior Stasi officer, Wilhelm Borostowski, directed them to a police garage in the centre of the city, where the weapons were handed to Weinrich and the ETA couriers in the middle of the night. With the arms hidden in the roof, the minibus was waved through the border at Marienborn after East German guards were instructed by the Stasi not to check its contents. 'I don't know if the ETA committed attacks for the Carlos group in exchange for arms deliveries,' Colonel Jäckel explained. 'Members of the ETA planned to use the weapons to support the fight for the liberation of El Salvador.'[30]

Further afield in the Communist family, Cuba offered a

helping hand to Carlos. Officers of Cuba's DGI intelligence service, posing as diplomats at embassies across the Warsaw Pact, supported South American and world revolutionary organisations. The DGI's man in East Berlin, Juan Miguel Roque Ramirez, met Weinrich repeatedly and in May 1980 Weinrich visited Cuba. But in 1981, perhaps influenced by President Reagan's high-profile crusade against terrorism, the Cuban party leadership decided to curtail relations with Carlos and decreed the island off-limits to him save for short stopovers.[31]

Of all the East bloc régimes that Carlos served, few were as nasty as that of the Romanian dictator Nicolae Ceauscescu and his wife Elena. And few of the crimes that Carlos carried out were as far removed from furthering world revolution as those the self-styled 'genius of the Carpathians' ordered in his determination to crush all opposition standing in the way of his personality cult. After negotiating with Ceauscescu's political police, the Securitate, Carlos committed himself in January 1981 to a bloodbath – the assassination of five Romanian dissidents and their families living in exile.[32]

On 3 February two very vocal critics of Ceauscescu living as exiles in Paris, former Interior Minister Nicolae Penescu and writer Paul Goma, received parcels in the post. The eighty-five-year-old Penescu opened his package and found a book written by Nikita Khrushchev. When he lifted the cover, the explosion of the bomb that had been hidden inside the gutted book wounded him in the face and hands. But Goma, who had received two death threats since seeking refuge in France four years earlier, sensed danger when he saw his parcel and called the police. Both packages had been sent on Carlos's instructions and manufactured with the help of Spanish Basque guerrillas of the ETA.[33] Carlos failed to carry out attacks on the three other dissidents and their families, including a former deputy-head of the Foreign Intelligence Service (DIE), General

Ion Mihai Pacepa, who had been condemned to death for defecting to the United States in 1978.

High on the Securitate's list of targets were two bedrocks of the propaganda battle between East and West, Radio Free Europe and Radio Liberty. Funded by the CIA and broadcast from Munich to the Soviet bloc in several eastern European languages, the station had been first with the news of Khrushchev's secret speech demolishing Stalin's personality cult. However, the coverage of the Solidarity trade union rebellion in Poland beginning in the summer of 1980 had prompted Communist régimes to redouble their efforts to stifle the broadcasts with heavy jamming.

In Romania surveys showed that three-quarters of the population tuned in regularly to the two channels. Jamming proved ineffective and so it was at the Securitate's behest that Carlos's accomplices parked a car packed with explosives outside the building that housed the stations on the edge of Munich's popular Englischer Garten park. The explosion late in the evening of 21 February 1981 devastated much of the building. Eight of the thirty people preparing news reports on that Saturday evening were wounded. But within an hour, Radio Free Europe was back on air.

The Securitate, which according to Hungarian intelligence had supplied the plans of the building, gave Carlos a triumphant welcome when he visited Bucharest shortly after the attack, even though it had not silenced Radio Free Europe. But there was more at stake than warm embraces and laudatory toasts. Carlos had delivered, at a price of $400,000 according to Western intelligence, and earned the gratitude of one of the East bloc's least savoury secret services. The Securitate refused him nothing. A safe house in the centre of Bucharest, sixty passports bearing false names (several of the passports were diplomatic), three rocket-launchers with eighteen projectiles, and Romanian-made remote controls.[34] He was even allowed a bank account in Bucharest, number 471 1210 3502, opened by Anna Luisa Kramer (alias Magdelana Kopp) at the Romanian Bank of Foreign Trade.[35]

In April 1980 Carlos had written a polite letter to the Hungarian leader, whom he called Comrade Janos Kadar, to signal his appreciation and thank him for 'the possibility to use Hungary to prepare for our international revolutionary actions', and for 'the safety, security and free passage' it provided. 'We have developed our international relations from Hungarian soil, contacting the revolutions of each nation, without being hampered by the Hungarian authorities . . . The socialist countries are allowing our combatants to pass freely, and are improving relations with our organisation,' he had written.[36]

But as Carlos's group grew more active the Hungarians began to get cold feet. In April 1981, two months after the Munich attack, Hungary's Varga told his East Berlin colleagues (Dahl, Jäckel and Voigt) that he had decided to expel Carlos and his accomplices by the middle of the following month.[37] On 15 May Andreas Petresevics, head of the Hungarian secret service's new counter-terrorism section, summoned Carlos and Weinrich to a meeting in his office. Petresevics had previously installed a concealed camera in the room behind the glass door of a cupboard. The grainy film of the encounter, which was held opposite a large portrait of Carlos's namesake Lenin, shows Petresevics and a subordinate warning their guests in Russian that Western intelligence was on their trail. They handed Carlos a notice by Interpol they had forged which reported his whereabouts in Budapest. 'You must liquidate your operational bases in our country,' Petresevics sternly admonished Carlos. 'You must stop using Hungary to lead your group, because there is a danger. Your operations can be jeopardised. What's more, if you were to remain, the interests of the People's Republic of Hungary could be threatened if we were associated with you.'

Carlos listened uneasily to Petresevics, fidgeting constantly, stuffing his hands into his pockets only to pull them out again, and obsessively chewing his lower lip. Weinrich, his pen racing, jotted down what was being said. Carlos reacted angrily: 'You are yielding to the imperialists. We had agreements and you are not respecting them.' Petresevics retorted that no written agreements existed, and in a conciliatory tactic suggested that Hungary might agree to Carlos passing through the country occasionally.

Wriggling in his seat and throwing nervous glances around the room, Carlos again burst out indignantly, this time in Spanish: 'Written contracts, I don't know what that is. The only paper I own is this!' He opened his jacket to show his gun resting in its holster. Carlos demanded access to East European intelligence reports on terrorist activity in West Germany, and then launched into a political speech laced with the rhetoric he liked to indulge in: 'If we have been fighting and spilling our blood for years, it is not to score a personal success but for socialism. We fight against the enemies of our camp, in the interest of all peoples and above all of the oppressed of the world. We have a common enemy to slay.' Such jargon was all too familiar to his hosts, but Carlos's negotiating skills, with their heavy reliance on threats, won him a reprieve.[38] The counter-intelligence service continued its surveillance however, and its listening devices recorded Carlos's reaction when he heard a radio report of the assassination of Egyptian President Anwar Sadat by Islamic radicals at a military parade on 6 October 1981. 'We've just lost a $4 million contract from Qathafi!' he exploded. 'Everything was ready.'

The Hungarians were not the only ones to grow wary of Carlos. His erratic personality irritated his East German handlers, and their verdict on his character was damning. Running through their reports – which inevitably reflect the Stasi's own paranoia – is an emphasis on Carlos's uncontrollable and unpredictable nature. His superiority complex and insecurity, the officers noted, meant he refused to suffer contradiction of any kind. If countered, he would lose control and seek revenge.

Although by late 1981 Carlos's force was estimated by the Stasi to number some forty members in Europe and two hundred or so associates in Arab countries, he was seen as so erratic that he could not be used even if the Cold War turned into a military confrontation. 'Mielke's belief was that in the event of war the disciplined members of West Germany's Red Army Faction could be used as a guerrilla force behind enemy lines, to blow up bridges and attack strategic installations,' recounted Wolf. 'But in Carlos's case no one, neither Mielke nor anyone else, trusted him. His behaviour showed that he could not be used for an operation. He was uncontrollable.'[39]

Nor did the Stasi, raised on Communist orthodoxy, have a good opinion of his idiosyncratic ideology. 'Carlos defines himself as a "Marxist" and a "Communist" but his views are simplistic and in part erroneous,' tut-tutted one study.[40] His long discourses on Communism and world revolution were confused, and his political aims were pseudo-revolutionary. As far as the Stasi could tell, Carlos's group did not quite live up to the different names with which it liked to drape itself: World Revolution, International Revolutionary Organisation, or Organisation of International Revolutionaries.

Carlos's flamboyant lifestyle was also not that of a terrorist hugging the shadows. He often chose to stay at the Palast Hotel. He dismissed pleas from the Stasi to keep a low profile and stay in his room out of trouble. Instead, Carlos whiled the nights away in the bar or in nightclubs, gun hung on his belt, drinking heavily and flirting with high-class prostitutes who doubled as Stasi agents. He made a habit of dining at expensive restaurants, where everything he ate was dutifully reported by the Stasi. Weinrich was just as fond as Carlos of costly female escorts, to whom he introduced himself as Doctor Salibi, supposedly an employee of OPEC. 'Mielke felt very uncomfortable about Carlos's stay,' related Wolf, who branded Carlos a 'human bomb' because of the potentially disastrous situation in which he might land his Stasi minders. 'Carlos did not follow the rules. It was terrible, unbelievable.'[41] The Stasi commented that Carlos was constantly 'at risk of being identified by commandos or specialists of Mossad'.

Mielke's concern was justified, at least in part. As early as August 1979 the West German Foreign Ministry had ticked off the Hungarian ambassador to Bonn for Carlos's presence in Budapest, even naming a hotel (the Intercontinental) at which it mistakenly believed him to be staying. But the reprimand was a light one, and was not followed up. West German intelligence, however, among the first to find out the whereabouts of Carlos and Weinrich some months later, censored itself from making such knowledge public because it did not want to jeopardise delicate relations between the two Germanies.

Assuming the Stasi had ever wanted to do so, arresting Carlos's associates even for a short time would have ensured that the rest of the team gave East Germany a wide berth. But the powerful friends that Carlos's group claimed to have in fifteen different intelligence services, in Arab countries especially, argued for caution on the part of the Stasi. 'The group was of particular importance because of the fact its members used Arab passports,' Colonel Jäckel explained. 'That's why diplomatic relations were always affected. More precisely, the majority of the passports used by the group were Syrian diplomatic passports. Before 1980 it was mainly Iraqi and Yemeni passports. Naturally this made our counter-terrorism much more difficult.'[42]

The Stasi sought advice from the KGB, but the latter was unhelpful. It told the East Germans little that they did not know already. The Stasi noted that 'our friends' (the usual phrase for describing the KGB) reported only that Carlos was a Marxist, and had studied at the Patrice Lumumba University. Moscow's attitude signalled that it was interested in his activities, but no more. Carlos was no Soviet agent. He wrote many years later: 'I was never an agent of an intelligence service, certainly not of the KGB, nor will I become one.'[43] In the thousands of Stasi files there is not a single word about Carlos being a KGB agent, even though Carlos and Weinrich were fond of hinting at powerful connections in the Kremlin, and repeatedly claimed that the KGB was kept informed of their activities.

The Stasi archives do record several trips that Carlos made to Moscow, but these were attempts to obtain the support of the Soviets. Carlos's professed commitment to the Palestinian cause undoubtedly led Moscow, as it had the East Germans, to give him a hearing because the Soviet Union's policy was to support both the mainstream PLO and the extremist factions of the Palestinian resistance. But the closest the Soviets ever came to giving him a helping hand was to allow the case of weapons which he sold to Spanish Basque guerrillas to transit via Moscow.

One Stasi document quotes Carlos as saying that only Moscow could help him to ensure warmer relations with Communist countries, and that he was thinking of submitting his grievances to Soviet leaders.[44] This bravado was typical of Carlos, who would have given much to be recognised by the KGB.

General Markus Wolf was regarded on both sides of the Iron Curtain as Moscow's man in the East bloc, and he was also a close friend of former KGB head and Soviet leader Yuri Andropov. Wolf rules out the possibility that Moscow took on board such a volatile charge at this time. 'Carlos is the last person that the KGB would have recruited,' Wolf reflects. 'Although it may have recruited him when he was a student at Lumumba, it would not have recruited him at a time when he was an active terrorist. Such a move would have been a very great danger for the KGB.'[45]

Among the Stasi files are copies of messages, many of which detail the planned movements of Carlos and his associates, complete with information on the weapons they were carrying. The messages were exchanged by the secret services of the Soviet Union, Hungary, Poland, Romania, Czechoslovakia and Bulgaria. Whether sent to Moscow or not, the messages were systematically translated into Russian, apparently for the benefit of the KGB officers stationed within each Warsaw Pact intelligence service.

The silence from Moscow did nothing to dispel the fear and mistrust that tinged Carlos's welcome by East bloc intelligence services. As concern mounted that if his whereabouts became known Western public opinion would finger Communist leaders as harbourers of terrorists, senior intelligence officers from East Germany and Hungary held regular meetings about Carlos. The minutes of these meetings too were translated into Russian for the benefit of the KGB.

The Hungarian secret service pleaded repeatedly for his departure, but the most it obtained was his absence for a few weeks or months whenever it used the pretext of Communist Party conferences, visits by foreign delegations, and even a world Lutheran assembly. But Carlos unfailingly returned. No active support or cooperation was ever granted Carlos or his group, Colonel Varga insisted. But he acknowledged that Carlos had the ability to plan attacks from his safe houses in Budapest, and added with only a hint of regret: 'With the benefit of hindsight, I think this was perhaps too much.'[46]

8

A Dirty, Private War

> The group is waging a dirty, private war with France until the day the prisoners are freed by combat.
>
> – Weinrich, questioned on arrival in East Berlin with fifty-three pounds of explosives

Carlos's private army had been operational for only a year and a half when he agreed to help stage an attack on French soil. In January 1982 he sealed an alliance with extremist Swiss environmentalists to enable them to strike at the Super-Phénix nuclear plant, then being built at Creys-Malville in central France. Until then, the unambitious Magdalena Kopp had played a minor role in her husband's organisation. But now she was assigned the task of supplying an RPG-7 rocket-launcher, a weapon which Carlos and Weinrich had used to no great effect against the El Al plane at Orly airport seven years earlier.

Fired from the other side of the River Rhône shortly before midnight on 18 January, five missiles hit the outer shell of the nuclear reactor. But they were not powerful enough to penetrate the metre-thick concrete casing, designed to hold even if a plane fell on it.[1] Despite the insignificant damage caused, Kopp later numbered the mission as her proudest achievement. 'The French had greatly deserved it because of their shit nuclear policy,' she proclaimed.[2] Carlos's wife was deemed to have proved herself.

Until then, Kopp's role had been limited to forging documents and helping Weinrich maintain good relations with European guerrilla movements such as the Basque ETA. A month after the attack on the nuclear reactor, Carlos sent her on a more difficult assignment. She was teamed with Bruno Bréguet, a recent Swiss recruit who combined the physique of a tall playboy with a long, mournful face. Bored with studying science at a lycée in Lugano, and infatuated by the legend of Che Guevara, Bréguet had left home at the age of nineteen in 1970 to travel to Lebanon and volunteer for the Popular Front – as Carlos had also done that same year. In June 1970, only a few weeks into his new career, Bréguet had disembarked at the port of Haifa with two kilos of explosives hidden under a heavy raincoat. He planned to blow up the Shalom Tower, a skyscraper in Tel Aviv. But he got no further than Israeli customs where officials thought he looked rather odd, wearing a raincoat despite the summer weather. 'I agreed to carry explosives into Israel for $5000,' he brazenly declared. But his luggage betrayed him: Soviet-made charges, German detonators, and brass tags bearing the initials 'PFLP'.

Freedom for Bréguet was among the demands that Haddad made when the Popular Front hijacked several planes to Dawson's Field in Jordan in September 1970. But Israel refused to yield. A less violent approach succeeded where Haddad had failed. A pro-Nazi Swiss banker with radical Palestinian sympathies, François Genoud, called on Bréguet's parents when he heard of the arrest and resolved to help his compatriot 'who had set out a bit like a boy scout. In an age in which so many young people are passionate about nothing, he had gone off to carry out, perhaps stupidly, something "interesting".' Genoud joined a humanitarian committee of the great and the good, alongside Jean-Paul Sartre, Simone de Beauvoir, Noam Chomsky and other intellectuals. As a result of this campaign the young Swiss militant – the first European sentenced in Israel for pro-Palestinian activities – was pardoned in 1977 after serving seven years of his fifteen-year sentence.

Acting on Carlos's orders, Kopp and Bréguet travelled from Budapest to Paris in February 1982, using false Austrian passports. But a thief stole Kopp's handbag which contained $50,000, her Austrian passport and two spare passports. Two days later, the pair were spotted in an underground car park close to the Champs-Elysées near a rundown Peugeot 504 which despite its age boasted new number plates. Security guards, intrigued by their behaviour and suspecting they might be thieves, demanded the car's papers.

The couple, who had no papers to show, were told to wait while one of the guards called the police. But Bréguet pulled out from under his jacket a 9mm Herstal GP35 automatic pistol of Belgian manufacture, ordered the guard to put the phone down, and then set off at a run with Kopp. Out in the street police caught up with Kopp and tripped her. Further ahead, Bréguet pointed his gun at a policeman and pressed the trigger. The gun jammed, and Bréguet was overpowered.

Among the woman's few belongings police found an envelope containing $2000. The gunman had two passports. 'I am a soldier,' he said in English to the policemen who handcuffed him. A search of the Peugeot was far more productive: four 500-gram packs of Pentrite explosives, an uncommon type at the time, two Czech grenades, an alarm clock set for half past ten that evening, a battery and electric wiring, as well as another GP35 pistol.

In the offices of the Brigade Criminelle at 36 Quai des Orfèvres on the River Seine the pair were unhelpful. Throughout hours of questioning they stuck to a single statement: 'We are members of an international revolutionary organisation. We had no intention of harming

French interests, nor of committing any action in this country.'

The French had no idea who the two revolutionaries were. They had soon discovered that the gunman's passports, in the name of Swiss national Henri Richoz and Frenchman Gilbert Durand, were both false. As for his partner – 'so plain nobody would turn round to look at her in the street,' one policeman said unkindly – she carried no identity papers, and there were none at her hotel either.

But with help from their colleagues at West Germany's Bundeskriminalamt police force, the French identified the pair and sketched out their backgrounds. Kopp's German file said she was wanted for supplying explosives to the Baader-Meinhof movement. Unknown to German police the file was out of date as it still had her down as Weinrich's girlfriend rather than Carlos's wife. Bréguet's shortened prison record also surfaced.

The Brigade Criminelle had little to go on. They found among Bréguet's possessions the address of a restaurant close to Paris's city hall, which counted mayor Jacques Chirac among its regulars. Perhaps the pair planned to blow up the restaurant. But no detonator was found in the car. Perhaps they were only delivering the equipment. The car was traced to its owner, Michel Jacquot, a Communist and an unemployed accountant with no background in terrorism. He shared a squat with a Corsican whom police thought might be a supporter of the separatists who bomb public buildings on the Mediterranean island.

It was a meagre harvest, and DST counter-espionage was partly to blame. The DST had known about Bréguet's presence in Paris thanks to a tip-off from West German intelligence, which had been monitoring his connections with West German and Palestinian extremists. French counter-espionage had also known about Bréguet's meetings with leftist militants in Paris, but it failed to pass on any of this either to police or to the investigating magistrate,

Jean-Louis Debré. By default, it was left to Carlos to enlighten the Brigade Criminelle.

When the news of the arrests of Kopp and Bréguet reached him within twenty-four hours of their misfortune, Carlos was in Budapest where the pair had started their ill-fated journey. The news also reached Hungarian State Security Intelligence, and its officers told Carlos on the day after the arrests, 17 February, that this time he really must leave. The Hungarians feared that French investigators would sooner or later find out who the couple were, and uncover their links with Carlos and Budapest. Carlos promised to go, but yet again won a delay of a few weeks.

Carlos summoned Weinrich and four other members of the group, and after a few hours of discussions on 23 February wrote a letter in French, dated two days later. It had taken Carlos a week to respond to the arrests. Still convinced that his grenade attack on the Drugstore Saint-Germain in Paris had forced a government climbdown eight years earlier, Carlos was ready to repeat his performance for his wife:

> His Exc. M. Gaston Defferre
> Minister of State, Minister of the Interior and of Decentralisation.
>
> I write to inform you:
>
> Firstly: that two militants of our organisation, MAGDALENA CACILA KOPP and BRUNO BREGUET, have been arrested in Paris by the French security forces.
>
> Secondly: that our militants were arrested during a mission which was not directed against France, following the orders of its [the organisation's] Leaders.
>
> Thirdly: that our militants do not deserve prison as retribution to its [the organisation's] dedication to the Revolutionary Cause.

Fourthly: that our organisation does not abandon, ever, its militants.

On the decision of our Central Leadership, I give you the following warning:

1) We do not accept that our comrades stay in prison.
2) We do not tolerate that our comrades be extradited to any country.

We ask of you:

1) An immediate stop to the interrogation of our militants.
2) The release of our militants within thirty days of the date of this letter.
3) That our militants be released with all seized documents.
4) That our militants be allowed to travel together, on a regular flight to a country and by the route of his choice. As carriers of French passes.

We are not at war against socialist France and I pray you, in all sincerity, not to force us to be.

I assure you that the content of this letter is considered by us as a secret of the organisation. However, we do not have no interest that it be publicly known (*sic*).

We hope that this affair will end soon and in a happy way.

By the ORGANISATION OF ARAB ARMED STRUGGLE – ARM OF THE ARAB REVOLUTION.

Carlos

PS: Below the prints of my thumbs to identify this letter.

Carlos gave the letter to Christa-Margot Froelich, a former schoolteacher living in Hanover in West Germany who had been introduced to him, like Kopp, by Weinrich. A former member of the Red Army Faction and of the Revolutionary Cells, Froelich had joined Carlos's group the previous year. She travelled to Budapest to take the letter from Carlos, and dropped it off at the French embassy in The Hague during the night of 26 February, together with a covering letter to the ambassador.

Both texts carried the full official title of the addressee. The French ambassador to the Netherlands was termed 'His Excellency M. Jean Jurgensen, Ambassador Extraordinary and Plenipotentiary'. In spite of jargon and spelling mistakes, the letter to the French minister struck a self-assured tone – the Stasi branded it 'conceited'. Few threats can have been couched so courteously. It was as if the thirty-two-year-old Carlos, sitting comfortably on the other side of Defferre's desk, were talking to him as an equal as they strove to resolve a delicate bureaucratic tangle.

The choice of the French embassy in The Hague was no coincidence. It was there that in September 1974 the Japanese Red Army, with Carlos's help, had taken eleven hostages, hoping to prise their accomplice Furuya out of jail. And Ambassador Jurgensen, whom Carlos addressed with such respect, had served in the same Second World War Resistance network as Defferre. Carlos's intelligence-gathering had operated efficiently.

Terrorism was slippery terrain for France's left-wing rulers. Ever since his election as the country's first socialist President in May 1981, François Mitterrand had been denounced by the right as being soft on crime. Western allies were also putting pressure on Mitterrand. Washington openly criticised the lack of progress in the investigation into the assassination that January of its deputy military attaché in Paris, Charles R. Ray. Italy accused the President of protecting members of the Red Brigades who had fled to France since his election. Defferre, known in his fiefdom of Marseille as 'the godfather' because of the iron hand with which he governed the city, had been appointed Interior Minister at the age of seventy-one to give the government a tougher image.

'I pray you,' Carlos had urbanely requested the French ambassador in The Hague, 'to take personal charge of sending this letter for M. Gaston Defferre as soon as possible. It is urgent! I thank you for your cooperation.' The ambassador obliged, and sent the letter straight to his former Resistance comrade. It was only later that he informed the Foreign Ministry of Carlos's threat through more orthodox channels.

With the police and secret service chiefs assembled before him, the Interior Minister blithely declared that he and Carlos had much in common. 'Defferre told us that Carlos had singled him out as one of his peers because he had himself been a very efficient terrorist when he led a Resistance network in Provence during the Second World War,' recalled Pierre Marion, then head of the SDECE intelligence service. 'He said that because of his past he was the only member of the government fit to talk to Carlos. We all stared wide-eyed at Defferre. I told him that he couldn't start talks, he must hit back. He didn't like that at all. For him Carlos was a brother in arms. He said he wanted to meet Carlos alone, "man-to-man".'[3]

Defferre's audience should have known better. That a government minister was ready to talk to a man most of France considered to be a terrorist was part and parcel of French political life. 'The French will never shut a door without trying something out first,' an MI6 officer reflected later. 'As a government, as a culture, the French are much happier to improvise when the chance arises.'

The letter's implications were not lost on Defferre. 'When you've received a letter like that, you don't need a second one to understand,' the Interior Minister growled. Within a few hours of Defferre receiving the letter, an extra police officer had been assigned to ride with him in his official car, and more bodyguards followed in a separate car.

The DST unearthed the Rue Toullier file to check the fingerprints. The file left no room for doubt as to the letter's author. Defferre gave strict orders that the letter must not be divulged, not even to the unfortunate Judge Debré who was struggling to investigate the arrest of Kopp and Bréguet. But on 5 March the popular daily *France-Soir* splashed the letter's contents across the front page. Defferre was so furious that 'he foamed at the mouth', according to one senior official. 'This is too serious,' Defferre raged. 'Carlos is a redoubtable man. His organisation exists. One can't fool around with this. Those who divulged the letter committed a very serious mistake. If tomorrow people are killed, they will be responsible.' He made a list of possible moles, but the culprit was never found. Publication of the letter incensed Carlos as much as it did Defferre.

The reason that Defferre gave for his – public – display of anger was that the leak might encourage Carlos to turn violent. The real reason for the anger of both men was that the leak threatened to blow the cover off their gentlemanly efforts to resolve their differences through secret negotiation. On the French government's part, this amounted to a cloak-and-dagger attempt to turn the country into a sanctuary safe from terrorism, even at the cost of placating a guerrilla wanted for the murder of two DST officers.

Much as he had wanted to, Defferre never did get to meet Carlos for a 'man-to-man' encounter. Instead he had to make do with his envoy, Jacques Vergès, France's most provocative lawyer.

Born in Thailand in 1925, Vergès had moved to France and built his notoriety as 'the devil's advocate' on a willingness to defend the indefensible, and to do so with a radical slant. The more outrageous his stand the better. The lawyer wrote a book about his strategy, published in the near-revolutionary days of 1968, in which he described what he called the *défense de rupture*, a subversive defence tactic which denied all legitimacy to the opposing side, judged the judges, and challenged the political establishment. Threats were a feature of Vergès's advocacy.

There was much about Vergès that appealed to Carlos.

In his youth a Stalinist student leader of the French Communist Party (Vergès's other heroes are Robespierre, like him an intriguing lawyer, and Napoleon), he had been editor of the Maoist journal *Revolution*; a gun-runner for guerrillas fighting Portuguese colonial rule in Mozambique and Angola; and a defender of independence fighters in the Algerian war and of Palestinian fedayeen. 'How can one understand a criminal,' Vergès wrote some time later, 'without having oneself, even by using one's imagination just once, tasted the roots of crime?'[4] Vergès converted to Islam to marry a 'freedom fighter', Djamila Bouhired, whom he had helped to save from the death penalty with a vibrant pamphlet in her defence.

A slice of Vergès's life, from the spring of 1970 to the end of 1978, is unaccounted for and he delightedly fans the mystery, saying that he had 'crossed to the other side of the mirror'. His student friendship with a young Kampuchean, Pol Pot, has led to speculation that perhaps he spent part of his time with the Khmer Rouge. Or, goes another theory, he served a lengthy spell in a jail in China, in the Soviet Union, or in Algeria. 'Your secret is your blood. If you give it up entirely, you die,' runs a Berber proverb that Vergès likes to quote.

According to French intelligence, Vergès may have first met Carlos during this period. Vergès has denied this, claiming that his knowledge of Carlos was based purely on accounts from Kopp and Bréguet whom he was appointed to defend. Years later, Vergès had a flattering view: 'Carlos is a very modern mix of idealism and man of action ... He was fascinated by the Cuban experience, by Che Guevara, a legendary figure, and decided in the end to fight with the Palestinians for the Arab cause.'[5]

The fifty-seven-year-old Vergès proved so dedicated in defending Kopp and Bréguet that he was described by the Stasi as 'one of the most important liaison individuals of the group'.[6] Vergès and other lawyers enabled Carlos to stay in touch with the prisoners, and keep abreast of the judicial investigation. Weinrich, who on at least one occasion met Vergès in East Berlin during this period used him to pass on money and messages, including an upbeat note to his ex-girlfriend: 'We hope you are okay ... Everything we are doing is aimed at getting you out of there.'[7]

Defferre instructed his legal affairs adviser, Roland Kessous, not to close the door on a possible approach from Carlos. As a result, Kessous and Vergès met about once every two weeks from March to August 1982. Kessous's portrait of the lawyer was slighting: 'I have the memory of a man standing in front of a mirror, soliloquising for half an hour while smoothing his hair. Apparently, he appreciated his own speech. He explained to me that a lawyer was an artist and the defence plea a work of art.'[8] Vergès told Kessous that it would not be 'in France's interest' to keep the two in jail and suggested 'direct contacts' with Carlos himself. Vergès even sought an audience with President Mitterrand but the head of his private office, Jean-Paul Colliard, rejected his request.

The threats hit home. Vergès twice met Louis Joinet, a magistrate and an adviser to Prime Minister Pierre Mauroy. Joinet received Vergès at his office the first time but then, given the delicate nature of their talks, invited him to breakfast at his home. 'I asked Vergès if he was in touch with Carlos, as he was making threats of reprisals in his name,' Joinet recalled. 'He told me that he communicated with him through coded advertisements in the newspaper *Le Matin de Paris*.'[9] Joinet reassured Vergès on the forthcoming trial of Kopp and Bréguet, guaranteeing that the government would lean on the judge to ensure any heavy sentence was suspended: 'The third chamber is the most reliable ... the government has the most influence.'

However, long before the case reached court, pressure was brought to bear on Judge Debré via the Paris public prosecutor Pierre Arpaillange. 'The public prosecutor would have liked me to think that this case did not deserve all the noise it was generating and in addition advised me not to be over-zealous because it was possible that an extra-judicial solution would be reached quickly,' Debré recalled.[10] Judge Debré's insistence that he did not bow to pressure does not tally with the judicial fate of Carlos's accomplices. One witness to Debré's meetings with Arpaillange remembers the judge 'simply took his orders from his superior'.

The policemen who caught Bréguet were adamant that he had tried to kill one of them, and Debré initially charged Bréguet with possessing arms and explosives as well as attempted homicide. By the rule-book, Bréguet should have been put on trial before an assizes court, an institution used only for the trial of felonies. But the judge later dropped the attempted homicide charge on the grounds of insufficient evidence. In fact, as a ballistics expert demonstrated, Bréguet had indeed pulled the trigger but the gun had failed to fire.

Debré's leniency ensured that Kopp and Bréguet were ordered to stand trial on 15 April before a magistrate's court where they would face lighter sentences than if they had been brought before an assizes court. 'Carlos's blackmail abruptly turned Kopp and Bréguet into a hot potato, and sent the government into a St Vitus dance,' explained Alain Marsaud, the deputy public prosecutor. 'The government – Defferre and Justice Minister Robert Badinter – pushed the judiciary into moving fast so that they would be released as soon as possible. The judiciary let itself be crushed.'[11]

To underscore Carlos's warnings, a bombing and shooting frenzy punctuated the negotiations in the two-month run-up to the trial. The targets, all French, were both in Europe and the Middle East. On 15 March a five-kilo bomb exploded inside the Villa des Dunes in Beirut, home to a French cultural centre. Five people were wounded. On 29 March at 8.41 p.m., four days after Carlos's ultimatum to

Defferre had run out, ten kilos of Pentrite high explosive blew up the Trans-Europe-Express train from Paris to Toulouse, the *Capitole*, as it sped through flat countryside north of Limoges. The explosion eviscerated a sixty-year-old woman and trapped her daughter under a seat. The body of one victim was thrown more than sixty metres from the train, and another passenger was decapitated. Five passengers died and thirty were injured. The train driver only just prevented the gaping carcass of bloodstained twisted steel from powering off the track.

'It is signed Carlos, obviously,' Mitterrand's special adviser Jacques Attali noted in his diary. 'The President took the news with *sang-froid*, his face set. It was expected, announced, inevitable: Carlos's love story with Magdalena Kopp costs France a great deal.'[12] As Defferre announced that police patrols in railway stations would be reinforced, the Police Judiciaire in Paris logged an anonymous telephone call from a man who spoke in French with no trace of a foreign accent. 'I claim responsibility for the *Capitole* attack in the name of the Terrorist International, a friend of Carlos. You free our friends Bruno Bréguet and Magdalena Kopp, otherwise we have other projects which are even more terrible.'[13] Terrorist International was a front for a guns-for-bombing deal. The Spanish Basque ETA helped to carry out the train bombing, which was planned by Weinrich on Carlos's behalf, in exchange for weapons.[14]

The bomb had been hidden in a Samsonite suitcase, which investigators believe was planted by Carlos's associate, Christa-Margot Froelich, just before the train's departure from the Gare d'Austerlitz in Paris. She placed the suitcase in carriage eighteen which was reserved for bearers of a special card issued to VIPs by the state-owned railway company. Paris mayor and former Prime Minister Jacques Chirac had planned to take the train on his way to the Corrèze region but he changed his mind at the last minute and flew instead. Carlos later wrote that the bombing was 'quite obviously' an attempt on Chirac's life.[15] According to Stasi files quoting from Weinrich's notes, Vergès had indirectly informed Weinrich that Chirac was against any deal with the group. Weinrich noted on the day of the bombing: '29.3. Capitole. Jirac (*sic*) had made a booking for the compartment.' But there is no evidence to prove that Carlos or Weinrich knew this when the bomb was placed on the train.

On 5 April the French embassy in The Hague, where Carlos had sent his letter to Defferre, received a threat couched in more political terms, and signed by the local wing of West Germany's Red Army Faction. Passed on immediately to the DST, it was never disclosed by French authorities, and highlights Carlos's very close relationship with the West German movement – as well as threatening more violence:

> To the French embassy to the Netherlands
>
> We declare our solidarity with the action of our comrade Carlos and the actions he will launch. We demand the immediate release of our comrades Bruno Bréguet and Magdalena Kopp. They are imprisoned in your country. If you do not fully satisfy this demand, we will for our part take powerful measures against you. These measures will be comparable to the measures taken by those who in your state tear liberty to shreds and of all those who seek to oppress human beings. This is a unique and ultimate message. If it is not accepted by your government, it will mean that it refuses dialogue. Our task is to stand by our comrade prisoners because where states persecute democracy through imprisonment, resistance becomes a duty. The revolution will triumph.[16]

The trial of Kopp and Bréguet had been due to start on 15 April, but a strike by prison guards forced a postponement. That evening in their Beirut home, non-commissioned officer Guy Cavallo, twenty-eight, an employee of the French embassy, and his twenty-five-year-old wife Marie-Caroline, a maths teacher who was seven months pregnant, were preparing dinner for some friends. 'These premises are placed under the protection of the French embassy', read the tricolour sticker on the door of the flat, located in an area controlled by Syrian and Palestinian forces.

When the doorbell rang Marie-Caroline glanced through the eyepiece set in the door, but could only make out a large bouquet of gladiolas and roses. So big was the bunch of flowers that she could not tell which of her guests had arrived early. She opened the door and stretched out both hands to receive the flowers. Two bullets fired with a silenced, 7.65-calibre pistol struck her body. Her husband rushed forward and was shot twice in the head. The first guests to arrive found blood seeping under the closed door. They forced their way in and discovered the dead couple, with Marie-Caroline still clutching the bouquet. Guy Cavallo was officially described as a coder at the embassy. In fact, he worked for the French SDECE secret service – more evidence of the strength of Carlos's intelligence-gathering network. Carlos now had the blood of France's two secret services, the SDECE and the DST, on his hands.

Kopp and Bréguet's task, when they were arrested in Paris, had in fact been the bombing of the Paris offices of the magazine *Al Watan al Arabi*, which two years earlier had published the long interview with Carlos.[17]

In a sadly prophetic scoop less than a week before the assassination of the French ambassador to Beirut, Louis Delamare, in September 1981, the magazine had reported that Syrian intelligence planned to kill Delamare in order to stop France pushing for the withdrawal of foreign troops on Lebanese soil – first and foremost the Syrian army. The Syrians conveyed their displeasure three months later, on

19 December. A TNT bomb was found on the fourth-floor landing outside the magazine's offices in Paris. The device had been programmed to explode at 8.14 p.m. and was deactivated by a bomb disposal expert at 8.13 p.m. Investigators discovered that Mokhail Kassouha, the cultural attaché at the Syrian embassy, had been involved in the bombing attempt.[18] But France had no desire to worsen its tense relations with Syria, and the Justice Ministry ordered prosecutors to shelve the probe.

That same December Carlos visited the Syrian capital Damascus where he stayed at the Hotel Méridien. On his return to Budapest, accompanied by two Syrians, he decreed another round of surveillance of *Al Watan al Arabi*.[19] Bréguet, who was part of the surveillance team, sent Carlos a detailed account of the routine of its editor, Walid Abou Zahr. A month after the arrests of Kopp and Bréguet, Carlos flew yet again to Damascus where he met Rifaat al-Assad, the Syrian President's brother and Carlos's patron. Carlos is also believed to have met his sponsor in Syrian air force intelligence, Colonel Haitham Sa'id, on this trip. A few weeks later, news leaked out that the French state-owned TF1 television channel would run a documentary in late April on the murder of the French ambassador to Beirut. Syrian intelligence considered bombing the broadcaster. But TF1 was deemed too big and too costly a target if the whole of it had to be blown up. The Syrians decided instead that *Al Watan al Arabi* should be the target. Syria wanted both to punish the magazine and to warn the new French administration against dabbling in Syria's Lebanese back yard after President Mitterrand demanded that foreign powers leave Lebanon in peace.

In early April Walid Abou Zahr was told by an Arab informer that a thirty-strong Syrian unit had arrived in Paris and was planning an attack. But the informer did not know what the target was. Abou Zahr tipped off the DST, and surrounded himself with nine bodyguards. Defferre sent police to patrol the editor's home and the inside of the magazine's offices. He did not think it necessary to station any men in the fashionable Rue Marbeuf, just outside the offices.[20]

On 19 April a brown-haired, forty-something woman with an unkempt appearance walked into the Hertz rental agency at Yugoslavia's Ljubljana airport and asked to hire an estate car. She presented a Swiss passport and a Swiss driving licence in the name of Margit Stadelmann, and said she was travelling to Vienna where she would return the car in a week's time on 26 April. She was handed the keys to an orange Opel Kadett with Austrian number plates.

The passport and driving licence were both false, and had been manufactured and supplied by the Stasi two days earlier when the woman had flown in to East Berlin en route to Ljubljana. The woman's real name was Christa-Margot Froelich. Three weeks earlier she had placed the bomb on the *Capitole* train. On the day she rented the car in Ljubljana, Froelich drove as far as the small town of Postojna, reputed among tourists for its grottoes and among guerrillas for pyrotechnists skilled in fitting out vehicles. Her instructions from Carlos were that she should drive the car to Paris and hand it over, filled with explosives, to an accomplice. On her route, via Trieste and Lyon, she used another two false identities, Marie Zimmerman and Beatrix Odenhal, to cover her tracks.[21]

On 21 April a bomb exploded outside the office of the military attaché at the French embassy in Vienna, where Carlos had paced the world stage during the OPEC raid. An Austrian policeman on guard duty was killed. On the evening of the same day the French television channel TF1 broadcast its documentary on the murder of Ambassador Delamare. The programme relayed the accusations against the Syrian secret service made by *Al Watan.* Late that night in Paris a man in his thirties with a thin moustache drove an orange Opel Kadett down the Rue Marbeuf and stopped outside the Tunisian restaurant Chez Bébert.

The driver, speaking in French, asked a waiter whether he knew who owned the Renault parked just in front of the restaurant. The stranger then walked up to the Renault's owner who was dining in the restaurant and asked him: 'Do you mind moving your car? I'm staying the whole night and I would like to park my Opel.' The Renault owner got up from his table and obliged. The driver of the Opel was Johannes Weinrich.[22] And three floors above the restaurant were the offices of *Al Watan al Arabi.*

In their cells at the Fleury-Merogis women's prison and at the Fresnes jail outside Paris, Kopp and Bréguet had spent more than two months waiting for their trial. Kopp passed part of the time knitting sweaters for Vergès. On the morning of 22 April the pair were brought into the dock sealed off with bullet-proof glass at the Palais de Justice on the Isle de la Cité. In a crowded courtroom guarded by members of the élite GIGN anti-terrorism unit wearing combat gear, Vergès greeted Kopp with a kiss on the cheek.

At 9.02 a.m. on the other side of the city from the law courts, Carlos's offensive ripped across the Rue Marbeuf during the morning rush hour. A few seconds earlier Nelly Guillerme, a thirty-year-old secretary dressed in a blue check suit, had reached into her bag for a letter she intended to put in the postbox next to Chez Bébert. When the twenty-kilo bomb hidden in the back of the nearby Opel station wagon exploded, a volley of steel shrapnel tore into the pregnant Guillerme and catapulted her body across the street. She died of her injuries.

As a fireball soared several storeys high, Philippe Rouaut, a messenger boy, was swept off the pavement, and thrown on to the bonnet of a car. Half his left leg was torn off. Nelly Barthomeuf, another young secretary on her way to work, had stopped to buy some croissants for breakfast at a nearby bakery. The explosion wounded her in the face and burned her leg. At the Boucherie Marbeuf, adjoining the restaurant, young butcher's apprentices ran to take cover at the back of the shop. Clad in their white aprons, the apprentices emerged, shards of glass crunching underfoot, to see billowing black smoke shutting off the sun, and fire devouring cars and the awnings of boutiques. As a shop alarm set off by the blast wailed lugubriously, ten people lay seriously wounded in the street, and another fifty-eight with lighter injuries stood or sat in shock, or struggled to flee.

Of the shattered Opel, only part of the front wheel-axle remained. The engine had punched its way into the car parked in front. Twisted pieces of the Opel's coachwork were found on the roofs of nearby buildings. A burned wing mirror landed on the terrace of a café on the Champs-Elysées, and the handbrake in the courtyard of the Europe 1 radio station nearby.

In the law courts, reports of the attack made no visible impression on the pale, fragile-looking Kopp and an apparently more robust Bréguet. Behind their bullet-proof glass, they stayed as mute as goldfish in a bowl throughout the trial. It was left to Vergès to speak for them, and for Carlos. As an appetiser, the lawyer accused Mossad of planting the explosives found in Kopp and Bréguet's car, and eulogised Carlos in vibrant and sardonic tones: 'In keeping silent and in awaiting your judgement, this man of audacity and courage shows that he knows how to keep the cool head of a great politician.'

The plea he launched into was characteristically forceful, and shocking: '[Kopp and Bréguet] are already beyond the court's judgement. They will leave jail ... They are soldiers, prisoners of a noble cause. They know that their friends will not rest as long as they are in prison. It is not possible that the Republic will keep them in its hands. Will they stay forty-eight hours, a month, three months in prison? The length of time raises the problem of the blood to be shed.'[23]

The speech was a public repetition of the warnings that Vergès had given government officials in the secret negotiations. The lawyer went one better and denounced France for failing to respect a tacit and mutual non-aggression pact with certain revolutionary movements. According to Vergès, the pact stipulated that 'If you don't commit any attacks on my territory, I turn a blind eye.' Carlos, Vergès concluded, 'demanded that this agreement be respected. Full stop.'[24]

As for the person who had leaked Carlos's letter to Defferre: 'It is this man who will carry or who already carries the responsibility for the blood spilled in presenting expulsion as an attitude of weakness.' This was one of the sharpest manifestations yet of Vergès's belief in the need to empathise with clients, to the extent of sharing their anxiety and anger. Vergès behaved 'like the spokesman of a terrorist movement', recalled the presiding judge, Jean-Georges Diemer. 'He multiplied provocations, he threatened us implicitly. So much so that for a time I was protected by police.'[25]

Like the investigation that had preceded it, the trial itself was stage-managed. The policemen who had arrested the pair were not called as witnesses, because authorities feared that they would insist that Bréguet had tried to shoot one of them. The ballistic report which showed that Bréguet had pulled the trigger was not produced in court. The sentences that the public prosecutor, who ultimately answers to the Justice Ministry, recommended were lenient: a minimum of three years in jail for Bréguet and two years for Kopp. In an ambiguous plea, he asked the court 'to take a significant but measured decision to respond precisely to the immoderation of the terrorists'.[26] On a day that had seen the Marbeuf bombing and a spirited plea by Vergès, the verdict handed down in the early afternoon was a little heavier. Five years for Bréguet and four years for Kopp, with a fine of 10,000 francs for each of them.

Within hours, Defferre condemned the bombing: 'The method employed is revealing of the mentality of the authors of this kind of outrage, who do not hesitate to make blood flow on French territory to settle scores which have nothing to do with France.' In the same breath, he announced the expulsion of two Syrian diplomats, naval attaché Colonel Ali Hassan and cultural attaché Mokhail Kassouha. The DST explained to the press that the two were not linked to the Marbeuf bombing but had been under surveillance for some time as Syrian spies. However, Kassouha had been linked to the bomb that had been defused outside *Al Watan*'s offices in December, while Hassan had in March organised a savage attack involving knives, pickaxes and truncheons on Syrian students demonstrating in the square outside the cathedral of Saint-Germain-des-Prés.[27]

At his next meeting with Weinrich and Issawe in East Berlin, Vergès berated them for planting the Marbeuf bomb. The attack, he said, had not helped Kopp and Bréguet. The lawyer need not have worried. Although French newspapers speculated that Carlos was behind the bombing, Defferre had no intention of letting it wreck the negotiations.

Defferre's orders to the head of the DST's counter-terrorism section, Commissaire Jean Baklouti, were clear: 'Defferre ordered me not to follow the Carlos lead, and to concentrate instead on the Syrians. Everything was done to make Syria carry the can. The diplomats who were expelled were scapegoats. It was a way of calming public opinion and shifting the police's attention away from the real authors of the bombing so that negotiations with Carlos could continue.' The DST defied the minister's instructions however: 'We went on investigating Carlos though. We knew that Vergès was travelling to Eastern Europe and was meeting a French Interior Ministry official, so we reached our own conclusions.'[28]

On the day after the Marbeuf bombing President Mitterrand summoned what Defferre called a 'war cabinet' on terrorism in his gilded office in the Elysée Palace. Facing the head of state were Defferre, Marcel Chalet, the DST chief, Pierre Marion, who had renamed the SDECE the Direction Générale de la Sécurité Extérieure (DGSE), and General Jean Saulnier, the President's chief of staff. Their decision was that Defferre should chair a weekly meeting on terrorism. But by late July these Wednesday evening meetings in the Interior Minister's office had lost all purpose. Far from launching a new anti-terrorism strategy, participants got bogged down in minutiae, such as the form residence permits should take, or Defferre's stories of his experiences in the French Resistance.

Less than a month after the Marbeuf bombing Carlos's offensive restarted. A rocket-propelled grenade struck the French consulate in Beirut, hitting a block of flats assigned to French diplomats. No one was hurt. In May twenty-five kilos of explosives hidden under a car blew up inside the French embassy compound in Beirut. Eleven people, including five embassy employees, were killed and another twenty-seven were wounded. Mitterrand's adviser Attali noted in his journal: 'A clear signal: in the eyes of many people, our presence is not needed here. Something is about to happen?'[29]

The butchery earned Weinrich a compliment from another of the Carlos group's lawyers, Swiss attorney Bernard Rambert: 'Graf [Rambert's code-name] has congratulated [us] for this action,' read a note by Weinrich, who had been despatched to Beirut by Carlos to prepare the attacks there. Weinrich's notes show that more attacks were planned. In the Lebanese capital the French and United States embassies and the French consulate were placed under surveillance. In Paris the home of Justice Minister Robert Badinter was also watched, while Rambert supplied Weinrich with details of the police security at the Justice Minister's home. Rambert, however, denies this. In Rome other members of the Carlos organisation considered an attack on the French embassy, housed in the Renaissance Palazzo Farnese.[30]

The nature of the targets owed much to Carlos's Syrian paymasters. 'To my knowledge, and this is a personal assessment, the Syrian secret services were indisputably behind Carlos,' the Stasi's Colonel Jäckel recalled. 'Especially at the time of the attacks in France and against France. More precisely, the secret service of the Syrian air force was involved ... For me, the members of the [Carlos] group were instruments.'[31]

Weinrich himself explained the purpose of the offensive when border guards challenged him on his arrival in late May at Berlin-Schönefeld airport with a heavy load of explosives tucked into a brown leather bag he was carrying as hand luggage on a mid-morning TAROM flight from Bucharest. Brandishing a false Syrian diplomatic passport in the name of Joseph Leon, he proudly declared: 'The group is conducting a dirty, private war with France until the prisoners Kopp and Bréguet are freed by combat.'[32] The Stasi, however, seized the explosives. At a later confrontation with Major Helmut Voigt, the head of the counter-terrorism section, and Colonel Jäckel, Weinrich explained just what kind of war he had in mind: 'Until now we have not moved from house to house in a Paris neighbourhood, killing everybody inside. We have the means to do this and to escape.'[33]

Carlos's 'dirty, private war' suffered a setback in June, only two months after the Rue Marbeuf blast. Froelich, who had driven the Opel Kadett to Paris, was arrested at Rome's Leonardo da Vinci airport carrying a suitcase artfully transformed into a portable arsenal: three and a half kilos of detonating/explosive cord had been neatly wound into a spiral to nestle underneath the inner lining. The suitcase also contained a cheap traveller's alarm clock turned into a timer for use with a bomb, and two electric detonators. Froelich, who also carried a false German passport in the name of Marie Zimmerman, spent the next six years in prison.

As bombings underscored Vergès's negotiations, Weinrich drafted a hard-hitting statement for the lawyer to recite if French government officials challenged him about the offensive. A note in Weinrich's handwriting read: 'Message for Vergès: If during his meetings with government representatives he is asked the question, he must answer in accordance with the directives from Michel [alias Carlos]: "We have undertaken a secret approach of Defferre and the answer was a public challenge to our organisation. We have accepted this challenge and we combat with the weapons of our choice, until such time as our comrades are returned to us in a definite manner." '[34] In a surreal exchange after one of Carlos's outrages, a French official turned to Vergès and remarked: '*Terrible*, this Carlos has no consideration for anyone, but perhaps he has a political obligation.' Vergès retorted: 'But Carlos, *Monsieur*, has no obligation in France.'[35]

The need to keep Carlos informed plunged Vergès into a complex procedure designed to shake off anyone shadowing him as he ferried messages to and fro, including one rousing recommendation for the prisoners: 'Your duty is to stay strong psychologically.' At least a week in advance of any trip to Berlin, Vergès was required to send a telex, signed 'Jean', to the Palast Hotel in East Berlin addressed to 'Mr Saeed', an alias that Weinrich used for receiving messages. Vergès's official cover for his travels, if discovered, was that he was visiting a West German national who had a child by Bréguet. If Carlos's team wanted to get in touch with Vergès it would send him a postcard with the meaningless message: 'Greetings . . . we are happy . . . to the sumptuous tower . . . affectionately – big kisses. Your Danielle.'

The sign-off was a private joke. Danielle was the name of President Mitterrand's wife.

In Berlin Vergès used the dead-letter technique tried and tested by spies of both East and West. He left the files of the judicial investigation into Kopp and Bréguet in a locker at the Friedrichstrasse station, gateway between West and East Berlin. Weinrich collected the papers, but not before a Stasi officer had passed by to copy them. Weinrich attempted to simplify the procedure by asking the Stasi's Major Voigt for help in facilitating the lawyer's trips through the Berlin Wall. Vergès, he pleaded in April 1983, 'has already done so much for the revolution'. The Stasi, which had opened a file on Vergès and put border posts on alert, turned Weinrich down. A sheepish Weinrich noted in his report: 'Shame: no visa for Vergès.'

Carlos stopped at nothing to free his accomplices. He even considered exploiting the last indefensible cause espoused by Vergès, that of Gestapo officer Klaus Barbie, known as 'The Butcher of Lyon' because of his unrelenting enforcement of Hitler's Final Solution. As head of the information section of the Gestapo in Lyon, Barbie had been ordered to wipe out the Resistance. Twice condemned to death in absentia by French courts, he was tracked down to Bolivia by French Nazi-hunter Beate Klarsfeld, and captured in February 1983. Vergès had joined de Gaulle's Free French forces at the age of seventeen, but he had no qualms about taking on the defence of a former enemy: 'No human being is all black or all white. There is in the heart of the worst criminal a secret garden, a kind of astonishing individual little paradise. There is in the heart of the most honest man a cesspit full of awful reptiles.'[36]

Weinrich and Carlos pondered a plan to kidnap the sixty-nine-year-old Barbie from the Saint-Joseph jail in Lyon. Weinrich's only reference to Barbie, in a letter to Carlos, underlined the Stasi's horrified reaction: 'Barbie affair is very interesting ... Don't worry I don't discuss about it with socialist camp but had a clash with Helmut [alias Major Voigt] longer time ago when they learned about it. He was furious.'[37]

Carlos's comments about his intentions are more telling. The revelations that he hoped to wring out of Barbie once he was captured would 'compromise Western régimes' and detail how the Nazi had worked for the American Counter Intelligence Corps in Germany after the war. To help prepare the kidnap, Vergès was expected to pass on details of Barbie's prison conditions to Carlos.[38] For all Carlos's enthusiasm, however, his group failed in its attempt to stage its own trial of the Gestapo officer. The kidnap was never attempted. Barbie was tried by a French court four years later, and sentenced to life in jail for crimes against humanity.[39]

But Carlos was not the kind to give up easily. If bombs failed, then he would arrange the escape from jail of Kopp and Bréguet. Again, Vergès's participation was required. The lawyer suggested that Kopp simulate a suicide attempt and make her getaway during the medical check-up that would inevitably follow. For Bréguet, the plan was to bribe a guard who would help him escape through the sewers.[40] The winter was deemed the most opportune season. The planned escape route led ultimately to Damascus, but Bréguet rejected this saying he wanted to be free to go where he liked.[41]

Carlos has told one of his lawyers that the KGB summoned him to Moscow about this time to warn him of a trap to capture him planned by the French secret service should either Kopp or Bréguet try to break out of jail. There is no evidence to substantiate this claim, but Carlos did drop both plans. Kopp and Bréguet stayed behind bars.

9

Licensed to Kill

I authorise you to kill only Carlos and Abu Nidal.
– President François Mitterrand to DGSE head
Pierre Marion

Given the revolving-door mechanism that usually prevailed at the top of the French secret service, the extrovert Count Alexandre de Marenches was an exceptional figure in post-war intelligence who endured as many as eleven years, from 1970 to 1981, at the head of the SDECE. His longevity remains unmatched by his successors.[1] It was de Marenches who first set the SDECE on Carlos's tail. De Marenches's gregariousness had come near to costing him not only his career but also his life in more youthful days. After escaping from wartime France, he had struck up a conversation with a well-dressed gentleman on a train bound for Madrid. Flush with success, the eighteen-year-old de Marenches related to the stranger how he had crossed the Pyrénées alone in driving snow, then kept silent under torture by Spanish Civil Guards, and would now enlist with General de Gaulle's Free French. 'Oh! Really? How interesting! That must have been difficult,' sympathised his courteous acquaintance. It was only when the train pulled into Madrid that de Marenches found out that he had recounted his triumphs to Baron von Stohrer,

Hitler's ambassador to Spain. Fortunately the baron never did trouble the would-be Resistance fighter.[2]

Picked to lead the SDECE, the aristocrat, who was dubbed 'Porthos' after one of the Three Musketeers because of his tall stature and robust girth, found himself at the head of what he likened to a gangsters' racket: 'Some agents were running drugs and guns; others were engaged in kidnapping, murder, and the settling of the most bloody scores.'[3] His purge of the SDECE weeded out most of the top brass and hundreds of lesser officers who were suspected of anti-Americanism, tainted by the scandals of the Algerian war of independence, or were simply deemed unworthy of his trust.

A unit in which de Marenches had complete confidence was the Action Service, the SDECE's clandestine operations arm. It was ordered to hunt Carlos. In late 1975, only a few months after his triple murder of the two DST secret servicemen and Moukharbal in Paris, Carlos was spotted in Algiers at his favourite nightclub, the chic Dar Salem. There the Action Service's Philippe Rondot watched him from a distance as, surrounded by female companions, Carlos sank into a drunken stupor. After consultation with the Action Service's chief, Count de Marolles, de Marenches suggested taking advantage of one of Carlos's drinking bouts to 'neutralise him'.

The nightclub was deemed an unsuitable venue for a kidnapping as it would have upset delicate diplomatic relations, given that the Dar Salem's owner was the brother of Algerian President Boumedienne. The Action Service rushed to make alternative arrangements. But by the time a team had assembled, the quarry described by de Marenches as 'an excellent young man, born of the champagne left and who always had primed grenades in his pocket' had disappeared.[4]

In 1976 Rondot managed again to track down Carlos, to the Eden Beach Hotel in Malta. The Action Service is said to have suggested murdering Carlos using a technique borrowed from Mossad, an explosive device concealed in the telephone of his hotel room. As de Marenches observed: 'When you're dealing with irregulars and terrorists, there are no more rules. Anything goes.' According to published reports, President Giscard d'Estaing refused to grant the SDECE permission to carry out the killing. But former members of the Action Service have denied such an assassination was on the cards, insisting that they wanted to catch Carlos so he could stand trial in France. However, tougher action would have been justified had Carlos put their lives at risk, they added. In 1977 Carlos was spotted in Colombia where his mother was living. But yet again the Action Service failed to capture him.

By the time of President Mitterrand's election in May 1981, France's attempts to catch Carlos had led nowhere. Murders and bombings on the streets of Paris in the spring and summer of 1982 marked Mitterrand's first confrontation with terrorism. Twenty-one attacks in the first six months of the year claimed a death toll of thirty and wounded 178 people, the price France paid for its interventionism in Lebanon and in the Arab-Israeli conflict. The Lebanese Revolutionary Armed Faction claimed the murders of the American Colonel Charles Ray and the Israeli diplomat Yacov Barsimentov; Carlos bombed French targets in Beirut; Carlos claimed responsibility for the *Capitole* train bombing; and the Carlos group, with the help of the Syrians, planted the Marbeuf bomb.

The list of attacks was lengthened when gunmen believed to have been sent by the terrorist Abu Nidal carried out a racist attack in the heart of Paris. Jo Goldenberg's kosher restaurant and delicatessen in the capital's Jewish neighbourhood, specialising in the diaspora fare of Eastern European Jews, was as crowded as ever at lunchtime on 9 August 1982 when a Czech-made grenade was lobbed through the window. Before customers and waiters, many of them wounded, realised what had happened, four or five masked men – the pandemonium was such that the exact number was never established – burst in and sprayed the room with machine-gun fire, killing four people and wounding another thirty, twelve of them seriously. A Moroccan waiter who tried to flee was pursued and executed in the kitchens. As the killers escaped into the street, they shot an elderly employee of the restaurant and a woman in her fifties who lived nearby. The investigating magistrate assigned to the case was Jean-Louis Bruguière, who happened to be one of the few Paris-based judges not away on holiday. Within hours of the massacre, he was in the restaurant looking for clues. It was Judge Bruguière's first introduction to terrorism after a career in which he had dealt mainly with the Paris underworld.

Eight days after the Goldenberg bloodbath, Mitterrand, still shaken by the shouts of '*Mitterrand assassin!*' and '*Mitterrand trahison!*' (treachery) chanted at him when he had visited the Jewish neighbourhood, turned his back on the existing anti-terrorism apparatus. For the first time in the history of the Republic, he created an operational counter-terrorism unit based at the Elysée Palace, reporting to him. The new unit was led by the energetic Colonel Christian Prouteau, who had headed the élite force of the para-military police, the Groupement d'Intervention de la Gendarmerie Nationale (GIGN).[5] Prouteau's force had previously ridiculed security at the Elysée by smuggling a bag of explosives into the Presidential office. Overnight, a purely action unit was entrusted with 'the mission of coordination, intelligence and action against terrorism'.

Prouteau's appointment not only amounted to changing the ship's captain in the middle of a storm, it also sowed confusion among established French police and intelligence forces. 'In the space of a few days, no one any longer knew who was doing what,' recalled former DST chief Marcel Chalet, voicing the dismay of many who wrote off

Prouteau's unit as gung-ho cowboys. 'Our foreign partners were dismayed that doubts were cast over existing procedures for sharing intelligence, and they threatened to turn off the tap.'[6] Prouteau's unit was already busy carrying out a discreet mission for Mitterrand, the illegal phone-tapping of politicians, film stars and journalists.

Mitterrand's creation of the anti-terrorism unit highlighted his long-standing lack of confidence in French intelligence, which had been dogged by a string of postwar scandals. The confidential report that the DST sent to Mitterrand after his election helped to devalue the secret services in his eyes. The report depicted one of his junior government members, Régis Debray, a revolutionary philosopher who served as intellectual companion to Che Guevara and recognised the 'strategic value' of terrorism, as Fidel Castro's stooge. French secret services, Mitterrand once confided, were nothing more than 'costly eyewash', and they suffered from 'a sort of intellectual submission to the Americans'.[7] To succeed de Marenches as head of the SDECE, Mitterrand looked outside intelligence circles and plucked Pierre Marion from the aerospace industry where he was on the verge of retirement.

In late August 1982, shortly after the Goldenberg carnage and four months after the bombing of the Rue Marbeuf, Pierre Marion strode across the courtyard of the Elysée. A tall figure with a piercing gaze and the dress and bearing of an English gentleman, he was escorted silently by the chief usher to the President's study. Marion was in confident mood: Mitterrand, he believed, was a man he could do business with. His conviction was born of the President's reaction to the Goldenberg murders. Mitterrand had immediately assembled the intelligence and police chiefs and declared terrorism public enemy number one, ordering them to wage war on it.

Marion had taken this as a go-ahead for action. Since

mid-1981 the Action Service had infiltrated informers into several terrorist support networks, and had drawn up a list of potential candidates for '*neutralisation*'. Carlos was not one of the names on the list, because Marion did not think him worth worrying about. 'We completely erased Carlos,' Marion admitted. 'He wasn't interesting for us. He had lost his aura. When I was at the secret service he was no longer considered dangerous, he wasn't a real terrorist.'[8]

Five targets had been located in Paris, and a total of another seven in Rome, Geneva, Frankfurt, Madrid and Brussels. Most of the individuals held Syrian, Libyan or Iraqi nationality, and professed to be diplomats. Partly on the basis of intelligence from Mossad and the PLO, Marion believed he had definite proof that ten of the targets supported terrorists. There were some doubts over the two remaining individuals, but, in Marion's eyes, France's right to self-defence meant that '*intime conviction*' (innermost conviction) was enough to justify their assassination.

Marion had selected volunteers from the 200-strong Action Service, 'perfectly disciplined, good observers, and precise executors'.[9] There was no shortage of candidates from the Cercottes training camp near Orléans run by the DGSE, formerly known as the SDECE. A four-strong team had been picked for each murder, which would be carried out with weapons that would point the finger at other terrorists. The teams were ready to strike. But Marion could go no further without consulting Mitterrand. What the secret service chief was seeking was an anonymous, blanket cover. All the President would know about was the number of targets involved, not their names.

Marion's witness-free meeting with Mitterrand – 'With more than two people, there are no more secrets,' the President was fond of saying – got off to a bad start. The President was in a foul mood, his handshake cold and his features set in stone. Handing Mitterrand his list of suggested operations, Marion told him that if anything went wrong or if news leaked out, the rule of the game was that he, Marion, would act as the scapegoat. The President, with the death-list in his delicate hands – Marion noticed they were as fine as those of a violin player – refused to give the green light for any of the assassinations.

Eight days later, in September, Marion asked for another urgent interview with Mitterrand. The encounter, also private, was just as strained. After another cold handshake, the President demanded roughly why the meeting was so urgent. When Marion suggested hitting an Abu Nidal base and a terrorist training camp in Beirut, the President grimaced and fell silent, the fingers of his right hand drumming the top of his desk. After a long pause, the President broke the tension: '*Non.* I authorise you to kill only Carlos and Abu Nidal.'

Marion retorted that both men were much too well protected. French intelligence believed (mistakenly) that Carlos was in a fortress in Czechoslovakia, armed to the teeth. Abu Nidal, who had turned his back on Arafat in the mid-1970s, was known to be in Syria. Regardless of its feasibility, for Marion there was nothing morally wrong with Mitterrand's order. The motto that the graduate of the Ecole Polytechnique publicly espoused was an eye for an eye, a tooth for a tooth. Marion's defence of state-commissioned murder, in a country that abolished the guillotine in 1981 (at Mitterrand's initiative), was unwavering: 'We are confronted by fanatics who stop at nothing to further their cause, to execute an order or to get a bonus ... In the end it is morally more legitimate to remove them than to give soldiers in a war the order to fire on other soldiers who may be engaged in a conflict only through patriotic discipline. And then there is the fact that such actions of neutralisation would be carried out outside the law. I have less scruples on this point. It is indeed for such actions that the secret services exist and they must, in exceptional cases, act outside the norms of law.'[10]

Marion's stand was representative of the secret service's thinking and practice. During the war against Algerian independence fighters, the service had used the cover of a shadowy organisation it had created, the Main Rouge (Red Hand), to assassinate nationalist leaders and arms traffickers across Europe and North Africa, and bomb the latter's ships or cargoes. One former alcohol and tobacco smuggler turned arms merchant based in Hamburg, Georg Puchert, was warned to stop supplying the Algerians in 1957. When he took no notice, three of his ships were bombed and sunk in as many months, and he was finally blown up. An associate was killed in a Geneva hotel with a poisoned dart fired into his neck. Nor were relatives spared: another German arms salesman, Otto Schluter, stopped supplying the Algerian nationalists after a car bomb killed his mother. According to a former Prime Ministerial adviser, Constantin Melnik, the Action Service assassinated 135 people in 1960 alone.[11]

One of Marion's successors, Admiral Pierre Lacoste, who was sacked after the French secret service bombed the Greenpeace ship *Rainbow Warrior*, would have gladly eliminated Carlos to satisfy Mitterrand: 'If I had had Carlos at the end of my rifle it's probable that I would have obtained permission to have him slain. I myself wouldn't have been reticent. But we never got close enough to the stage where I could ask Mitterrand for authorisation to kill him.'[12]

Biographers have invariably assumed that the socialist President Mitterrand always refused to sanction state killings. As well as abolishing the death penalty, he is widely believed to have turned down such plans known in France as '*operations humides*' (wet jobs) or '*actions homo*' (short for homicide), and to the CIA as 'operations to terminate with extreme prejudice'. In fact, the Action Service was still active during Mitterrand's long reign.

France's ambassador to Beirut, the 59-year-old Louis Delamare, knew that his life was in danger. He had received death threats. But he had refused bodyguards and an armour-plated car, saying that an escort would be pointless and would only mean that several people would die instead of just one.

Delamare was alone with his driver when his car, French tricolour flapping in the wind, was ambushed in West Beirut on 4 September 1981. Four gunmen sprang out of the white BMW which had blocked the way and, while the driver cowered on the floor, one of them took aim at the ambassador and fired through the window. Six bullets struck Delamare at point-blank range in the head, heart, and stomach.

Witnesses including Delamare's driver related that the gunmen had initially run up to the ambassador's car and tried to open the doors. But the doors were locked from the inside. Only a few dozen yards away, Syrian soldiers and intelligence officers looked on from a Syrian army check-point. When the white BMW sped away with the killers, the Syrian soldiers let the car through the check-point.

Three of the killers of Louis Delamare were slain – by members of the French Action Service. Within hours of the assassination of the ambassador, Marion had ordered his spies in the Middle East to identify and find the killers. Initial reports from Lebanese, Palestinian and Syrian sources all pointed to Damascus. In an investigation lasting several months the French confirmed that Syria had commissioned the murder, although the original plan had been for Syria to hold Delamare hostage, as it had held a Jordanian diplomat a few months earlier, to put pressure on France.

The French spies discovered that the killers were members of the Red Knights, a new paramilitary organisation set up that summer and deployed in Lebanon by the Syrian President's brother, Rifaat al-Assad. The gunmen had trained at a camp in Syria run by Rifaat al-Assad's special forces, the 50,000-strong Defence Brigades.

After the ambassador's murder the gunmen were escorted by the Syrian secret service to Damascus where they were held and questioned before being released.

The French were able to identify only three of the assassins and tracked them down in late 1982 to a village in Lebanon's Bekaa Valley. Marion sent a team of a dozen Action Service recruits which shot two of the killers dead, and wounded the third. The commando contacted Marion to seek the go-ahead to complete their assignment. Marion gave them clearance, and a French officer followed the badly wounded man to his hospital bed, and wrenched out the oxygen and other tubes linking him to a life-support machine, 'so that he would have no more memories', as one senior intelligence officer put it. Mission accomplished, the team radioed back to Paris.

Carlos escaped having a similar fate inflicted on him by the Action Service, but the rival DST which had lost two men to his bullets was more than willing to step into the breach and execute him.

In December 1982 the CIA's Paris station chief John Siddel telephoned the new head of the DST, Yves Bonnet. They had urgent business to discuss, insisted Siddel, whom Bonnet had nicknamed 'von Siddel' because the American carried himself as stiffly as a Prussian officer. The CIA officer brought his French colleague a magnificent Christmas present: a chance to seize Carlos. Bonnet, a career civil servant, had been in the job barely a month, but that had been long enough to realise how much the CIA's information mattered to his service: 'I found the DST still very traumatised by the Rue Toullier shootings. Carlos had become a mythical beast; he was undoubtedly public enemy number one for the DST.'[13]

Siddel was convinced that the CIA's source, a Syrian, was reliable. Carlos, who had been located in Damascus, apparently planned to travel in the next few days to the

Swiss resort of Gstaad, favoured haunt of the European jet-set, and would stay there in a hotel over Christmas. Siddel had the name of the hotel and the date on which Carlos was due to arrive. Bonnet's superior, Interior Minister Defferre, jumped at the opportunity to get even with the man he had tried to placate through negotiation, only to see a bombing and shooting campaign strike France and French targets abroad. 'We'll take the risk of catching him, we'll gun him down,' Defferre enthused to Bonnet. 'I take full responsibility. My duty isn't to ask the President; he cannot order this assassination.'[14]

Technically, the DST had no right to carry out such a mission. Its brief was national, as clearly underlined in the decree defining it as 'responsible for detecting and preventing, on the territory of the French Republic, the activities inspired, engaged in or sustained by foreign influences of a nature that threatens the security of the country'. Foreign operations were the DGSE's domain. Countless DST chiefs had manoeuvred to gain wider powers, only to be obstructed by their rival.

As there was no question of the DST passing on the American tip to the Action Service of the DGSE, Defferre had little choice but to turn to Colonel Prouteau, the officer promoted only five months earlier to head Mitterrand's new anti-terrorist unit. Thirsty for a coup to legitimise his unit in the face of intense criticism from the French police and secret services, Colonel Prouteau personally led a team to Gstaad where the athletic paramilitary team merged with some difficulty with the resort's jewel- and fur-clad revellers.

Colonel Prouteau found no sign of his quarry, in the hotel or on the slopes. 'If a famous terrorist was present in this town, which we have not been able to prove, in no case was it Carlos,' he reported in a confidential note to Mitterrand, adding a sybilline reference to the President's order to catch Carlos: 'It is certain that in your mind, given the danger Carlos represents, it was important, as soon as he had been located, to do what was necessary so that he could no longer do harm.'[15]

An irritated Bonnet challenged Siddel following the operation's failure. 'You took us for bloody idiots,' the Frenchman protested. 'No, no. We were certain. We'd put the informer through a lie-detector test,' Siddel answered. Yet again the CIA had paid the price of its reliance on polygraphs, widely decried by other intelligence services and by critics within the CIA itself. 'Some cultures polygraph more effectively than others,' remarked a politically incorrect Clarridge, who had made his own attempt at neutralising Carlos in the mid-1970s. 'Americans, because of our puritanical tradition of right and wrong, are good subjects. Arabs and Indians, for example, are notoriously difficult, because lying under certain circumstances is culturally acceptable.'[16]

In the year that followed Carlos's wave of terror against French targets, the missions launched by France's secret services amounted to little more than boxing with his shadow. The closest either Marion of the DGSE or Bonnet of the DST came to Carlos was in the quirky 'para-diplomacy' which they – separately – attempted with his chief sponsor of the time, Syrian intelligence. Bypassing the cumbersome diplomatic apparatus is nothing exceptional in France, where politicians, chairmen of state-owned companies, and secret service chiefs alike regard managing personal networks of foreign contacts as part of their job.

At his September 1982 meeting with Mitterrand, Marion had sought and obtained permission from the President – 'Yes, but hurry' – to try to secure a pledge from Syria's Rifaat that there would be no more Syrian-sponsored terrorist attacks in France. The Syrian was not an easy individual with whom to negotiate. The previous year, in February 1981, Rifaat al-Assad had crushed a revolt by the fundamentalist Moslem Brotherhood. The rebels had managed to seize the ancient city of Hama north of Damascus before Rifaat sent in troops backed by a tank division. Some 10,000 members of the Brotherhood and civilians are believed to have perished in the bloodletting that followed.

Marion had already shown the Syrians that he meant business. Five days after the Rue Marbeuf bombing an Action Service squad which had been despatched to Madrid fired a volley of shots at Hassan Dayoub, the Syrian cultural attaché, as he arrived home. Dayoub was suspected of masterminding the murders of Syrian opposition figures exiled across Europe. He survived unharmed. The Action Service had been ordered to wound but not kill, but failed even in that limited task.

Following the Presidential go-ahead, Marion arranged a meeting with Rifaat al-Assad later that September at a luxurious villa owned by the Syrian on the edge of the Saint-Nom-la-Bretêche golf course in Paris's western suburbs. Locals reported that whenever Rifaat, a skilled golfer, strode around the course, a swarm of bodyguards would follow. Marion was told not to bring any of his own bodyguards, but DGSE officers were unobtrusively deployed within eyesight of the villa. Accompanied only by his driver, Marion was greeted by a row of Syrian bodyguards armed with machine-guns.

In two five-hour rounds of talks, Rifaat angrily and repeatedly denied any links to terrorists. Marion wielded carrot and stick. The carrot was the prospect of warmer relations with France, the stick a threat to strike at the terrorists' support networks in France and other European countries, including Syrian so-called diplomats, even though Mitterrand had refused to grant Marion permission to do just that. The bluff was not called, and the two shook hands on a mutual non-aggression pact. 'You can count on my word,' Rifaat said. 'Abu Nidal will no longer act against you.'[17]

No mention was made of Carlos. 'The negotiations did

not concern Carlos,' Marion recalled. 'In the DGSE's assessment, he wasn't yet supported by Syria. Carlos wasn't even considered operational by the Syrians.'[18] In fact, as Carlos himself was shortly to demonstrate, he was at the time a key element in Rifaat al-Assad's stable. The DST chief Yves Bonnet was similarly duped by the Syrians. Several months after Marion's meeting with Rifaat, Bonnet flew to Damascus for his own attempt at diplomacy.

The two French intelligence chiefs made no attempt to coordinate their initiatives. 'I never had the habit of asking the DGSE for permission when I went on foreign missions,' Bonnet sniffed.[19] In the words of an MI6 observer: 'The French secret services keep their sharpness and tautness more by jousting and competing with each other than by cooperating.' The feud between the two intelligence agencies was rooted in the Dreyfus scandal which had spawned mistrust of the secret services among French leaders and public opinion. In the intelligence community the decision prompted by the Dreyfus affair to strip the military of its domestic counter-espionage role bred lasting resentment. The army-linked secret service, of which the DGSE was the heir, jostled continuously with its civilian counter-intelligence rival (now the DST), which gave as good as it got.

Like Marion, Bonnet had to sit through a monologue, a two-hour denunciation of French meddling in Lebanon by General Mohamed Al-Khuli, the head of Syria's élite secret service, the air force intelligence corps. Relations between the two men soon warmed, however, and the heavily built general, friend and personal adviser to President al-Assad, pulled on a cigar as he took Bonnet for a stroll through the streets of Damascus, surrounded, Bonnet remembered, 'by his likeable mates with bulges at their sides'. In the Omayyad Mosque, he pointed out the mosaics to Bonnet, as their escort, minus shoes but still with bulges under their jackets, strolled nearby.

Bonnet was evasive about the other figures he met in Damascus on his visits in 1983 and 1985. He admitted to seeing 'people from the Abu Nidal group – not unpleasant but stirred up. People who have an unrealistic vision.' But he denied meeting Abu Nidal himself. It seems surprising, however, that the head of France's DST, on a visit to the Syrian capital to see General Al-Khuli, should have to deal with an obscure subordinate of Abu Nidal's. The fact that in 1985 Abu Nidal sent Bonnet a personal message of sympathy, verbally and through an intermediary, on his dismissal from the DST – 'You have left but you remain our friend' – would suggest otherwise.[20]

Like Marion, Bonnet claimed credit for a two-year pause in Syrian-backed terrorist attacks in France, which by his own admission was won on entirely selfish terms: 'The terrorist attacks continued in other countries, but France was the only one that was spared. The truce was based on balanced relations – an exchange of information and a mutual non-aggression pact with no attacks on France and French interests abroad. At the same time, the message was: "If you conduct operations against your opponents, I don't care as long as it's not in France." The Arabs were interested in information about their opposition figures in France. But I gave nothing that led to anyone's death. I have no deaths on my conscience.'[21]

Yet again, Carlos was not part of the deal. 'Operationally, Carlos was of no interest. I was more concerned by Soviet spying,' Bonnet recalled. 'When I asked Al-Khuli about Carlos, he told me: "Don't get excited about a guy who represents nothing." Palestinian groups told me that Carlos was completely wrecked by drugs and alcohol. Abu Nidal's people said the same thing.'[22]

Unoperational, and addicted to drink and drugs. Not a flattering portrait. Nor an accurate one. Both Marion and Bonnet's diplomatic efforts were missed opportunities to restrain the hand guiding Carlos. The Stasi files spotlight Rifaat al-Assad, General Al-Khuli and his deputy Haitham Sa'id as Carlos's direct contacts in Syrian intelligence from the mid-1970s onwards.

Some eighteen months after first visiting East Berlin, Carlos had established direct contact with the Syrian ambassador to ask for help. In the winter of 1980 the ambassador received Carlos, his wife Magdalena Kopp and Johannes Weinrich – all of whom carried Syrian diplomatic passports – for a half-hour interview in his office. After the meeting, the ambassador ordered the third secretary in charge of security, Nabil Shritah, to 'look after' the group. Soon afterwards, the Syrian Foreign Minister sent a coded telegram from Damascus ordering the embassy to give Carlos support.[23]

The thirty-year-old Nabil Shritah served as President al-Assad's interpreter during the head of state's visits to German-speaking countries, but in the eyes of the East German Stasi Shritah was a Syrian spy. The tasks that Carlos and Weinrich requested of him were initially mundane. Letters of recommendation for visas to Hungary, Romania and Czechoslovakia. Currency swaps, hotel and car-hire bookings. Weinrich's accounts detail various sums of money given to him by the diplomat. A few days after the first meeting with the Syrian ambassador in East Berlin, Weinrich asked Shritah to store a Samsonite suitcase containing guns and explosives packed in perfume boxes. The ambassador, Weinrich said, had told him he had no objections. Later, Weinrich's armoury of submachine-guns, automatic pistols, ammunition, detonators and other items was placed in a large safe in Shritah's office. Weinrich helped himself from it once a month.

Weinrich was always sure of a warm welcome at the Syrian embassy. He was on first-name terms with the ambassador, Amin Askari (and from 1981 onwards his successor Faisal Summak), who served as Carlos's inter-

Marxist lawyer José Altagracia Ramírez Navas with two of the three sons he named after the father of the Bolshevik Revolution, his favourite Ilich (left) and Lenin (right), in Venezuela in 1954.

Carlos's mother Elba Maria Sánchez, who would take him to mass while her husband's back was turned. According to a friend, Elba was 'the only thing Carlos really loved'.

On the eve of Carlos's first trial since his capture after two decades on the run, Ramírez Navas holds a photograph which his son sent him from a Paris jail.

'El Gordo' (Fatso), the schoolboy who would answer taunts with the cry 'The whole world will hear of me!', at sixteen. Ilich's identity card from the Fermin Toro school in Caracas.

LFT
REPUBLICA ... VENEZUELA
LICEO FERMIN TORO
DIRECCION
CARACAS
30
No.
Director
CARNETS S. R. BOUZO - T. 553598

Carlos photographed by French counter-espionage (the DST) in the Latin Quarter in Paris in June 1975. The service under-estimated Carlos, with fatal results in the nearby Rue Toullier a few days later.

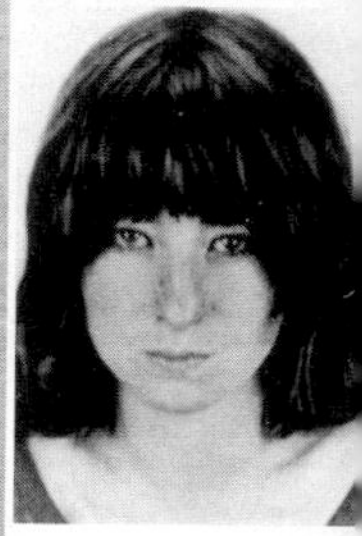

Gabriele Kröcher-Tiedemann, who at Carlos's side in Vienna demonstrated how mistaken Interpol had been in describing her as 'submissive'.

'Tell them I'm from Venezuela and my name is Carlos. Tell them I'm the famous Carlos.' Carlos, minus Che Guevara beret, at Algiers airport in the last moments of the OPEC raid, the most audacious coup of his career.

The bombing of the Paris-Toulouse Capitole express, one of Carlos's opening shots in a 'dirty, private war' to force the release from jail of his wife and an accomplice.

Rue Marbeuf, off the Champs-Elysées avenue, devastated by a car bomb on 22 April 1982, the day set for the trial of Carlos's partners. 'Carlos's love story with Magdalena Kopp costs France a great deal,' an aide to President Mitterand noted in his diary.

'Usually, I fire three bullets in th nose which kills immediately'. Carlos on his attempt to murder the president of Marks and Spencer, Joseph Edward Sieff, pictured recovering on his hospital bed with his wife.

Count Jacques Senard, the French ambassador to The Hague, taken hostage by the Japanese Red Army in an operation which Carlos helped to plan. 'I don't understand why the Japanese didn't kill their hostages one by one.' Carlos commented later.

Louis Delamare, France's brave ambassador to Beirut, was ambushed and assassinated in September 1981. French intelligence hunted down the murderers, and granted itself a licence to kill in a mission that has remained secret until now.

Two French counter-espionage officers sent to their deaths in the Rue Toullier blunder which humiliated the DST: Algerian war veteran Raymond Dous (left) and young recruit Jean Donatini (right).

Carlos's right-hand man Johannes Weinrich, described by the Stasi as a coward and 'a soft-boiled egg', five months into detention at a Berlin prison after he was captured in Aden.

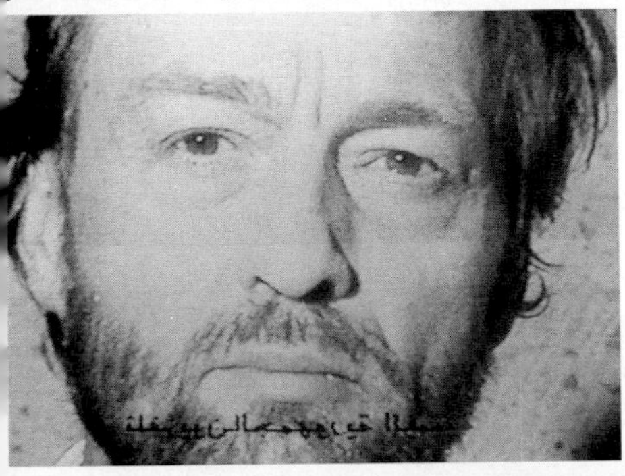

'My character is simple. I am a father first and foremost.' Mr and Mrs Ramírez Sánchez (alias Carlos and Magdalena Kopp) and their daughter Elbita.

The Jackal's lair. The Bayswater home of Angela Otaola, who described Carlos as 'a friend – well, a former friend now' after a bag he had asked her to keep for him was found to contain Semtex explosives, hand grenades, pistols and rubber coshes.

Carlos lived like a man of the world in Hungary, and the secret service supplied him with women behind Kopp's back. The service feared Carlos's associates would declare 'Allah's revenge' on Hungary if something happened to him.

Carlos lived like a king in Hungary

HUNGARY, which once sheltered Carlos and has rare television pictures of him, has dropped an investigation into him because of insufficient evidence.

The inquiry into links between Carlos and the country's former communist

Carlos's villa on the Hill of Roses in Budapest, from which he was allowed to run a private army with bases across the Soviet bloc.

Carlos's last refuge in the Sudanese capital Khartoum. 'He was a very lovable guy,' a neighbour said of him. 'Entertaining and nice to everybody.'

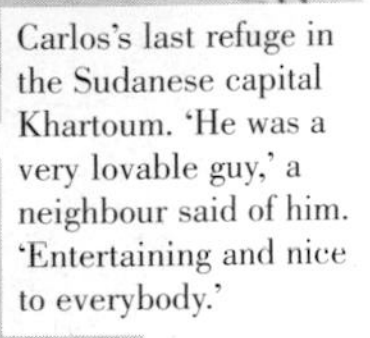

Carlos's living room. His high-ranking friends ensured a generous supply of alcohol in a country ruled by a military dictatorship which had turned Sudan into a Moslem fundamentalist bastion.

Reading matter for the world's most wanted man, who kept himself well-informed on current affairs and the Arab-Israeli dispute.

A passport photograph of Carlos, supplied by Venezuelan police to the French DST in 1975 after the Rue Toullier killings.

The photograph on one of Carlos's false passports, with which he posed as a Peruvian economist by the name of Carlos Martinez Torres.

A Polaroid snap of Carlos in his Paris jail cell, cheerful and dapper before his trial. The Spanish message translates as: 'For my dear old man from a son and comrade.'

mediary with Rifaat al-Assad. In a letter to Carlos, Weinrich wrote that to establish contact with Rifaat he was supposed to call someone in the latter's office in Damascus and say: 'I am Steve [one of Weinrich's aliases] from Carlos. Best regards from Amin Askari, Germany.'[24]

The explosives that the Stasi had taken from Weinrich at East Berlin's airport on 31 May 1982 – prompting Weinrich's declaration that Carlos was waging 'a dirty, private war with France' – had sent alarm bells ringing. The explosives, neatly wrapped in small packs, were analysed by the Stasi's Operative Technical Sector, which identified them as Nitropenta weighing in at 24.38 kilos. The Stasi concluded the Nitropenta had been supplied by the Securitate, the Romanian political police. At tense meetings with Major Voigt, head of the Stasi's counter-terrorism section, Weinrich repeatedly demanded his property back. But he refused to enlighten the East Germans on how the explosives might be used, beyond saying that they would be shared out among 'liberation movements'.

Irked by Weinrich's refusal to cooperate, Voigt ordered junior officer Borostowski to search his room at the Hotel Metropol. There were plenty of clues as to how the explosives might be used in Weinrich's briefcase. Plans of the Maison de France, which housed the French consulate and a cultural centre on West Berlin's smartest avenue, the Kurfürstendamm. Together with notes in Weinrich's hand detailing the results of surveillance of the consulate by two members of the group. Other searches revealed plans for an attack on the home of the general commanding French troops stationed in West Berlin, a kidnap in Beirut, the blowing up of a university building and the Hotel Méridien in the French Riviera capital Nice, attacks on the French and American embassies in Beirut, and the French embassy in Bonn.[25]

Carlos's private army was so large and well deployed that it could contemplate more or less simultaneous attacks in both Western Europe and the Middle East. The time-consuming process of watching the three embassies in Beirut and Bonn had already been undertaken by members of the organisation. Borostowski reported in a prophetic memo: 'As far as other attacks are concerned, the plan is for the gang in all cases to free its two members [Kopp and Bréguet] through pressure … The longer their imprisonment lasts, the more brutal must the attacks be … The group has the intention of carrying out actions until the prisoners are released.'[26]

Carlos's organisation suffered its first defection in mid-1983 when the Kurdish refugee Jamal al-Kurdi turned his back on the group after he was arrested in Switzerland as an illegal immigrant. Since 1979, when he had refused to assassinate the journalist who had interviewed Carlos for *Al Watan al Arabi*, al-Kurdi had refused to carry out several other operations for Carlos. Unconfirmed reports reached Weinrich that al-Kurdi had betrayed the organisation in testimony to Swiss authorities, because he feared that he would become the target of reprisals. But the news did not worry the organisation unduly, because it was felt that al-Kurdi did not know enough about its workings to put it in jeopardy. Similarly, the Stasi, which found out about al-Kurdi through its surveillance of Weinrich, concluded that there was little risk that East Germany would be identified as one of the group's safe havens.

After more than a year's lobbying by Weinrich, Major Voigt finally ordered Borostowski in August 1983 to fetch the Nitropenta explosives from the Stasi's arms store where they had been placed and return them to Weinrich. This was despite Borostowski's warning of future attacks, and in violation of the usual practice whereby explosives seized by the Stasi were destroyed. Weinrich recovered his precious consignment with only a cautionary word from the Stasi: he must not use the explosives in a way that might allow Western nations to track any member of the Carlos group down to East Germany. On the evening of 21 August 1983 Weinrich added the explosives, together with a detonator, to his armoury in the Syrian embassy.

The previous morning one of Carlos's associates in Damascus, Mustafa Ahmed El Sibai, had flown from the Syrian capital to Berlin-Schönefeld airport. The Lebanese-born Sibai then checked in at the Metropol Hotel in East Berlin, conveniently situated across a leafy square from the Friedrichstrasse station. He was given room 1108, two doors down the corridor from Weinrich's room.[27] Sibai's travel plans were already known to the Stasi, which had been tipped off a day earlier by the Hungarian secret service in a telegram about Sibai, branded the 'Kamikaze candidate'. A few days earlier Carlos's Syrian lieutenant, Ali Al Issawe, had taken a room at East Berlin's Palast Hotel.

On the morning of 25 August Weinrich called again at the Syrian embassy just behind the ruined Reichstag building. He asked Nabil Shritah, the third secretary in charge of security, to fetch the brown leather bag containing the Nitropenta explosives from the big safe in his office. Weinrich then asked a favour: would the third secretary ferry the bag across the Berlin Wall? Uncertain as to how far he should go in helping Weinrich, Shritah sought advice from Ambassador Summak. The ambassador was unhelpful, telling Shritah that it was his affair. Shritah refused the request.

But Weinrich had little difficulty finding another courier. Reluctant to walk even a short distance carrying the heavy explosives, Carlos's second-in-command took a taxi to the Friedrichstrasse station, a key link between East and West Berlin in both fact and fiction. The man he had picked as his alternate courier, Issawe, was awaiting him. Moments later, Issawe crossed unchallenged into West Berlin with the explosives. Issawe had used a Syrian diplomatic passport. Shortly after Issawe had walked through the heavily guarded border, he met another member of Carlos's organisation, Sibai, who had previously crossed over into West Berlin.

During the morning of 25 August someone on the third floor of the Maison de France, where the cultural centre, offices and a restaurant were located, saw a well-dressed man, carrying a loud, fluorescent-coloured travel bag, pressing to his chest something wrapped in brown paper. The same figure was spotted a short time later on the fourth floor, which was virtually empty because of maintenance work.

At twenty minutes past eleven an explosion tore the roof off the Maison de France, destroyed the fourth floor, where the bomb had been left, and caused part of the building to collapse. Michael Haritz, who a few days earlier had joined the Youth for Peace church group and was about to deliver a petition to the French consul protesting against French nuclear tests in the South Pacific, was buried alive under the ceiling of the third floor. The twenty-six-year-old Haritz died of asphyxiation. Twenty-two other people who were in the building and in the street below, including a baby girl and a five-year-old boy, were wounded by flying blocks of concrete, shards of glass and debris.

Twenty-five minutes after the blast, which was later estimated by police as involving explosives weighing between twenty and thirty kilos, Sibai, who had planted the device, and Issawe crossed back from West to East Berlin at the Friedrichstrasse station. At lunchtime, Weinrich again visited the Syrian embassy in East Berlin. He told Shritah to listen to the one o'clock news bulletin on the radio. 'That's my work,' Weinrich smirked when the bombing was reported.[28]

On 1 September Carlos wrote a letter, in English, which he had an emissary of his organisation deliver a few days later to the West German embassy in Saudi Arabia. The threat he made to the West German Interior Minister Friedrich Zimmermann echoed the threat made to France's

Interior Minister Gaston Defferre soon after Magdalena Kopp and Bruno Bréguet were arrested in Paris:

> Your Excellency,
>
> In the name of our Central Leadership:
>
> 1) We have destroyed the French Consulate in West Berlin at 11h50 on 25th August last. This operation enters in the cadre of the armed conflict imposed upon us by the French Regime. A drawing and some explanations regarding the operation are attached.
>
> 2) The choice of West Berlin is a warning to desist from the activities engaged by your predecessor against our organisation. Mrs Gabrielle Kröcher-Tiedemann, who has never being (*sic*) a member of our organisation, is being extradited by Federal Germany for her presumed involvement in the OPEC operation of 21st December, 1975. Any judicial or police initiative against Mrs Kröcher-Tiedemann (or against anybody else) on the grounds of presumed or actual involvement in the activities of our organisation would be considered a wanton aggression to which we would answer accordingly.
>
> For the Organisation of the Arab Armed Struggle – Arm of the Arab Revolution:
>
> Carlos

As usual, Carlos added his thumbprints below the signature. He also slipped into the envelope, in case there were any doubts as to the veracity of the claim, a plan he had drawn of the fourth floor of the Maison de France. Entitled *Sketch of the 4th floor at time of explosion*, it was a precise drawing, with captions including 'Toilet (locked)' and 'Locked glass doors to empty art gallery'. An arrow pointed to 'Smaller storage room', with the words '25kg of high power plastic explosive placed here'.

With Syrian help, a chivalrous Carlos had struck a blow not only for the jailed Kopp and Bréguet – part of what Carlos called 'the armed conflict imposed on us by the

French Regime' – but also for his female comrade Kröcher-Tiedemann. Two months earlier public prosecutors in the West German city of Cologne had requested that Kröcher-Tiedemann be extradited from Switzerland, where she was imprisoned. As was her habit when cornered, she and an accomplice had started a gunfight when Swiss police had stopped her as she crossed the border from France in December 1977. Two border guards were wounded before Kröcher-Tiedemann and her accomplice surrendered. The Cologne public prosecutors wanted her to be extradited so that she could be tried in West Germany for her two murders in the opening minutes of the OPEC raid. Eventually, Kröcher-Tiedemann did walk free but not because of Carlos's intervention. Witnesses refused to testify about the Vienna killings at her trial in 1992 and the court in Cologne was forced to release her.

From Belgrade, where he had flown two days after the Maison de France bombing, Weinrich (alias Peter) sent an account of the attack to Carlos (alias Michel), who was in the Romanian capital Bucharest. Under the heading 'Berlin Operation', Weinrich wrote: 'The operation had a greater impact than I'd expected. I send you some pictures.' The dispatch, a twenty-seven-page round-up of activities past, present and future, reflected Weinrich's self-confidence. '[The Palestinians] known that you are in Bucharest, I learned this from their questions about you. My reply was: "We are everywhere and nowhere at the same time. People can find us only in the underground."' Weinrich concluded his letter with the words: 'Dear Michel, I try to keep everything around here under control. I want to meet you, the sooner the better. Please take care of yourself and the comrades. We need everybody ... a big kiss for you, yours, Peter.'[29]

10

Forced Out of the Cold

> From today's viewpoint, everything looks different. At the time, we were all scared that by putting too much pressure on the group, we would become victims.
>
> – Stasi Colonel Günter Jäckel

Ever since Carlos had taken the oil ministers hostage in Vienna, Colonel Qathafi had been generous in his support. While Carlos was still based in South Yemen in 1979, the Libyan leader had ordered a high-ranking Libyan army officer, Major Abdullah Zekri, to approach Weinrich.[1] The intermediary the Libyan used was a senior official at the South Yemeni Foreign Ministry, Abdel Mohsen Assaf, who had helped Carlos's group settle in the country and had since given several of Carlos's associates diplomatic passports. Carlos had been invited to Tripoli where he was welcomed by intelligence chiefs and Qathafi himself. The Stasi files noted that Carlos met Qathafi on several occasions.

Funds, weapons and equipment were all supplied to Carlos by the Libyans. In one consignment in 1980, they delivered Ingram submachine-guns, pistols fitted with silencers, and hand-grenades.[2] Inventories drawn up by Carlos and Weinrich also refer to receivers for Libyan remote-control detonators, timers and other weapons. In return, Carlos's organisation was drafted in to help Qathafi's purge of 'stray dogs', political opponents in exile. In one of his earliest missions for Qathafi, Carlos sent several subordinates to Switzerland to prepare the ground for an attack on a leading critic of the Tripoli régime, Omar Yahiah. Yahiah was placed under surveillance for several days at his villa on the edge of Lake Geneva, but the assassination never took place.

Qathafi also requested attacks on US and Israeli military and diplomatic targets, and the assassination of Saudi Arabian officials including diplomats in Paris. In May 1981, Carlos organised several surveillance operations for the Libyans in Beirut, where potential targets included the US and French embassies. Few attacks were carried out, however, and for a time Carlos and the Libyan Colonel slowly drifted apart. It is possible that Carlos's prices were too high. Tripoli was unenthusiastic about Carlos's idea of assassinating President Reagan for a hundred million dollars, an operation which would have involved a getaway submarine.

But at one of his regular meetings with Weinrich in East Berlin in 1983, an officer of the Libyan secret service, Major Salem Abu Shreda, took Carlos's lieutenant to task. The Major reproached Weinrich for not working for Tripoli any more. The Major promised that if the group agreed to carry out attacks for Tripoli, it would obtain significant resources from Libya and its intelligence service. 'More than from Syria, Yemen and Moscow put together,' the Libyan officer told Weinrich.

This alluring offer persuaded Carlos to work again for Qathafi. The Saudi ambassador to Greece narrowly escaped death in June when a team sent by Carlos, at the behest of Libyan intelligence, bombed his convoy in Athens. A car crammed with explosives blew up as the Saudi ambassador's motorcade sped by. 'Why the two in the first car were not killed on the spot is strange. Maybe George [one of the members of Carlos's group] pushed a fraction of a second too early,' Weinrich wrote to Carlos, adding hopefully: 'Anyway perhaps they are killed.'[3] Weinrich had scrutinised the newspapers hoping to supply Carlos with press cuttings, and photographs of the damage: 'The newspapers lie about the ambassador, saying that he took extra security steps [such] as never going by car to the embassy but leaving it one km away and approaching on foot. A clear provocation.' Partly because of the failed attack, Carlos's relations with Tripoli worsened in the months that followed.

In his lengthy letter to Carlos following the Maison de France bombing, Weinrich could hardly contain his glee at having, he thought, pulled the wool over the Stasi's eyes. Major Helmut Voigt 'was always warning us not to have an operation in the west ... directly from east and returning,' Weinrich wrote to Carlos in his rudimentary English. 'We always denied and kept hidden how we transported the bag to the west. They seemed to me not to be sure if we have done it ... We have always done what we wanted, even if they have tried to sabotage our activities. It will perhaps serve them as a lesson when they will have the official confirmation that it was us. I don't have the intention of using Berlin for very long and that will be the best of the lessons I could give them.'[4]

So full of fight was Weinrich that he drew up a list, code-named Waterloo, of more French targets: the French military command and the French library in West Berlin; the French consulate in Düsseldorf; and in Switzerland the French embassy in Berne and the French consulate in Zurich. Weinrich's upbeat letter to Carlos was tempered only by a brief note of concern at the Stasi's reaction: 'It seems obvious that their aggressive attitude could lead them to betray us.' But the overly confident Weinrich quickly dismissed this.

Carlos's dirty, private war to free Kopp and Bréguet, so far removed from his proclaimed ideal of world revolution as endorsed by the Stasi in its first reports on him, irritated the secret police. As the Stasi's day-to-day contact, Weinrich had since mid-1982 made himself increasingly unpopular with his lengthening list of demands: arms, explosives, travel documents, visas for contacts visiting East Berlin, logistical assistance for ferrying arms across the Iron Curtain, safe houses, and guarantees of protection and asylum in East Germany should the 'enemy' launch reprisals. After a confrontation with Major Voigt in October 1982 Weinrich had scrawled furiously in his notebook: 'If the time comes, where is my submachine-gun and my silencer?'[5]

The more Weinrich demanded, the more the Stasi judged his requests a threat to the security of the East German state and refused them. Meetings turned acrimonious, with Weinrich accusing his hosts of weakness as they did not take up his suggestion that the Stasi should strike against NATO bases in West Germany. 'If you don't want us, say it: "Leave!" ' he yelled. Apparently, an impatient Voigt was taking less and less care to mask his true feelings for Carlos's right-hand man whom he called 'a political nutcase and a megalomaniac'.

The East Germans rebuked the Carlos group for its lack of caution, and its personally motivated attacks which did not even pay lip service to the revolutionary ideology officially espoused by the Communist state. The Stasi concluded that the group was completely uncontrollable, due to the personality of Carlos who was judged 'brutal and contemptuous of human life'. This was an authoritative criticism, coming from a Soviet bloc secret service with a notoriety second only to that of the KGB. The East Germans noted Carlos's self-assurance based on 'an overestimation of his capacities', and his fondness of appearing in public. In certain circumstances he was liable to lose all self-control and became totally unpredictable.

'Carlos was a totally destructive person. I'm not sure that he had a real ideology,' Stasi General Markus Wolf reflected years later. 'Perhaps he had one at an earlier stage but now his actions were only a means to destroy. I make a distinction between Carlos and Che Guevara: although I don't think that Che was helpful or had a chance of success, his way was more thought out and more honourable than Carlos's.'[6]

For all Weinrich's attempts at keeping the group's involvement secret, it did not take the Stasi long to find out the truth about the bombing of the Maison de France in August 1983, and the Syrians' role in harbouring the explosives. A report signed by Voigt drew the unavoidable conclusion: 'The West Berlin attack has shown that the Carlos group uses the resources put at its disposal for terrorist ends although we have informed it of our security problems. It will therefore be necessary to reinforce measures of control and surveillance and to continue requiring that this group respect discipline.'

Surprisingly, the Stasi held back from expelling Weinrich and his partners.[7] The strongest action it took was to seize the gun he carried without a licence. The gun was later returned to Weinrich who placed it in the safe at the Syrian embassy. The Stasi did however tighten surveillance of the rebellious organisation. The East Germans resorted to a tactic that mirrored the handsome Romeo spies employed to such good effect by General Wolf in foreign intelligence-gathering – the closest that spying, labelled the world's second oldest profession, came to what is reputedly the oldest, prostitution.

The tailing of Carlos's two lieutenants, Weinrich and Issawe, revealed that they had several East German lovers. The two men divulged nothing about their real activities to their girlfriends, posing instead as businessmen. Having uncovered these relationships, the Stasi decided to exploit them. Stasi officers approached several of the women and attempted to recruit them as agents. One was a young East German, Wilhelmine Götting. But a stratagem which worked wonders in the heart of the West German government or at NATO headquarters in Brussels made no headway in East Germany. Worse, it backfired on the Stasi. Götting fell for Carlos's talk of world revolution and instead became a fully fledged member of the group and, effectively, Weinrich's secretary.

Carlos's realisation that the Stasi had tried to penetrate his network drastically worsened relations between the two. An incensed Carlos began to consider the East Germans potential enemies. He threatened to occupy the East German embassy in Paris if the Stasi did not help him win freedom for Kopp and Bréguet. Security at that embassy was reinforced. Shortly afterwards, Weinrich drafted plans for a bomb or machine-gun attack on a target within East Berlin. The plans were discovered by the Stasi during a routine check of Weinrich's belongings.

The Stasi took the threat seriously, and many Stasi files show that the all-powerful secret police exaggerated, intentionally or not, the importance and the true capabilities of the Carlos group, and especially its ability to strike East German interests. 'From today's viewpoint, everything looks different,' Jäckel testified.[8] 'At the time, we were all scared that by putting too much pressure on the group, we would become victims... In general, our aim was to temper the group, even verbally. Neither Weinrich nor Issawe would stray from their pig-headed attitude.' A mighty security service, feared at home and abroad, had been brought to its knees by the threats of a small private army for hire.

In late December 1983 Weinrich wrote a short phrase in his pidgin English in his notebook. 'The action: to blow Marseille.' The jotting was linked to the letter that Carlos had sent French Interior Minister Gaston Defferre after the arrest of Magdalena Kopp and Bruno Bréguet in February 1982. The proposed operation centred on the Mediterranean port-city where Defferre served as mayor.

The Paris-bound, high-speed *Train à Grande Vitesse* (TGV) which pulled out of Marseille's recently opened Saint-Charles station early in the evening on the last day of 1983 was almost empty. Three passengers consoled themselves with a drink in the bar of the sleek train. The hostesses wished everyone, a little early, a happy New Year. None of the dozen travellers in carriage number three had noticed the person who had lifted a heavy suitcase on to a luggage rack before slipping away.

At 7.43 p.m., as the TGV neared the sleepy town of Tain-l'Hermitage in the Rhône Valley, the bomb exploded. The explosive ripped wide holes through the roof and the sides of carriage number three. Had the bomb gone off thirty-five seconds earlier, it would have exploded just as the train passed another TGV hurtling in the opposite direction towards Marseille at 130 kilometres an hour. Designed to resist 'normal' accidents such as a derailing or an external shock, the carriage became a jagged-edged mess of curled steel, upturned seats, glass and pools of blood through which the hostesses gingerly picked their way to give a dozen injured passengers first-aid. Two women died instantly, including the wife of an entrepreneur who a day later also died of his injuries without having regained consciousness.

At 8.05 p.m. the TGV from Paris halted beneath the huge glass roof of the Saint-Charles station in Marseille. Well-wishers, many of them North Africans who had settled in the port-city, surged forward to greet the new arrivals. Four minutes later, an explosion in the left-luggage area blew to pieces two immigrants who had been walking past, an Algerian and a Yugoslav, and injured another thirty-four people. In the main hall a trail of blood streaked around the Christmas tree heavy with flashing lights and decorations. The station clock froze.

Both the place and timing of the two bombs, carried out with sophisticated, military-type high-explosive devices to ensure maximum casualties, left the French government with few doubts as to whom the bloody message was addressed. The bombs had exploded as President Mitterrand appeared on television to deliver his traditional New Year address to the nation. As he had done after the bombing of the *Capitole* train in March of the previous year, Interior Minister Defferre responded with a promise that security on trains would be strengthened, this time with extra police accompanying passengers.

According to Magdalena Kopp, both bombs were planted by Weinrich.[9] The day after the bombings Weinrich travelled from Zurich to Budapest, using a false British passport in the name of Gerald Anthony Allen. Anxious as ever to sign his deeds, Carlos claimed credit for the explosions in the name of the Organisation of Arab Armed Struggle no less than three times. Letters were sent to the Paris and West Berlin offices of the news agency Agence France-Presse, and to the Reuters office in Tripoli in northern Lebanon. In his schoolboy handwriting, Carlos passed the attacks off as revenge for a raid the previous month by French Super-Etendard jets on a training camp for Moslem militias in Baalbek in eastern Lebanon. The French military had been riven by recrimination after the bombing run because it had resulted in fewer casualties than had been hoped for. But there were more than enough victims to sting Carlos into action. Or so he said in his letters: 'We will not tolerate our children being the only ones to cry for the blood of the martyrs of Baalbek.' A day later a bomb wrecked the French cultural centre in Tripoli. The attack was later attributed to the Carlos group.

Throwing caution aside, Carlos (or a member of his group) had posted his letter to the West Berlin office of

Agence France-Presse from East Berlin. This forced Honecker's government to deny vigorously that Carlos was in East Berlin. However, the Stasi was still unsure how it should treat the Carlos organisation. After Weinrich and Issawe bragged in front of Stasi officers of supposed relations with the Soviet Union, the East Germans tried to verify the claims. In February 1984 the Stasi sent a message to the KGB asking for any information it might have on Carlos. The request went unanswered.[10]

By May 1984 the Stasi's counter-terrorism section had good reason to feel even less well disposed towards Carlos. Another wing of the Ministry of State Security, the HAIII division in charge of spying within West Germany, discovered that the 'enemy' was well aware of Carlos's bases in East Berlin and other Soviet bloc capitals.[11] The Stasi now knew that at any moment it might be exposed to Western public opinion as Carlos's protector – a threat that hung like a sword of Damocles over the East German secret police.

Fear of a public reprimand by the West was common to all Carlos's Communist sponsors, and was fanned by the intervention of the United States administration in 1984. Relations between Washington and the East bloc had recently begun to thaw as President Reagan gradually softened his 'evil empire' stance. Eastern European countries were pressing the United States to boost long-neglected economic ties. The State Department was willing to lower barriers to closer political and trade links. But not at any price.

In mid-1984 the ambassadors to Washington of five Warsaw Pact countries – Bulgaria, Czechoslovakia, East Germany, Hungary and Romania – were summoned to the State Department, to meet Mark Palmer, deputy assistant secretary responsible for Eastern Europe and the Soviet Union. What he had to say cast a chill over his guests. The United States, Palmer reported, had discovered that Carlos and other guerrillas were being protected and given asylum by the countries the ambassadors represented. No East bloc country should expect better relations with Washington unless it put a stop to sponsorship of international terrorists and to spying activities. For Palmer, Carlos was a symbol of the Soviet bloc's support for terrorism.

Several of the ambassadors, who had listened to Palmer's comments in stony-faced silence, were quick to deny his allegations. Palmer had very strong feelings about the issue, and he took malicious pleasure in retorting: 'These denials are, quite simply, totally unacceptable and unjustifiable. If your governments want a balanced, positive relationship with the United States, then they must stop protecting terrorists.' The ambassadors never did make such a commitment to Palmer. 'The East Europeans were very elusive, they would never say that such protection would be halted,' Palmer recalled. 'But it wasn't as if we were making a huge request. There were bigger things we wanted of these countries, such as that they change their spots and move from Communism to democracy.'[12]

Palmer kept the source of his information about Carlos secret, but it was the CIA which had told him that it had very detailed intelligence about Carlos's movements, down to details about the hotels at which he stayed during his visits to Eastern European countries. It is possible that the agency benefited from information passed on by the West German secret service. Palmer suggested to his superiors that such intelligence be used to capture Carlos, or, failing that, to assassinate him. 'I've always felt that the failure to do something against a Hitler, a Stalin or a Saddam Hussein should teach us something,' Palmer explained. 'Carlos is a criminal. Civilisation needs to protect itself from people like that. It needs the political will and the technical means to remove them.'[13] But although the CIA was then directed by Bill Casey, who during his tenure spearheaded an aggressive expansion of clandestine activities, the plan was turned down. The agency argued that such a mission had no chance of success, and that the American people would in any case not support it.

The CIA's refusal to intervene echoed the stance of another Western intelligence service which had also become aware of Carlos's bases. Like the CIA, the British MI6 decided to take no action. 'If we had gone in to East Berlin to get Carlos, we would have started a world war,' an MI6 member recalled. 'If we had gone in SAS-like we wouldn't have got out again. Or we would have risked the plane getting shot down. You couldn't seize Carlos there like the ex-Nazis in Bolivia. We had, or we thought we had, our hands tied.'

On 22 September 1984 the patience of the Stasi finally snapped. Its officers informed Weinrich that he was banned from East German soil. The official reason was 'the dangers and risks which might threaten the security of the German Democratic Republic'.[14] Carlos, however, had no intention of giving up on East Berlin. Told of the ban, Carlos swiftly substituted Weinrich, his second-in-command, with Issawe, the recruit from Syrian intelligence. Just as promptly, the Stasi threatened to ban Issawe too. The East Germans told Issawe that his presence would be tolerated only if he could prove that he was a guest of the Syrian or any other embassy.

Following the reproaches made to their ambassadors by Mark Palmer in Washington, an increasing swathe of East European states cold-shouldered Carlos. His relations with Romania had deteriorated since the bombing of Radio Free Europe. The Securitate did ask Carlos to arrange the murder of the manager of the giant French aluminium firm Pechiney in Greece – 'I like it,' chirped Weinrich in a letter to Carlos[15] – and to attack the French embassy in Athens, but neither request was followed up. By 1984 Carlos's emissaries in Bucharest were complaining of intense surveillance in the Romanian capital. In April 1985

Czechoslovakia declared itself out of bounds to the Carlos group. As the doors of the East bloc started closing on him, Carlos returned to one of his first sanctuaries, the South Yemeni capital Aden, for a few days. He took part in a meeting of Palestinian extremists at the Hotel Frantel, but he had long lost what little he ever had in common with the fedayeen.

Early in the morning of 4 May 1985 Jacques Vergès arrived at the gates of the Fleury-Merogis women's prison on the outskirts of Paris clutching a large suitcase. The lawyer had come to collect thirty-six-year-old Magdalena Kopp – 'my favourite client alongside Klaus Barbie' – who was due out that morning. Her detention had caused bloody havoc in the world outside, but in jail Kopp had been a model prisoner and earned maximum remission for her demure behaviour.

Unknown to Vergès, French counter-espionage had also been preparing for Kopp's release. The previous day the DST head Yves Bonnet received a call from police chief Pierre Verbrugghe, appointed two years earlier by President Mitterrand with anti-terrorism as his priority.

'Magdalena Kopp has been granted remission. She's out tomorrow. We don't want her in France,' Verbrugghe told Bonnet.

'That's fine by me but she has the right to stay.'

'She has to go.'

'Then we won't do it by the book. We'll grab her as she comes out of the jail and we'll send her to West Germany.'

'Okay.'

'But what if she comes back?' asked Bonnet.

'Never mind. It won't be your fault.'

Bonnet immediately called his counterpart at West German counter-intelligence in Bonn, the BfV (Bundesamt für Verfassungsschutz, the Federal Office for the Protection of the Constitution) to announce that he would be sending a parcel the next day, 'a parcel called Magdalena'. The BfV chief said that she would be made welcome, but only on one condition. 'I'll take your girl but not before nine o'clock in the evening. We don't want her in broad daylight.'

On the day of her release Magdalena Kopp was woken an hour earlier than usual. She had been due to leave the prison at eight o'clock, and was surprised to hear from her wardens that she would be set free earlier than scheduled. Another surprise awaited her when, clutching her few belongings and waiting for the metal gate to swing open, two men and a woman jumped on her, pinned her arms to her body and thrust her into a waiting car. Too bewildered to react, Kopp offered no resistance. She was forced down, head out of sight, on to the back seat of the car as it sped out of the prison, followed by two other cars. She did not see Vergès, suitcase in hand, standing waiting for her.

A safe distance away from the prison, Kopp's captors, officers of the DST, introduced themselves and revealed that their orders were to take her to Hoffenburg in West Germany. But they had fourteen hours to waste before parting company with her. Kopp was treated to a snail's-pace crawl around the Paris suburbs. The officers drove all day, going around in circles, doubling back on their route, stopping for snacks. Bonnet had feared that Kopp might lodge a complaint accusing the DST of kidnapping, torture, or even rape. 'I put the woman in the team so that she would not accuse us of rape because it would have to be really perverse to rape her with a woman present,' Bonnet explained.[16]

He need not have worried. Kopp was quiet throughout the long drive, and made no formal complaint after she was finally handed over to West German police at nightfall. She was briefly held for questioning, then allowed to go and stay with her mother, Rosina, in the town of Neu-Ulm where she had been born. On the evening of Kopp's arrival at her mother's house, the telephone rang; Carlos had already tracked her down and was calling to find out how she was. 'It was a wonderful time,' Rosina recalled. 'She stayed here and relaxed. She had to get a new driver's licence and a passport because everything was gone. We rode our bikes together to my husband's grave. I hoped she would stay but she said she had to go to Frankfurt. I assumed she had gone back to Carlos.'[17] Not that the two women ever talked about the man in Magdalena's life. They had a tacit understanding not to.

Rosina had guessed correctly, but Frankfurt was not Magdalena's final destination. Carlos, who was visiting Damascus at the time, ordered Issawe to accompany her to the Syrian capital. All Carlos's bombing and shooting frenzy had achieved was to knock a year off his wife's sentence. Five months later, in September, Kopp's erstwhile partner in crime Bruno Bréguet was also released before completing his sentence, for 'excellent behaviour' in detention during which he had taken several examinations to qualify as a draughtsman and geometer. Bréguet's refusal to rejoin Carlos, despite the 'dirty, private war' waged partly on his behalf, must have tasted of ingratitude to the group's leader. Like Kopp, Bréguet returned to his partner, a German woman with whom he had been living before his arrest, in Lugano.

After meeting his patrons in Damascus, Carlos flew back with Kopp to Budapest. But they were allowed only a few months to celebrate their reunion. In late August 1985 the US State Department stepped up the pressure on Carlos's backers, this time on Hungary in particular. In the office where the previous year he had received five Soviet bloc ambassadors, Mark Palmer met the Hungarian chargé d'affaires in Washington privately. The two men discussed bilateral relations, and it was only when they shook hands at the end of their meeting that Palmer broached the key point on his agenda. 'Oh, by the way,' Palmer, all smiles, casually remarked. 'I've heard it said that Carlos was in Budapest recently. I hope that he enjoyed himself!'[18]

Palmer's unexpected aside stung the Hungarians into action. A few days later Carlos was notified of the State Security's decision to evict him and his organisation from their safe houses, and ban them from its territory, this time for good. Carlos's pleas fell on deaf ears. Weinrich flew to Bucharest on 4 September, followed a day later by Issawe. Kopp flew to Damascus on 13 September, and Carlos to Baghdad the following day. On 18 September a relieved Colonel Jozsef Varga of Hungary's counter-espionage unit told officers of the Stasi that Budapest was rid at last of the Carlos group.[19] Romania eventually yielded to pressure from West Germany, and expelled Weinrich and Issawe.

Conscientious to the last, the Stasi officers recorded Carlos's comment on the East bloc régimes that had abandoned him: 'The Communists are terrible, they are worse than the imperialist adversaries. The [East] German Communists are the worst.'[20] The Stasi had finally shaken itself free of Carlos, a state of affairs it could have engineered many years earlier. As is to be expected from a former Stasi general, Wolf plays down the East German links with Carlos: 'Minister Mielke was labouring under an illusion. He thought that control of the Carlos group could ensure that nothing would tie the German Democratic Republic to the group's terrorist acts in Western countries. There was no direct support from the Stasi for the group through knowledge of such terrorist acts, but of course I have to recognise the Stasi's responsibility.'[21]

The fact that the Stasi handed explosives back to Weinrich knowing that he planned to use them to bomb a target in West Berlin demonstrates that Wolf's assertion is untrue. Wolf's cheeks flushed when this was pointed out to him. He pleaded ignorance, and the Stasi's good faith. Wolf's prodigious memory, a vital asset in his intelligence career, was lacking in this regard: 'With this knowledge you have now, you may say that there was complicity on the Stasi's part. But I do not think such acts were committed with the clear will of someone in the ministry to give support to terrorists. I cannot explain the reasons why the explosives were seized and then given back. I did not see details of all the activities of the counter-terrorism section.'[22]

Forced to abandon his bases in Eastern Europe, Carlos searched for a new refuge, just as he had done when he set up his organisation a few years earlier. He tried to improve his fraught relations with Libya, and sent Issawe to Tripoli on an exploratory mission. Issawe returned shortly afterwards with discouraging news. Carlos had been sidelined because of the influence enjoyed by the short, bald Sabri Khalil al-Banna, alias Abu Nidal, as much a recluse as Carlos was a showman. In the late 1970s, when he was under Iraqi patronage, Abu Nidal had apparently felt only respect for his colleague. 'My comrade Carlos defies all the police forces of the world,' Abu Nidal told an interviewer at the time. 'With him, I support all actions directed against American imperialism, the destruction of the reactionary régime of Lebanon and of Saudi Arabia. The ultimate objective is to establish a democratic state in Palestine.'[23]

But halfway through 1985 Abu Nidal had shifted his faction's headquarters from Damascus to Tripoli where, as reported by the official Libyan news agency, he met Qathafi and enjoyed shelter, aid and the use of training camps in exchange for services rendered. It was Abu Nidal who elbowed Carlos out of Qathafi's favours by bad-mouthing him behind his back so as to rid himself of a rival.[24] In January 1986 a triumphant Abu Nidal praised the Libyan leader for having been 'of great help to us ... an honest man with whom we have strong ties'. To make things worse for Carlos, his tenuous link to the fight for a Palestinian homeland was fast losing credibility. In November 1985, and after the hijack of the cruise ship *Achille Lauro* by a Palestinian gang led by Abu Abbas had ended in the callous murder of a paraplegic Jew, Leon Klinghofer, the PLO's

Yasser Arafat renounced any 'military action' committed by Palestinians outside Israel.

Beyond the Middle East, Carlos tried to breathe new life into relations with Cuba and the Direccion General de Inteligencia (DGI) secret service which had reached a low point in 1981 when Fidel Castro allowed the group only short stopovers on the island. In early 1982 Cuba was ready to renew links and Carlos met a DGI spy in Hungary to discuss a possible partnership. But no agreement was reached and the talks came to a sudden end.[25] Carlos made another attempt to woo his Latin American cousins in the summer of 1983. Weinrich re-established relations with the DGI station chief in East Berlin, Juan Miguel Roque Ramirez, and the Cuban became the liaison officer between Carlos and Havana. The group kept Roque Ramirez informed of its activities. '[We] organised the Marseille explosion in answer to a French air attack on a Lebanese village,' the Stasi files quoted Weinrich as telling Roque Ramirez in February 1984, before adding that there would be further similar actions.[26] But despite a visit to Cuba which Carlos made shortly afterwards, the relationship did not improve. Unknown to Carlos, Roque Ramirez had also been passing on the information that he had gleaned from Weinrich to his colleagues at the Stasi.

The Syrians had long proved the most steadfast of Carlos's allies, and it was in Damascus that he found asylum after his expulsion from Eastern Europe. Among the honours that had in the past been showered on Carlos, according to the Stasi archives, was a six-hour private audience in 1983 with President al-Assad.[27] Acting on the head of state's orders, intelligence chiefs now helped Carlos establish himself in the Syrian capital. Carlos and his partners flew in their arsenal and false papers, along with Weinrich's files and accounts.

The Syrians drove a hard bargain, and had plenty of ideas on how Carlos should repay their hospitality: strikes against opposition figures abroad, especially the Moslem Brothers in West Germany; attacks to intimidate 'reactionary Arab régimes acting against President al-Assad'; attacks to be committed in an offensive launched jointly by Syria and Iran against Saudi Arabia and other Gulf states; and attacks against Israeli and other anti-Syrian forces in Lebanon. The Hungarian and East German archives reveal that Syria's task-list also included the kidnapping of a president (they do not say which) for a ransom of $10 million.

The sudden closure to Carlos's organisation of the Hungarian and Czech borders had caught him unprepared, forcing him to abandon sizeable sums of money in bank accounts in both countries. Carlos was in no mind to lose this wealth. On 10 June 1986 Carlos, Kopp, who was seven months pregnant at the time, and a bodyguard flew to the Czech capital Prague, carrying Syrian diplomatic passports bearing false names. But the Czech secret service soon discovered their real identities, and three days after their arrival several intelligence officers called at the married couple's hotel room. Carlos nervously smoked cigarette after cigarette as his visitors begged him to leave. The encounter was so tense that every time Carlos was about to reach in his pocket for another cigarette, he would signal to his bodyguard in case the latter concluded that he was reaching for his gun.

A telephone call to the PLO's representative in Czechoslovakia persuaded Carlos that there was no point in staying in Prague. Carlos was photographed in Kopp's company at the airport, a shot highlighting his aquiline nose and his jutting chin. Dressed in a suit and tie, the heavily built Carlos looked to all appearances like a businessman pulling a sour face after a hard day at the office as he loaded a trolley with hefty suitcases. The only giveaway was the suitcases' contents, his customary arsenal which led to a brief dispute with the pilot before it was accepted on board the plane. The plane flew to Moscow, from where Carlos and his companions caught another flight back to the Middle East.

To casual acquaintances in the Syrian capital Damascus, Carlos introduced himself as a Mexican businessman dealing with the Arab world, although he held Syrian passports in the name of Michel Khoury and Michel Assaf. His hosts loaned him a flat with a large terrace on Al-Akram Ben Sayfi Street in the city's smart Mezzeh district. The tightly protected residential neighbourhood was home to the heavyweights of Syria's political establishment, and officers from the military political academy lived just opposite Carlos's new home.

Many streets in Mezzeh, lined with trees and jasmine bushes, were closed to non-residents. Among those living in Carlos's neighbourhood was the world's most wanted Nazi criminal, Alois Brunner, blamed for the deaths of 120,000 Jews including more than 46,000 who were deported from Salonika to Auschwitz in 1943. Like Carlos, Brunner – who once told a German interviewer 'That junk [the Jews] deserved to die' – was wanted by France which had twice sentenced him to death in absentia for his work as Adolf Eichmann's right-hand man.

As detailed in a rough map scrawled by Carlos, his first-floor home had a pleasant view over orchards, was down the street from a women's teaching institute, and conveniently close to the airport. The only reminder of Carlos's long-lost revolutionary ideals was the Kalashnikov – perhaps the most common firearm ever made, but snubbed by Carlos himself – carried in desultory fashion by the bodyguard who escorted him whenever he emerged from the block of flats. In the evenings, up to six bodyguards watched over him.

The Stasi files report that among the well-wishers who visited Carlos in Damascus was Vergès. The lawyer has always denied that he met Carlos in Syria or earlier. 'Even if it were true that I had met Carlos, that would be within the framework of my profession,' Vergès once said. 'When a woman is arrested, I have the right to see her husband. If her husband is the object of legal proceedings, I don't have the right to help him in his activity, but I have the right to meet him.'[28]

The East Germans were still keeping watch over Carlos and his organisation, albeit from a distance. The Stasi files record a visit which Vergès is alleged to have made to Damascus in July 1986. As in the case of his visits to East Berlin, it was shrouded in secrecy and benefited from intricate precautions devised by Weinrich. Vergès sorted out the bureaucratic formalities for his journey with the Syrian ambassador to Paris and the embassy's first secretary. The plan was for the lawyer to travel under the official pretext of meeting three of his clients, Lebanese nationals living in Damascus. Vergès was told to check in at the Hotel Méridien in the city and wait for a call from Weinrich or Issawe.[29]

On 17 August 1986 Kopp gave birth to a daughter – in Beirut, according to French intelligence.[30] Carlos named the child after his own mother and Kopp's – Elba Rosa. The words of Carlos's Lebanese friend, Assam El Jundi, may be a guide to his reaction to the birth of a baby daughter: 'His relations with children are bizarre. When he has them before him, he seems stunned. And when a friend's children are introduced to him, he spends the best moments of his life. A mix of sorrow torn by sadness and deep pride appears in his eyes when he is with children.'[31]

The Nazi who had stood by Carlos ever since they met in the early 1970s, the retired Swiss banker François Genoud, regularly flew to the Syrian capital to see him. The 'Black Banker' was an unlikely figure for the left-wing Carlos to identify with as a fellow revolutionary. Genoud helped fugitive Nazis after the war, and claimed rights on writings attributed to Adolf Hitler, Martin Bormann and Joseph

Goebbels, whom he published. He had a strong sympathy for extremist Palestinian movements – for him, Nazism was part of 'a global war against Zionism'. Genoud himself admitted to visiting Carlos and Weinrich in Damascus, describing them as guests of the Syrian government which had welcomed them as 'brothers of the Palestinian revolution'.[32]

Carlos's hungering for adventure was slowly draining out of him. Over recent years the world's press had continued to see Carlos's shadow lurking behind a host of attacks. In September 1980 it was immediately assumed that he had shot dead the ousted Nicaraguan dictator, Anastasio Somoza, in the centre of Asunción in Paraguay. That same year he was credited with masterminding the hostage-taking at the United States embassy in Tehran. And in December 1981 he was believed to be about to lead a six-man commando to assassinate President Reagan. In July 1984 he was arrested by the Israelis, seized by gunboats, according to the *Evening Standard*, when they intercepted a ferry from Cyprus, the *Alisur Blanco*, on its way to Beirut. Two years later, in February 1986, his obituary was written when the Israeli newspaper *Davar* reported his execution and burial several feet under the sands of the Libyan desert, at the hands of Libyan agents. According to a senior Israeli military intelligence officer, General Yehoshua Saguy: 'He knew too much, and his intimate knowledge of the involvement of Arab leaders and their security services in international terrorism posed a danger to them, so they got rid of him.'

In fact Carlos was alive but his Syrian sponsors showed less and less interest in using his private army. Over the years Carlos became resigned to the idleness of a twilight existence. As little Elbita, whose chubby features echoed those of her father, grew up, Carlos would walk her through the streets, holding her by the hand, a bodyguard trailing not far behind them. Carlos and Kopp often dined at the

Golden Star restaurant on the fifteenth floor of the Cham Palace Hotel, which boasted a slowly rotating floor which gave diners a 360-degree view over the city. For a holiday, Carlos would take his family to the seaside.

The fire had long gone out of Kopp, whose telephone calls and letters to her family, including a collage of holiday snaps of Elbita playing on the beach, and Elbita blowing out the candles on her birthday cake, were intercepted by German police. 'I'm well. Everything is well with us,' Kopp told her sister in one call. In a letter posted from Cyprus, she wrote: 'I now need a new pair of glasses. I'm beginning to get old.' She may have thought the same of her husband.

Soon Carlos's hosts warned him against any temptation to break out of his domestic routine. The investigation into the bombing of a Pan Am jumbo jet over Lockerbie in Scotland in December 1988 had exposed the role believed to have been played by Syria.[33] As the West put pressure on Damascus, President al-Assad tried to demonstrate that he was cold-shouldering terrorists and ordered several gangs out of the Syrian-controlled Bekaa Valley in Lebanon. Carlos was told that his presence in the capital would be tolerated only on condition that he remain inactive. One suggestion that Carlos made in 1989, for an attack on an American base in Greece, was turned down. Only Weinrich, who spent much of his time in the South Yemen capital Aden, was still active. He was an instructor at camps in Syria, Lebanon and on the Indian Ocean island of Socotra.

Not yet forty years old, Carlos had effectively been forced into early retirement by the régime that had for so long rained money and weapons on him. As an MI6 officer observed, the late 1980s was a time when Carlos 'went off the boil'. The lack of interest shown by several Western intelligence agencies threatened to make a travesty of the title Carlos had long been honoured with: 'the world's most wanted man'. Most wanted by whom? For the CIA, Carlos in the late 1980s was a has-been. To Vincent Cannistraro, the agency's head of counter-terrorism until 1990, Carlos was only 'a historical curiosity … a rather sad character. A Communist whisky barrel who doesn't believe in God and who was no longer of use to Moslem governments. Operations were blamed on him because the truth was people didn't know who had committed them. In Damascus, he was dead drunk most of the time.' Mossad judged Carlos practically irrelevant to its counter-terrorism efforts, despite his links to Palestinian movements, as he had attacked no Israeli targets since his failed rocket attack on an El Al jet in 1975.

Even the DST was taking little notice of the fugitive who had shot two of its officers dead and wounded a third. 'We considered him to have retired,' said a former director of the service. 'We always knew more or less where he was. Some of our agents went through the neighbourhood where he lived in Damascus; we knew which was his block of flats. But we didn't need a potential target. And in any case we never got President Mitterrand's green light to jump on him in Damascus.'

The boisterous crowd which, a million strong, streamed across the Berlin Wall during the night of 9 November 1989 tasted freedom for the first time in twenty-eight years. It thronged West Berlin and gaped at the glittering boutiques of the Kurfürstendamm. On that heady night young Germans from both sides of the Iron Curtain stood on the soon-to-be-demolished Wall, and sprayed each other with champagne.

In the weeks of turmoil that followed the East German decision to allow unrestricted travel through the Berlin Wall, the KGB predicted that the revelry would turn nasty. Mikhail Gorbachev was warned that East Berliners might attack the Red Army's barracks in the city. As it turned out, they made for a more feared and hated testimony to Communist rule: the headquarters of the Stasi. On 15 January 1990 a furious mob swarmed across its sinister complex of offices on the Normannenstrasse, in a bleak working-class district of East Berlin known locally as Stasigrad.

Hundreds of rioters raced down the long corridors of the tall and lifeless buildings. They daubed slogans – 'Nazi swine' and 'Gestapo' – and urinated on the walls. Windows were smashed, locked doors knocked down, and thousands of files scattered about. Rumoured to have been masterminded by the West German secret service, the Bundesnachrichtendienst (BND), the assault ensured that many files were saved from destruction. The archives revealed that for years neighbours had spied upon neighbours, friends upon friends, and even wives upon husbands.

As the Berlin Wall collapsed, so did the system that had shielded Carlos for so long. The East Germans who streamed across the Wall not only buried Marxism and the Cold War, they also rewrote the rules of international terror. Deep in the archives of the Ministry of State Security, and stacked in neatly bound folders on rows and rows of shelves, were thousands of reports, photocopies of letters and transcripts of bugged conversations which detailed Carlos's years in the East bloc's embrace.

11

Exorcising the Ghost

> Carlos was a priority every day. Every time we met someone in a position to know something, there was always the question at the end: 'Do you know where Carlos is?' or 'Can you help us get to him?' We had a moral duty to ask.
>
> – Former DST chief Jacques Fournet

Barely two weeks after Iraq's Saddam Hussein ordered his tanks to roll across the desert sands into neighbouring Kuwait on 2 August 1990, Western secret services suddenly shone the spotlight on Carlos. Reports from across the Middle East suggested that in the wake of his invasion Saddam Hussein was preparing a global terror campaign against the United States and its allies. According to Mossad, it would feature Abu Nidal whom the Iraqi President had called in from Tripoli to launch the operation. But the leader whom Saddam Hussein had picked to coordinate the campaign, said the Western intelligence reports, was Carlos.

'The public appeals which Saddam Hussein made for a *jihad*, a holy war against the enemies of Islam, got us worried about attacks in Britain or against British troops out in the Gulf,' an MI6 officer acknowledged. 'We were concerned about guns for hire so we sent out people to track them down, including Carlos.' In fact, the possibility that Carlos should suddenly put himself at Saddam Hussein's beck and call was unlikely given that he was still living in Damascus and that Syria had denounced Iraq's invasion of Kuwait. The Gulf War that followed the invasion, however, breathed new vigour into the hunt for Carlos. And it was the CIA which jolted the French into making a new attempt to capture him.

Like many other Arab states, Syria had been forced into a less hostile stance towards the West by the collapse of the Soviet empire. Saddam Hussein's aggression threw Syria on to the side of the Western allies and as part of that budding partnership President al-Assad decided to abandon Carlos. The question that puzzled Western secret services was not so much why Syria had finally decided to abandon him, but why Syria had supported Carlos for so long. By all accounts he had outlived his usefulness several years earlier.

While half a million US troops, together with forces from a host of allied countries, massed in Saudi Arabia to prepare to fight Iraq, Syrian intelligence helped the CIA and the DST to plan a joint attempt to catch Carlos. To preserve a minimum of dignity in their treachery, the Syrians refused to allow a Franco-American team to grab their longtime guest from his home. Syrian involvement had to appear minimal, and the best opportunity was deemed to be Carlos's next trip out of the country.

The life of leisure imposed on Carlos by President al-Assad had dried up commissions as a source of income, and in late 1990 Carlos decided to visit Hungary and Czechoslovakia to withdraw the funds that remained in numerous bank accounts. News that Carlos planned to fly to two of his former havens in the Soviet bloc reached Syrian intelligence, and it passed the information on to the CIA. But the Americans had their hands tied because there were no judicial proceedings pending against Carlos in the United States. Under the Omnibus Crime Act of 1986 the

CIA could only seize terrorists in foreign lands if they had committed attacks on US citizens.

However, there was nothing to stop the CIA giving an old ally a little help. As it had done in 1982 when it mistakenly placed Carlos among the Christmas skiers in Gstaad, Langley chose to cooperate with the French secret service that had suffered most at Carlos's hands, the DST. The French harboured no ill feelings for the Gstaad fiasco, and working in tandem with the Syrians the two services prepared to ambush Carlos on his arrival in Eastern Europe. But the kidnap attempt was called off because Carlos postponed his trip, worried that the impending Gulf War would make it difficult for him to find his way back into Syria. 'We located him, we saw him, and we missed him,' was all Jacques Fournet, the head of the DST, would say about the new failure.[1]

The DST was forced to be patient. But the alliance of French, American and Syrian intelligence was to hold good. With their first glimpse of a new Syrian stance, Fournet and his service scented success and from then on the chase became obsessive: 'Carlos was a priority every day. Every time we met someone in a position to know something, there was always the question at the end: "Do you know where he is?" or "Can you help us get to him?" We had a moral duty to ask.'[2]

The arcane workings of the French judicial system had been far from Carlos's mind as he struggled to find a safe home outside the Warsaw Pact, and then to establish himself as best he could in Damascus. Nor, for many years, was there much reason to worry because most of the investigations into his crimes were as good as buried. The probes into the *Capitole* train bombing, and into the twin bombings of the high-speed TGV train and the Marseille railway station had been split up among provincial investigating magistrates who had little or no experience of terrorism.

The investigators failed to liaise and lacked an overview of Carlos's organisation. So much so that all three investigations were closed due to lack of evidence. It was only in response to relentless pressure from the victims of terror that French justice finally found a voice.

One such was Françoise Rudetzki who, two days before Christmas 1983, strolled out of the restaurant Le Grand Véfour by the noble arches of the Palais Royal Gardens in Paris with her husband with whom she had spent the evening celebrating their tenth wedding anniversary. Rudetzki was an attractive law graduate of Polish origin who now worked for a clothing company. The couple had a young child whom they had left at home. The bomb which exploded as they walked away from the restaurant slammed her down on to the ground, shards of debris tearing into her legs. Her husband suffered burns and a burst eardrum. Another eight people were hurt.

Françoise Rudetzki's injuries were so serious that doctors suggested amputation of both legs, but she refused. As she fought to be able to walk again, she lost her job and found herself abandoned both by the French state and by French justice. Confined to a wheelchair, she was told by a welfare officer that no benefits existed for victims of terrorist attacks. Nor did she ever find out who had planted the bomb in the restaurant.

Rudetzki's frustration led her to create a forum for those who, like her, had the day, month and year of a terrorist outrage branded into their minds and bodies. SOS Attentats (SOS Attacks) was created in her sitting room 'by victims and for victims'. After a year in which more than a dozen bombings by pro-Iranian Lebanese guerrillas rocked France, starting with an attack on the Galeries Lafayette and Printemps department stores in Paris in December 1985, pressure from SOS Attacks and from judges sympathetic to its cause finally gave France the judicial apparatus it needed if it were ever to bring Carlos to trial.

In what was no less than a legal revolution, a public prosecutor's office set up in Paris in 1986 to deal specifically with counter-terrorism investigations nationwide seized responsibility for probes into all attacks attributed to Carlos. Under the reform, terrorism was finally given a legal definition, police were allowed to detain suspects for four days without charge, and a special assize court was created in which magistrates replaced jurors after one prisoner of the Action Directe guerrilla movement emptied the jury bench with a barrage of threats.

SOS Attacks was granted the right to be represented as a civil plaintiff in any anti-terrorism investigation, allowing it to defend victims with funds from the Justice Ministry, and to follow an enquiry's progress day by day and to speak out if it threatened to stall. Following appeals from Rudetzki, President Mitterrand created a special fund to give victims of terrorism in France, whether French or foreign, the same benefits as those earmarked for individuals wounded in war. The rights won in France for victims of terrorist attacks, and their families, are unmatched in other European countries. 'Victims have mobilised and are waging a battle without hatred or desire for vengeance,' Rudetzki explained dispassionately. 'They are the victims of a new war, but they are all too often forgotten and despised.'[3] After grafts and re-education, she now walks using crutches.

Within a few years the judicial proceedings launched when Carlos shot dead two DST officers and Moukharbal in Paris were finally completed. In late 1990 prosecutors in Paris's anti-terrorism section disinterred a warrant for Carlos's arrest drawn up on 9 January 1976. In July 1991 policemen from the Brigade Criminelle returned to the flat in Rue Toullier – his last known address – with the hopeless aim of notifying him, as the law required, of his upcoming trial. Tried in his absence, he was sentenced in June 1992 to life imprisonment for the Rue Toullier killings, the first sentence ever imposed on him. In a separate investigation into the Rue Marbeuf bombing, lawyers working for SOS Attacks monitored progress and prodded the investigating magistrate to ensure leads were followed up.

Apart from the knowledge that a life behind bars was awaiting him if he were caught on French soil, Carlos must have felt the noose tightening. In late 1990 articles had appeared in the French and German press revealing first the neighbourhood in which he lived in Damascus and the false name he had assumed, and then his precise address together with a photograph of the block of flats, watched over by a scruffy gunman.[4] The sudden spate of stories about him flattered Carlos's ego, but the coverage should have served as a warning. It echoed publication of the address of his Damascus neighbour, Nazi war criminal Alois Brunner, by French Nazi-hunter Serge Klarsfeld. The aim had been to raise the pressure on President al-Assad to expel Brunner.

Carlos's whereabouts had also become of interest to another secret service which, unknown to him, had joined the CIA and the DST in the hunt. In 1991 German intelligence obtained confirmation that Johannes Weinrich was in the Syrian capital with Carlos. Weinrich was betrayed by an empty packet of not-so-lucky Lucky Strike cigarettes which he threw into a wastepaper basket at a Mercedes showroom in Damascus. The empty cigarette packet was retrieved, and passed on to German spies who found his fingerprints on it.

Among the passengers on the Syrian Airlines jumbo jet that landed in Tripoli on the evening of 21 September 1991 were five travellers who had no desire to visit the Libyan capital. But they were careful not to show it. Four of them carried diplomatic passports, the fifth was a five-year-old girl. Their luggage included two Beretta pistols, two hand grenades, ammunition, jewels and a million dollars in cash.

At Tripoli airport a tall figure with a podgy face and a thick moustache handed a Yemeni diplomatic passport in the name of Nagi Abubaker Ahmed to Libyan police. 'We are Palestinians who have been chased out of Syria and we want to settle in Libya,' the diplomat told passport control.[5] As far as the policemen could tell from the passports they were shown, the other adults in the group were Moroccan and Yemeni diplomats. It was an odd jumble of nationalities, and the diplomats were ordered to open their suitcases for inspection. The contents of the suitcases, far from resolving the policemen's doubts, raised yet more questions. The policemen summoned the Syrian consul to the airport, but his intervention failed to win right of entry for Nagi Abubaker Ahmed.

Libyan officials insisted after the episode that they had no idea at the time that the diplomats were in fact Carlos, his wife Magdalena Kopp, his mother Elba Sánchez, and his right-hand man Johannes Weinrich. Only Weinrich, who boasted the best Libyan contacts of the group, was allowed into the country. Tripoli had no desire to accept the others, whom Syria had slyly tried to discard, giving no advance notice of their arrival. Abu Nidal, who had settled in Tripoli after his expulsion from Damascus, was already more than enough for Libyan intelligence to have to cope with. And Qathafi's relations with Washington, at daggers drawn at the best of times, had hit a particularly rocky stretch following the Bush administration's accusations that Libyan nationals carried out the bombings of Pan Am Flight 103 over Lockerbie and a French UTA DC10 over the Sahara.

Carlos owed his (albeit aborted) expulsion from Syria to President al-Assad's hopes for warmer relations with Washington. The role played by Syrian forces in the Gulf War, although it had little military impact, had done much to improve relations with Washington. But Syria was still on the State Department's list of state sponsors of terrorism, a ranking which banned Syria from trading with or receiving aid from the United States. Withdrawing support from the likes of Carlos would also help Washington accept Syria as a player in Arab-Israeli peace talks. Over recent months Carlos's Syrian handler, Colonel Haitham Sa'id, had made it increasingly clear that his presence was a burden. For Carlos, this uncomfortable situation echoed the way the secret services of the Soviet bloc had put pressure on him before evicting him a few years earlier.

Following the débâcle at Tripoli airport, Carlos was made to feel less than welcome on his enforced return to the Syrian capital. The next day incensed Syrian intelligence officers wrecked a Libyan Airlines plane at Damascus airport. Equally enraged by his humiliation – 'we were kicked out like dogs,' was how Kopp later described it – Carlos refused to make things easy for the Syrians. He rejected their suggestion that he settle, at least temporarily, in Lebanon. After only a couple of days in Tripoli, Weinrich had quickly realised that nothing would make the Libyans go back on their decision, and he flew back to join Carlos in Damascus.

After searching for another Arab country that might welcome Carlos, Syria sent him and Kopp in December 1991 to Yemen, which had been unified the previous year when leaders of the Soviet-allied south and of the pro-Western north had agreed to share power in a new state. The couple got as far as the VIP lounge at the airport outside the capital San'a. Appeals from the Yemeni Socialist Party failed to sway the new country's leaders, and within twenty-four hours husband and wife were sent back to Damascus on the same plane. It was only after Carlos had left Yemen that Western intelligence learned of his brief stay. 'We missed him because the Yemenis did not tell us in time,' acknowledged an MI6 officer.

Again with false Yemeni passports – Carlos's, issued by the Yemeni embassy in Damascus, had diplomatic status as usual, this time in the name of Abdurabo Ali Mohamed – he and his family slipped unnoticed and with Syrian complicity into Jordan in late 1991. No one bothered to seek the permission of the authorities in the Jordanian capital Amman. It was not until the summer of 1992 that the Jordanian secret service discovered Carlos's presence. The authorities then granted him a trial period in the country of a few months. But an incident in which, according to his lawyers, Carlos murdered an Iraqi national, soon convinced the Jordanians that he should not be allowed to stay.

Carlos's thirteen-year marriage to Magdalena Kopp, which had been marked by her imprisonment and which had cost France so much suffering, unravelled as their nomadic existence became increasingly precarious. It was Carlos who took the decisive step, abandoning his partner in life and crime for a much younger woman, an attractive Jordanian almost half his age. Although the marriage was effectively in ruins, Carlos was in no position to file for a divorce, even if he had wished to do so. No ugly courtroom battle buried the union in whose name Carlos had waged a dirty, private war. Carlos and Kopp parted as friends within a few weeks of arriving in Jordan. They agreed that Kopp should keep custody of their daughter Elba.

Still on good terms with Carlos's family, the jilted Kopp, accompanied by her daughter and Carlos's mother, flew to Venezuela. Kopp settled in a chic district of Caracas in the east of the city. Carlos's mother, who had been separated from her husband Ramírez Navas for many years, moved in as a neighbour. While the local secret service kept casual watch over the new arrivals, the Carlos clan rallied round Kopp, a single parent in a foreign country. Carlos's father lobbied unsuccessfully for Kopp and her daughter to be granted Venezuelan nationality. Carlos's brother Lenin, who had opted for a more settled career as an electrical engineer, helped Kopp sort out her financial situation.

Carlos's new lover was only twenty-three years old. The

striking and slender Abdel Salam Adhman Jarrar Lana was impressed by the charisma and experience of the forty-two-year-old Venezuelan. Born in Amman and of Palestinian origin, Lana was studying at Damascus University to become a dentist. It is possible that Carlos had met her in the Syrian capital before his move to Jordan. As there was no question of divorcing Kopp, Carlos decided to marry his new love in the Moslem tradition – which permits polygamy – within weeks of his wife and daughter flying to Latin America.[6]

Carlos's travels were far from over. After a short visit to Cyprus, where he renewed his links with Palestinian extremists, Carlos approached the Iranians, but they refused to accept him. Instead, according to his lawyers, they gave him $1.2 million and advised him to try another Moslem fundamentalist country, Sudan. Issawe's separate negotiations with guerrillas of the pro-Iranian Hezbollah, and with the extremist Hamas movement to find Carlos a home in Lebanon's lush Bekaa Valley wedged between snow-peaked mountains, also failed. Syria, the master of the valley which had long also been fertile ground for a host of guerrilla movements, scuppered Issawe's attempts. With nowhere else to go, Carlos finally flew to Sudan with Lana, Weinrich and Issawe in the autumn of 1993.

For the fun-loving Carlos, Sudan was a particularly insalubrious place to end up. A thinly populated territory that is mainly desert and has few natural resources, Africa's biggest nation stretches across nearly 1.5 million square kilometres south of Egypt and Libya, and has a short strip of coastline on the Red Sea. A Cook's guidebook published in 1929 had praised attractions such as big-game hunting in the swamps and jungles of the White Nile. The mud-walled native towns and coarse-thatched villages, the Cook's guide enthused, 'convey that sense of Africa which formerly could only be experienced by hardy travellers and explorers'. Prosperity and peace marked the entire territory, then administered by Anglo-Egyptian authorities, 'and wherever that authority runs a traveller may penetrate without fear of molestation'. The capital Khartoum was also deemed worthy of an accolade: 'the rapidity of its economic and social advance has transformed it from a waste to one of the most agreeable residential cities of Africa'.[7]

By 1993 Sudan had little in common with those rosy days when the population was 'peaceful and contented'. The military dictatorship which seized power in June 1989 in a pre-dawn coup had turned the country into the biggest Moslem fundamentalist bastion in Africa and the Arab world. Its rulers dreamed of spreading revolution across Moslem lands and beyond in partnership with Iran. Alcohol and adultery, no strangers to Carlos, were punished by flagellation and stoning to death under Sudan's 'an eye for an eye, a tooth for a tooth' penal code based on the Islamic Shari'a law.[8] This harshness was a corruption of the austere, mystical and tolerant version of Islam which had endured in Sudan for many decades.

Since the 1989 *coup d'état* Sudan's authorities had perpetrated, in the words of an Amnesty International report, virtually every kind of human rights violation, with widespread torture of prisoners of conscience in what locals gruesomely called 'ghost houses'. Popular techniques of torture included crushing the testicles of detainees with pliers, and stabbing pins or screwdrivers into genitals.[9] United Nations observers described summary executions, disappearances, torture and a child slave trade.[10]

The poverty-stricken population in the south of the country, an area mostly controlled by the rebel Sudan People's Liberation Army (SPLA), a mainly Christian movement, was burdened with one of Africa's ugliest civil wars. In the past decade this racist and religious conflict between an Islamic Arab north and an African Christian and animist south had claimed 1.3 million lives. There were few prisoners since both sides routinely killed any captives taken during combat.

A pariah state, its isolation compounded by its support for Iraq in the Gulf War, Sudan appeared in August 1993 on the American State Department's list of state sponsors of terrorism, alongside Syria, Iran, Iraq, Libya, North Korea and Cuba, and as a result Washington halted all aid save for emergency humanitarian relief. The State Department's annual report on global terrorism trends for that year identified Sudan as a sanctuary for Abu Nidal, Hezbollah, Hamas and the Palestinian Islamic Jihad, making it 'a convenient transit point, meeting site and safe haven for Iranian-backed extremist groups'.[11]

The official Sudanese version of Carlos's arrival was that he furtively entered Khartoum on a Jordanian diplomatic passport using a false name. A dusty city with about six hundred thousand inhabitants, the Sudanese capital boasted broad boulevards lined by trees and by buildings whose features often harked back to Britain's imperial presence. On the outskirts of Khartoum, refugees from the civil war crowded into vast slums. The Sudanese claim they knew nothing of Carlos's real identity, and opened a file on the mysterious individual under the code-name 'The Ghost'. Sudanese security agents who investigated the visitor, according to this version, were alerted by his 'suspicious activities and plans for terrorist plots against some foreign institutions in Sudan'. It was only thanks to French intelligence at a later stage, the Sudanese maintained, that they found out who the Ghost was.

The truth is that the Sudanese identified Carlos themselves, with the help of a vigilant prostitute who, intrigued by his accent, reported him to the police without knowing who he was. Carlos was welcomed with open arms as a noble defender of the Palestinian cause by the country's power behind the throne: sixty-one-year-old Sheikh

Hassan al-Turabi, an ideologue who had drafted the new penal code. Blackballed by most Arab and African governments as the leader of an Islamist international movement fostering armed rebellion in Egypt and in war-stricken Algeria and Afghanistan, the slender, bearded al-Turabi was a confusing blend of Western education and Moslem fundamentalist doctrine. Educated in London and at the Sorbonne, a law professor, author of religious treatises – *Prayer and its incidence on the life of individuals*; *Prayer, pillar of religion*; and *Dialogue of religion and art* – he freely admitted to borrowing from Machiavelli to shape his conviction that the end justified the means, where the end was the reign of Islam.

The support of al-Turabi, whose power derived from the Moslem Brothers activists whom he had infiltrated into the government, the military and academia, opened Khartoum's doors to Carlos. Al-Turabi appointed his own security adviser, Sadik Mohamed Babikri, to look after Carlos's needs.[12] Initially Carlos and Lana stayed at the Grand Hotel overlooking the Blue Nile, but Carlos was soon provided with a large flat on Africa Road in a new district near the airport. The flat was disappointingly ugly. Decorated with cheap prints of still-life paintings, the sitting room had as its main feature a large metal bookcase straining under the weight of boxes of Johnnie Walker whisky and packs of beer cans.

Al-Turabi asked Carlos to use his contacts to help supply arms to the government troops fighting the rebels in the south. Carlos also lectured at the local military academies where he was billed as an expert on strategic affairs. However, Carlos hoped that from his new base in Sudan he would be able to work for the Iranians, plotting attacks against opposition figures abroad or at the worst helping to train guerrillas in the Sudanese camps run by the Iranians.

Carlos came alive at night. He and his new wife led a busy social life in Khartoum, posing as a Jordanian couple,

Lana and Abdallah Barakhat. In love and making no attempt to hide the fact, according to friends, they flitted from nightclubs to parties and wedding receptions, driven by an armed bodyguard. Both Carlos and Lana were regulars at the exclusive clubs reserved for foreigners and the Sudanese establishment, where contraband alcohol could be purchased under the table for an extravagant fee. At the Armenian and Syrian clubs in the New Extension area south of the city centre, and at the Greek Apollo club, Carlos would order a bottle, tip the waiter generously, then fall into conversation with his neighbours for whom he would pour a drink. The Armenian nightclub was Carlos's favourite haunt, where he would sip whisky while Lana performed a belly-dance. Fridays usually saw him at the Filipino club for the weekly cockfighting.

Benedict Fultang, the local representative of the UN's World Food Programme who lived above Carlos and Lana, ensured that both were accepted at the Diplomats' Club. With his youthful experience of such gatherings in London, Carlos fitted in easily. 'He was a very lovable guy. Entertaining and nice to everybody,' Fultang said of him. Judging by his lifestyle, Carlos felt safe in Khartoum. But his infatuation with Lana eventually waned somewhat, and he started a public affair with a middle-aged general's widow, Zeinab Sulieman, who owned a crafts and jewellery shop.

After the failure to catch Carlos during the Gulf War, the Central Intelligence Agency had promised its French allies that it would not let the trail go cold. Within weeks of Carlos's arrival in the Sudanese capital, the Syrian secret service told the Americans of his whereabouts.

Sudan was unfamiliar and hostile territory for the Central Intelligence Agency. To check the Syrian report that Carlos was living in Khartoum, Langley's Directorate of Operations, the clandestine wing whose actions have made the CIA notorious, sent a team of black officers to the Sudanese capital. They spent several weeks following Carlos and even managed to get acquainted with him. After a round of drinks at the Armenian club, one of the CIA spies pocketed Carlos's empty glass when he had his back turned. The fingerprints on the glass were sent for analysis and gave the CIA unit positive confirmation that the man it had tailed, and had had a few drinks with, was Carlos. However, the rules barring the Americans from too pre-eminent a role as US justice was not concerned with Carlos still applied, and there was no question of sending him exploding cigars or any similar offerings, as the agency had once tried to do with Fidel Castro. It was therefore time to tell the French who, it was felt by American intelligence, more than deserved a favour after their help in the Gulf War.

To help track down Carlos, the CIA had also recruited an informer with a murky past. The agent, who has not been precisely identified, was a retired terrorist who had been involved in two bombings in Europe in the mid-1980s. The casualties of those attacks included Americans. As Clarridge, who two decades earlier had tried to hire an informer to assassinate Carlos, explained: 'Sometimes in the spy business you don't have a choice with whom you deal; unfortunately, it is often the unsavoury individuals who have the critical information.'[13]

Long before Carlos's arrival in Khartoum, the Sudanese and French intelligence communities had forged discreet links. Despite Sudan's status as an outcast nation, and ignoring Washington's disapproval, the French DGSE secret service had negotiated a secret agreement in 1989 to help the new Sudanese government in its war against the southern rebels.

The pact forged by Colonel Jean-Claude Mantion of the DGSE provided the Sudanese army with a right of way along a ten kilometre-wide corridor running through the Central African Republic, a country where the colonel officiated as viceroy in all but name as a special adviser to President André Kolingba. In exchange for the chance to harass the rebel forces from behind, Khartoum pledged not to spread its Moslem fundamentalist crusade to the Central African Republic. The pact held, even when the Sudanese army deliberately shot down a plane belonging to the charity Médecins Sans Frontières (Doctors Without Borders), killing three French doctors who had volunteered to work in the disputed south.

True to its tradition of poaching on its rival's territory, the DST had also befriended the country which was at the crossroads of Islam and black Africa. Counter-intelligence chief Jacques Fournet, who established those ties, believed that talking with the devil was always better than having to deal with him in other ways. 'I have a saying,' Fournet candidly explained. 'There are no true friends, there are no true enemies, but there are common interests.'[14] For the French, Sudan was of more than passing interest because it bordered Chad and the Central African Republic, both seen as part of Paris's self-attributed zone of influence in Africa. American and British hostility towards Sudan was all the more reason to leap into the breach. From an uncertain beginning, the contacts prospered.

Both the DST and the DGSE invited senior members of the Sudanese intelligences services – the Directorate of Military Intelligence, and the civilian Foreign Security Service – to Paris. The DST both trained several Sudanese officers, who were particularly interested in communications equipment, and supplied information on the latest systems and sold French-made equipment to the Sudanese. Not to be outdone, the DGSE supplied the Sudanese with satellite photographs of positions held by the rebels. The tip-off from the CIA on Carlos's whereabouts gave the French a chance to exploit their special relationship with the Sudanese.

There was no question about which French intelligence

officer should latch on to Carlos. Philippe Rondot, the spy who had followed Carlos's trail to Algiers, Colombia and Malta in the 1970s, and had never given up on the possibility of catching him, was a natural choice for the mission. Rondot's army début in the Algerian war, after graduating from the prestigious Saint-Cyr military school, fanned a passion for the Arab world which he had inherited from his father, who had set up the Syrian police force when the country was under a French mandate. Rondot's Middle Eastern expertise was among the qualities that got him into the French secret service. And it was Rondot's task of monitoring pro-Palestinian guerrillas as a member of the Action Service that first prompted his interest in Carlos.

But Rondot's career in French intelligence was chequered. Shortly after the botched attempt to catch Carlos in Algiers, about which he had protested on his return to Paris, Rondot had suffered his greatest blow. SDECE chief Count de Marenches sacked Rondot in 1977. The official reason for the dismissal was that Rondot had failed to justify an absence of forty-eight hours from his office as deputy station chief at the French embassy in Bucharest. But as the episode was ten years old, it is more likely that Rondot was the victim of a plot by rivals within the intelligence service. Rondot's demand in the early 1980s that he be reinstated by de Marenches's successor, Pierre Marion, was rejected, partly because of his reputation among Marion's closest aides as a fiercely independent spirit with a caustic, often cutting wit. It was not until 1984 that Rondot's name was cleared.

In the meantime the spy turned scholar. Rondot took a doctorate in political sociology and published university manuals on Syria, Jordan and Iraq, contributed to a *World Atlas of Activist Islam*, and to a French encyclopaedia. A year after his name had been cleared he was back in print with an essay entitled 'On the Correct Usage of the Special Services' in which, quoting John le Carré among others, he defended French intelligence in the wake of the scandal prompted by the sinking of the Greenpeace ship *Rainbow Warrior*, arguing that covert operations 'are no better nor worse than the foreign policy which they are designed to support'.[15]

A spy for all seasons at the service of governments of right and left, Rondot was so dedicated to the French state that he wrote the word 'France' in capitals in his letters and proclaimed himself ready to take responsibility if things went wrong: 'It is an inescapable law ... People like me must under no circumstances, in a critical situation, risk compromising the government.'[16] He had carefully avoided doing so on several delicate assignments. President Mitterrand sent him to negotiate with Iraqi intelligence after the 1982 Goldenberg restaurant killings and Rondot helped to engineer the expulsion of Abu Nidal – whom he is said to have met – from Baghdad to Damascus. A decade later, in August 1991, promoted as adviser to the Defence Minister and given the rank of general, he saved the life of General Michel Aoun, extracting him from Beirut where he had been held hostage by the Syrians. Rondot's successes persuaded the DST to hire him in 1993 as a Middle East troubleshooter, the only military officer in the counter-espionage service. In the words of the DST chief who took him on board, Rondot was 'tremendously mysterious but he has a fabulous visiting card – his Arab contacts'.[17]

None of Rondot's varied pursuits had distracted him from keeping a watching brief on intelligence reports involving Carlos, and when the DST requested Rondot's assistance he had no doubt about whether he should accept. The fifty-seven-year-old Rondot packed his bags and flew to Khartoum. Shadowing Carlos from a safe distance, and on one occasion sitting in a café only a few tables away, Rondot watched for any routine that he could exploit. The Frenchman noted Carlos's habit of leaving Lana at home while he sought female company in nightclubs, and his purchases of bottles of Scotch which he paid for with new, large-denomination dollar bills. 'If I had drunk as much as he did, my liver would have bust,' Rondot said later. 'I've gone undercover myself, and it's not by going whoring that you stay hidden.' The officer noted Carlos's stay in a private Khartoum hospital where he underwent liposuction to remove fat from around his waist.

It quickly became obvious to Rondot that Carlos was in Khartoum with the consent of the Sudanese authorities, and his enquiries soon revealed that the men to talk to were Sheikh Hassan al-Turabi and General Hachim Abou Zeid, the head of the Sudanese military secret service. However, Rondot's first contacts with the Sudanese authorities were disappointing. When he explained what had brought him to Khartoum, the Sudanese denied any knowledge of Carlos's presence.

Rondot needed proof of Carlos's presence. He found it by taking a photograph of Carlos with a concealed camera fitted with a telephoto lens. The picture shows a puffy-faced, paunchy man with a moustache and tousled hair, spectacles hanging from a chain around his neck, as he crosses between two parked cars in the street outside the Ibn Khaldoun hospital. Carlos is looking down and his brow is slightly furrowed in a worried expression. It was a grainy picture, but clear enough to counter the denials of the Sudanese. Together with the evidence supplied by the CIA, the photograph enabled the French army officer to make progress. The Sudanese officials were forced to admit, at least implicitly, that they had been lying. The French were ready to talk business.

If there is one remark for which the earthy Interior Minister Charles Pasqua will be remembered by his French countrymen, it is the gruff pledge he made in a parliamentary speech at the time of the mid-1980s bombings: 'We must terrorise the terrorists.'

The chance to do just that with Carlos was timely for the ambitious sixty-seven-year-old 'Charlie la matraque' (Truncheon Charlie), who had his eye on the prime ministership. The right-wing Pasqua built his reputation as the scourge of Moslem and other terrorists with controversial coups such as the bloody liberation of hostages held in a grotto in New Caledonia in 1988. Many such successes were due to Pasqua's opaque network of personal and business links which stretched across much of Africa and the Middle East.

Pasqua's idiosyncratic negotiating skills baffled the CIA. 'Pasqua was flexible when dealing with terrorists, or with countries supporting terrorists. It depended on France's relations with that country: he could either be tough, or he could cut a deal. You never knew if there wasn't another level on which things were going on,' said the CIA's Clarridge, who had dealt with Pasqua in the mid-1980s.[18] When Paris was rocked by a series of bombings the Americans helped to supply Pasqua, who was Interior Minister at the time, with the technology to find a large cache of explosives hidden by Shiite fundamentalists in the Fontainebleau Forest south of the French capital. Despite the CIA's pleas for discretion Pasqua publicly thanked Washington for its assistance. The affair left Clarridge embittered. But a decade later Langley was in forgiving mood, and it was to the DST – which answered to Pasqua – that the Americans revealed their knowledge of Carlos's refuge.

Publicly, Pasqua described Carlos as 'a true professional of terrorism, a mercenary' and 'one of my priority objectives for a long time'. But he explained his failure to catch him somewhat weakly: 'In the course of his adventures, he often changed countries. He never stayed long enough for us to spot him and act'.[19] The truth was that Pasqua had so far shown little interest in Carlos. But now the DST was telling him that Carlos might be caught, if the right price were paid.

With Pasqua's encouragement, negotiations with the Sudanese secret service were intensified shortly after the first sighting of Carlos in Khartoum. Pasqua, notorious for his crackdowns on Moslems suspected of fundamentalist sympathies, has admitted that he met the Sudanese intelligence head, General Abou Zeid, when the latter was invited by him to Paris in December 1993.[20] Carlos was the main item on the agenda. Pasqua's initiative ruffled feathers in the French intelligence community and much further afield. As former DGSE head Claude Silberzahn observed: 'The official Republic should not negotiate on such a subject with a country which has become one of the essential supports of terrorism (it is no coincidence that Carlos found refuge there!).'[21] The American State Department's assistant secretary for African affairs, George Moose, lodged a protest on a visit to Paris in January 1994, spotlighting the training given to Sudanese intelligence officers whom the United States believed to be behind terrorist attacks.

On the evening of 30 December 1993, on the eve of New Year celebrations, the office of Prime Minister Edouard Balladur issued a communiqué over which it had been prevaricating for months. It announced that he had decided not to extradite two Iranian terrorists to Switzerland, Ahmad Taheri and Mohsen Sharif Esfahani, who had been held in a French jail since their arrest in November 1992. Instead they were put on a flight to Tehran. The announcement meant freedom for two suspected murderers who, according to Swiss investigators, were part of the thirteen-strong squad that had ambushed a prominent critic of the Iranian régime, Kazem Rajavi, as he drove through the Swiss canton of Vaud at midday on 24 April 1990. Seconds after two cars blocked his way, six bullets tore into his body. Kazem Rajavi was a former Iranian ambassador to the United Nations, a gifted orator and a tireless challenger of Tehran's human rights record.

The French decision was baffling, not least to the Swiss who had been notified the previous month to expect the two Iranians soon. All the paperwork had been completed. Prime Minister Balladur had signed a decree in August ordering their extradition, the Swiss were told, after French courts recommended such a move. But the handover had been delayed twice. In Swiss eyes, a positive response to their request for extradition was all the more natural as Switzerland had some two years earlier braved Iranian anger to send France two Iranian agents linked with the stabbing to death of the shah's last Prime Minister, Shapour Bakhtiar, at his home outside Paris.

The Swiss were so shocked that they dropped their ever-cautious neutrality to complain that they 'deeply regretted' such a flagrant violation of international legal convention, although promptly adding that they considered the incident closed, and that there was no question of it jeopardising the country's excellent relations with France. Iranian dissidents who had sought refuge in France were less willing to forgive and forget, and accused Balladur of effectively encouraging more assassinations within their ranks.

'The national interest' was the mysterious explanation. 'I ask to be trusted on this point, if it is not asking too much,' murmured the urbane Prime Minister. Unnamed 'sources' within the government told the press that France was desperate to avoid any repetition of the Iranian-sponsored terrorist onslaught on the streets of Paris which had left thirteen people dead and another 300 wounded in 1985–6. Washington demanded an explanation. 'Keep your secrets secret,' Pasqua replied, adding sardonically: 'I am not an employee of Mr Clinton.' The explanations were a smokescreen, and the reticence of the French leaders natural. For 'the national interest' read 'Carlos'.

While Rondot conducted his negotiations in Khartoum, Pasqua had opened another front to prise Carlos out of the city. The Interior Minister did not need to look very far in his search for a potential ally. The only régime that might intervene, he concluded, was Iran. The ideology of its mullahs had much in common with that of the Sudanese leaders, and Iran treated Sudan as its bridgehead on the African continent. Iran regularly sent to Sudan guerrillas belonging to Hezbollah – which had carried out the October 1983 suicide bombing on US marine barracks in Beirut, killing 241 American and fifty-eight French soldiers – to train and prepare for attacks on the 'Godless West'.

Several training camps in Sudan were run by Iran's Revolutionary Guards, and according to US intelligence Sudan helped Tehran smuggle arms to Moslem fundamentalist guerrillas in Algeria. French intelligence believed Sudan was the only country to send army officers and air force pilots to train in Tehran. Iran and Sudan had common enemies: the United States, Egypt and Saudi Arabia. Iran supplied Sudan with petrol and economic aid, and paid for its purchases of arms from Communist China.

Prime Minister Balladur's decision to send the two Iranian suspected murderers home (which earned him a sharp but ineffectual reprimand from France's highest administrative court, the Council of State) was in fact the result of hard lobbying by Pasqua. As described by officials involved in the Carlos negotiations, the Interior Minister's secret gamble followed signals from Iran that the safe delivery of the pair would encourage them to urge Sudan to abandon Carlos. 'The Iranians are difficult partners, they don't give anything for nothing,' a senior Sudanese official who took part in the Carlos negotiations remarked. Iran had few links with Carlos, and stood to lose little should he ever decide to talk about his past.[22]

In early July 1994, after playing the Iranian card, Pasqua had finally succeeded in meeting Carlos's chief protector. Sheikh Hassan al-Turabi had played hard to get, and mediators had shuttled back and forth for months until he at last accepted an invitation to meet Pasqua in Paris. At their encounter, al-Turabi protested that giving up a guest who had sought asylum amounted to treachery. Pasqua promised diplomatic help to break Sudan's isolation if Carlos were handed over, saying that France would lobby on Sudan's behalf within the International Monetary Fund and the World Bank to ensure that loans were granted to Sudan despite the objections of the United States. A promise to gradually erase Sudan's foreign debt was also thrown in.

Pasqua had over-reached himself. The pledges which the Interior Minister made were in fact within the domain of the French Foreign Minister, Alain Juppé. Had Pasqua sought the endorsement of his counterpart with whom he had poor personal relations, he would have been certain of a frosty reception. The Foreign Ministry gave short shrift to any challenges to its jealously guarded supremacy over the nation's global interests. The promises Pasqua made were effectively stillborn. As one of Pasqua's favourite sayings ran: 'In politics, promises commit only those who believe in them'.

The French were not alone on Carlos's trail. The Egyptian secret service, which was much more hostile to the Sudanese, had also discovered his whereabouts. The pressure on the Sudanese mounted. 'The fact that several secret services knew about Carlos meant that resolving his fate became a race against time,' explained a Sudanese official. 'Carlos became a bomb waiting to explode, and what's more at a time when the Americans and the Egyptians were accusing Sudan of sheltering terrorists. We could give Carlos to a Western country, or we could keep him and run the risk that his presence would be exposed and Sudan would be denounced.'

It was from Cairo that Rondot obtained a video made secretly by an Egyptian spy at a private party. It gave Rondot a chance to study his quarry at leisure. Rondot played it back again and again, looking for any clues and etching Carlos's physique and mannerisms into his mind.

The video shows a reception in which middle-aged guests are jammed elbow-to-elbow at long narrow tables in a marquee. The women wear their jewels, the men are mostly in suits. A couple of children run around restlessly. There is no alcohol on the tables, only bottled mineral water clustered around a single white carnation. The camera pans across the crowded tables and stops, zooming in on one couple who stand out because the man is better groomed than the other male guests, and she is quite simply the most beautiful young woman there.

There is no trace of the would-be Che Guevara look-alike. Carlos's greying hair is cropped short and neatly combed, his face has filled out and his looks and bearing are those of a flashy Mafioso rather than a revolutionary. His pale face has been well scrubbed and the stiff, spotless collar of his white shirt cuts slightly into his fleshy bull-neck, around which he has tied a polka-dot ascot scarf. In the breast pocket of his dark jacket is a matching handkerchief. A long white cigarette dangles from his mouth. Lana, a smooth-skinned brunette with long hair and a small pert nose, is wearing a low-cut white dress and a brown jacket, with a gold necklace. She sits with her lips pursed, and her big dark eyes roll across the room with a soulful expression. She looks bored.

Carlos suddenly springs to life. He has caught sight of the camera, and abruptly raises his right hand. To his companions it looks as if he is simply hailing a friend. But at the same time he leans backwards in his chair to hide behind his neighbour. It is a crafty move: the gesture to grab the cameraman's notice, and the shift backwards to show that he has no wish to appear on film. The camera swings away, but Carlos has shaken off the unwelcome attention only temporarily and when the lens is again pointed at him, he no longer seems to care, staring into the camera for a time.

When he escorts Lana to the dance floor, Carlos walks in a stiff, dignified way a few feet behind her. Totally at ease, he waves at a friend who has just called out to him. The music has little in common with the tunes he danced to as a young man in Paris's Latin Quarter, but after fussing with the handkerchief in his breast pocket he sways to Arab pop music with a smug smile on his face, a thickset man with a receding hairline and a sweaty forehead towering above the slim young Lana who every so often self-consciously shakes away a strand of hair which has fallen across her face.

It was not the only time that Carlos was captured on camera in Khartoum. At another private party in June he was filmed for two minutes by an amateur who caught him swinging his hips to the Lambada. Aware of the camera but apparently not unduly worried, Carlos however does make sure he never faces it.[23]

Carlos's drinking, partying and his all-too-public love affairs were too much for al-Turabi. In the first half of August the Sudanese leader gave up on any hopes of using Carlos. 'We're going to deliver Carlos up in the next few days,' al-Turabi told a senior Sudanese official. 'We welcomed him as a combatant, someone who had fought for the Palestinian cause, for noble causes. Now he's a hoodlum, his behaviour is shameful. He drinks and goes out with women so much that I don't even know whether he's a Moslem. Given that his presence has become a real danger we are going to hand him over. We have no regrets. Because of his behaviour, we are absolved from blame.'

A year after Carlos's arrival in Khartoum the Sudanese bowed to French demands, but insisted that no harm should befall Carlos because they feared that reprisals might follow their decision to abandon him. The French had proved themselves the highest bidders, and Rondot and the DST were given the green light. Carlos was theirs.

12

Betrayal and Revenge

> If you know the enemy and know yourself, you need not fear a hundred battles. If you know yourself and not the enemy, for every victory you will suffer a defeat. If you know neither yourself nor the enemy, you are a fool and will meet defeat in every battle.
> – Sixth-century BC Chinese General Sun-Tzu,
> *The Art of War*

For all her charms and the love she showed him, Lana could not make up for the loss of Carlos's daughter, hustled away by Magdalena Kopp to Venezuela. Little Elbita wrote letters in Spanish overflowing with childish affection for her 'Uncle Ilich'. According to his friends, Carlos had always loved having children around and the loss of Elbita greatly affected him. Carlos made no secret of his desire for another child, and Lana was more than willing to bear him one.

Vanity had brought the forty-five-year-old Carlos to the operating theatre for liposuction a few months earlier, but now he discovered he must return to hospital if he were to have any chance of starting a second family. Doctors at the Ibn Khaldoun hospital in Khartoum had diagnosed a low sperm count, caused by varicocele in his right testicle, a condition not unusual in middle-aged men, where the veins of the spermatic cord multiply and become distended rather like varicose veins. Carlos agreed with alacrity to undergo a minor operation, all the more so given that the hot weather heightened the pain caused by the varicocele, giving rise to a dragging sensation in the affected mass of veins which doctors inelegantly likened to a bag of worms.

A short stay in hospital was no reason for Carlos to relax his guard. He was given permission to station bodyguards in the corridor outside his private room, and in another waiver of hospital rules Lana was allowed to spend the night before the operation with him. The surgery, carried out under general anaesthetic during the afternoon of Saturday, 13 August went well and Carlos was wheeled back to his room where Lana watched over him as he emerged from the anaesthetic.

Carlos had still not completely recovered his senses when a uniformed visitor walked past the bodyguards and into the private room. He introduced himself as a member of Sudan's criminal investigation department. Even in his dazed state, Carlos realised that the news that the officer imparted was worrying: Sudanese police had uncovered a plot to murder Carlos. As Carlos needed time to recover from the operation, the officer urged him to agree to be transferred under armed escort to a military hospital where he would be better protected. It was only a temporary measure, the officer assured him. His sketchy answers to the questions put by Carlos and Lana left them none the wiser about the murder plot, but Carlos could not refuse the offer of improved protection.

An armed escort awaited the couple outside the Ibn Khaldoun hospital, but it did not take them to the military hospital. Someone in authority had apparently ordered a last-minute change of plan. Instead Carlos and Lana were whisked to the Sudanese State Security headquarters. There, Dr Nafaa, a deputy director whom Carlos had never met before, gave them a few more details of the plans for their improved security. Again with Carlos's agreement, a convoy took him and his young wife to an empty villa in the Taif neighbourhood on the edge of Khartoum, which Carlos knew to be close to the home of Sheikh Hassan al-Turabi.

Carlos and Lana were far from enthusiastic about their refuge. Although the villa looked fine from the outside, it was in poor condition and shabby inside. The only possessions they had with them were what they had taken from the hospital. They spent an uncomfortable night with Carlos suffering from the stitches in his testicle. On Sunday morning both were eager to return home. But insistent questioning of the bodyguards lounging about the villa proved pointless. Nor was Carlos given any information by a doctor who called briefly to check on his recovery. The couple eventually accepted they would be spending a second night in unfamiliar surroundings. About ten o'clock that evening when the sweltering heat of the day had abated, Carlos, in no state to go himself, despatched Lana with a driver to fetch some belongings from their flat on Africa Road.

Lana did not return quickly, and, still suffering from the after-effects of surgery, Carlos gave up waiting for her and went to bed. It was about three o'clock in the morning when he felt the breath punched out of his lungs and his limbs were pinned to the mattress. Shock and fear snapped him fully awake but he was given no opportunity to reach for the gun that he always kept by his bedside. As he writhed impotently beneath the weight of his assailants, Carlos recognised his Sudanese bodyguards among the dozen or so men crowding into the bedroom. His arms were forced behind his back and handcuffs clicked shut on his wrists. Fetters were clamped around his ankles. A hood was slipped over his head. However, the hood was too thin to stop him following what was happening.

Carlos made out a Sudanese army doctor – he noted that he bore the rank of major – approaching him clutching a hypodermic syringe. Carlos, who had never lost his childhood fear of needles, was forced to lie motionless as the doctor stabbed the needle into his thigh. Poison, he thought for a brief moment. But one of his assailants reassured him that it was only a tranquilliser. Within minutes Carlos felt its effect start to take hold as he was picked up and carried out of the villa to a waiting van. Unceremoniously, he was bundled inside and laid on a stretcher.

After a short drive at high speed through Khartoum's deserted but ill-lit streets, the van pulled up abruptly. By this time the tranquilliser should have sent Carlos to sleep, but somehow he had steeled his body to fight the drug and managed to stay awake. His mind racing for clues to his fate, Carlos heard the whine of jet engines. When the rear door opened he saw that the van was parked on the tarmac of Khartoum airport near a small plane with no markings. All he could tell was that it was an 'executive-type' jet. A few moments after he had been carried up the steps and the door banged shut behind him, the plane taxied to the runway and took off.

As the jet climbed sharply, the men watching Carlos finally realised that the hood was too thin. Another, woollen hood was placed over his head. When Carlos motioned that he was suffocating, the new hood was lifted slightly to free his mouth. The gesture was only a brief respite. With one more affront to his dignity, Carlos was inserted feet first into a large, thick jute sack. With only his head sticking out of the sack, leather thongs were pulled tight around his feet, knees and shoulders. ('He was tied up like a sausage' one of Carlos's lawyers related later.)

The last thing his abductors wanted was for Carlos to recover his strength, and throughout the six-and-a-half-hour flight no food or drink was offered to him. Still battling against the effects of the tranquilliser and trying to work out who had snatched him, Carlos heard people talking in low voices in English. 'Well done,' Carlos said, struggling to make himself heard above the drone of the jet's engines.

'You must be Americans.' But the brusque answer he received was French, and revealed a trace of Gallic pride: '*Non.* You are on French territory.'[1]

Carlos was in the hands of General Philippe Rondot and a team from the DST. The plane flying him to Paris was a Dassault Mystère Falcon of the GLAM fleet, the Groupement de liaison aérienne ministérielle, officially reserved for government ministers and, as was later revealed in a minor scandal, all too often used unofficially for their wives or mistresses who disdained commoner, public forms of transport.

To have the team initially speak English was a perfidious touch of Interior Minister Charles Pasqua. A country whose governments wage continuous war on perceived Anglo-Saxon linguistic and cultural imperialism had exceptionally ordered the secret servicemen to speak English, to trick Carlos into thinking that Mossad had come for him. 'Carlos had flattered himself before his arrest that he had killed Israeli spies,' Pasqua explained. 'With the DST men speaking English he could think that he was in the hands of the Israelis, who are credited with this kind of operation more readily than the French.'[2]

But when the counter-espionage team saw that their operation was drawing to a successful close, one of them could not help crowing: '*Ça y est, Pascal, on y est!*' (That's it, Pascal, we're there!). Moments later the Mystère landed at Villacoublay, a military airport outside Paris. Rondot handed Carlos over to a fresh DST team, who threw him into an estate car. Someone covered Carlos with a blanket, and two men sat on top of him. One of them gripped his head tightly, forcing it down against the floor of the car although Carlos was still trussed up in the jute sack.

It was not until the car was inside the DST's headquarters, in the shadow of the Eiffel Tower, that France formally revealed itself to Carlos as the power that had captured him. He was served with a national arrest warrant issued by Judge Jean-Louis Bruguière, the investigating magistrate who had been specialising in anti-terrorism ever since the massacre at the Goldenberg restaurant in 1982.[3] For the DST there was no question of Carlos going straight to prison. The sight of a cowed Carlos brought through its gates in handcuffs and shackles, nineteen years and forty-nine days after the shooting of Commissaire Herranz, Inspector Dous and Inspector Donatini, was too gratifying to miss.

In its desire to settle old scores, the DST did not hesitate to take several liberties with French law, before hastily attempting to mask its cavalier approach. According to the official records of Carlos's abduction drawn up by the DST, he boarded the flight to the Villacoublay military airbase of his own volition. In the first report, Commissaire Poussel writes that he was on duty at counter-intelligence headquarters on 15 August when at a quarter past ten in the morning he was 'advised by our hierarchy that an individual who might be identifiable as Ilich Ramírez Sánchez alias Carlos, born in 1949 in Caracas, Venezuela, originating from Sudan, was reportedly at Villacoublay'.[4]

According to Poussel's report, he reached the airport at half past ten and, having found out that the traveller carried no passport nor any other identity papers, ordered his transfer to headquarters.[5] Poussel's report makes no attempt to explain how he was able to check whether Carlos was carrying any documents at the time, given the fact that the suspect 'resting' on the tarmac at the foot of the Mystère's steps was trussed up in a narrow sack that covered him up to his neck, his hands handcuffed behind his back, and his head covered by two hoods.[6]

France had violated both national and international law. It had failed to demand Carlos's extradition from Sudan by legal means, and there was no French arrest warrant to justify his seizure. The arrest warrant issued for the Rue Toullier killings was out of date, and that for the Rue

Marbeuf bombing – the only Carlos probe that had not been shelved – was valid only within France.

It is an interesting coincidence that Judge Bruguière had issued the Marbeuf warrant only three months earlier, in June. By issuing a national warrant, the process of going through Interpol to obtain Carlos's extradition from Sudan was avoided. To do so would have given Carlos plenty of time to slip away.

At midday, confronting members of the DST for the first time since he had shot three of them in the Rue Toullier, Carlos was in combative mood. 'I am an international revolutionary,' he proclaimed proudly.[7] His fingerprints were taken – something that could have been done at the jail – and compared to those found on the whisky glasses in Rue Toullier, and to those on the threatening letter he had written to Interior Minister Defferre after the arrests of Kopp and Bréguet. By two o'clock in the afternoon the DST was sure it had the right man. Carlos was escorted to the maximum-security prison, the oddly named La Santé (Health) jail some way south of the Latin Quarter and Rue Toullier.

This was much too hasty, according to Yves Bonnet, the DST chief who had tried to assassinate Carlos in a Swiss Alpine resort in 1982. Elected to parliament as a conservative in 1993, he was careful not to spoil the DST's celebrations at the time of the snatch and kept his misgivings to himself. But later he gave vent to his frustration. 'The only thing which interested us in Carlos, and which justified our arresting him instead of liquidating him physically, was the identification of his accomplices, the people who got him out of France after Rue Toullier,' Bonnet argued. 'Instead of bringing him back with a great fanfare, we should have concealed him somewhere and questioned him. A villain, a bastard like Carlos, we should have beaten him up and tortured him. I have no problems with him being hit with a truncheon. It would have lasted a month or three months, but Carlos wouldn't have left the DST cellars without spilling the beans. Now we will never know.'[8]

The news of Carlos's capture pulled Pasqua out of bed at half past four that Sunday morning. But Pasqua begrudged no one the lack of sleep. With Carlos not yet at La Santé, the Interior Minister called a news conference. Pasqua did not have to share the spotlight since Rondot had firmly declined an invitation to join him.

Pasqua spoke in the biggest and most regal reception room of his ministry. His elbows resting on a table draped in imperial red, he charged through a prepared statement, pausing only to lick his lips and to throw a commanding glance at his audience of some fifty journalists. The briefing given by the *premier flic de France* (France's top cop) was a crude exercise in news management. The frankest admission he made was: 'Several times, we hoped that Carlos would be handed to us. Several times, our hopes proved vain.' Only a brief reference was made to the 'friendly services' that had helped France.

The Interior Minister's version of events was that he had been informed earlier in the year of Carlos's possible presence in Sudan, and that he had then ordered appropriate measures to verify the information with 'irrefutable proof'. The previous morning, on 14 August, the Sudanese authorities told France that they had themselves identified Carlos and that they were ready to respond immediately to French arrest warrants. The DST, Pasqua concluded, had apprehended Carlos at the Villacoublay airbase. No other information would be released as the government had thrown a national security secrecy cover over the episode. In fact, Pasqua had known that Carlos was in Sudan since the previous year, obtained 'irrefutable proof' from the CIA, negotiated with the Sudanese for months, and sent a DST team to supervise his abduction in Khartoum.

Pasqua ensured that the price paid for Carlos, namely the return of two suspected murderers to Tehran and various promises made by the Interior Minister to Khartoum, stayed a closely guarded secret. Any rumour that he had paid for Carlos, be it in the form of intelligence cooperation with Sudan or anything else, he thundered, was 'a tissue of lies, disinformation, scandalous'. Only 'twisted minds' could imagine that France had negotiated with Sudan. Had not Pasqua, when outlining his anti-terrorism formula in November 1986 after attacks had rocked Paris, declared: 'Neither negotiations nor bargaining'? Pasqua's insistence that he had learned of Carlos's whereabouts only earlier in the year was an attempt to nip in the bud any speculation that Iran might have played a part in the capture.

In what was to all appearances a concerted public relations campaign, Sudan rushed to echo Pasqua's protestations. 'It was not a deal and the aim was not to obtain grants or aid,' declared President Hassan Omar al-Bashir, conceding however that 'it had a positive effect on the relations between Sudan and France'. Any suggestion that Sheikh Hassan al-Turabi might have been involved was mistaken, the President added brazenly. 'Doctor al-Turabi does not intervene in such affairs at all.'[9]

So relieved was Pasqua that Sudan had at last yielded to his entreaties that he tried to redeem the country of its poor reputation. In handing over Carlos, Pasqua said, Sudan had broken with terrorism. But Washington, still no great friend of the French Interior Minister, tempered his enthusiasm with a deadpan comment that Sudan would stay on the State Department's blacklist. It was only much later that Pasqua acknowledged his debt to Washington and the Central Intelligence Agency. 'The Carlos operation has its roots in the warming of relations between the United States and Syria,' he admitted. 'The United States leaned on Syria to force it to stop supporting terrorists. It's true that certain elements from the CIA helped us in pinpointing

Carlos. They located him.' But he could not resist hurriedly qualifying his gratitude. 'We located him too,' he added. And he was even less keen on sharing the credit with Rondot, about whom he would say nothing. On the other hand, he had no qualms about recognising the desire for revenge that had motivated the DST: 'When a secret service is subjected to a serious setback like Rue Toullier, when that setback results in several deaths, the service must avenge itself, it must avenge its dead, it must never forget. Since Carlos killed the DST officers, it had never given up on the idea of arresting him and making him pay.'[10]

The DST had tasted revenge because Carlos's sponsors betrayed him. The silence of the Arab leaders who had sheltered, supported and hired him over the years was deafening. Of all his patrons, only one of his former mentors, George Habash of the Popular Front, protested at the sell-out of his movement's ex-recruit. Habash, partially paralysed by a stroke, protested at such bad manners, 'a cheap action against an international fighter who served liberation movements. The Sudanese government could have asked Carlos to leave the country had his presence constituted a danger or had it faced any pressure.'[11]

Aside from the Palestinian extremists, only one other voice spoke out for Carlos. A friend phoned his elderly father, Ramírez Navas, to tell him that his son's life on the run had come to an end. Ramírez Navas broke down and wept at the news, just as he had done when Carlos had told him two decades earlier of his decision to become a guerrilla. His first call was to his estranged wife. Only atheism, and sympathy with his son's political views, the retired lawyer explained, had carried him through the constant anguish he had felt about his fate. Ramírez Navas had tried to find sanctuary in his homeland for his vagrant first-born. But his appeals to former President Ramon J. Velasquez had fallen on deaf ears, especially after France, which got wind of the attempt to give Carlos a safe haven, threatened to stop selling Venezuela spare parts for its Mirage fighter planes.

Ramírez Navas had long given up on the chances of revolution ever coming about, and over the past years he had been reduced to penning vibrant denunciations of political corruption in his homeland. He expressed his frustration in poems, including one called 'Vindicta', which he read only to close friends. 'I too fight for a more just society,' claimed the wiry Ramírez Navas, as neatly turned out in his seventies as in his more youthful days. 'It's not that I'm tired or anything like that but I'm convinced that there are too many forces against that. The only certainty is that Ilich will die the death he wants. He may be the only one who achieves that.'[12]

In the days following Carlos's capture Ramírez Navas chained a heavy lock to the grey gates of his modest zinc-roofed home, in which hanging bedsheets replaced doors, and names and telephone numbers had been scribbled on the wooden walls, to share the confinement inflicted on his first-born. 'My son is the greatest hero in the world,' Ramírez Navas affirmed. 'He's a great man who does everything out of conviction ... I only live for my sons, my three boys, although some think I only live for one of them.'[13] From jail, Carlos later sent his father a photograph of him standing in his prison cell in front of a picture of a peaceful rural scene hanging on the cell wall. Carlos scrawled a message for his father: 'To my old man, in spiritual communion.'

Carlos's mother kept her feelings to herself. When French officers of the Brigade Criminelle flew to Caracas to investigate Carlos's youth, Elba at first rejected their summons, saying that she was suffering from the after-effects of dental treatment. But she later decided to accompany her divorced husband and Carlos's brother Lenin (a millionaire who managed a construction company) to the law courts. She had nothing to say to the

French police officers, aside from affirming her right not to be interrogated under a provision in the Venezuelan constitution which exonerates citizens from testifying about relatives.[14]

Only Carlos's younger brother Vladimir, an engineer, was willing to talk, although he was more than guarded in his responses. 'I don't know,' was his stock response to the French investigators. Stretching brotherly loyalty somewhat, he said he knew little of Carlos's love affairs: 'I only know of his relationship with Magdalena Kopp, a union out of which my niece Elba was born.'[15]

One of the first people whom Pasqua had called after hearing the good news from Sudan had been France's anti-terrorism supremo, Judge Bruguière. '*Bonjour, Monsieur le juge.* I have a parcel for you,' the minister told Bruguière, whom he had informed three months earlier of the negotiations under way with the Sudanese. From then on the judge, who was to meet the prisoner countless times over the next few years, became the face of the French state for Carlos and as such his sparring partner.

Born in the Basque Country to a family boasting six generations of magistrates – among his ancestors were eighteenth-century parliamentarians from Toulouse who had opposed Louis XIII – the fifty-one-year-old Bruguière was not the kind to suffer fools, or contradiction, gladly. His thin lips part more willingly for a pipe or a Wild Havana cigar than to impart confidences. But when he does share a secret he mumbles it with reluctance out of the corner of his mouth. When crossed, the wrinkles on his brow deepen and his chin juts out in a prelude to a burst of ice-cold rage, which he is adept at faking if that helps him get his way.

Over the past twenty years the judge had grilled the pimps of the Paris underworld, the high-society brothel-keeper Madame Claude, Japanese gangsters, a Japanese murderer who ate his Dutch girlfriend, the last Frenchman to be sentenced to death, gun-runners frustrated in their attempt to ferry arms and explosives from Libya to the Irish Republican Army, Arab guerrillas and Libyan spies. The judge narrowly escaped an assassination attempt when a bodyguard discovered a primed grenade tied to the door of his flat by a nylon thread. 'The risks of the job,' Bruguière commented wryly. For ten years he had carried a Magnum .357 pistol, a type said to be so powerful that one bullet could bore its way through the boot of a Cadillac, kill the driver and smash against the engine. The gun had earned him the nickname 'The Sheriff', not totally unsuited to a man who had on one occasion – before road-rage was given a name – brandished it to wave a motorist out of his way, and who liked to show colleagues and lawyers his quick-draw talents.

Bruguière had earned himself another nickname, 'The Admiral', when he commandeered a French navy warship and tried to enter Libya in order to investigate the bombing of a French DC10 airliner in September 1989. He was turned away by Colonel Qathafi. As part of the same probe, he himself piloted a Transall military heavy transport plane over the Sahara, and after handing over the controls parachuted in combat gear to hunt for parts of the downed DC10. 'I don't keep to the beaten paths,' the solitary judge confessed. 'I'm subversive because I use the law, the law pushed to the limit. That necessarily leads to conflicts, institutional conflicts.'[16]

Carlos was Judge Bruguière's most notorious prize to date, and he had long been preparing for the confrontation. Since he had heard that an abduction was a possibility, the judge had stepped up his efforts to acquire the files of the Stasi. Two years earlier the DST chief Jacques Fournet had sent an envoy to Berlin to draw up a report summarising the contents of the files relating to Carlos. Fournet is by no means convinced that the envoy was shown all there was to see. 'There was a kind of euphoria when the Berlin Wall fell. We all thought that all the archives had come out,' explained Fournet, a former adviser to President Mitterrand. 'Some did come out, but it didn't last. The Germans wanted to preserve national cohesion, and blocked the release of the files after a few months. We were able to verify lots of things, but we don't know what we didn't get. Perhaps there are files on Carlos and the KGB which will come out only in twenty years' time.'[17]

Copies of the original Stasi dossiers had started trickling into Judge Bruguière's chambers in July, and he was in upbeat mood as he readied to meet Carlos – in the Palais de Justice, because the judge wanted to do battle on his own territory rather than at the prison. As the magistrate leading the investigations into all Carlos's crimes on French soil, it was Bruguière who under French judicial procedure would now be responsible for questioning Carlos about these crimes. It was also Bruguière who would gather and assess any evidence to support charges against Carlos, and then make a recommendation to the indicting chamber of the court of appeals as to whether Carlos should stand trial.

Judge Bruguière had heard about the defiance Carlos had shown at DST headquarters the previous day, but he was surprised by the bonhomie oozing from Carlos as he stepped through the armour-plated doors into the judge's chambers. He looked, the judge thought, none the worse for his first night in French custody. The moustachioed and balding visitor was dressed as if for a summer cocktail party in spotless white trousers, white shirt and a wine-coloured jacket, his hands handcuffed behind his back.[18] The reputed master of disguise, said to have undergone plastic surgery, was a less handsome, podgier but still easily recognisable version of the passport mug-shots which the world's police forces had painstakingly collected.

Earlier that sunny August morning a convoy had picked Carlos up from La Santé and, sirens blaring, escorted him across Paris. The convoy's progress was hampered by a swarm of photographers and television cameramen on motorcycles. The large van carrying Carlos had several big windows and although no one could see in, Carlos was able to watch the landmarks he knew so well pass by: the leafy banks of the River Seine and their picturesque *bouquinistes*, and the Cathedral of Notre-Dame. Black-clad sharp-shooters perched on rooftops stiffened as the van swung into the Quai des Orfèvres and then entered the law courts.

The trip apparently did not ruffle Carlos. The prospect of spending the rest of his life behind bars had either not yet hit home, or perhaps he was putting on a show. Judge Bruguière had braced himself for a confrontation, but Carlos's relaxed attitude ensured a steady flow of idle banter. As the two men studied each other, Carlos was careful to betray neither fear nor anxiety.

His first words as he neared the judge's chambers were for his escort of four armed officers of the gendarmerie police, who wore bullet-proof vests over their black uniforms. 'We too had FAMAS [assault rifles] in Lebanon. That's good,' Carlos told them, speaking French with a heavy South American accent.

Then, catching sight of Bruguière: 'And here's *Monsieur le juge*. How are you?' Carlos called out teasingly. 'And you?' asked the judge. 'Still alive, and for a long time,' the man whose obituary had been written so many times answered with a smile. Carlos spoke with a hint of both relief and defiance, before turning to the armed officers and pointing towards Bruguière. 'He's a star, he is!' Carlos quipped.

Throughout the two-hour session Carlos treated the judge, with whom he shared a taste for cigars, as an equal. He talked politics, women, and philosophy, and about his memories of Khartoum. Carlos's in-depth knowledge of the state of the investigations into his past surprised Bruguière. In flippant mood, Carlos offered to take the judge out to lunch at the Lutétia, a luxury hotel on the Left Bank, to tell him about his exploits. The judge politely declined. Unabashed, Carlos confided: 'We're cut of the same wood, you and I, we'll get on well together.' When the judge asked Carlos which lawyer he wished to name for his defence, Carlos announced that he chose Jacques Vergès, the attorney who had represented Magdalena Kopp. 'I nominate Vergès because he is a greater terrorist than I am,' Carlos told the judge. 'He is responsible for more deaths than I am. He is a terrorist who scares me.'

Carlos was less laid back when the judge formally charged him with planting the bomb outside the offices of the *Al Watan al Arabi* magazine in Paris in 1982, and brushed aside Carlos's allegation that he had been kidnapped from Sudan. Carlos raised his voice, insisting that he had been leaped on by Sudanese security officers who had protected him until then, that he had been drugged and then flown to Paris. But Bruguière was determined to steer clear of this legal minefield, and soldiered on as he outlined the charges against Carlos. The Carlos who emerged from Bruguière's chambers had lost much of his good cheer. 'We're both professionals,' the judge remarked later with a broad smile. 'Carlos didn't confide in me, but he must have realised that he was at the end of the road. He's lucky to finish up like this, because his end could have been much darker, and more sudden.'

13

The Jackal Caged

My character is simple. I am a father first and foremost.

– Carlos in a message spirited out of La Santé jail

Carlos was taken to 42 Rue de la Santé. In a rare distinction, he was greeted by the governor of the greystone prison on his arrival in the main courtyard which had once been graced by Dr Guillotin's bloody invention but where the only dash of red now was that of geraniums in window-boxes. Carlos's fingerprints were taken yet again, he was searched, and with a sheet and blanket under his arm he was led to his new life as, in prison jargon, a *détenu particulièrement surveillé* (specially guarded inmate).

A model establishment when it was built in 1867 in accord with the latest American theories on prison design and little changed since, La Santé was close to the heart of Paris. Too close for the comfort of the poet Guillaume Apollinaire, held briefly in 1911 on suspicion of stealing works of art, who penned a few lines on his stay at La Santé:

I listen to the sounds of the city
And, prisoner without a horizon,
I see nothing but a hostile sky
And the naked walls of my prison.

La Santé had played host to an impressive range of

political beliefs. Anarchists, communists, royalists, Resistance fighters during the Nazi occupation of Paris, Nazi collaborators after the capital's liberation, and Algerian nationalists had all despaired behind its filthy walls. In April 1919, it had welcomed Henri Landru who had recruited his female victims (chiefly war widows lured by his promises of matrimony) through lonely hearts columns. The women were dismembered and cooked.

The exploits of more recent inmates had forged the jail's reputation for spectacular escapes. Only a week before Carlos's arrival a rapist had sawn through the bars of his cell, and thrown an electric cable fitted with a metal hook across to the outer wall. He had then slid to freedom, commando-like, along the cable by hanging on to a brass tube. Eight years earlier the gangster Michel Vaujour was plucked from a roof of the jail by his wife Nadine who was flying a helicopter. And in 1978 another gangster, public enemy number one Jacques Mesrine, used a warder's uniform, a gun and tear gas to make his getaway.

According to Carlos's fellow inmates, security at La Santé was usually not too oppressive. 'Compared to other jails I've been to like Fresnes and Fleury-Mérogis near Paris,' one prisoner said after he had served a year of his five-year sentence for armed and violent robbery, 'La Santé is very good, it's cool. At Fresnes the atmosphere is different. You're not allowed cigarettes there, and you have to walk along a yellow line painted on the ground close to the walls, with your arms hanging down at your sides.'[1]

But the prison governor was taking no chances with Carlos. A unit of CRS anti-riot police carrying submachine-guns was deployed outside the jail during Carlos's first few weeks there. Warders were ordered to glance through his cell's eyehole every seven minutes. Because of his weighty pedigree, Carlos was spared the promiscuity – and in some cases, consequent sodomy[2] – which hoodlums and petty drug dealers among La Santé's 1500 inmates were forced to endure, packed six strong to a twelve-square-metre cell, with only a waist-high wall partly concealing the lavatory in the corner.

From the Soviet empire and a wide swathe of the Middle East, Carlos's domain had shrunk to cell number 258187 in the isolation division. Behind a door painted a pastel shade of green the cell was ten square metres large, with most of the space taken by a bed, a metal chair, a concrete table built into the wall, a sink and a lavatory. Carlos could make out nothing through the plexiglass window barred with iron rods and wire meshing so thick that not even a cigarette could be pushed through it. His immediate neighbours were rapists, murderers and Corsican separatists. Two floors above him was the wing reserved for VIPs, including politicians and business tycoons who had been felled by corruption investigations. 'Ten square metres, twenty-three hours out of twenty-four. I wouldn't put my dog in it,' summed up one of those VIPs, the garrulous former soccer boss and government minister Bernard Tapie. 'A prison is a machine to crush a man. People treat you like shit. It's not surprising that after six months some want to kill everyone when they get out.'[3]

The routine suffered only a few exceptions. A wake-up call at around seven o'clock by a guard to whom Carlos would hand his mail, then coffee and bread for breakfast, followed by a quick clean up of the cell and an hour's exercise which Carlos usually skipped in favour of a lie-in. The wait for his daily shower in a small cubicle at the end of the corridor must have irritated a man obsessed by personal hygiene. Lunch was described by Captain Bob Denard, a mercenary, as cold and 'smelling like a corpse'.[4] Afternoons included mail distribution and another hour set aside for exercise, with lights out at eleven o'clock.

Only the television Carlos was allowed to rent – he had to wait several days for it and thus missed seeing himself lead the news bulletins – and the three books he could borrow from the prison library each week varied the routine. Visitors were banned save for his lawyers. Nor was he allowed to join in the games of soccer that prisoners played against warders in a forty-five-square-metre yard. French, drawing and painting classes were also out of bounds as was the Thursday mass available to other inmates.

Every time Carlos had to leave his cell guards were mobilised to clear corridors, as regulations dictated that only prison warders should lay eyes on him. 'You don't move Carlos the way you shift a petty thief who has stolen a hen from a farm,' explained prison governor Yves Tigoulet.[5] The governor, however, was ready to indulge some foibles of his most notorious prisoner. The privileges that Carlos sought were in keeping with the lifestyle he had previously enjoyed. He pleaded that the regulation-issue sheets irritated his skin, and was granted permission to sleep in silk sheets instead. He had his guards fetch him Cuban Cohiba cigars – the most expensive money can buy, and Fidel Castro's favourite – from an exclusive boutique in Paris. The silk sheets and cigars were purchased with money sent by Carlos's father. His cigar-cutter, which should have been banned, was another exception to prison rules. And when he heard that a former politician in the VIP wing had been granted permission to use a dictaphone, Carlos instantly demanded the same perk.

If detention took its toll, Carlos was careful not to show it. He impressed a senior official at the jail with his attitude: 'Carlos took it all pretty lightly. He was convinced that he still had a market value.' He was cheerful with the warders to whom he chatted non-stop as, too unfit for press-ups, he took perfunctory exercise in one of the cramped, so-called 'Camembert' courtyards (which owe their name to the fact that they have a triangular shape, like portions of the pungent cheese). He talked a great deal about women, about Lana and Magdalena Kopp, and boasted about the beautiful women he had had. Carlos also liked to list the Arab heads of state whom he had met. 'For him, death is nothing,' reported one jailer. 'He talks of the people he has killed and of those he will kill. When I asked him how far back this past went back to – I didn't say "terrorism" because that's not what he calls it – he told me: "Since I was thirteen years old."'[6] To another warder Carlos advised: 'You earn 9000 francs a month. You should get another job.' The guard replied: 'I'm fine as I am. I'd rather be where I am than where you are.'

After grabbing $30,000 that Carlos had hidden away in their Khartoum flat, Lana had flown to Paris. In the French capital she lobbied judicial authorities for permission to see her husband, but her requests were fruitless. Carlos soon found out about Lana's journey to Paris, but this was the last he heard of her: 'It's when he talks about losing Lana that Carlos realises what he has lost with his imprisonment,' one of Carlos's lawyers related later. Lana was the second lover to vanish out of Carlos's life. Back in London after his studies in Moscow in the early 1970s he had spent months trying to find his Cuban girlfriend, Sonia, but without success.

The maverick lawyer Jacques Vergès was more than happy to defend a prisoner whom he termed both 'a myth and a legend', a courageous idealist who faced, in his words, a public lynching. Vergès added that he was not in the business of defending Mother Teresa. Two days into Carlos's captivity Vergès issued a rosy bulletin on his client's state of mind: 'He has excellent morale, he is in good shape and he's cracking jokes ... From now on he will justify his actions. He will justify his politics in general, his ideological struggle. There is no question of disavowing the actions he is reproached with.' Nor of showing any remorse. 'Carlos is a human being,' Vergès explained. 'He is very sorry about people who die, people who are wounded. But at the same time he thinks that his fight was in a very violent atmosphere.'[7]

Now, Carlos wanted the world to know that he did not feel beaten. He had started to nurture that image with his relaxed behaviour in the judge's chambers. Angered by the way the media had covered his capture, with colourful reports that he was addicted to alcohol, had been operated on to trim his waistline, and had slept with prostitutes, Carlos spirited a message out of La Santé. Published by a French newspaper two weeks after his arrest, Carlos's statement sought to polish his tarnished image:

> I was seized in the truest Mafia style. But now that I have been neutralised, instead of assassinating me physically, people are carrying out a moral assassination. I don't understand. Why do people try to make me out as an alcoholic? All this is wrong, I've never been a drunkard. Why do they say I underwent a liposuction when I went to hospital for an operation on a varicocele? I don't understand. My character is simple. I am a father first and foremost. My wife and daughter live normal lives in Venezuela, in the heart of my own family. They live in a house next to my mother's.[8]

For all his resentment at his betrayal by the Sudanese and other régimes, Carlos had no intention of behaving like those states and informing on his sponsors. 'I am one of the founders of the Organisation of Internationalist Revolutionaries, and I am still a member,' Carlos proclaimed in the message that he smuggled out of prison. 'In my organisation, we shoot traitors. So don't count on me to betray friendly countries and name names.'[9] Much later, he hinted darkly that the plan 'to neutralise "Carlos"' (he wrote about himself in the third person) had been masterminded by the Americans, in coordination with the French and with Israeli and Saudi financial support. Only French authorities, he said, had been ready 'to transform a kidnapping – the result of state betrayal – into a due process of law'.[10]

Soon after Carlos's imprisonment Vergès swore to sue the French courts, arguing that his client – whom he liked to hail with a resounding 'Don Carlos' – had been kidnapped and should therefore be freed. If that failed, he would take the case to the European Court of Human Rights. It was the same argument that Vergès had used in his defence of Gestapo officer Klaus Barbie. Arrested by Bolivian police for failing to pay a sizeable fine following the bankruptcy of one of his companies, Barbie was put on a French air force Hercules C130. Two officers of the DGSE's Action Service took charge of him and he was served with an arrest warrant when the plane touched down in French Guiana. From there, he was flown on to mainland France.

Other victims of French high-handedness had fared no better. In the case of Colonel Antoine Argoud of the OAS movement of military conspirators who resisted Algerian independence, France refused to admit to any part in his kidnapping in Munich in February 1963. The official version held that Argoud, a brilliant officer and the army's youngest colonel, was discovered, following an anonymous telephone call, bound by chains in a van parked conveniently close to the headquarters of the Brigade Criminelle police unit, not far from Notre-Dame. 'See what French police have done to a French officer!' exclaimed the former Free French fighter when a police officer arrived at the scene.

Vergès's defence of Carlos was however soon undermined by leaks to the press about his past links to the prisoner. As if guided by some invisible hand, extracts from the East German Stasi files found their way into some newspapers. Vergès counter-attacked and alleged that he had been the subject of an assassination order by President Mitterrand, a claim ridiculed by the head of state's aides and by the heads of the secret services. Carlos joked to his attorney: 'Soon it'll be you who's charged in my place, then I'll go out and bring you oranges.' There was speculation in the press that Judge Bruguière was considering an investigation of Vergès – bringing about a situation in which the lawyer defending the main suspect would himself be under judicial scrutiny – because of reported contacts with Carlos, in the East German files.

For all his past work for the cause, Vergès was to disappoint Carlos. In an incautious admission, Vergès wrote in a book that was published in November 1994 that Carlos was guilty of the Rue Toullier shootings. 'In Paris, Rue Toullier, he did indeed do something which was regrettable in order to avoid arrest. It was his liberty as a combatant,' Vergès wrote. 'The indicator he shot down was the head of the Popular Front network who had turned Mossad agent and was being protected by French police.'[11] The admission angered Carlos, but it was when Carlos finally realised that there was no prospect of release that relations between the lawyer and his client deteriorated beyond repair. Carlos came to distrust Vergès and at the beginning of 1995 Carlos dropped him. Vergès diplomatically explained that the two had conflicting opinions on defence strategy and the role of an attorney.

Vergès was not the only lawyer to clash with Carlos. Mourad Oussedik, a Franco-Algerian appointed to work with Vergès, had made his reputation defending Algerian independence fighters, and Carlos's former patron Georges Habash, when he was briefly detained in Paris in January 1992. The official reason for his rift with Carlos was a problem with 'lawyer-client relations'. In fact, in a closed courtroom hearing and before an impassive Vergès, Carlos had in February 1995 accused one of the lawyers in Oussedik's office of spying for the French police. A furious Oussedik, together with his aggrieved colleague, called on Carlos early the next morning at La Santé. 'Terrorists like you, I shit them every day!' Oussedik shouted at Carlos in the visiting room. After telling a deputy governor, 'I leave you this stupid bastard,' Oussedik stormed away. Carlos watched him leave in sullen silence.

Within months of his arrest Carlos's private army had faded away. Soon after the capture French intelligence estimated that the group numbered no more than a dozen members, several of whom had been identified in Beirut, Amman and Damascus. Officers of France's DGSE spotted the forty-eight-year-old Johannes Weinrich, still sporting his moustache, in early 1995 as he passed through Djibouti on the Horn of Africa before crossing the Gulf of Aden in a fishing boat bound for Carlos's former Marxist sanctuary. But a civil war fought the previous year, in which the Marxist secessionist rebels of South Yemen were crushed, and the unification of North and South Yemen reaffirmed, meant Weinrich was on less safe terrain. Living in Aden under the aliases John Saleh and Peter Smith, he desperately tried to retrieve all the records he had kept so meticulously from several hiding places, and from the dispersed members of the now leaderless organisation. No fewer than three different secret services – the DGSE, the CIA, and the German BND – managed to identify Weinrich in Aden. Vital evidence was supplied by the fingerprints that Weinrich left on a plate in a restaurant.

German intelligence insisted that it should be the service that tried to catch its countryman, Germany's longest-sought fugitive. The Central Intelligence Agency had no more grounds to seize Weinrich than they had had to seize Carlos, and took a back seat. The French felt that Carlos was enough for them to have to deal with, and were more than happy to leave Weinrich to the Germans. From a safe distance, BND officers watched Yemeni police arrest Weinrich in an Aden suburb in June 1995, almost a year after Carlos's abduction. Treated much more gently than his leader – something Weinrich must have appreciated, as he was described by the Stasi as 'a soft-boiled egg' – he was restrained only by handcuffs when he boarded a German air force plane.

The charge sheet awaiting Weinrich on his arrival at Berlin's old Moabit jail – where fellow inmates included Erich Mielke, the former head of the East German Stasi – compared quite respectably with Carlos's: the first of the two bungled missile attacks at Orly airport, a failed attempt on the life of the Saudi Arabian ambassador in Athens, and the bombings of Radio Free Europe in Munich, the TGV train and the Marseille railway station, and the Maison de France in West Berlin. From his cell in Paris, Carlos could not resist writing an epitaph for the fallen 'comrade Weinrich', pronouncing him 'one of the greatest revolutionaries produced by the German nation'. Describing Weinrich as his right-hand man, as one French magazine had done, belittled his contribution to the cause, and amounted to insulting Carlos's friend and companion.[12]

Only a few months later another middle-aged Carlos soldier fell. Christa-Margot Froelich had driven to Paris the car used to bomb the Rue Marbeuf in 1982. She had apparently been intent on bombing another French target when she was arrested at Rome's Leonardo da Vinci airport in June of that year as she prepared to travel to Paris with several kilos of explosives in her suitcase.[13] After six years in an Italian jail, she had long broken with the Carlos organisation and was living a quiet life in her native Germany when he was seized in Sudan. Fearing that her past involvement with Carlos might catch up with her, she prudently and naïvely asked Italian authorities whether she would be arrested again if she made another of her regular visits to see her husband, a member of the Red Brigades jailed in Rome. The answer given to her lawyers was that there was nothing pending against her in Italy. It was a devious answer.

When Froelich arrived in Rome late one Saturday in October 1995 for a meeting with her husband, she was arrested because Judge Bruguière had issued an international warrant for her. Her husband struggled in vain to fight the French extradition request. She refused to talk and was ordered to await her trial in a French prison. Had she remained in Germany she would undoubtedly have remained free. German examining magistrates had launched an investigation into her past, based on the East German and Hungarian intelligence records, but concluded there was insufficient evidence on which to charge her. Her file was closed. 'Froelich was arrested with the sole purpose of extraditing her. We had nothing else on her,' a senior Italian police officer admitted.[14] Only Carlos's other chief lieutenant, the Syrian Issawe, escaped. He vanished so completely that not even Weinrich in his last months as a fugitive, let alone Western intelligence services, were able to find him.

Long before her husband's arrest, the jilted Magdalena Kopp had traded in her meagre revolutionary credentials. Both in Venezuela and in Bavaria, where Kopp moved in late 1995 to give her nine-year-old daughter Elba a German upbringing and to be near her elderly disabled mother, her only concern was for Elba's future. There was none of the ideological brainwashing that Carlos's father had inflicted on him, and no private tuition. In her mother's home town of Neu-Ulm, Elba studied at the local state school. She was a hard worker whose parents had raised her to speak English and Spanish as well as German.

When Judge Bruguière sent investigators to question her, Kopp invoked her right under German law not to testify against the man who was legally still her husband despite his marriage to Lana.[15] But it was her concern for the child's future, together with a consuming desire to be left in peace, which led her to take one of the most dramatic decisions of her life. The betrayal not only of her husband Carlos, but also of her former lover Weinrich.

'The war is over but Carlos hasn't realised it,' the woman for whose sake Carlos had masterminded a string of bloody attacks to prise her out of jail told Berlin investigating magistrate Dieter Mehlis in December 1995. Although the revelations she made to the Berlin judge related specifically to Weinrich, they obviously hurt Carlos. 'From the way she spoke about Weinrich,' noted one investigator, 'it was only logical to conclude that nothing happened without Carlos knowing about it or ordering it to happen.' Her questioners however refrained from pressing her about Carlos's involvement in various crimes since he was her husband and the father of her daughter.

It was Weinrich, Kopp explained, who had parked the explosive-packed orange Opel in the Rue Marbeuf in Paris in 1982. And it was again Weinrich, possibly with the help of others, who planted the suitcases containing the bombs that went off within minutes of each other in a high-speed TGV train and at the Marseille railway station the following year.

Kopp seemed nonplussed by the impact of her indiscretions. 'Whatever I tell you, Carlos and Weinrich will spend the rest of their lives in jail,' she confided to Judge Mehlis, who could only agree with her. Carlos himself was unable to discover what had made her talk. When one of his lawyers reached Kopp on the telephone and asked the reason why, the only answer she gave was: 'I don't know.' Carlos concluded that as she had no source of income and was under the thumb of the German police, she had no choice but to cooperate with the authorities. In a magazine interview which she gave later in return for a hefty payment, she branded Carlos a megalomaniac obsessed by power, and capable of killing without batting an eyelid. 'Carlos fought for no one,' Kopp said. 'Only for himself. I would be delighted to see his myth destroyed.' She added bitterly: 'He never really loved me.'[16]

Even in prison, Carlos continued to look after his appearance, and to play Don Juan. In his first months in detention his laundry was done by Vergès's maid, but apparently this was not good enough for Carlos and he began sending it to a local dry cleaner's, the only prisoner to do so. He earned a reputation as one of La Santé's cleanest and best-dressed inmates. At a meeting with Judge Bruguière, Carlos turned to the attractive blonde secretary and suavely asked her what her name was. 'Isabelle,' answered the bewildered secretary, blushing slightly. 'What a beautiful name,' Carlos cooed as he bent down to take her hand and kiss it, too quickly for her to pull it away. His female lawyers were also fair game for gallantry, and the forbidding surroundings of La Santé did nothing to suppress his spirited shows of affection. A warder discovered one of Vergès's colleagues, Marie-Annick Ramassamy-Vergès (no relation to the lawyer), sitting on Carlos's knees in the visiting room. The warder sternly urged her 'to adopt an attitude more in keeping with the premises'.[17]

At another time, as armed police escorted him to a van in the prison courtyard, with motorcycle outriders revving their engines and the road outside blocked by yet more police, Carlos stopped in mid-stride. He had recognised another of his female lawyers, Isabelle Coutant-Peyre. With a wide smile and to the bafflement of his guards, Carlos walked up to her and kissed her hand in greeting. She was impressed by him. 'He has many qualities,' she said later. 'He is very intelligent, immensely cultivated, and his memory is impressive. One feels good with him.'[18] So good that in La Santé's cramped visiting room the two made a habit of pulling on fat Cuban cigars as they discussed his defence strategy.

In the autumn of 1995 an elderly gentleman showed his

Swiss passport at the gate of Fresnes jail outside Paris and was ushered to a visiting room which was almost certainly bugged. He was joined there by Carlos, who had been transferred to Fresnes temporarily. The two men spent just over an hour together. Carlos confided to the visitor that his morale was good although he was convinced that he would never again see his homeland Venezuela, and he still had no news of Lana.

The visitor was the 'Black Banker' François Genoud, the Nazi friend of Carlos who was the only person aside from his lawyers granted permission to visit him in prison by Judge Bruguière. It was to Genoud that Carlos wrote to proclaim his commitment to world revolution. In Genoud's archives Carlos's letters sit among others from Martin Bormann, Klaus Barbie, Emma Goering and Oswald Mosley. The missives from the self-styled revolutionary show that the Nazi Genoud, who denied that the Holocaust had taken place, was a father figure to Carlos.[19]

Genoud had once boasted that he had planted 'a small bomb' against British forces in Palestine, and in 1969 he appeared at Vergès's side to defend three members of the Popular Front who had attacked an El Al plane in Zurich. Three years later Genoud helped to hijack a Lufthansa plane for a $5 million ransom from the airline.[20] Such acts earned him the everlasting gratitude of his Palestinian friends. In later years Genoud made no effort to hide his appreciation of Carlos. For Genoud, 'Carlos threw himself heart and soul into the Palestinian struggle and he risked his life many times for it. He is a courageous man of action whose deeply held convictions are beyond doubt. He was never scared of gambling his skin for a cause which was not his. Remember the OPEC ministers hostage-taking. I admire him for that.'[21]

In one of the first letters to 'my dearest comrade' from jail, dated 4 December 1994, Carlos thanked Genoud for a gift of 10,000 francs and expressed admiration for an interview that Genoud had given to a Swiss newspaper. In the interview Genoud had admitted to his friendship with Carlos for the first time. 'I admire your fearlessness in denouncing ignominy just after my abduction by the Sudanese authorities,' Carlos wrote, assuring his friend that he was in good health and that his morale was holding well. Censure of the Sudanese regime was more than justified in Carlos's eyes, but he cautioned Genoud against weakening Arab nations in general: 'Condemnation of the betrayal of Hassan al-Turabi does not imply condemnation of the true Islamic revolutionaries which form the vanguard of the struggle against imperialism and Zionism. Regarding other Arab governments, it is my opinion that any accusation of treachery should be weighed against the impact it could have on the ability of the Arab peoples to face the enemy.'[22]

Carlos advised Genoud against visiting him in prison, which he called 'a great school for revolutionaries'. A visit to the jail, Carlos wrote, 'could give room to attack you as a symbol of resistance against Zionist lies and calumnies. And anyway we would not have any privacy to allow us to speak freely and at leisure.' The latter was a reference to the strong likelihood that the visiting room at the jail was bugged. Carlos asked Genoud to try to contact Lana because he had had no news of her since his capture, and signed his letter: 'Yours in revolution'. Genoud later flew to Beirut and then Amman to try to track down Lana, to find money for his friend's defence and to pass on messages to friends of Carlos. Lana, however, had vanished without trace.[23]

In his next letter to Genoud, dated 19 January 1995, Carlos again thanked him for sending money to the jail, this time 5000 francs. Soon there would be no need for such gifts, Carlos wrote, because he was awaiting help from his family. Carlos proudly announced that he had begun to set up a group of lawyers to assure his defence. These attorneys 'have not sold their souls to the devil and truly cherish justice'. He thanked Genoud for a letter 'full of militant ardour, which has really raised my spirits'. In a long and effusive letter dated 18 March Carlos told Genoud that he was the only person, aside from his close family, with whom he corresponded from jail. 'If we never meet again, we shall wait for the Valhalla of revolutionaries where we shall share the moments of complicity with our dearly missed martyrs ... I shall be happy to arrive at your ripe age with only a tenth of your indomitable spirit. I want you to know that I truly admire you, trust you and cherish your friendship.'

On 30 May Carlos asked his friend to suggest a French lawyer who could help defend him and who would not betray him to the enemy. 'Like every true revolutionary, I am an optimist but I do not expect that the treacherous enemy will allow me to reach Venezuela alive ... Nevertheless, I shall persevere in my struggle until my last breath.' Genoud's friendship with Carlos led Judge Bruguière to question the retired banker on 6 July 1995. Genoud simply explained that he had pro-Arab sympathies and that this was the reason why he supported Carlos. Genoud was faithful to Carlos, so much so that the last trip he ever made was to keep a promise to Carlos to travel to Venezuela and try to convince Magdalena Kopp not to return to Germany. Genoud kept his promise, but failed to sway the estranged wife.

The letter that Carlos wrote to Genoud on 30 August 1995 showed that Carlos saw himself as akin to Moslem fundamentalist guerrillas: 'Our materialistic conception of the world did not prevent us from seeing years ago that a new kind of militant, the Islamic revolutionist, has joined the vanguard of Revolution of which he is now the spearhead. This new state of affairs was not accepted by most fellow revolutionaries at the time out of dogmatism.'

Carlos's correspondence with Genoud drew to a close in the spring of 1996. On 30 May Genoud gathered friends around him at his home in Pully, a leafy eastern district of

Lausanne, where one of his proudest possessions was a watercolour painted by Hitler in Vienna in 1913 when he was a talentless artist. Watched by members of Exit, a pro-suicide group he had joined the previous year, he drank a cocktail of drugs and then lay down to await death. He had decided to choose the time of his death in order 'to leave in a dignified way without physical deterioration'.

Carlos's closeness to the banker who had paid for the defence of Adolf Eichmann and Klaus Barbie was due at least in part to an undercurrent of anti-Semitism common to both men. In Carlos's case, it echoed the beliefs of his father, Ramírez Navas. When media in San Cristobal denounced one of Carlos's brothers, Carlos's father branded one of the journalists involved 'that dirty Jewess'.[24] Relatives of Carlos have testified to his racial leanings. 'He believed in a free state of Palestine and he detested Jews,' according to his cousin Luis Sánchez, a dance professor.[25] Much later, and before a Jewish lawyer of his, Carlos pejoratively referred to his former OPEC accomplice Hans-Joachim Klein as '*enjuivé*' (a non-Jew who pretends to be Jewish). His prejudice also surfaced in court. Needled by the campaign waged by lawyers representing victims of his attacks, he denounced Françoise Rudetzki, the head of the French association SOS Attacks, as 'the heiress of Vladimir Jabotinsky', one of the pioneering figures of Zionism.[26]

As the months, and then the years passed, the confinement and isolation which Carlos himself called *tortura blanca* (white torture) began to take their toll. His belief that his stay in jail was only temporary evaporated, and on some occasions so did his self-confidence. Late one evening in June 1996, as two prisoners discussed television programmes by shouting to each other from one cell window to another, a high-pitched whine broke into their conversation: 'I am Carlos! It's me, Carlos!' The wail for recognition fell flat when one inmate yelled back: 'Carlos who?'

But when the prisoners realised who the cry had come from, they fell silent. No one answered Carlos and there was no need for prison warders to order quiet. 'His voice made people feel ill at ease,' recalled the mercenary Bob Denard, who was in a cell two floors above Carlos. 'It was as if his voice came from the beyond. He was isolated, he wanted to talk. We didn't speak about him among us, he was almost taboo. He had quite a lot of blood on his hands, and that surprised people, even common criminals.'[27]

Carlos's frustration exacerbated a feature of his character which had been noted by his guardians in the Stasi several years previously: the superiority complex mixed with insecurity which made him incapable of tolerating contradiction. The few individuals allowed to approach Carlos at La Santé described him as pleasant, convivial and warm-hearted, but capable of flying into a rage if anyone showed him a lack of respect.

Prison warders and guards who escorted him to and from the law courts for his interrogations by Judge Bruguière were the butt of his tantrums. When on one November day in 1996 the guards insisted on stripping him of his belt before he left La Santé, as regulations dictate, Carlos started yelling at them. They promptly handcuffed his arms behind his back, seized him by the shoulders and legs, and heaved his burly frame into the van. Awaiting him at the law courts with the judge was a team from Scotland Yard which had finally obtained permission to question Carlos after first making a request soon after his capture. The British officers looked on in quiet amazement as the guards, still bearing their load, struggled through the narrow armoured doors. The judge struggled vainly to calm Carlos down.

Carlos refused to make a sworn deposition, but politely assured the Scotland Yard team that the incident had nothing to do with their presence. Back in jail, Carlos demanded a medical examination because of a bruise on his arm caused by one of the guards using a truncheon to carry him. So incensed was Carlos that he had his lawyer send a letter of protest to the Venezuelan consul in which he charged that his manhandling meant that he had been unable to present himself before the judge 'in decent posture', and that this was a violation of the European Convention of Human Rights.'[28]

When the Scotland Yard officers returned to Paris a month later, determined to question Carlos on the shooting of Joseph Edward Sieff, the president of Marks and Spencer, in December 1973 and on the bombing of the Israeli bank a month later, they learned little new. He protested that Britain was yielding to a Zionist lobby in dusting down investigations such as the Sieff murder. When they told him that one of the revolvers found in a cache of his in Paris in the summer of 1975 was the one used to shoot Sieff, Carlos pretended to be clueless about ballistics studies and asked how they could tell.

Carlos's insistence on respect for his rights landed him in another row when one prison warder, a plump black man, refused to take a letter from him. 'You gnu, you!' Carlos shouted. The prison authorities launched proceedings against Carlos, and his protestation that 'gnu' was merely the name of an African antelope, and not an insult, failed to sway the governor. Carlos was given a suspended ten-day spell in a disciplinary cell, which he would have to serve if he offended again.

Carlos would often consult the copy of La Santé rules which he kept in his cell, and liked to quote from it chapter and verse. 'My father is a lawyer. I have the greatest respect for the law. I want the law to be observed in all cases,' he said at one closed court hearing. The fact that the prison intercepted and delayed his correspondence with his family particularly irritated him, and he once slammed his fist down on the desk of Judge Bruguière as he raged about this infringement of his privacy.

Since the light-hearted banter at the start of their first

encounter, Carlos's relationship with Judge Bruguière had rapidly soured. Debonair, Carlos would arrive at the chambers with a yellow scarf thrown around his neck and a booklet of crossword puzzles peeking out of his jacket pocket. At first he refused to answer questions, in protest at the way he was seized. 'I'm not here, I don't exist, so you can't investigate me,' he scoffed. But Bruguière persisted and the temptation to talk was soon too much for Carlos, and he began telling the judge at length about his youth and the start of his career. Questions about specific outrages, however, were met for the most part with a stony silence or with unsmiling repetition that as an officer leading the commando unit of a revolutionary organisation he could not speak for its actions.

Under questioning, Carlos was in Bruguière's eyes 'a mixed bag of fascination, attraction and repulsion – and of anxiety. He was always lively, a braggart, provocative, manipulating, charming and threatening. All at the same time.' The judge's plodding approach, and his habit of asking lengthy questions that virtually filled a whole page, irritated Carlos, who would reply with a single sentence. When Carlos was in a more verbose mood, the pair got bogged down in verbal jousting as neither was prepared to give an inch over the wording of the testimony, which Carlos couched in the literary French he had learned at school. On one occasion the two clashed for forty long minutes over one word, with Bruguière, a classicist, invoking its Latin or Greek etymology, and Carlos its English or Spanish translations.

After three years in jail, Carlos launched a personal attack on the judge, casting doubt over his independence and impartiality because of his links with the victims' association SOS Attacks, which under French law has access to investigation files as a civil plaintiff. Carlos took Judge Bruguière to task for attending a ceremony at the Père Lachaise cemetery in Paris to commemorate the victims of the bombing of a French UTA DC10 airliner six years earlier with Françoise Rudetzki, the president of SOS Attacks. One of the association's lawyers has acknowledged that its representatives met the judge as often as once a week, but this in itself is not illegal under French law.[29]

In the first few years following Carlos's arrest, France showed no desire to give him a chance to proclaim publicly that his arrest had been illegal. His rare and brief court appearances, at hearings prompted by his appeals against his detention on the grounds that he had been kidnapped from Sudan, were with one exception behind closed doors. His manner was private theatrics. When the judge entered, Carlos would stand in the dock, join his hands together and bow forward slightly to proffer the traditional Arabic greeting *Salam Alaykum* (May peace be with you). Robbed of an audience, these were for Carlos only dress-rehearsals for the public performance that was yet to come.

Carlos's determination in pressing the kidnap suit won him a judicial triumph. On the day that he was hauled to France, the Justice Ministry had made it clear that it had no intention of investigating the circumstances of the abduction, as these were classified a state secret. An investigating magistrate invoked 'technical reasons' to justify his refusal to follow up Carlos's plea. But in June 1996, almost two years after his capture, an appeal court found in Carlos's favour. The verdict was a public slap in the face for both Interior Minister Pasqua and Judge Bruguière. The arrest had taken place 'outside any legal framework, and without either an international warrant or an extradition convention between France and Sudan'.[30] The court ordered an investigation into 'events that may have involved French nationals aboard a French plane and on French territory'.[31] The ruling was however only a fleeting victory for Carlos, as it was later crushed by the supreme court.

14

The Trial

> There is a Carlos myth and it is blown up out of all proportion. Carlos is here, Carlos is there, he is a Soviet agent, he is making a nuclear bomb to blow up New York...
>
> – Carlos at his trial

The Paris assizes court is the most ornate and daunting in the Palais de Justice which stretches across the entire Ile de la Cité, with the Brigade Criminelle at one end and the Conciergerie where Queen Marie-Antoinette spent her last hours before she was guillotined at the other. Below the blue, white and gold coffered ceiling, a huge fresco covering almost an entire wall shows red-robed cardinals and nobles paying homage at the coronation of the child-king of Navarre, Henry IV, a ceremony as solemnly orchestrated as the trials that take place in the courtroom.

Two life-sized lions carved out of white stone tower above the large door through which the judge and jury file into the court, and smaller lions, mouths gaping and teeth bared, are carved into the oak panels that line the walls. The box destined for the accused is large enough to accommodate twenty people on its hard wooden benches. Emile Zola had sat there just short of a hundred years ago in 1898, on trial for penning the virulent manifesto *J'accuse* in defence of the Jewish officer, Alfred Dreyfus. Many of the senior French officials accused of collaborating with the

Nazis during the war had also sat in the dock, as had the last man sentenced to the guillotine (who was spared by President Mitterrand).

The forty-eight-year-old Carlos who strolled into the box just after one o'clock on Friday, 12 December 1997 looked for all the world as if he were stepping into a café for a pre-lunch *apéritif.* Among all the crimes he was charged with, French justice had chosen the shooting in Rue Toullier of three DST officers and Michel Moukharbal – for which Carlos had been given a life sentence in absentia five years earlier – as the first case to come to court since his abduction from Sudan in August 1994.

Dressed in khaki trousers, a white shirt and a beige jacket, Carlos sported a grey ascot scarf with yellow stripes. His handcuffs had been taken off moments before. He carried a plastic shopping bag, swaggering slightly as he made for the front bench. He glanced at the public gallery as if to seek out friends. Gold-rimmed spectacles hung from a cord around his neck. Carlos was to all appearances in good health. But his hair was thinner and greyer, and his face paler and more wrinkled than in the video taken by the Egyptian spy which had shown him dancing in Sudan.

Carlos had brushed his hair back, and trimmed his moustache down to the thin line of a dandy. Were it not for his commanding nose and his deep-set, piercing grey eyes, his round face and solid build would have given him a genial air. The sharp looks of his youth were almost gone. Betraying no sign of tension other than a slight flush in the face, he sat down, leaned forward to rest his arms on the wooden ledge, and looked around him. He chatted quietly with his lawyers who were sitting in front of him.

The layout of the courtroom set the stage for head-on confrontation. Carlos sat with his back to the wall, flanked by three grim-faced gendarmes clad in black who would also stand, arms folded, every time Carlos got up to speak. Glass partitions separated the box from the jury at one end, and from the public gallery at the other. On the opposite side of the courtroom, facing him, were the relatives of the DST men shot in Rue Toullier: Commissaire Jean Herranz, and inspectors Jean Donatini and Raymond Dous. Herranz, the only man to survive the assassin's bullets, had died of cancer four years earlier.

To Carlos's right, on a raised dais facing the room, sat the presiding judge, Yves Corneloup. Unlike his counterparts in Anglo-Saxon courts, the judge would play the main role in the trial, exercising his right to question the accused and the witnesses himself, and reading out testimony gathered by investigators. Any questioning of Carlos or of a witness by lawyers for the civil plaintiffs or by the public prosecutor had to be channelled through him.

'Surname, first name, date and place of birth, profession, and address,' recited the judge. Carlos stood up. 'My name is Ilich Ramírez Sánchez. I was born in Caracas, Venezuela on 12 October 1949. My profession is "professional revolutionary", in the Leninist tradition. My last address? Listen, the world is my domain, I am an internationalist professional revolutionary, but my last address is Khartoum, Sudan.' The packed courtroom laughed when Carlos gave his profession. His voice was steady and self-assured, and he spoke in French with a heavy Spanish accent that often made it difficult to understand him. His French was otherwise excellent, and he was able to follow closely the intricacies of the debates.

Dipping into a large urn, Judge Corneloup picked the names of nine people who, together with himself and two professional magistrates, would constitute the jury. Temporarily occupying the benches reserved for the press opposite Carlos, some forty potential jurors, chosen at random from electoral registers and at least twenty-three years old, sat waiting for the selection to end. The twelve jurors would decide whether Carlos was innocent or guilty of the murder of Donatini, Dous and Moukharbal, and of the attempted murder of Herranz. In the case of a guilty verdict, the jurors would also set the penalty. As the death sentence had been abolished in 1981, the heaviest penalty was life imprisonment.

The six women and three men chosen haphazardly by the judge walked past Carlos to take their places at either side of the judge and the two professional magistrates, facing the courtroom. Again involuntarily, Carlos had prompted laughter in the public gallery and the press box when he gave a broad smile to one juror, a blonde woman wearing an electric blue suit, as she walked past him. The jurors swore 'not to betray the interests of either the accused or those of the society that accuses him ... to give way to neither hatred nor spite, neither fear nor affection ... to keep the deliberations secret, even after the conclusion of your functions'. Young and casually dressed for the most part, they looked uncomfortable in such august surroundings and from then on took copious notes, careful to hide their feelings as required by law.

One of the jurors later agreed to be interviewed for this book and so reveal aspects of the trial that would otherwise remain secret, on condition that his or her identity would not be published. Juror X, as this person will be referred to, found out a few weeks before the trial of the possibility of being among those deciding Carlos's fate. 'Like everybody else, I had heard this terrorist mentioned over the years,' Juror X explained. 'But I hadn't read anything much about him in particular, and so much time had gone by since the attacks to which he had been linked.'[1]

Juror X had been impressed by reports that the members of the jury would be placed under police surveillance. In fact, Juror X and other jurors were each offered two bodyguards for the duration of the trial. The security was somewhat limited, however: the bodyguards simply accompanied the jurors from their homes to the law courts in the morning and back again every evening. 'I very quickly realised that the police protection was aimed above all at protecting me from possible pressure from the media,' Juror X related. 'Thanks to that protection, I could feel free to listen to proceedings. I could also live my daily life outside the Palais de Justice as normally as possible.' From then on, Juror X was absorbed by the unfolding trial: 'I felt like an actor rather than a spectator, passionately keen on hearing and remembering everything. I took dozens of pages of notes, and at night I dreamed of the trial. I could hear Carlos speaking.'

Carlos lost no time in making it clear that he would remain master of his own defence, and that his lawyers would only play a minor role. After worrying the microphone to make sure that he could be heard, he apologised for his strong accent. 'I have been prevented from taking French language lessons. I have tried to learn to speak properly by watching the bad television you have in France and by reading the newspapers.' It was a deceptively mild opening gambit. Carlos revelled in his chance to perform, seizing every opportunity to speak, and giving clenched-fist salutes to sympathisers in the audience, including four youths wearing Arafat-style chequered scarves around their necks.

Carlos appeared to be completely at ease, taking swigs from a bottle of Badoit mineral water which he had carried into the box, breaking into a wide grin when one of his lawyers described him in a sarcastic tone as 'the man said to be the world's number one terrorist', and asking the judge to supply him with a miniature microphone which he could attach to his lapel. In no mood for banter, the judge reprimanded Carlos for his slack posture as he stood in the dock. Carlos had leaned his foot on the bench, and was resting an elbow on his thigh. Carlos answered with a smile: 'I am an old gentleman of forty-eight. I am not sitting where you are, and it's not comfortable here.' The judge rarely called Carlos to order, mostly letting him talk as much as he wanted.

Within minutes of the trial starting, Carlos demanded that it be cancelled and explained why: he had been kidnapped in Sudan and his imprisonment in France was therefore illegal. 'I live in a legal void,' Carlos proclaimed. 'Today I challenge the right of French justice to try me. But I am forced to answer before you because I do not want to fall into a trap.' The lawyer's son could not resist the temptation to let himself be dragged into the judicial arena. Should the judge reject Carlos's plea, he should at least ban the SOS Attacks association from supplying the two lawyers who represented the victims' relatives. Legally, the association could only represent victims of terrorism, and the Rue Toullier shootings had nothing to do with terrorism, Carlos argued.

Worse, Carlos charged, the association (whose president, Françoise Rudetzki, is Jewish) exploited the suffering of the families 'in the name of the most ignoble of ideologies, revisionist Zionism'. SOS Attacks therefore represented the enemy he had been fighting since, he claimed, the age of fourteen. 'I am a political militant,' Carlos proclaimed. 'Our enemy is the enemy of humanity, of the French people, of the Palestinian people – US imperialism and its avatar, the Zionists. In the name of the suffering of the Jewish community during the Second World War, they lay claim to occupying a Holy Land which belongs to all humanity and fundamentally to the Palestinian people.'

When the judge asked him about the purpose of the Popular Front, Carlos answered, to laughs from the public: 'Buying tulips in the Netherlands.' But then he abruptly turned serious, slapping the edge of the dock with his palm as he raised his voice: 'We waged war against the Zionists, all over the world. We were at war!' He had no hesitation in admitting that this battle involved hijacking planes, taking hostages and carrying out 'executions' – all crimes that were justified because they were part of a war. 'I am morally responsible before the whole world, before history, before our martyrs and before the Palestinians, for all the military operations carried out by Palestinians. And I am politically responsible for all the operations carried out by the Popular Front.' Whether the Rue Toullier shootings were part of those operations, and whether it was he who had pulled the trigger, was an issue that Carlos side-stepped. There was no reason for him to plead innocent or guilty, he argued, as he was illegally imprisoned.

Carlos couched his commitment in revolutionary jargon that sounded outdated but then, in Magdalena Kopp's phrase, he did not realise that the war was over. 'For thirty years I have waged war with the pen, the gun, the bomb and the noose. It is a permanent struggle . . . I must continue my struggle. Today I fight with my tongue. If I was a lowly combatant I would sit here and not open my mouth, but I am a leader. I must fight until my last sigh.' One exchange was particularly revealing of Carlos's refusal to turn the page. Could Carlos confirm that he served as Moukharbal's right-hand man, the judge wanted to know. After all, this question related to events more than two decades ago. 'It's a delicate question,' retorted Carlos. 'The Popular Front still exists, this is not history but current affairs.'

The second day of the trial, Monday, started with a defeat for Carlos. Judge Corneloup announced that he had decided to reject Carlos's appeals. The European Court of Human Rights had refused to consider Carlos's plea that he had been illegally kidnapped in Sudan, and therefore he could be tried by a French court. As for the demand that SOS Attacks be expelled from the courtroom, the judge decided to rule on the matter later. In the meantime, the trial must continue.

Carlos had changed into smarter clothes, and looked like a flashy yachtsman, dressed in a blazer, white Lacoste polo shirt, and blue jeans, with a white silk handkerchief poking out of his breast pocket. His mostly urbane manner, however, alternated with thinly veiled threats worthy of a Mafioso. Carlos complained about the three gendarmes standing by him in the dock; another twenty were stationed around the courtroom. He urged the jury not to let themselves be impressed by such heavy security. 'I'm used to weapons, and it doesn't impress me,' Carlos assured the jurors. 'Quite the contrary, it makes me feel nostalgic. No revolutionary movement has ever dreamed of putting pressure on jurors. *You are not in danger.* You are in danger of being manipulated. It's true that magistrates were bumped off, several times, but I don't regret that' (author's italics). Facing the judge, Carlos added for his benefit: 'You are taking on a great responsibility, Your Honour. I'm not under orders from you. Don't forget who I am.'

If Carlos had failed in his first attempt to halt the trial, he still had plenty of other tricks up his sleeve. Cast out of the limelight by her client on the first day, Carlos's chief counsel, Isabelle Coutant-Peyre, a spiky, militant left-winger with curly black hair who had helped represent Magdalena Kopp fifteen years earlier, now took centre-stage. The court, Coutant-Peyre charged, had yielded to pressure from the DST, which she termed 'the political police', in failing to call any of the eye-witnesses who were present in the Rue Toullier flat at the time of the crime. The Rue Toullier affair was part of a plot by the DST, in partnership with Mossad, which she said had recruited Moukharbal, to shatter a mutual non-aggression pact between French authorities and Palestinian organisations. However, no evidence was produced to back this claim.

The investigating magistrate, Judge Bruguière, Coutant-Peyre said, had made mistakes in transcribing the names of the surviving eye-witnesses on his official warrants to ensure that police in Venezuela, where the witnesses were presumed to reside, would be unable to track them down. French justice dictated that proceedings in an assizes court must be based on a verbal confrontation between witnesses and the accused, and robbing Carlos of that confrontation meant that this would not be a fair trial, but a Stalinist trial. What was more, only part of the evidence had been brought before the court, and the originals of many key documents were missing. There were therefore sufficient grounds for calling a stop to this trial.

The counsel for the victims' relatives, Francis Szpiner, countered in booming tones that this was in no way a Soviet-style trial with a foregone conclusion. 'Ladies and gentlemen of the jury, when you judge Carlos you must answer a single question: Did he kill the DST inspectors? The only basis for your decision must be your intimate conviction.' The proof of Carlos's guilt lay in his confessions, in the experts' reports and in accounts by eyewitnesses – the Latin Americans at the party in the flat, and Herranz – taken down in the hours that followed the crime. If Carlos had not yet been confronted with the witnesses, it was for good reason: he had been on the run for more than two decades. As for French justice, it had done everything in its power to find the witnesses and bring them to court.

Judge Corneloup blamed the bad grace of the Venezuelan political establishment for the lack of witnesses in court. It was not France's fault, the judge said, if Venezuelan politicians considered Carlos a national hero. The judge refused to postpone proceedings to seek out witnesses and again ruled against the defence. Coutant-Peyre promptly declared that she refused to prostitute herself (an unfortunate turn of phrase for which she later apologised) in a trial unworthy of French justice, and she stormed out of the courtroom halfway through Monday's proceedings. She refused to obey the judge's order that she serve as a barrister appointed by the court. After Carlos protested repeatedly that he had been left without a counsel, the judge had no alternative but to appoint two young lawyers who were given only a night to read the ten volumes of judicial proceedings on Rue Toullier.

There was nothing that the assizes court could do to force witnesses to come to the bar. Amparo Silva Masmela, the Paris girlfriend whose flat Carlos had turned into an arsenal, was tracked down by Interpol in Spain but she refused to come and testify. Angela Otaola, his London lover who was jailed for looking after more of his weapons, also stayed away. 'Who is she?' Carlos asked ingenuously when the judge read out her name. She sent a medical certificate to the court which invoked her economic situation, professional considerations and the fact that she had needed psychological treatment for eight years 'to be able to tackle daily life'.

Carlos's tactics delayed proceedings considerably, and it was only on Monday evening that the jury were finally given an initial outline of the events they had been called to judge. The reading of the sixteen-page indictment by the clerk of the court apparently failed to move Carlos. Head bowed, he followed the clerk by reading a copy of the text resting on his knee. He stroked his moustache when the clerk came to the passage describing the points of entry and exit of the bullet which had killed Dous. When the proceedings were adjourned shortly afterwards, Carlos turned as usual towards the public gallery before he walked out. But rather than the defiant clenched-fist salute that he usually gave, he only managed a weak wave of the hand.

Commandant Daniel Aberard of the Brigade Criminelle, who took the witness stand on Tuesday morning, was the first person called to testify. A short and stout fifty-year-old, he read out the biography of Carlos he had compiled from reports by the police and secret services of France and other countries. Reminders of Carlos's love life flattered him, and when one of his London students was quoted as saying that he had constantly tried to chat her up, Carlos threw his head back and laughed silently to himself.

According to Juror X, none of this impressed the women in the jury, and nor did the fact that Carlos had kissed the lawyer Coutant-Peyre on the hand at close of business in the evenings: 'The female jurors were surprised to read in the newspapers that Carlos was supposedly a great seducer, or had been in the past. The women in the jury thought he was more like a horrible Latin-American.'

When Judge Corneloup questioned Carlos about the biography that had just been read out, Carlos picked holes in the account, reprimanding Aberard for what he said were a host of factual mistakes. Carlos denied that he had felt embarrassed by his childhood nickname 'El Gordo' (Fatso) as Aberard had reported. Nor had he ever set foot in Cuba, although he had some family there: 'You know, *Monsieur le Président*, I have children everywhere.' Carlos also denied ever giving an interview to the magazine *Al Watan al Arabi*, in which he had claimed responsibility for the Rue Toullier murders and several other attacks and bombings.

'Professional revolutionary.' In almost his first words to the court Carlos had set the tone of his defence. When the judge questioned him about his political commitment, Carlos insisted that the war to free Palestine was by definition a war that had to be fought outside Palestine, a world war. He felt only pride for the battle he had fought: 'I am a man of a proud nature. I am proud of my struggle, of my ideology, of the hundreds of militant revolutionaries whom I trained and who will train hundreds of others and continue the struggle after my death.' Just as he was proud of the one hundred passports and the fifty-two different aliases which, by his own reckoning, he had used during his years as a fugitive.

At no time did he display any trace of regret, let alone remorse. Only once, late on Tuesday, did Carlos play down his role in the war he had waged: 'It is wrong to personalise a revolution. There is a Carlos myth and it is blown up out of all proportion. Carlos is here, Carlos is there, he is a

Soviet agent, he is preparing a nuclear bomb to blow up New York ... My comrades in India have sent me stories by women who told of their torrid nights with me. I have never seen these women.'

Carlos had no problem recognising the only witness from his past life whom France managed to bring before the court. A few hours before his former London girlfriend, and assistant, Nydia Tobon was due to testify on the fourth day of the trial, Carlos announced that he had recruited her into the Popular Front. But now, he said, Nydia lived in France as a paid agent of the DST which would never allow her to appear at his trial. He was proved wrong when Nydia did enter the courtroom early on Wednesday afternoon.

Sprucely turned out in grey trousers, red sweater, a double-breasted blazer and a necklace of large coloured beads, she looked younger than her fifty-nine years. Carlos faced her and smiled as she walked past him on her way to the witness stand, but she stared straight ahead so as not to catch the eye of the man for whose sake she had spent a year in a British jail. As she was entitled to, she did not speak on oath. In low, demure tones, and with a Spanish lilt, she described how their paths had first crossed. 'We went out several times to have fun. Once I was going up an escalator at Holborn Tube station. It's very high there. I looked up and I saw him halfway up the stairs. I started running up the stairs to say hello because I liked him very much.' Carlos smiled at the recollection. 'Once, in a restaurant,' Nydia continued, 'he told me that he was happy because he had found a cause to fight for – Palestine. I told him that for me Latin America and my country were the most important. I told him that I respected his choice. I have a great deal of esteem for him.'

The judge, the first to question Nydia, wanted to know about her relations with Carlos at the time of the Rue Toullier murders. How did she find out about the killings?

By reading the *Guardian*. Did Carlos not telephone her soon after the murders? He did, but she was out and he left a message for her with a friend which said: 'Tell Nydia that André [alias Moukharbal] is dead.' Was it true that she had written a book on Carlos in 1978? Yes. 'It was foolish of me. I wanted to make the book more spicy, more marketable, so I took material from newspaper articles and put it in. I wrote that Carlos called me and told me that he had assassinated André. But that is not true.'

Her statement threatened to weaken the prosecution's case. In the book, Nydia had written that she had spoken to Carlos by telephone after the triple murder, and that during this conversation he had confessed to the killings. The judge was anxious that the jury should hear the relevant extract from the book, whatever Nydia had to say about it, and an interpreter translated from the Spanish: 'I had to do it. Moukharbal was a coward, the police took him and he sold us. I had to make a way for myself by shooting. There was no way of avoiding him ... It was him or me. I think that if I had fallen into their hands I would have been killed.' Carlos helped the interpreter with her translation, suggesting a word when she stumbled.

The judge turned to Nydia. 'So, *Madame*. What do you have to say?'

'All that was taken from newspaper articles to write a kind of novel,' she answered.

'Three years after the event,' the judge insisted, 'at a time when you are seeking political asylum in France, you write a novel which can only concern the authorities? You say you were a friend of Carlos, and yet you write things which can only put him in a terrible situation? How could you, a lawyer, write such lies about your friend?'

Nydia was on slippery ground, and she hesitated before answering. 'It was thoughtless of me. But here you see him as a terrorist, an assassin, a cold-blooded mercenary. If you talk to people from my country Colombia, or from

Venezuela, you will see how they see him there.'

Pressed further by the judge, Nydia protested lamely that she was sorry and that this questioning was painful for her as it reminded her of a traumatic period of her life. The judge upbraided her sharply: 'The "torture" of testifying before the assizes court twenty-two years on is nothing compared to the suffering of those who waited twenty-two years to understand why their father or why their husband died.'

Like his lawyers, Carlos had the right to question witnesses provided that he put his queries through Judge Corneloup – a condition which in practice was waived, so that Carlos's interventions amounted to cross-examination. When his turn came to question Nydia, Carlos greeted her with a show of deference, using the title by which lawyers are addressed in France: '*Bonjour Maître Tobon*.' Both hands resting on the edge of the dock, he leaned towards her slightly. 'I am delighted to see you again after all these years, to see you in good health and elegant. She is almost sixty years old but look, she is an elegant woman.' Nydia stood rigid at the witness stand, making no move to acknowledge the compliment nor to look in Carlos's direction.

With fond recollection, Carlos recalled their idyll: 'I was rather a good looker. It's true, we were lovers. Nydia Tobon has no need to hide a sexual peccadillo with me.' As Carlos questioned her about their relationship and her political commitment, like a lawyer sternly cross-examining a witness, he went back on his earlier assertion that he had recruited her for the Popular Front. Perhaps this was his reward for the help that she had given him in her testimony. The book she had written about him, Carlos concluded, was cheap, pulp fiction.

Nydia Tobon was the first and last acquaintance of Carlos to testify. The defence was deprived of a clash with the three students who were in the flat at the time the shots were fired. Instead, Carlos had to make do with battling police and DST officers, as well as medical, graphology and ballistics experts.

With virtually all the witnesses, Carlos tried to cast doubt over the official DST version which said that the men he was accused of shooting were unarmed. But as with many of the allegations that Carlos made in court, he had no proof. Commissaire Jean Lafargue of the Brigade Criminelle, a friend of Donatini who had played soccer with him a week before he saw his body stretched out in the Rue Toullier flat, dismissed Carlos's allegations.

Late on Wednesday, Lafargue testified that a DST official told him shortly after the murders that the guns of the three secret servicemen were at headquarters. During one recess, Dous's son Gilles recalled that Dous had telephoned his wife to say that he had to leave headquarters for a short while but that he would return home straight afterwards, without going back to his office. Had he carried a weapon, he would have had to hand it in for the weekend. 'Even if one of the DST men had a weapon, it wouldn't have made much difference,' Gilles Dous remarked.[2]

The shortage of exhibits provided the defence with an easy target, which it sought to exploit on Thursday. Better investigations had been carried out into the deaths of tramps in the Métro, reckoned one defence lawyer. Captain Pascal Loriot of the Brigade Criminelle acknowledged that Scotland Yard had agreed to supply the original letter sent by Carlos to his girlfriend Angela Otaola in London, on condition that French prosecutors made a specific request for it. It was in this eighteen-line letter, written hours after the killings, that Carlos wrote in a reference to Moukharbal: 'As for the "Chiquitin" [little baby], I have sent him to a better world, because he was a traitor.'

Despite the importance of such an exhibit, no request to Scotland Yard for use of the original letter during the trial had been made. A French graphologist, Pierre Feydeau, was given only a photograph of the letter as a basis for determining whether it matched Carlos's handwriting. Feydeau told the court that he had concluded that it did, but this was not good enough for Carlos who shouted as he vented his exasperation, or perhaps pretended to, at the court: 'You cannot go on like this! Where are the originals? They don't exist. The expert has worked on a photograph which is supposedly of the letter. He says it is written by me. He is lying!'

Judge Corneloup read out another alleged confession by Carlos, an extract from his interview to the magazine *Al Watan al Arabi* in which he described shooting Moukharbal 'between the eyes'. Carlos again denied giving the interview, and challenged the judge: 'Do you believe what you have just read? It's not me, I don't speak like that. Someone who knew this information passed it on.' Carlos's lawyers argued that 'secrecy, silence and the shadows' had been his only guarantees of survival, and for that reason it would have been absurd to expect him to sue the magazine. But in an unguarded moment, perhaps tired by the effort of following proceedings in a foreign language, Carlos admitted that the writing on the back of his photograph given to the author of the interview – the message read: 'To a wonderful poet from an apprentice poet' – could well be his own.

Clashing with another witness, Pierre Leport, an expert in forensic medicine, Carlos sought to undermine his testimony. Leport's role, Carlos stressed, had been limited to summarising the reports of studies carried out by other doctors on the bodies of the dead men and on the wounded Herranz. Using one of his lawyers as a stand-in, Carlos – who described himself as an arms expert – cheerfully shaped his hand like a pistol and pointed it at various points of the man's head to dispute the findings on the paths taken by the bullets. Seconds later, Carlos roared at the judge: 'This is not an expert's report, it is lies!' The judge ordered him out of the courtroom so he could calm down but Carlos sat down and refused to move. 'That's the end of it,' the judge said testily. 'It's only beginning,' Carlos muttered audibly.

Carlos was right. The DST's attempt later on Thursday to salvage what it could of the dignity it lost in the Rue Toullier mayhem further weakened the prosecution's case. Jean-François Clair, head of the DST counter-terrorism unit, was the only secret serviceman called to the bar, and no effort was made to mask his identity. At the time of the killings the fifty-three-year-old Clair was the head of research in the counter-terrorism unit and a subordinate of Herranz, and as such might well have been sent to his death in Rue Toullier had he not been on holiday at the time. Carlos treated him with the respect due, as he put it, from one intelligence professional to another. Clair was 'a seasoned officer whom we know well'.

In sending Clair before the court, the directors of French counter-intelligence entrusted him with a thankless mission which he had to accomplish in a glare of publicity. To present the events leading up to the murders in as favourable a light as possible, Clair pleaded that in the mid-1970s the DST was inexperienced in dealing with terrorism. It was only after Mossad blew up Mohamed Boudia that the DST found out that he was the Popular Front's man in Paris. As for the grenade attack on the Drugstore Saint-Germain, the DST linked it with Carlos only when it discovered a similar device in the flat of his ex-girlfriend Amparo after the Rue Toullier bloodbath. Nor did the secret service at the time have any idea who had carried out the failed attacks on Israeli planes at Orly airport in January 1975.

The toughest part of Clair's assignment was to explain why the DST, given all the information it had about Moukharbal within hours of his arrest in Beirut, treated him as a low-ranking activist. The first that the DST heard of Moukharbal, he declared, was when it learned that he would fly from Beirut to Paris on 13 June 1975. Moukharbal was described as a liaison agent of the Popular Front. He was preparing attacks against the Israeli ambassador to Paris among others.

How had the DST found this out? The judge demanded. From a source that must remain secret because the DST had an obligation to protect it, Clair responded.

Did the DST not know about Moukharbal's arrest in Beirut? It only found out after the killings from Amparo whom he himself had questioned, Clair testified.

Just as the DST had used the same tactic to hide the circumstances of Carlos's capture in Sudan, so it threw a national security secrecy cover over its information. The source that Clair was so keen to protect for 'deontological reasons and as a matter of principle' was the former DST officer Jean-Paul Mauriat, who had helped the Lebanese Sûreté question Moukharbal in Beirut. Mauriat had fully briefed the DST about the arrest, and it was in consultation with the DST that Moukharbal was put on the Paris flight. If Clair refused to reveal his source, it was to shield the DST. Clair also did not say that Moukharbal had spoken about Carlos (albeit as his hitman Nourredine) to his Lebanese interrogators, and that the DST knew he had done so. As Clair said during his testimony: 'I am a human being but I must ensure that the decision of the state prevails.'

For six days the relatives of the murdered officers had been forced to hold back their anger as Carlos's defence tactics (including the return of the lawyer who had previously stormed out, Isabelle Coutant-Peyre) ensured that the trial went ahead at a snail's pace. The families were finally given a chance to speak out on Friday. The court listened in silence. Carlos sat staring quietly, stroking his moustache, taking notes, and at times looking moved by what he heard. Gilles Dous, in his late thirties, was the first to take the witness stand, and managed only a few sentences in a faint voice. 'My father always brought me up to respect other people. I find it very difficult to speak of him. He never spoke to me of arms or violence. All he wanted was that men should be better.' Louis Donatini, a retired police officer, spoke with more assurance but his voice shook with both sadness and pent-up rage: 'Jean Donatini was my little brother. He was the victim of an abominable murderer. On my advice, perhaps unfortunately, he joined the police and then he joined the DST. He was assassinated on an official assignment and I ask you simply, when you have unmasked the murderer, to condemn him to live in jail.'

Jean-Noël Herranz, a sports photographer from Toulouse, stood stiffly, arms folded across his chest: 'I have come to try and represent the memory of my father out of solidarity with the people who died at his side. He suffered both mentally and physically from this shooting, but mainly mentally. I was eight years old at the time. The shooting changed quite a few things, including family relationships, but I would rather not talk about that. He would have been the only eye-witness today, so it is important for me to be here.'

The French victims were at the heart of the first summing-up speech by the relatives' lawyers on Monday. For a week, the attorney Jean-Paul Lévy said, the relatives of the men shot in cold blood by a professional killer had endured the scorn of the accused, his boastful nature, his threats, his sniggers and his playacting. The accused had tried to turn the court into a grotesque theatre, but he had not succeeded. You, the jury, said Lévy as he faced the dais, know nothing of the men who were shot that evening. Jean Herranz had taken part in the liberation of Paris and was decorated for dragging his commanding officer from a blazing vehicle. Jean Donatini was the son of an Italian builder who emigrated to France before the Second World War. Raymond Dous disliked carrying a weapon so much that he was reprimanded several times by his superiors. At eight o'clock on the evening of that fateful Friday Dous telephoned his wife to say he would be late home. At two o'clock the following morning she was told that he had been shot dead. For the next fifteen years she suffered from an obsession, seeing her husband everywhere she went.

Lévy glowered at Carlos, who had been nervously chewing his lower lip, a hunted look in his eyes as he listened. 'It would have been easy for you to spare them, to hold them at gunpoint. You say you were the first in your commando training camp. The truth is that you are above all an experienced gunman and that you shoot to kill.' Carlos looked down, the first time that he had failed to hold an opponent's gaze in the courtroom.

The chief attorney representing the families, Szpiner, jumped up to launch into a passionate harangue that in a British or US court would have been given by the public prosecutor. 'Once these boys were told that their fathers had been honoured posthumously, once they were told that the assassin was Carlos, what did they live through? A nightmare. In 1976 they saw this man carry out the OPEC raid, and then be given asylum in Algeria. For years they knew that the man who caused their misfortune was alive, and a legend was born. For twenty-two years he thought that he could kill with impunity. His mistake was to kill police officers of the Republic, and the Republic never forgets the assassinations of police officers.'

The three officers had gone to Rue Toullier simply to trace an organisation, and for that reason they had gone unarmed, Szpiner continued, pacing up and down in front of the dock and pausing to lay a hand on the shoulder of Donatini's brother. The defence claimed that the bodies were moved shortly after the shooting, which was true. But not to take guns off them. The bodies were moved by the emergency medical team to find out if the men could be saved. 'Only one thing bothered Carlos: the fact that he shot at men who were unarmed. That was cowardly and it harmed his legend.' Carlos had shot the men like dogs, and the evidence of his guilt was beyond doubt: the depositions of four eye-witnesses including Herranz, the confessions that Carlos had made to his lovers and in a magazine interview, and his fingerprints which were found at the flat. Carlos had pressed the trigger because he believed that Moukharbal had betrayed him. Carlos knew that he faced the guillotine if caught. Today, the jury should impose the maximum sentence, life in jail.

'I have followed Carlos since 1983, I collect all that is written about him,' Szpiner concluded. 'For all these years I have imagined him here. And now he is here. I respect his rights; this is no lynching and no Stalinist trial. As a man who proclaimed himself a professional revolutionary, Carlos has, I admit, surprised me. I thought he would either challenge French justice or say the truth: "I was twenty-six years old, I shot them, I was at war." But you, Carlos, have resorted to the path of pettiness and insult. You have insulted the victims. You said at the start of the trial that you were not a chicken thief. Let me tell you that you defend yourself like a chicken thief, and not like a revolutionary. This trial will show you for what you are, the myth will be tarnished and democracy will have scored a victory in revealing those who combat it for what they really are.' Carlos, a mocking smile on his face, clapped silently. He made the same gesture when the public prosecutor ended his plea after also asking the jury to impose the heaviest sentence possible.

With three of his lawyers down to speak before Carlos himself, the last day of the trial, Tuesday, was entirely dedicated to the arguments of the defence. They argued that the accusations against their client were a fabrication, and that the fingerprints found at the flat had been tampered with. The fact that the DST refused to reveal the source that had led it to Moukharbal perhaps implied that there had been a deal between the DST and the informer. 'Carlos is being investigated for four other attacks, so he will in any case stay in jail for a long period of his life, perhaps even for all his life,' attorney Oliver Maudret told the jury. 'You cannot cancel this trial. But I suggest that you sanction the fact that the rights of the accused have been violated as he was not confronted with his accusers. The only way you can do this is by acquitting Carlos. I ask this of you not for Carlos but for us, for this country, for the rule of law, and for truth.'

'Carlos Final Act', quipped a reporter on Tuesday evening as Carlos, clutching a red plastic folder and a bottle of Badoit, stepped into the dock. His first court appearance had sapped little of his self-confidence, and he paused at length to smile at the public gallery. Two days earlier he had declared dramatically: 'Carlos is a dead man. He will never leave France alive. If I get out of France in a hostage swap, I will die riddled with lead. I am proud because I chose this path at fourteen, and I want to die standing like a revolutionary, not on my knees but on the pedestal of the Revolution.'

His last speech was intended for a wider audience than the twelve members of the jury who would withdraw to consider their verdict as soon as he finished speaking. 'The world must hear me, because the world is also present here,' Carlos said with a glance at the public gallery and at the press box. At one point he interrupted himself to ask the public gallery whether he could be heard clearly. Several people shouted '*Non!*' so Carlos moved to another microphone. So at ease was Carlos that at one point he paused to mime playing a cup-and-ball-game as he recalled an episode with his brother Lenin.

It took Carlos almost four hours to work his way through the points he had noted in the red folder which he rested on the edge of the dock as he spoke. In his rambling speech he reiterated the points he had made over the past eight days: there were no witnesses and no evidence, Nydia's book was fiction, the experts were not qualified to testify.

The trial had been a conspiracy to hide the truth from beginning to end, a judicial stampede in which evidence was discussed but not shown. The trial had been an attempt to destroy the Carlos myth, he insisted: 'The myth brought hundreds of millions of dollars to the Palestinians. Everyone benefited from it. I don't give a damn about the Carlos myth, it's not me who created it.' Portraying himself as a victim rather than the accused, Carlos denounced the lawyers who he said had betrayed him since his capture, the isolation in jail which constituted permanent harassment, and the withholding of his private correspondence.

Carlos admitted that he knew part of the truth about Rue Toullier, alleging that it was a plot by the DST in partnership with Mossad. But he refused to say what he knew, because to do so would amount to collaborating with American hegemonism, and its Israeli metastases. The odds were stacked against him, and this would be his last chance for a long time to defend his record: 'I heard people talk of a bloodthirsty mercenary. I am not bloodthirsty, I waged war for thirty years. A mercenary is a hired killer, someone who does things for money. Never did we do anything for money, never did we act at the service of someone else. We fought for an ideology, for the most noble of causes, Palestine.' His war was a world war, a war to the death against, in his bizarre jargon, 'the McDonald-isation of humanity, against American neo-barbarism'. But Carlos had no doubts as to his fate: 'I am getting old, the end approaches. I will join my comrades in paradise where all revolutionaries are.'

When Carlos sat down, Judge Corneloup congratulated him on his physical condition, pointing out that he had spoken for a considerable length of time. Carlos acknowledged the compliment with a smile. Shortly after nine o'clock on Tuesday evening the jury withdrew to consider its verdict, and the punishment it would impose on Carlos if he was found guilty. Early on in the trial Carlos had confided to one of his lawyers: 'They are going to jail me for life because I am Carlos.' And during his last speech he had told the jury: 'You can sentence me to life in prison, that doesn't scare me.'

The eight-day trial had been an exhausting experience for the jury, so much so that one woman, according to Juror X, asked Judge Corneloup for a pause in proceedings on the last day as she felt that she was about to faint. For Juror X as for other jury members, the Rue Toullier affair had revealed itself in a confusing fashion, punctuated by flashbacks as each witness or deposition 'added an extra piece to the jigsaw puzzle'. The constant adjournments prompted by the procedural battles fought by Carlos's lawyers had also weighed heavily on the jurors. 'Coutant-Peyre's strategy, the fact that she left the trial and then came back, was as far as I could tell a ploy to seek some ground for an appeal to the Supreme Court after the trial finished,' Juror X said.

Juror X had found Carlos's attitude towards the jurors and the victims respectful, but felt he had been less deferential towards the witnesses. 'To me he rarely seemed vehement or aggressive,' Juror X related. 'If I had been risking my freedom, I would have been much more aggressive than Carlos. I found him neither hateful nor likeable, leaving aside the horror of the crimes he was accused of. That's not true of all the jurors. Physically, he looked older than his age, apparently worn down by drinking and smoking too much.' Carlos's Palestinian and revolutionary commitments were unconvincing: 'He never told us what this commitment consisted of exactly. He seemed more like a gun for hire who had been abandoned by everyone.'

The jury's deliberations are covered by a strict secrecy rule. Juror X, however, raised several questions which show that at least one member of the jury had grave doubts about the conduct of the trial. As Juror X put it: 'Did France as a democracy give Carlos a fair trial?' Juror X pointed out that this trial was highly unusual given that it dealt with events that happened more than two decades earlier, and given that it relied more on written depositions than on witnesses testifying in court: 'I find it surprising that a supposedly oral procedure relied on so few witnesses.'

Juror X was shocked by the lack of physical evidence in court, and by the DST's insistence on keeping its source secret: 'What was the point, twenty-two years later? The DST refused to admit it, but the secret servicemen and Moukharbal were all sent to the slaughterhouse. It was a coup for nothing, like a bad film which makes you want to say "Start again".' As for Judge Corneloup's marshalling of proceedings, Juror X found him 'often relatively impartial', adding however that 'this was no ordinary case. Behind this case there was the French state, the honour of the DST, the fear that we all have that terrorism will start again.'

The jury's deliberations began with Judge Corneloup guiding the jurors, who sat around a large table, through the entire sequence of events that had led up to the murders at Rue Toullier. According to Juror X, the jury was encouraged to ask as many questions as possible by the judge, who urged them to participate to the full in what he called 'a common meditation'.

At Judge Corneloup's request, each juror marked on a clean sheet of paper the word '*Culpabilité*' (Guilt), and next to that the word '*Oui*' or '*Non*' according to his or her innermost conviction. The papers were then folded and dropped into a large urn. Under French law, the first juror to have been picked on the first day of the trial then began fishing papers out of the urn. A minimum of eight votes for pronouncing Carlos innocent, or the contrary, was necessary before a ruling was deemed to have been reached. If a guilty verdict was reached, the procedure was repeated to establish the penalty.

After deliberations that lasted three hours and forty-eight minutes, the jury filed back into the assizes court for the last time, shortly after one o'clock in the morning on Wednesday. Judge Corneloup announced that the jury had found Carlos guilty on all counts, and that his punishment would be a life sentence. Carlos raised his left fist and shouted '*Viva la revolucion!*' (Long live the revolution!) Breaking into a smile, and his eyes shining, Carlos raised his fist again four times, his farewell to the court, before he was escorted outside and back to his prison cell. According to Juror X, the jury had needed to vote only once to reach the verdict, and once more to settle the penalty.

15

Epilogue

> I could make Qathafi fall from power if I wanted to. I have a million things on him.
>
> – Carlos to one of his lawyers

Carlos's lawyers drew a blank when they tried to extract a convincing ideological stand out of him, solid enough to exploit in court and portray him as a political victim. 'It's impossible to make him think something up,' remarked one lawyer. 'I don't know what there is up there in his head, but he's not Fidel Castro.' Revolution for Carlos meant a state of mindless euphoria, chasing after women and luxurious living. The definition of himself that he came up with after his arrest – 'professional revolutionary' – smacks of a business career path rather than heady idealistic inspiration.

The battle lines of the Cold War supplied Carlos with a convenient rationale for his organisation, and more importantly with the shelter and resources necessary to strike deep within the opposite camp. The collapse of the Soviet empire took the wind out of his Marxist sails. The launch of peace talks between Arabs and Israelis, culminating in the birth of a new Palestine, did the same for his early commitment as a fedayeen. The empire forged by Ilich Ramírez Sánchez's namesake had withered away, and one of his patrons, Nicolae Ceausescu, lay mangled in his grave after he was shot by his own soldiers for genocide of the

Romanian people. Not that Carlos ever acknowledged that a page had been turned. Three years after his arrest he still defined himself as 'a revolutionary militant dedicated to the most noble of causes, the liberation of Palestine within the context of the World Revolution'.[1]

This irrepressible belief in the righteousness of his personal cause, and the refusal to acknowledge that the cause had become a historical irrelevance, were sources of strength for Carlos after his capture. His public performance at his trial for the Rue Toullier murders underscored his refusal, or perhaps his inability, to accept defeat. Uncowed, he defiantly waged a war of attrition against French justice which forced the judge to appoint new defence lawyers and extend the trial, and which helped to sow doubts about the validity of the prosecution's case in the mind of the jury. Carlos might have achieved much more had he limited himself to his claims that he had been illegally kidnapped and that the case against him was a travesty of justice. There were plenty of shortcomings to pinpoint in the French investigation, and Carlos often showed he was more than a match for the sharp legal minds pitted against him. But Carlos overplayed his hand in admitting that he knew part of the truth about the Rue Toullier killings, and in boasting in repetitive monologues of the importance of his violent contribution to the causes of an independent Palestine and world revolution.

'Many people would prefer Carlos dead,' French Interior Minister Charles Pasqua had said after hauling in his prize. In fact, all the signs are that the masters whom Carlos served as a foot soldier, whose names are listed in the files of the East German and other Soviet bloc intelligence services, will continue to sleep soundly. Only the Romanians have launched an investigation into the links of former Communist rulers (in this case, the Securitate secret police) with Carlos. Despite Judge Bruguière's reputation as a fearless bulldozer of diplomatic conventions, the

Libyan, Syrian and other Arab patrons who hired Carlos and his group have so far been spared judicial proceedings. On a visit to Tripoli as part of his investigation into the blowing up of a French DC10 aircraft, the judge interrogated many Libyan secret service officers but, as he himself admitted, he did not question them about Carlos. For the bombing, Bruguière blamed six Libyans, including Colonel Qathafi's brother-in-law.

The judge pledged to see the probe into the car-bomb attack on the magazine *Al Watan al Arabi* in 1982 through 'to the end'. But no action was taken against the Syrian intelligence heads, of whom President al-Assad's brother Rifaat was one and without whom Carlos would never have existed. Carlos himself made no secret of his subservience at one court hearing. In a stunningly frank admission, he described himself as 'a senior officer of the Syrian secret services'.[2] But France was in no mood to turn against Syria. President al-Assad, welcomed to the Arab-Israeli negotiating table, was wooed by a President Chirac anxious to carve France a role in the Middle East without which, he believed, like his inspiration General Charles de Gaulle, it could not match the superpowers. Washington too treated Syria with kid gloves, despite intelligence reports that the country served as a refuge for a myriad of Palestinian, Turkish and Lebanese guerrilla groups, and that Moslem fundamentalists trained in the Syrian-ruled Bekaa Valley.

German justice, bolstered by all the evidence from the East German Stasi files, tried but failed to take on Damascus. At Berlin's request Faisal Sammak, who had been Syria's ambassador to East Berlin from 1981 to 1989 and had allowed Weinrich to store weapons and explosives in his embassy, was arrested in Vienna in August 1994 shortly after Carlos's capture. But Summak was released only five weeks later. Syrian President al-Assad had telephoned Austrian President Thomas Klestil to intercede on behalf of the one-time ambassador, who happened to be a relative of the Syrian head of state. Summak, who now managed Syria's state tobacco industry, was declared a bona fide diplomat – a sudden upgrading, given the fact that he had entered Austria as a tourist – entitling him to that caste's immunity from prosecution.

Judge Bruguière obtained many intelligence reports from Berlin, but much less from Hungary. With bad grace, Budapest supplied only an unsigned, undated six-page summary of its copious records on Carlos (which amount to thirteen thick dossiers) on the grounds that handing over any more 'would violate important security interests of the Hungarian nation'.[3] Other clues to Carlos's past must lie in the archives of Moscow, Bucharest, Prague and Havana. The French judge has said he has no desire to travel to Moscow, but although Carlos was no agent of the KGB its files are likely to contain copies of the reports about him sent in by the Soviet Union's Communist cousins.

It is improbable that Carlos himself will lift the veil. In private meetings with his lawyers he has bragged that he met Libya's Colonel Qathafi, Syria's al-Assad and Iraq's Saddam Hussein among other heads of state. Were Carlos ever to renege on his pledges not to betray his masters, the Libyan leader would apparently be the first in the firing line. 'I could make Qathafi fall from power if I wanted to,' Carlos told one of his attorneys. 'I have a million things on him.' In public, however, a different Carlos speaks: 'I have never worked for the countries behind the Iron Curtain nor in any other part of the world.'[4] Exposure of the patronage, be it in the former Soviet bloc or in the Middle East, must be the priority for investigators if they are ever to make both Carlos and those who aided and abetted him pay for their crimes.

For too long during Carlos's career the refusal of Western intelligence services to jeopardise delicate relations with Soviet allies or with Arab dictatorships guaranteed him impunity. His aura was so great that one French security service, the Renseignements Généraux, used his name in September 1980 to ambush two leaders of the Action Directe guerrilla movement, Jean-Marc Rouillan and his girlfriend Nathalie Ménigon. An Egyptian informer was paid to tell them that Carlos needed them to help blow up the Aswan dam. It was a pretty outlandish proposal, but the bait worked. When Rouillan and Ménigon turned up for what they expected to be a rendezvous with the Jackal himself in a Paris flat, they were greeted not by the outstretched hand of the world's most wanted man but by the cocked guns of the police.

When the secret services did decide to intervene against Carlos it was often to attempt to assassinate him – a democracy adopting the same tactics as his private army for hire. Typically, the former chief of the French DGSE, Claude Silberzahn, claimed a '*droit de mort*' (licence to kill) for his service. The President may have de facto lost his right over life and death with the abolition of the death penalty, Silberzahn reflected, but the intelligence agency enjoyed the 'privilege' of killing certain murderers, notably terrorists, which should be exercised only on foreign lands. On French territory, guerrillas should not be eliminated because they could be captured.[5]

In shying away from a public accusation of the régimes that protected and used Carlos, Western secret services deprived themselves of an effective means of putting pressure on his sponsors. In 1986 the CIA had decided to adopt just such a tactic against Carlos's rival Abu Nidal. The agency's publication of *The Abu Nidal Handbook*, which included an organisational chart and listed members, accomplices and crimes, led several European governments, including East Germany, to break off relations with Abu Nidal. The files of Eastern European intelligence services show that the fear of being revealed as a haven for Carlos played a large part in the decision to expel him.

Much of the blame for Carlos being free to wreak havoc

for so long must be laid at the door both of Western secret services and of Western governments. Counter-orders by French leaders led to the scuppering of several attempts to seize him. President Mitterrand's abrupt creation of an ill-prepared counter-terrorism unit under his personal authority sowed confusion among established security forces, and set the clock back considerably as far as France's fight against terrorism was concerned. A few years later, the directors of the DGSE and the DST attempted separately to negotiate an end to Syrian-backed attacks in France, but both French intelligence services had failed to discover that Carlos was among those under Syria's protective wing. The fact that two Iranians accused of murder were released as part of the price for catching Carlos in 1994, and that he was abducted in violation of international laws, is no credit to the French state.

That Carlos was able to harness his personal cause to that of totalitarian regimes must rank as one of his greatest achievements in ensuring the survival of his private army for so long. As a military commander, he showed loyalty to his soldiers and attempted to free those held by the authorities: Hans-Joachim Klein, Magdalena Kopp, Bruno Bréguet and Gabriele Kröcher-Tiedemann. In contrast to Haddad, Carlos did not lose any members of his organisation during operations. As the Stasi noted, Carlos ran his group with an iron hand, successfully resisting an attempt by the East Germans to infiltrate the organisation, and he suffered only one defection.

Several of the operations that Carlos launched did not fulfil their objectives: the failed murder of Joseph Edward Sieff, the failed murders of the OPEC Oil Ministers, the failure to obtain the release of his imprisoned subordinates. But on a wider level he severely jolted several governments of Western and Eastern Europe and ensured that one state (France) attempted to negotiate a truce with his emissary. And it is because of the likes of Carlos that heavier security has had to be deployed at airports, government buildings, embassies and other potential targets worldwide. But on the organisation's own terms, and as highlighted by the often gleeful tone of Weinrich's reports to Carlos, the mere fact of killing and maiming civilians, or destroying buildings, made for the success of an operation. Violence became an end in itself – Carlos and his group are responsible for the deaths of twenty-four people, and the wounding of another 257.

Carlos's era was that of state-sponsored terrorism, a practice that suffered a knock when the Cold War ended. As Sir Colin McColl, for five years the head of MI6, noted: 'State-sponsored terrorism is one of the things that suffered from the end of the Cold War, during which several states involved in terrorism had support from the Soviet Union or their allies. That stopped so they became exposed. They were worried about military attacks and also about whether they would qualify for financial support and investment in the new world that followed financial and economic deregulation.'[6]

But Carlos does not represent a bygone era. True, the fall of Communism tore to shreds the left-wing banners waved by Carlos's colleagues in the Red Army Faction, the Red Brigades, and the Japanese Red Army. But they have to a large extent been supplanted by religiously motivated groups – Moslem fundamentalists in Algeria and Egypt, the Hamas and Islamic Jihad in the Middle East – or by autonomous groups such as those responsible for the Sarin poison gas attack on the Japanese underground, the Oklahoma bombing, or the siege of the Japanese embassy in Peru. The scale of these crimes make Carlos's car or train bombings appear modest in comparison. He did not massacre sixty tourists at an Egyptian temple, blow up a Manhattan skyscraper or gas tens of thousands of people in the Tokyo underground. It is too early, however, to write the epitaph of state terrorism as espoused by Carlos. The suicide-bombers of the Hezbollah have Iran to thank for the explosives that enable them to accomplish their missions.

Carlos has told his lawyers that he has already written his memoirs, that he had finished them in 1992, two years before he was caught. They have been sold, he revealed, to a publisher for an undisclosed sum. But he is in no hurry to publish pages that he has said contained 'many disturbing things'. 'They are publishable only after my death,' he confided to one attorney of a work which is probably marred by the ego of the author, and by his failure to grasp the magnitude of the changes that have curtailed his life's ambitions.

That Carlos should prefer to think about the past rather than the future was understandable. Ahead lay at least five years of trials for the crimes he is accused of committing in France: the first rocket attack on an El Al plane at Orly airport, the bombings of the Rue Marbeuf and the *Capitole* express train, the bombings of the TGV train and of the Marseille railway station. Although he is likely to collect several life sentences, there is no guarantee that Carlos will spend the rest of his life behind bars. His crimes were committed long before France passed a law allowing judges to cast their sentences in stone, with no possibility of early remission. The norm is for life sentences to translate into some twenty years of detention. Perhaps he will emerge blinking in the sunlight at the age of seventy around the year 2020. He might stand a chance of release even earlier if he did ever decide to betray his former employers. His lawyers still talk of a 'solution' to the Carlos case.

Today Carlos's greatest fear is that his own end will be a violent one. More than spending the rest of his life behind bars, it is death by poisoning that he most fears.[7] To one of his lawyers he has declared: 'I will stay in jail for ever or I will be shot dead if I get out. I will not get out of France alive.' Much earlier in his life as a fugitive he had confided to a friend that he feared being murdered: 'Listen, my friend, I love life. I love living at full speed because I don't know when I will be assassinated. I only know that I will be assassinated one day. That's why you notice my fanatical desire to live."[8] Perhaps he dreamed of a death that would crown the myth spawned in his lifetime, and freeze it as execution without trial did for Che Guevara, the *guerrillero heroico.*

Fate will surely be less kind to the Jackal.

Notes

1 MARX AND THE HOLY CROSS

1 Interview with José Ramírez Navas published by *La Nacion* on 16.8.94.
2 Quoted by the *Sunday Times* on 21.8.94.
3 Interview with Ramírez Navas, op. cit.
4 Ibid.
5 Interview with Mireya Gonzalez de Ruiz published by *La Nacion* on 19.8.94.
6 Interview with Ramírez Navas, op. cit.
7 Interview with Carlos published by *Al Watan al Arabi* on 30.11.79.
8 Interview with Carlos carried out by *Al Watan al Arabi* and published by *Le Figaro Magazine* on 15.12.79.
9 Testimony by Carlos to Judge Bruguière on 28.10.94.
10 Interview with Carlos, *Al Watan al Arabi*, 30.11.79.
11 'A good case for a shrink', added Hans-Joachim Klein in an interview published in *Le Nouvel Observateur* on 23.2.95.
12 Testimony by Carlos to Judge Bruguière, 28.10.94.
13 Carlos before the Cour d'assizes de Paris on 16.12.97.
14 Interview with Carlos, *Al Watan al Arabi*, 30.11.79.
15 Ibid.
16 Interview with Emir Ruiz published by *La Nacion* on 19.8.94.
17 Interview with Carlos, *Al Watan al Arabi*, 30.11.79.
18 Carlos before the Cour d'assizes de Paris on 16.12.97.

19 Testimony by Carlos to Judge Bruguière on 15.11.94.
20 Interview with Carlos, *Al Watan al Arabi*, 30.11.79.
21 Testimony by Carlos to Judge Bruguière on 28.10.94.
22 Letter from Pedro Ortega Diaz sent to Venezuelan judicial authorities, dated 27.3.96.
23 Interview with Carlos carried out by *Al Watan al Arabi* and published in *Le Figaro Magazine*, 15.12.79.
24 Christopher Dobson and Ronald Payne, *The Dictionary of Espionage* (Harrap, London, 1984) and, by the same authors and in more detail on this episode, *The Carlos Complex: A Study in Terror* (Hodder and Stoughton, London, 1977).
25 Michel Poniatowski, *L'avenir n'est écrit nulle part* (Editions Albin Michel, Paris, 1978).
26 Testimony by Carlos to Judge Bruguière on 15.11.94.
27 Ibid.
28 A few years later he used the name Torres on one of his false passports, a homage to the Latin American revolutionary.
29 Brigade Criminelle, Inspecteur Divisionaire Daniel Aberard, *Enquête de CV concernant Ilich Ramírez Sánchez*, 22.5.95. Aberard's requests for information on this supposed episode, sent to Havana via Interpol, went unanswered.
30 Questioning of Vladimir Ramírez Sánchez by Caracas investigating magistrates on 15.7.96, as reported by French police officers Hugues Saumet and Claude Legros of the Brigade Criminelle in report dated 1.8.96 on their mission to the Venezuelan capital.
31 Brigade Criminelle, Aberard, op. cit.
32 Interview with Carlos carried out by *Al Watan al Arabi* and published in *Le Figaro Magazine*, 15.12.79.
33 Carlos before the Cour d'assizes de Paris on 16.12.97.
34 Ibid.
35 Testimony by Carlos to Judge Bruguière on 28.10.94.
36 Testimony by Carlos to Judge Bruguière on 15.11.94.
37 Carlos before the Cour d'assizes de Paris on 16.12.97.

38 Letter from Pedro Ortega Diaz, op. cit.
39 Carlos before the Cour d'assizes de Paris on 16.12.97.
40 Author interview with Kirill Privalov on 4.9.97.
41 Ibid.
42 Interview with Carlos published by *Al Watan al Arabi* on 14.12.79.
43 Ibid.
44 Testimony by Carlos to Judge Bruguière on 15.11.94. Before the Cour d'assizes de Paris on 16.12.97, Carlos admitted that he still had 'family' in Cuba.
45 Interview with Carlos carried out by *Al Watan al Arabi* and published by *Le Figaro Magazine*, 15.12.79.
46 Interview with Gustavo Machado in the documentary *Carlos, terroriste sans frontières* broadcast on France 3 on 2.3.97.
47 Carlos before the Cour d'assizes de Paris on 16.12.97.
48 Testimony by Carlos to Judge Bruguière on 28.10.94.
49 Interview with Hans-Joachim Klein published in *Libération* on 5.10.78.
50 Interview with Carlos, *Al Watan al Arabi*, 30.11.79.

2 TRAINING FOR TERROR

1 Author interview with Carlos obtained through a third party on 17.6.97.
2 Interview with Ramírez Navas published in *La Nacion* on 16.8.94.
3 Interview with Hans-Joachim Klein published in *Libération* on 5.10.78.
4 Ibid.
5 The letter, marked *Secret-confidential/Particularly important/Special file*, was unearthed in the Kremlin archives by former Soviet dissident Vladimir Boukovsky. Dated 23.4.74, it is published in Vladimir Boukovsky, *Jugement à Moscou: Un dissident dans les archives du Kremlin* (Robert Laffont, Paris, 1995).

6 Testimony by Carlos to Judge Bruguière on 15.11.94.
7 Interview with Carlos published by *Al Watan al Arabi* on 7.12.79.
8 Bassam Abu-Sharif and Uzi Mahnaimi, *Tried By Fire: The Searing True Story of Two Men at the Heart of the Struggle between the Arabs and the Jews* (Little, Brown, London, 1995).
9 Ibid.
10 Interview with Carlos published by *Al Watan al Arabi* on 7.12.79.
11 Testimony by Carlos to Judge Bruguière on 15.11.94.
12 Abu-Sharif and Mahnaimi, op. cit.
13 Testimony by Carlos to Judge Bruguière on 15.11.94.
14 Ibid.
15 Ibid.
16 Ibid.
17 Testimony by Carlos to Judge Bruguière on 19.12.94.
18 Abu-Sharif and Mahnaimi, op. cit.
19 Interview with Carlos carried out by *Al Watan al Arabi* and published by *Le Figaro Magazine* on 15.12.79.
20 Testimony by Carlos to Judge Bruguière on 15.11.94.
21 Abu-Sharif and Mahnaimi, op. cit.
22 Interview with Carlos, *Al Watan al Arabi*, 7.12.79.
23 Ibid.
24 Testimony by Carlos to Judge Bruguière on 15.11.94. In fact, other foreigners who joined the Popular Front at about this time included a future associate of Carlos, the Swiss Bruno Bréguet.
25 Abu-Sharif and Mahnaimi, op. cit.
26 Testimony by Carlos to Judge Bruguière on 19.12.94.
27 As demonstrated by the signature of Elba Maria Sánchez on her testimony to Caracas investigating magistrates on 18.7.96, part of a report, dated 1.8.96, by Brigade Criminelle officers Hugues Saumet and Claude Legros on their mission to the Venezuelan capital.
28 Scotland Yard, SO13 anti-terrorism branch, *Preliminary report by Detective Inspector David Cooper after international*

rogatory letter from Judge Jean-Louis Bruguière dated 22.5.95 and sent by the Brigade Criminelle and the Police Judiciaire, 7.7.95.

29 Ibid.

30 Nydia Tobon, *Carlos: terrorista o guerrillero* (Grijalbo, Barcelona, 1978).

31 Nydia Tobon at Carlos's trial before the Cour d'assizes de Paris on 17.12.97.

32 Tobon, op. cit.

33 Brigade Criminelle, Inspecteur Divisionaire Daniel Aberard, *Enquête de CV concernant Ilich Ramírez Sánchez*, 22.5.95.

34 Testimony by Carlos to Judge Bruguière on 19.12.94.

3 THE DRUGSTORE SAINT-GERMAIN

1 Testimony by Inspecteur Général Jean-François Clair of the DST's counter-terrorism unit before the Cour d'assizes de Paris on 18.12.97.

2 Testimony by Carlos to Judge Bruguière on 29.3.96.

3 Nydia Tobon, *Carlos: terrorista o guerrillero* (Grijalbo, Barcelona, 1978).

4 Interview with Carlos published by *Al Watan al Arabi* on 14.12.79.

5 Ibid.

6 Ibid.

7 Ibid. Carlos also recounted that he had used a getaway car in both attacks. A Scotland Yard check on his real name, Ilich Ramírez Sánchez, and on his date of birth, 12.10.49, threw up the driver record number RAMIR 410129 199 SJ which to all appearances (the first number mirrors his date of birth with the month and day in the middle) once belonged to Carlos. Detective Inspector David Cooper, Scotland Yard's SO13 anti-terrorism branch, report on *Case papers regarding Carlos*, dated 29.8.96.

8 Testimony by Carlos to Judge Bruguière on 19.12.94.

9 Interview with Ramírez Navas published by *La Nacion* on 16.8.94.
10 Ibid.
11 Interview with Carlos published by *Al Watan al Arabi* on 30.11.79.
12 Interview with Ramírez Navas published by the *Observer* on 15.2.76.
13 Interview with Ramírez Navas, *La Nacion*, 16.8.94.
14 Interview with Barry Woodhams published by Reuters on 16.8.94.
15 Testimony by Amparo Silva Masmela as quoted by Judge Bruguière in his questioning of Carlos on 27.2.97.
16 Nydia Tobon, op. cit.
17 Ibid.
18 Interview with Carlos, *Al Watan al Arabi*, 14.12.79.
19 Ibid.
20 Author interview with Pierre Ottavioli on 28.1.97.
21 Commissaire Broussard, *Mémoires*, (Plon, Paris, 1997).
22 Ibid.
23 Interview with Carlos, *Al Watan al Arabi*, 14.12.79.
24 Ibid.
25 Brigade Criminelle, Inspecteur Divisionaire Daniel Aberard, *Enquête de CV concernant Ilich Ramírez Sánchez*, 22.5.95.
26 Interview with Carlos, *Al Watan al Arabi*, 14.12.79.
27 Ibid.
28 Bizarrely, Fares Raghdan, alias Omar, was not charged despite his confession. Detained by Venezuelan authorities for entering the country illegally on two occasions, in August 1975 and in May 1976, he told local judicial authorities that he was one of the authors of the second Orly raid, and gave a detailed description of events. Colleagues of Venezuela's notorious export were apparently entitled to mercy. Brigade Criminelle, op. cit.
29 Interview with Carlos, *Al Watan al Arabi*, 14.12.79.
30 Quoted by *L'Aurore* on 21.11.75.

31 Father Louis Vades-Gonnet as quoted by *Le Monde* on 22.11.75.
32 The guerrillas were surreptitiously photographed by DST spies, according to testimony by Inspecteur Général Jean-François Clair, op. cit. Clair added that none of those photographed looked like Carlos.
33 Author interview with Pierre Ottavioli, 28.1.97.
34 Interview with Hans-Joachim Klein in *Les années Carlos: Klein: Un cas allemand*, broadcast by Arte on 23.2.95.
35 Ibid.

4 SECRETS AND LIES

1 Marcel Chalet and Thierry Wolton, *Les visiteurs de l'ombre* (Editions Grasset & Fasquelle, Paris, 1990).
2 Author interview with Jean-Paul Mauriat on 26.2.97. Mauriat wrote a six-page report on subsequent events which he entitled *A Propos de l'Affaire Carlos* (About the Carlos Case). The head of the DST refused to grant him permission to publish it in the internal newsletter.
3 Testimony of Amparo Silva Masmela to investigating magistrate Christian Gallut of the Cour de sûreté de l'état on 30.7.75.
4 *Procès-verbal* by Commissaire Principal Jean Herranz on testimony of Michel Moukharbal, 22.6.97.
5 *Procès-verbal* by Inspector Jean Laffargue of the Police Judiciaire on testimony of Luis Urdaneta Urbina, 28.6.75.
6 Interview with Angela Armstrong by Don North of Canadian Television, quoted in Christopher Dobson and Ronald Payne, *The Carlos Complex* (Coronet, London, 1978).
7 *Procès-verbal* by Commissaire Guido Spiessens on testimony of Leyma Palomares, 28.6.75.
8 Interview with Carlos published by *Al Watan al Arabi* on 14.12.79.
9 *Procès-verbal* by Spiessens, 28.6.75.
10 *Procès-verbal* by Inspector Michel Calvet of the Police

Judiciaire on testimony of Edgar Marino-Muller, 28.6.75.

11 *Procès-verbal* by police officer Bernard Lefevre on testimony of Olivier Martel, 28.6.75. And *Procès-verbal* by Inspector Calvet on new testimony by Martel, 2.7.75.

12 *Procès-verbal* by Commissaire Divisionaire Pierre Ottavioli to the Paris public prosecutor's office on 27.6.75. Ottavioli failed to indicate the time at which he filed his report.

13 *Procès-verbal* by Commissaire Daniel Marcout at 10.20 p.m., 27.6.75.

14 Author interview with Ottavioli on 28.1.97.

15 The weapon Carlos used was identified as most likely a CZ Vzor 52 automatic, and not a Russian-made Tokarev pistol as widely reported, by forensic police expert Pierre Deloume in an interview with the author after his testimony before the Cour d'assizes de Paris on 19.12.97.

16 *Procès-verbal* by Ottavioli, 27.6.75.

17 Nydia Tobon, *Carlos: terrorista o guerrillero* (Grijalbo, Barcelona, 1978).

18 *Procès-verbal* by an unnamed officer of the Direction de la Police Judiciaire, 17.7.75. The letter was dated Paris, 28 June, and was sent by express airmail on the same day.

19 Report by Inspector Marc Terrasson of the Brigade Criminelle, *Compte rendu de commission rogatoire en Grande Bretagne*, 21.7.75.

20 Testimony by Angela Armstrong to Judge Gallut on 25.7.75. Testimony by her friend Ann Ellen Hamburger to Scotland Yard Detective Sergeant Fickling, 15.7.75. And testimony by another friend, Igor Rodor, to Scotland Yard Detective Constable Phillips, 16.7.75.

21 *Procès-verbal* by Ottavioli on the search of the flat at 11bis Rue Amélie by the DST, 4.7.75.

22 Report by Inspector Jacques Imbert of the Police Judiciaire's Section technique de recherches et d'investigations de l'identité judiciaire, 28.7.75. The report found two prints of Carlos's right index finger on a bottle of J&B whisky and on a glass on the table, two prints of his

left index on the aniseed bottle and on a glass in the bathroom, and a print of his right little finger on a bottle of Johnnie Walker.

23 Cour de sûreté de l'état, *Procès-verbal* on testimony of Amparo Silva Masmela to Judge Gallut, 30.7.75.
24 Printed in the *Guardian* Letters column, 18.8.94.
25 Interview with Barry Woodhams published by Reuters on 16.8.94.
26 The true extent of her knowledge was revealed by Nydia Tobon herself in her book, op. cit.
27 Testimony by Carlos to Judge Bruguière on 27.2.97.
28 Brigade Criminelle, Inspecteur Divisionaire Daniel Aberard, *Enquête de CV concernant Ilich Ramírez Sánchez*, 22.9.95.
29 Author interview with Jean-Paul Mauriat on 26.2.97.
30 Author interview with Jean-Noël Herranz on 22.12.97.
31 *Procès-verbal* by Commissaire Daniel Marcout, timed 10.20 p.m. on 27.6.75.
32 *Procès-verbal* by Ottavioli, 27.6.75.
33 Author interview with Valéry Giscard d'Estaing on 23.10.96.
34 Dr Le Breton, *Rapport d'examen du sang-dosage de l'alcool*, 30.6.75.
35 Interview with Carlos, *Al Watan al Arabi*, 14.12.79.
36 Results of autopsy carried out by Inspector Gerard Loir of the Police Judiciaire, 28.6.75.
37 Testimony by Carlos to Judge Bruguière on 23.1.96.
38 Ibid.
39 Testimony by Carlos to Judge Bruguière on 19.4.96.
40 Testimony by Carlos to Judge Bruguière on 7.6.96.
41 Claire Hoy and Victor Ostrovsky, *By Way of Deception: A Devastating Insider's Portrait of the Mossad* (Stoddart Publishing, Toronto, 1990).

5 AN AWFUL PARTY

1. *Fiche de signalement sur Kröcher-Tiedemann, Gabriele Brigitte Hildegard Frieda*, drawn up by the International Criminal Police Organisation/Interpol, April 1975.
2. Interview with Hans-Joachim Klein published in *Libération* on 5.10.78.
3. Interview with Hans-Joachim Klein published in *Der Spiegel* on 7.8.78.
4. Quoted in Hans-Joachim Klein, *La mort mercenaire: Témoignage d'un ancien terroriste ouest-allemand* (Seuil, Paris, 1980).
5. Author interview with Sidney Weiland, who was covering the OPEC session for Reuters, on 18.8.97.
6. Interview with Hans-Joachim Klein in *Les années Carlos. Klein: Un cas allemand* broadcast by Arte on 23.2.95.
7. Ibid.
8. Interview with Klein, *Libération*, 5.10.78.
9. Interview with Klein broadcast by Arte, 23.2.95.
10. Interview with Ahmed Zaki Yamani published by *Saudi Review* on 5.1.76 and 6.1.76.
11. Ibid.
12. Ibid.
13. Klein, op. cit.
14. Ibid.
15. Interview with Yamani, op. cit.
16. Account by Foreign Ministry adviser Dr Türk as related in *Die Vorfälle vom 21 und 22 Dezember 1975 (Überfall auf die Teilnehmer der OPEC-Konferenz)*, published by the Austrian government in the wake of the OPEC raid.
17. Ibid.
18. Interview with Yamani, op. cit.
19. Interview with Yamani, op. cit.
20. Speech by Bruno Kreisky to the Austrian parliament on 27.1.76.
21. Interview with Yamani, op. cit.

22 Tony Benn quoted Amouzegar in an extract from his diaries published by the *Guardian* on 18.8.94.
23 Author interview with Bernard Edinger, who witnessed the scene for Reuters, on 25.7.97.
24 Interview with Yamani, op. cit.
25 Interview with Carlos carried out by *Al Watan al Arabi* and published by *Le Figaro Magazine* on 15.12.79.
26 Interview with Yamani, op. cit.
27 Interview with Carlos, op. cit.
28 Interview with Yamani, op. cit.
29 One of the journalists, Julian Nundy, who at the time worked for Reuters, told the story in an article published in the *Independent* on 16.8.94.
30 *Comte-rendu d'enquête* by Inspecteur Gérard Loir to Commissaire Pierre Ottavioli, head of the Brigade Criminelle, on 9.1.76.
31 Interview with Klein broadcast by Arte, 23.2.95.

6 THE RENEGADE REVOLUTIONARY

1 Andropov in a letter, dated 16.5.75, to Soviet leader Leonid Brezhnev, which detailed the nocturnal supply by the KGB of fifty-three submachine-guns, fifty pistols, and 34,000 cartridges and bullets: 'This delivery of arms, which was illegal, was carried out in neutral waters in the Gulf of Aden, without any identifiable contacts, in conditions of rigorous secrecy, using a patrol boat of the Soviet war flotilla.' Vladimir Boukovsky, *Jugement à Moscou: Un dissident dans les archives du Kremlin* (Robert Laffont, Paris, 1995).
2 Author interview with Duane R. Clarridge on 19.6.97.
3 Ibid.
4 Duane R. Clarridge, *A Spy for All Seasons: My Life in the CIA* (Scribner, New York, 1997).
5 Author interview with Clarridge, 19.6.97.

6 Interview with Hans-Joachim Klein published in *Le Nouvel Observateur* on 23.2.95.
7 Letter from Carlos to *Le Nouvel Observateur* published on 5.6.97.
8 Interview with Hans-Joachim Klein in *Les années Carlos. Klein: Un cas allemand* broadcast by Arte, 23.2.95.
9 Interview with Hans-Joachim Klein published in *Der Spiegel* on 7.8.78.
10 Interview with Carlos carried out by *Al Watan al Arabi* and published by *Le Figaro Magazine* on 15.12.79.
11 Interview with Magdalena Kopp published by *Stern* on 11.12.97.
12 Interview with Carlos, op. cit.
13 Note by the Stasi dated 7.5.84.
14 The anecdote is told by Klein in his interview in *Libération*, 5.10.78.
15 Interview with Klein broadcast by Arte, 23.2.95.
16 Quoted in Bassam Abu-Sharif and Uzi Mahnaimi, *Tried By Fire: The Searing True Story of Two Men at the Heart of the Struggle between the Arabs and the Jews* (Little, Brown, London, 1995).
17 Carlos as quoted by one of his lawyers, who has refused to be named, in an interview with the author on 27.5.97.
18 Interview with Klein broadcast by Arte, 23.2.95.
19 Ibid.
20 Abu-Sharif and Mahnaimi, op. cit.
21 Böse as quoted by one of the hostages, Michel Cojot, in an interview with *Le Monde* published on 8.7.76.
22 Interview with Klein broadcast by Arte, 23.2.95.
23 Interview with Pavle Celik published by *Globus* on 26.8.94.
24 Ibid.
25 Ibid.
26 Interview with Klein broadcast by Arte, 23.2.95.
27 A note by the Stasi dated 17.4.79 refers to Carlos's contacts with a senior Iraqi intelligence officer, Saddun Shaker.
28 Brigade Criminelle, op. cit.

29 Interview with Klein, *Der Spiegel*, 7.8.78.
30 Testimony by Carlos to an international commission in the presence of Frankfurt prosecutor Volker Rath, and Bundeskriminalamt (BKA) officers Michaela Ragg and Guido Schneider.
31 Andrawes's behaviour in particular, and the hostage-taking in general, was also described by one of the hostages, Ernö Kiraly, in an interview published by *L'Express* on 24.10.77.
32 Brigade Criminelle, op. cit.
33 Speech published in *Democratic Palestine*, May 1986. Quoted in Xavier Raufer, *La Nébuleuse: le terrorisme du Moyen-Orient* (Fayard, Paris, 1987).
34 Interview with Shigenobu Fusako published by *Al Mostakbal*, June 1985. Quoted in Raufer, op. cit.
35 The episode is recounted by Magdalena Kopp herself in her testimony to Berlin investigating magistrate Dieter Mchlis in December 1995.
36 Interview with Kopp, *Stern*, 11.12.97.
37 Ibid.
38 Author interview with Alain de Gaigncron de Marolles on 21.7.97.
39 Charles Villeneuve, Jean Pierre Péret, *Histoire secrète du terrorisme: Les juges de l'impossible* (Plon, Paris, 1987).
40 Philippe Thyraud de Vosjoli, *Lamia* (Little, Brown, London, 1970).
41 Philippe Rondot, 'Du bon usage des services spéciaux', published in *Politique Internationale*, autumn 1985.
42 Author interview with Valéry Giscard d'Estaing on 23.10.96.
43 Author interview with Alain de Gaigneron de Marolles on 17.2.97.
44 In his memoirs, Giscard wrote that he revealed four secrets to his successor: that Brezhnev had chosen his heir, that France and the United States were working together on a nuclear project, that the Elf-Erap firm was testing an oil detection system, and that Egypt was plotting to overthrow

Colonel Qathafi. He did not mention in his memoirs that he also told Mitterrand about the Carlos mission. Valéry Giscard d'Estaing, *Le Pouvoir et la Vie* (Compagnie 12, Paris, 1988).

45 Author interview with Giscard d'Estaing, 23.10.96.

7 A MATCH MADE IN HELL

1 Brigade Criminelle, Inspecteur Divisionaire Daniel Aberard, *Enquête de CV concernant Ilich Ramírez Sánchez*, 22.5.95.

2 Markus Wolf, with Anne McElvoy, *Man Without a Face: The Autobiography of Communism's Greatest Spymaster* (Jonathan Cape, London, 1997).

3 Author interview with General Markus Wolf on 29.9.97.

4 The peace treaty, which followed the 1978 Camp David Accords, meant Egypt no longer had a role to play in the Arab-Israeli conflict. Egypt, however, failed to win any firm pledges from Israel on the West Bank, Gaza or East Jerusalem.

5 Note by the Stasi dated April 1979.

6 Report by the Stasi dated 8.5.79.

7 Note by the Stasi dated May 1979.

8 Letter from Carlos to *Le Nouvel Observateur* published on 5.6.97.

9 The draft bill, dated 26.6.80, was approved by General Mielke.

10 Author interview with Wolf, 29.9.97.

11 Note by the Stasi dated 19.1.81.

12 One note in Weinrich's handwriting, dated 25.6.84, refers to presents for his mother and father each costing 80 and 245 marks.

13 Interview with Jozsef Varga published in *L'Evénement du Jeudi* on 25.8.94.

14 Ibid.

15 Interview with Andreas Petresevics, former counter-terrorism chief, broadcast by Hungarian state television's *Panorama* news programme on 7.7.90.
16 The C79 files amount to thirteen volumes according to a report by Commissaire Caprioli of the DST sent to Paris public prosecutors on 28.8.91.
17 Interview with Varga, op. cit.
18 Interview with General Miklos Redei, broadcast by Hungarian state television's *Panorama*, 7.7.90.
19 Note by the Stasi dated February 1981.
20 Carlos's friend told the story to Robert Fisk of the *Independent* on condition that he not be identified. The interview was published on 20.8.94.
21 Author interview with Walid Abou Zahr on 2.5.97.
22 Note by the Stasi dated February 1981.
23 Author interview with Zahr, 2.5.97.
24 Hungary's C79 files, quoted by DST counter-terrorism chief Jean-François Clair in a report to Judge Bruguière dated 3.6.94.
25 Ibid.
26 Note by the Stasi dated May 1984.
27 A Stasi note dated September 1983 reports that Issawe had 'close relations' with Rifaat al-Assad.
28 The arms shipment is detailed in the Berlin public prosecutors' indictment of Nabil Shritah and Wilhelm Borostowski, dated 29.3.94, for the bombing of the French cultural centre in West Berlin on 25.8.83.
29 Testimony by Günter Jäckel to Judge Bruguière, Berlin, on 22.3.95.
30 Ibid.
31 Note by the Stasi dated 7.5.84.
32 Minutes by the Stasi referring to meetings with Hungarian counterparts on 24.4.81 and 25.4.81. Report by Caprioli, op. cit.
33 Report by Caprioli, op. cit.
34 Inventory drawn up by the Stasi in February 1981.

35 Note, seized by the Stasi, in Carlos's handwriting dated 24.10.81.
36 The letter, part of the Hungarian C79 files, is dated 2.4.80.
37 Minutes by the Stasi referring to meetings with Hungarian counterparts, op. cit.
38 The film was broadcast by Hungarian state television's *Panorama*, 7.7.90.
39 Author interview with Wolf, 29.9.97.
40 Note by the Stasi dated February 1981.
41 Author interview with Wolf, 29.9.97.
42 Testimony of Jäckel, op. cit.
43 Unpublished right of reply drafted by Carlos in answer to an article in *Le Point* (2.11.96), made available to the author by one of his lawyers.
44 Note by the Stasi dated May 1984.
45 Author interview with Wolf, 29.9.97.
46 Interview with Varga, op. cit.

8 A DIRTY, PRIVATE WAR

1 The attack was 'carried out by a Swiss extremist group on instructions from Carlos who led the operation from an eastern European country', according to a report by Commissaire Caprioli of the DST to the Paris public prosecutor on 28.8.91.
2 Interview with Magdalena Kopp published by *Stern* on 11.12.97.
3 Author interview with Pierre Marion on 21.10.96.
4 Jacques Vergès, *De la stratégie judiciaire* (Editions de Minuit, Paris, 1968).
5 Jacques Vergès, *Le salaud lumineux: Conversations avec Jean-Louis Remilleux* (Editions Numéro 1/Michel Lafon, Paris, 1990).
6 Note by the Stasi dated 7.5.84. The note refers to Vergès's attempts to obtain the release of Kopp and Bréguet. The

Stasi files and Weinrich's notes refer to Vergès under the code-names 'Herzog', 'Gabriel', and 'Jean'.

7 Direction de la Surveillance du Territoire, Commissaire Divisionaire Michel Guérin, *Rapport d'exécution de la commission rogatoire delivrée par le juge Jean-Louis Bruguière se rapportant à Marbeuf*, 3.10.95.

8 Letter dated 12.6.92 sent by Roland Kessous to the DST.

9 Quoted by *Le Monde* on 19.8.94.

10 Interview with Jean-Louis Debré published in *Le Figaro* on 23.8.94. Debré later served as Interior Minister.

11 Author interview with Alain Marsaud, later France's chief anti-terrorism investigating magistrate (1986–9), on 17.10.96.

12 Jacques Attali, *Verbatim I: Chronique des années 1981–1986* (Fayard, Paris, 1993).

13 Brigade Criminelle, Inspecteur Divisionaire Daniel Aberard, *Enquête de CV concernant Ilich Ramírez Sánchez*, 22.5.95.

14 According to a report by Caprioli, op. cit.

15 Letter from Carlos to *Le Nouvel Observateur* published on 5.6.97.

16 Text translated from French-language version sent by Ambassador Jurgensen on 5.4.82 in a coded telegram, marked Secret, to the Foreign Ministry in Paris.

17 A note by the Stasi dated 22.4.82 says the Carlos group was about to assassinate Walid Abou Zahr when Kopp and Bréguet were arrested. As well as the couple, Issawe and Luc Groven, described by the Stasi as in charge of international relations at the ETA, were helping to prepare the attack.

18 Author interview with Marsaud, 17.10.96. According to Marsaud, the Brigade Criminelle found that the cardboard box, in which the device had been concealed, originally contained Sony electronics equipment purchased by Kassouha.

19 Brigade Criminelle, op. cit.

20 Author interview with Walid Abou Zahr, 2.5.97.
21 Froelich's odyssey was reconstructed by the DST, on the basis of Stasi and Hungarian files, as detailed in the DST's report to Judge Bruguière dated 3.6.94.
22 Testimony by Magdalena Kopp to Berlin investigating magistrate Dieter Mehlis, December 1995.
23 Quoted in *Le Monde* on 24.4.82.
24 Ibid.
25 Quoted in *Le Journal du Dimanche* on 21.8.94.
26 Ibid.
27 Nezar Hindawi, sentenced to a record forty-five years in prison for hiding a bomb in the luggage of his pregnant Irish girlfriend in an attempt to blow up an El Al plane over London in April 1986, told Scotland Yard that Carlos's sponsor in Syrian air force intelligence Colonel Haitham Sa'id had ordered the Marbeuf bombing. Sa'id told Hindawi that he had ordered the Marbeuf bombing to prove that he was a serious terrorist, according to Hindawi. Report on the investigation by Judge Yves Corneloup into the Marbeuf bombing to the public prosecutor at the Parquet du tribunal de grande instance de Paris, dated 15.9.87.
28 Author interview with Jean Baklouti, head of DST counter-terrorism from 1977 to 1984, on 6.5.97.
29 Attali, op. cit.
30 Notes by the Stasi dated 28.4.83 and 11.5.83. Bernard Rambert has branded the report that he supplied details of security at the Justice Minister's home as 'absurd, and invented from A to Z'.
31 Testimony by Günter Jäckel to Judge Bruguière, Berlin, on 22.3.95.
32 Note by the Stasi dated 31.5.82.
33 Quoted in the Berlin magistrate's indictment of Johannes Weinrich for the bombing of the Maison de France, West Berlin, issued by the Staatsanwaltschaft bei dem Kammergericht on 3.12.95.

34 Direction de la Surveillance du Territoire, op. cit.
35 Ibid.
36 Vergès, *Le salaud lumineux*.
37 Weinrich's letter to Carlos, dated August 1983.
38 The plan is detailed in notes including a Stasi report dated May 1984.
39 Vergès has dismissed what he called a disinformation campaign by the Stasi. The idea of kidnapping Barbie was ridiculous, he said, adding, 'When I defend a client, I do it with complete devotion, whoever the client is.' Interview with Jacques Vergès broadcast on the television channel LCI (La Chaîne Info) on 27.8.94.
40 'The documents I had seized at Weinrich's home showed that Vergès wanted to bribe prison officials,' Stasi officer Borostowski said in his testimony to Judge Bruguière in Berlin on 22.3.95.
41 The plans are detailed in notes by the Stasi dated 17.8.83 and 7.5.84. According to the former 'Vergès was also busy organising the escape of the prisoners Kopp and Bréguet through the corruption of members of the prison personnel.' The second note says: 'According to manuscript notes which have been seized, the group worked to prepare the escape of Kopp, activities in which Vergès was totally implicated in supplying information on certain matters of detail. According to him, the escape of Kopp should thus take place during a medical consultation.'

9 LICENSED TO KILL

1 In the decade following de Marenches's departure, no fewer than five spymasters succeeded each other at the head of the DGSE.
2 Christine Ockrent and Alexandre de Marenches, *Dans le secret des princes* (Stock, Paris, 1986).
3 Alexandre de Marenches and David A. Andelman, *The*

Fourth World War: Diplomacy and Espionage in the Age of Terrorism (Morrow, New York, 1992).

4 Interview with Alexandre de Marenches published in *Le Nouvel Observateur* on 17.8.96.

5 The Gendarmerie Nationale is a police formation and is placed under the responsibility of the Defence Ministry.

6 Marcel Chalet and Thierry Wolton, *Les visiteurs de l'ombre* (Editions Grasset & Fasquelle, Paris, 1990).

7 Quoted in Pierre Favier and Michel Martin-Roland, *La décennie Mitterrand: 1. Les ruptures (1981–1984)* (Editions du Seuil, Paris, 1990).

8 Author interview with Pierre Marion on 21.10.96.

9 Ibid.

10 Pierre Marion, *La mission impossible, A la tête des Services Secrets* (Calmann-Levy, Paris, 1991).

11 Constantin Melnik, *La mort était leur mission, le Service Action pendant la guerre d'Algérie* (Plon, Paris, 1996).

12 Author interview with Admiral Pierre Lacoste on 5.3.97.

13 Author interview with Yves Bonnet on 22.10.96.

14 Ibid.

15 *Note à l'intention de Monsieur le Président* by Christian Prouteau, dated 11.1.83.

16 Duane R. Clarridge, *A Spy For All Seasons: My Life in the CIA* (Scribner, New York, 1997).

17 Marion, op. cit.

18 Author interview with Marion, 21.10.96.

19 Author interview with Bonnet, 22.10.96.

20 Ibid.

21 Author interview with Bonnet, 28.1.97.

22 Author interview with Bonnet, 22.10.96.

23 Testimony of Nabil Shritah to Judge Bruguière, Berlin, on 22.3.95.

24 Direction de la Surveillance du Territoire, Commissaire divisionaire Michel Guérin, *Rapport d'exécution de la commission rogatoire délivrée par le juge Jean-Louis Bruguière se rapportant à Marbeuf*, dated 3.10.95.

25 The results of the searches are described in reports by the Stasi dated 28.4.83 and 11.5.83.
26 Report by the Stasi dated 9.6.83.
27 Public prosecutor's office at Berlin appeal court, Indictment of Nabil Shritah for his involvement in the Maison de France bombing, dated 29.3.94.
28 Years later, Major Voigt protested before a Berlin court: 'I trusted Weinrich and believed his promises. He basely deceived me.' The judge sentenced him none the less to four years in jail as an accomplice to murder for ordering the explosives be handed back to Weinrich, an act which the verdict said amounted to 'a free rein to carry out the bombing'.
29 Letter from Johannes Weinrich to Carlos, sent from Belgrade and dated August 1983.

10 FORCED OUT OF THE COLD

1 Note by the Stasi dated 11.3.81.
2 Note by the Stasi dated 6.1.81. Another Stasi note refers to a payment to the Carlos group by the Libyans of 10,000 dinars.
3 Direction de la Surveillance du Territoire, Commissaire Divisionaire Michel Guérin, *Rapport d'exécution de la commission rogatoire delivrée par le juge Jean-Louis Bruguière se rapportant à Marbeuf*, 3.10.95.
4 Weinrich's letter to Carlos, August 1983.
5 Note in Weinrich's handwriting, dated 20.10.82.
6 Author interview with Markus Wolf on 29.9.97.
7 According to Jäckel, the policy of asylum continued partly because the Stasi officers did not see eye to eye on how best to follow instructions from the East German politburo. Jäckel testified: 'Dahl and I had different ideas ... Dahl, with his counter-espionage background, had established direct contacts [with Carlos's group]. In 1980 it had become very clear what kind of people were masquerading

as diplomats. That's why they had to be chased out. I considered the members of this group to be psychopaths, whom we must imperatively get rid of.' Jäckel's explanation however smacked of self-justification and there is little evidence in the Stasi files to back his claim. (Testimony of Günter Jäckel to Judge Bruguière, Berlin, on 22.3.95.)

8 Testimony of Jäckel, 22.3.95.
9 According to justice sources interviewed by the author, Kopp made the revelation to Berlin investigating magistrate Dieter Mehlis in December 1995.
10 Message by the Stasi sent on 7.2.84.
11 Report by the Stasi dated May 1984.
12 Author interview with Mark Palmer on 25.2.98.
13 Ibid.
14 Report by the Stasi dated 18.1.85.
15 Weinrich's letter to Carlos, August 1983.
16 Author interview with Yves Bonnet on 22.10.96.
17 Reuters, 17.8.94.
18 Author interview with Palmer, 25.2.98.
19 Mark Palmer served as US ambassador to Hungary from 1986 to 1990. 'I'm sure that I met Carlos's sponsors during this time,' Palmer said. 'I got to know senior intelligence officers and party leaders. But my information was that Carlos was no longer in Hungary.' Author interview with Palmer, 25.2.98.
20 Direction de la Surveillance du Territoire, op. cit.
21 Author interview with Wolf, 29.9.97.
22 Ibid.
23 Interview with Abu Nidal published by the *Middle East Review* in July 1978.
24 Note by the Stasi dated 21.5.85.
25 Note by the Stasi dated 16.4.82. It refers to the DGI officer only as 'Granados'.
26 Direction de la Surveillance du Territoire, op. cit.
27 Indictment of Johannes Weinrich for the bombing of the Maison de France drawn up by Berlin prosecutors,

Staatsanwaltschaft bei dem Kammergericht, dated 3.12.95.

28 Interview with Jacques Vergès published by *Le Monde* on 27.8.94.

29 Arrangements for the visit are detailed in Weinrich's letter to Carlos, August 1983. A note by the Stasi dated 7.8.86 confirms that Vergès's visit took place.

30 Brigade Criminelle, Inspecteur Divisionaire Daniel Aberard, *Enquête de CV concernant Ilich Ramírez Sánchez*, 22.5.95.

31 Interview with Carlos published by *Al Watan al Arabi* on 30.11.79.

32 Transcript of interview with François Genoud carried out by French writer Pierre Péan for his biography of Genoud, *L'extrémiste: François Genoud, de Hitler à Carlos* (Fayard, Paris, 1996).

33 Investigators believed at first that the bombing of the plane had been linked to the Popular Front for the Liberation of Palestine – General Command, led by Ahmed Jibril and based in Syria. But in 1981 the investigators blamed the regime of Libya's Colonel Qathafi when a microchip, part of the device that detonated the bomb, was found to be similar to those carried by Libyan intelligence officers arrested in February 1988 at Dakar airport in Senegal. The officers carried Semtex plastic and TNT explosives, weapons and detonators.

11 EXORCISING THE GHOST

1 Author interview with Jacques Fournet on 13.1.97.

2 Ibid.

3 Author interview with Françoise Rudetzki on 28.10.96.

4 The articles appeared in *L'Express* (December 1990) and in *Stern* (May 1991).

5 According to an article by Pierre Péan published in *Libération* on 28.11.91.

6 Brigade Criminelle, Inspecteur Divisionaire Daniel

Aberard, *Enquête de CV concernant Ilich Ramírez Sánchez*, 22.5.95.

7 Roy Elston, *The Traveller's Handbook for Egypt and the Sudan* (Simpkin, Marshall, London, 1929).

8 Human Rights Watch/Africa, *Sudan: New Islamic Penal Code Violates Basic Human Rights*, published on 9.4.91.

9 Amnesty International, *The Tears of Orphans: No Future Without Human Rights*, 1995.

10 Gáspár Biró, Special UN Rapporteur, *Situation of Human Rights in the Sudan*, submitted to the Commission on Human Rights on 30.1.95.

11 US State Department, *Patterns of Global Terrorism*, August 1993.

12 Jacques Vergès, *Intelligence avec l'ennemi: Conversations avec Jean-Louis Remilleux* (Editions Michel Lafon, Paris, 1994).

13 Duane R. Clarridge, *A Spy for All Seasons: My Life in the CIA* (Scribner, New York, 1997). Following charges that the CIA was involved in human rights abuses in Guatemala, and under pressure from Congress on the ethics of hiring 'unsavoury' agents, the agency cut ties over the next two years with more than a thousand quaintly named 'human assets' on the grounds that they were tainted by crimes (assassination, kidnappings and terrorism), human rights abuses and torture, or that they were just unproductive. A new guideline issued by CIA director John Deutch early in 1996 generally banned officers from hiring informants with a criminal record, although there was a loophole that senior officers could exploit if national security was deemed to be at stake.

14 Author interview with Fournet, 13.1.97.

15 Philippe Rondot, 'Du bon usage des services spéciaux', in *Politique Internationale*, autumn 1985.

16 Quoted under the alias 'Menuet' in Charles Villeneuve and Jean-Pierre Péret, *Histoire secrète du terrorisme: Les juges de l'impossible* (Plon, Paris, 1987).

17 The words of Yves Bonnet, in an interview with the author on 22.10.96.

18 Author interview with Duane R. Clarridge on 19.6.97.

19 Interview with Charles Pasqua published by *Paris-Match* on 25.8.94.

20 Author interview with Charles Pasqua on 7.3.97.

21 Claude Silberzahn with Jean Guisnel, *Au coeur du secret: 1500 jours aux commandes de la DGSE (1989–1993)* (Fayard, Paris, 1995).

22 Such bargaining by the French was nothing new. In 1990 President Mitterrand had similarly waited for a public holiday to release the Armenian Anis Naccache, who was serving a life sentence for trying to assassinate former Iranian Prime Minister Shapour Bakhtiar. It was part of a deal – brokered by Pasqua's Corsican lieutenant, Jean-Charles Marchiani – to obtain the release of three French hostages in Lebanon.

23 According to Richard Butcher, who was working with relief agencies in Khartoum and who had it edited, the film was made in June with the tacit consent of Carlos. Author interview with Richard Butcher on 25.3.97.

12 BETRAYAL AND REVENGE

1 Sources for the details of Carlos's capture include his own manuscript plea to the European Commission of Human Rights, Strasbourg, registered as plea number 28780/95 on 26.9.95; the Commission's ruling issued on 24.6.96; lawyer Mourad Oussedik's plea to the Chambre d'accusation de la cour d'appel de Paris.

2 Author interview with Charles Pasqua on 7.3.97.

3 Issued on 6.6.94, the warrant ordered Carlos's arrest for 'complicity in voluntary destruction ... having led to the death of one person ... homicide and voluntary blows and injuries' in the Rue Marbeuf bombing.

4 *Procès-verbal* drawn up by Commissaire Alain Poussel of

the Police Judiciaire, at 10.15 a.m. on 15.8.94.

5 Ibid.

6 Letter from Carlos to Judge Yves Corneloup, president of the Cour d'assizes de Paris, dated 23.9.97. The letter's schizophrenic author signed it twice: first as 'Carlos' and then, below, with a scrawl standing for Ramírez Sánchez.

7 *Procès-verbal* by Commissaire Eric Bellemin-Comte of the Police Judiciaire, at 13.30 p.m. on 15.8.94.

8 Author interview with Yves Bonnet on 22.10.96.

9 News conference by President Hassan Omar al-Bashir, Tripoli, on 1.9.94.

10 Author interview with Pasqua, 7.3.97.

11 According to a spokesman for the Popular Front as quoted by Reuters on 17.8.94.

12 Interview with Ramírez Navas published by *La Nacion* on 16.8.94.

13 Ibid. Ramírez Navas entreated the newspaper's envoy not to publish any of his remarks: 'Don't even say that you visited me. You weren't with me because I don't give interviews.' The newspaper published his comments over an entire page. 'He gave me his hand when we parted,' concluded the reporter. 'I smile at him and deeply regret that perhaps, after this is published, he won't give me a second opportunity because he beseeched me not to say anything and made a friend responsible that it should not happen.'

14 Testimony of Elba Maria Sánchez before Venezuelan investigating magistrates on 18.7.96, in the presence of Brigade Criminelle officers Hugues Saumet and Claude Legros, as detailed in their report dated 1.8.96 on their mission to Caracas.

15 Testimony of Vladimir Ramírez Sánchez before Venezuelan investigating magistrates on 15.7.96, op. cit.

16 Author interview with Jean-Louis Bruguière on 10.9.96.

17 Author interview with Jacques Fournet on 13.1.97.

18 Sources for Carlos's first exchanges with Judge Bruguière

include former Reuters court reporter Nathalie Prevost, who witnessed Carlos's arrival.

13 THE JACKAL CAGED

1 Author interview with an inmate at La Santé, who cannot be named under prison regulations, on 6.12.96.

2 According to former French state railways chief Loik Le Floch-Prigent, who after a six-month stint in La Santé for alleged corruption, told *Le Nouvel Observateur* in an interview published on 23.1.97: 'Prison is above all destructive of the individual and his dignity: my nights are haunted by the noises I heard over there, the worst of which are undoubtedly the howls of inmates, especially of the newcomers sodomised as soon as they arrived by their cell-mates, without our being able to intervene.'

3 Quoted in *Le Monde* on 5.4.97.

4 Author interview with Bob Denard on 30.9.96.

5 Author interview with Yves Tigoulet on 20.11.96.

6 Author interview with a warder at La Santé, who cannot be named under prison regulations, on 27.11.96.

7 Author interview with Jacques Vergès on 17.8.94.

8 The statement was published by *InfoMatin* on 30.8.94.

9 Ibid.

10 Author interview with Carlos through a third party obtained on 17.6.97.

11 Jacques Vergès, *Intelligence avec l'ennemi: Conversations avec Jean-Louis Remilleux* (Editions Michel Lafon, Paris, 1994).

12 Unpublished right of reply drafted by Carlos in answer to an article in *Le Point* (2.11.96), and made available to the author by his lawyers.

13 According to a report by Commissaire Caprioli of the DST dated 5.9.91: 'Her arrest probably prevented the carrying out of a bombing in France.'

14 Author interview with Antonio Vecchione, secretary to Italy's police chief, on 8.1.97.

15 Custody ruling by Chambre d'accusation de la cour d'appel de Paris, 30.9.96.
16 Interview with Magdalena Kopp published by *Stern* on 11.12.97.
17 The episode is described in a confidential report from La Santé governor Yves Tigoulet to Judge Bruguière dated 13.11.94, and published by *Le Point* on 21.1.95. The lawyer has said that she only pretended to sit on Carlos's knees, with two colleagues and a warder present, to protest against the lack of chairs.
18 Author interview with Isabelle Coutant-Peyre on 13.10.97.
19 'I absolutely do not believe that there was a will for a Final Solution to eliminate [the Jews],' Genoud told one interviewer. 'They were mobilised to work but they were not systematically killed ... I have the impression that when people were no longer productive, perhaps their departure was hastened. That is possible.' Transcript of interview with François Genoud carried out by Pierre Péan for his biography *L'extrémiste: François Genoud, de Hitler à Carlos* (Fayard, Paris, 1996).
20 According to Genoud, he delivered a message from Haddad to the headquarters of Lufthansa in Cologne. The company followed Haddad's instructions to the letter, and a Lufthansa representative met Haddad's envoys in Lebanon and handed over the ransom in exchange for the hijacked plane, a Boeing 747 which had taken off from New Delhi, and its 188 passengers. Transcript of interview with François Genoud, op. cit.
21 Interview with François Genoud published in *La Tribune de Genève* on 18.8.94.
22 The author is indebted to Pierre Péan, who was given Carlos's letters by François Genoud, for permission to quote from them. Carlos wrote the letters in longhand and in English.
23 Péan, op. cit.
24 Interview with Ramírez Navas published in *La Nacion* on

16.8.94. The journalist's name was Sophia Imier.

25 Interview with Luis Sánchez published in *El Pais* on 23.08.94. The sixty-two-year-old Sánchez, speaking of his cousin Carlos in the past tense as if in mourning after his capture, also testified: 'I never saw any criminal tendencies in him. Quite to the contrary. He spoke to me with bitterness of poverty and social injustice. He loved birds and flowers. He was gallant with women.'

26 Author interview with Jean-Paul Lévy on 24.7.97.

27 Author interview with Denard, 30.9.96.

28 Letter from Carlos's lawyer Frédéric Pariente sent on 2.12.96 to the Venezuelan consul, Paris.

29 Author interview with Lévy, 21.10.96.

30 Ruling by the Chambre d'accusation de la cour d'appel de Paris on 10.6.96.

31 Ibid.

14 THE TRIAL

1 Author interviews with Juror X in January and February 1998. The testimony is also based on a text written by Juror X for the author in January 1998.

2 Author interview with Gilles Dous on 18.12.97.

15 EPILOGUE

1 Letter from Carlos to Judge Yves Corneloup, president of the Cour d'assizes de Paris, dated 23.9.97.

2 As quoted by Jean-Paul Lévy in an interview with the author on 21.10.96.

3 According to a spokesman for Istvan Nikolits, the minister responsible for the civilian secret service, 'the handover of such documents [to foreign countries] is unusual in international practice and is not provided for in the bilateral legal aid agreement either.' Quoted by MTI news agency on 27.6.97.

4 Letter from Carlos to *Le Nouvel Observateur*, 5.6.97.
5 Claude Silberzahn and Jean Guisnel, *Au coeur du secret: 1500 jours aux commandes de la DGSE (1989–1993)* (Librairie Arthème Fayard, Paris, 1995).
6 Conference on terrorism *Europe horizon 2000: nouvelles menaces, nouveaux terrorismes*, organised by the International Group for Research and Information on Security, and the Paris Criminology Institute, Brussels, 28.11.96.
7 Author interview with one of Carlos's lawyers, who has refused to be named.
8 Interview with Carlos published by *Al Watan al Arabi* on 14.12.79.

Acknowledgements

When Carlos was seized in Sudan in August 1994 he was brought, courtesy of French counter-espionage, to within walking distance of where I was living in Paris. But the problems involved in trying to establish contact with him meant that he might as well have been on another planet. Buried in the isolation section of La Santé jail, Carlos was officially forbidden any contact with other prisoners or with visitors other than his lawyers, and his mail was censored by prison authorities.

French magistrates rejected my request for an interview with Carlos in jail, and seized a letter I wrote to him. 'By all means see whoever you want to see,' one anti-terrorism investigator told me, 'but I don't want anyone doing a parallel investigation.' When Carlos was informed of this through a third party, he drafted a reply to my (unseen) letter, sending his 'best revolutionary regards'. It took many months of lobbying, a copy of my first book, and oddly enough a curriculum vitae which Carlos had requested, to establish contact with him. Carlos's obsessive prudence, verging on paranoia, punctuated our exchanges. He seemed a sharp-minded but manipulative character whose egocentric nature led him to take offence quickly at anything he perceived as a slight.

I wish to thank the many people without whom this book could not have been written. I am deeply indebted to those who, at considerable risk to themselves, granted me access to the secret files of France's long-running investigations into the shootings and bombings that Carlos is accused of committing in this and other countries. These files amount to thousands of pages and include the testimony of Carlos himself, as well as that of his accomplices, friends, girlfriends and family. They also include reports by the French secret services which tracked him episodically over the years, and investigations by foreign police forces including Scotland Yard.

I am also very grateful to those who allowed me to consult the Cold War archives of the East German secret police, the Stasi. They are vital to retracing Carlos's career, and form a fascinating, virtually day-by-day snapshot of Carlos and his group in the years when they were based in East Germany, Hungary and other Soviet satellite states. Common to the defence of many who feature in the Stasi files is the argument that their contents cannot be blindly accepted as fact. But the officers who drafted the reports did so for their own superiors, often indicating whether what they wrote had been established beyond doubt, with no idea that one day their work would fall into the hands of Western intelligence agencies or be used in trials. Standard practice at the Stasi was to use a plethora of informers who did not know of each other's existence but whose assignments overlapped. Corroboration was provided by house searches, by hidden microphones and by telephone taps.

Carlos's capture loosened the tongues of many who had been on the receiving end of his threats, including members of the DST and of the Stasi. Many intelligence sources, several of whom agreed to be quoted on the record for the first time, gave me invaluable guidance. Virtually all the former DST chiefs who dealt with the Carlos file shared with me their time and confidence: Jacques Chartron, Bernard Gérard, Yves Bonnet and Jacques Fournet. Jean-Paul Mauriat and Jean Baklouti, who both headed the

DST's counter-terrorism section, shared their insiders' knowledge, and their criticisms of France's actions.

I also wish to thank several former chiefs of the French DGSE secret service: Pierre Marion, Admiral Pierre Lacoste, and Claude Silberzahn. General Alain de Gaigneron de Marolles, the former head of the clandestine Action Service, was of great assistance in recalling its operations. I am indebted to the association of retired DGSE officers for tracking down several former members of the service. Thanks also to Yves Bertrand, head of the Renseignements Généraux. I am particularly grateful to Duane R. Clarridge for lifting the veil on the CIA's attempt to have Carlos murdered. Serving members of MI6 were unwilling to be identified, but my thanks go in particular to the one who casually asked me at our first meeting: 'Do you know what I do?'

On the road to Berlin, Patrick Moreau gave me the benefit of his expertise on the Stasi. At the Gauck Commission responsible for the Stasi files, Johannes Legner and Tobias Wunschik both gave me much of their time. I am grateful to General Markus Wolf for agreeing to talk about Carlos in more detail than he had previously done. Those in Berlin who helped me, but declined to have their names published, also deserve my gratitude.

In Paris, many of the lawyers hired by Carlos after his capture (several have since been fired) were willing to talk about their client: Mourad Oussedik and his colleague Martine Tigrane, Antoine Comte, Isabelle Coutant-Peyre, François Honorat, Olivier Maudret, and Frédéric Pariente. I am also grateful to Magdalena Kopp's lawyer Manuel Mayer, and to Christa-Margot Froelich's former attorney Jean-Jacques de Felice.

Françoise Rudetzki, president of the victims association SOS Attentats (SOS Attacks), and the association's lawyer Jean-Paul Lévy both dedicated much time to me. Several relatives of Carlos's victims, in particular Jean-Noël

Herranz and Gilles Dous, were willing to recall painful events. Kirill Privalov described his university years as a contemporary of Ilich Ramírez Sánchez, and Walid Abou Zahr, the editor of *Al Watan al Arabi*, shared memories of Carlos's bombing of his magazine, and granted me permission to quote from its interview with Carlos.

This book would have been the poorer without the help of many who served in the administrations of Presidents Valéry Giscard d'Estaing and François Mitterrand. I am particularly grateful to Giscard d'Estaing for making an exception to his rule that he never gives interviews to writers. Charles Pasqua, the former Interior Minister, Gilles Ménage, the former head of Mitterrand's private office, and Hubert Védrine, formerly diplomatic adviser to Mitterrand and secretary-general at the Elysée Palace, all gave me precious leads. At the Defence Ministry, I am grateful to Pierre Conesa, Nathalie Fustier and Cécile Jolly. Officials of the Foreign Ministry, who have declined to be identified, were also helpful. In Washington, Mark Palmer, formerly of the State Department, described with delight the occasion on which he upbraided Soviet bloc ambassadors for protecting Carlos.

Of the investigating magistrates who have dealt or still deal with the Carlos case, I must thank Jean-Louis Bruguière, Alain Marsaud and Irène Stoller. At the Brigade Criminelle, Pierre Ottavioli recalled the various times he had followed in Carlos's footsteps. I must also thank Daniel Aberard, who prepared a biography of Carlos for the investigating magistrates, Jacques Poinas, head of the inter-ministerial anti-terrorism body Uclat, and, across the Channel, a member of Scotland Yard's counter-terrorism unit.

I am grateful to Pierre Pédron at the Justice Ministry, Yves Tigoulet, the governor of La Santé jail, and his deputy André Varignan, for a long and detailed tour of the prison which included conversations with Carlos's guards. Thanks also to one of Carlos's former fellow inmates, Captain Bob

Denard, and to two other prisoners who cannot be named here.

Many people helped me to track down the rare footage which has been filmed of Carlos. I am grateful to Véronique Lambert de Guise at Kuiv Productions, Camille Michel at Arte, Cyril Lollivier at France 2, Joël François-Dumont at France 3, and Richard Butcher. I also have staff at several institutions and publications to thank, including Nicolas Gleizal at the Institut des Hautes Etudes de Sécurité Intérieure (IHESI), the periodicals section of the Bibliothèque Nationale de France, the library of the Centre Georges Pompidou, Françoise Lauters at the clippings library of *L'Express*, the archive department of the *Guardian*, the Council of Europe, the International Group for Research and Information on Security, Fabio Riccardi at the Communità di Sant'Egidio, Médecins Sans Frontières, Amnesty International, the International Federation of Human Rights Leagues, and Human Rights Watch. I am also grateful to Lee Silverman of the El Al press office and Charlotte Smith of the Marks and Spencer archive.

Pierre Péan allowed me to use extracts from letters sent by Carlos to François Genoud. Péan also gave me the transcript of the interviews with Genoud he carried out before the latter's death. Among my own colleagues I must also thank Robert Fisk, Antoine Glaser, Cristina Gonzàlez de Rodrìguez, Serge Grangé, Tim Livesey, Xavier Raufer, William José Vivas Cano and Mary Yates. Several friends and colleagues helped me with translations, including Lauren Taylor who kindly dedicated many hours to the task, Giampaolo Cadalanu and Elidar Zolia.

Colleagues and friends at Reuters were exceptionally generous. Bernard Edinger, John Morrison and Sydney Weiland recalled their coverage of the OPEC raid in Vienna and its epilogue in Algiers. Thierry Lévèque was a great help in guiding me through the French legal labyrinth, while Christian Curtenelle led me through the police establishment. Irwin Arieff and François Raitberger both gave me very useful advice during Carlos's trial. David Cutler tracked down material and verified facts, Wilfrid Exbrayat was a constant source of encouragement and suggestions, and Tony Mora recalled the attacks at Orly airport. I must also thank François Duriaud at Reuters in Paris for encouraging me in this project at a very early stage, and Izabel Grindal and David Rogers for letting me off the hook early so that I could devote more time to the book. Similarly, Peter Greiff and Fred Kapner granted me extra time to pursue this project.

Ion Trewin and Ravi Mirchandani, my publishers at Weidenfeld and Nicolson, showed great enthusiasm from very early days, and I am grateful for the professionalism and patience which they demonstrated in turning the manuscript into a book at impressive speed. My thanks also to Rachel Leyshon, Elsbeth Lindner, Roy Furness, Isabel Best, Valerie Duff and Morag Lyall. Arthur Goodhart, my agent, championed the project from day one, and painstakingly worked his way through several drafts of the manuscript with heart-warming zeal.

I am very thankful to family and friends who gave me support and hospitality during the research and writing of this book, and who made valuable suggestions on the manuscript. The fear that Carlos still inspires despite his imprisonment means that many of those who helped me cannot be identified, but my gratitude to them is undiminished. To one person in particular I owe more than words can say.

Paris, May 1997 – Rome, May 1998

Bibliography

FRENCH AND FOREIGN OFFICIAL AND OTHER DOCUMENTS

Files of the judicial, police and secret service investigations into the Rue Toullier shootings, including:

Brigade Criminelle, Inspecteur Divisionaire Daniel Aberard, *Enquête de CV concernant Ilich Ramírez Sánchez*, 22.5.95

Brigade Criminelle, Commissaire Divisionaire Pierre Ottavioli, *Procès-verbal* summing up the first stage of the investigation sent to the Paris public prosecutor's office on 27.6.75

Brigade Criminelle, Commissaire Divisionaire Pierre Ottavioli, *Procès-verbal* on the search of the flat at 11bis Rue Amélie by the DST, 4.7.75

Brigade Criminelle, Commissaire Guido Spiessens, *Procès-verbal* on testimony of Leyma Palomares, 28.6.75

Brigade Criminelle, Inspecteur Marc Terrasson, *Compte-rendu de commission rogatoire en Grande-Bretagne*, 21.7.75

Cour d'appel de Paris, Tribunal de grande instance de Paris, *Réquisitoire définitif de transmission des pièces au Procureur Général*, 7.1.91

Cour d'appel de Paris, Deuxième chambre d'accusation, *Arrêt prononcé en chambre du conseil le 9 juillet 1991.* The ruling ordered Carlos to stand trial before the Cour d'assises de Paris

Cour de sûreté de l'état, *Procès-verbal* on testimony of Angela

Armstrong to investigating magistrate Judge Christian Gallut on 25.7.75

Cour de sûreté de l'état, *Procès-verbal* on testimony of Amparo Silva Masmela to Judge Gallut, 30.7.75

Direction de la Surveillance du Territoire (DST), *L'affaire Moukharbal-Carlos*, August 1975

Direction de la Surveillance du Territoire, Commissaire Principal Jean Herranz, *Procès-verbal* on testimony of Michel Moukharbal, 22.6.97

Direction de la Surveillance du Territoire, Sous-directeur Jean-Paul Mauriat, *A propos de l'affaire Carlos*, undated

Police Judiciaire, Inspecteur Michel Calvet, *Procès-verbal* on testimony of Edgar Marino-Muller, 28.6.75

Police Judiciaire, Inspecteur Jean Laffargue, *Procès-verbal* on testimony of Luis Urdaneta Urbina, 28.6.75

Police Judiciaire, Dr Le Breton, *Rapport d'examen du sang-dosage de l'alcool*, 30.6.75

Police Judiciaire, Inspecteur Gérard Loir, *Rapport d'autopsies sur les corps de Michel Moukharbal, Jean Donatini, et Raymond Dous*, 28.6.75

Police Judiciaire, Section technique de recherches et d'investigations de l'identité judiciaire, Inspecteur Jacque Imbert, report, 28.7.75

Police Nationale, Officier Bernard Lefevre, *Procès-verbal* on testimony of Olivier Martel, 28.6.75

Police Nationale, Commissaire Daniel Marcout, *Procès-verbal* on scene of Rue Toullier shootings, 27.6.75

Scotland Yard, SO13 anti-terrorism branch, *Preliminary report by Detective Inspector David Cooper after international rogatory letter from Judge Jean-Louis Bruguière dated 22.5.95 and sent by the Brigade Criminelle and the Police Judiciaire*, 7.7.95. This report includes *Statement of witness Lynn Simmonds* (12.7.95) and *Statement of witness Hillary Cowan* (11.7.75).

Scotland Yard, *Statement of witness Ann Ellen Hamburger*, taken by Detective Sergeant Fickling, 15.7.75

Scotland Yard, *Statement of witness Igor Rodor*, taken by Detective Constable Phillips, 16.7.75

EM2 (Home Office) Branch, Forensic Explosives Laboratory, *PP.6985. Explosives recovered from 24B Hereford Road, W2, on 1st July 1975*

Files of the investigations into the Rue Marbeuf bombing, including:

Brigade Criminelle, Inspecteur Divisionaire Hugues Saumet, *Compte-rendu d'interrogations par le juge Jean-Louis Bruguière* on testimony of former Stasi officers Helmut Voigt, Harry Dahl, Günter Jäckel, Eberhard Kind and Wilhelm Borostowski, and of Nabil Shritah, dated 20.4.95

Cour d'appel de Paris, Judge Yves Corneloup, Report on the investigation into the Rue Marbeuf bombing to the public prosecutor at the Parquet du tribunal de grande instance de Paris, dated 15.9.87

Cour d'appel de Paris, Chambre d'accusation, *Réquisitoire* on bombing of *Capitole* train, dated 16.9.94

Direction de la Surveillance du Territoire, *Etat des investigations de la DST sur les récents attentats terroristes*, August 1982

Direction de la Surveillance du Territoire, *Rapport sur François Genoud*, dated 22.3.95

Direction de la Surveillance du Territoire, Commissaire Caprioli, *Rapport* on C79 files of Hungarian intelligence, sent to Paris public prosecutors on 28.8.91

Direction de la Surveillance du Territoire, Inspecteur-Général Jean-François Clair, *Synthèse des éléments relatifs à Marbeuf*, 3.6.94

Direction de la Surveillance du Territoire, Commissaire divisionaire Michel Guérin, *Rapport d'exécution de la commission rogatoire delivrée par le juge Jean-Louis Bruguière se rapportant à Marbeuf*, dated 3.10.95

Files of the judicial investigations into the Maison de France bombing, including:

Staatsanwaltschaft bei dem Kammergericht, Berlin, Indictment of Nabil Shritah, dated 29.3.94

Staatsanwaltschaft bei dem Kammergericht, Berlin, Indictment of Johannes Weinrich, dated 3.12.95

Documents on Carlos's capture:

Chambre d'accusation de la cour d'appel de Paris, Ruling on Carlos's plea that he was kidnapped, 10.6.96

Police Judiciaire, Commissaire Eric Bellemin-Comte, *Procès-verbal*, 15.8.94

Police Judiciaire, Commissaire Alain Poussel, *Procès-verbal*, 15.8.94

Ilich Ramírez Sánchez, Plea filed to the European Commission of Human Rights, registered by the Commission on 26.9.95 as plea number 28780/95

European Commission of Human Rights, Ruling dated 24.6.96, on plea number 28780/95 filed by Ilich Ramírez Sánchez

On Sudan:

Amnesty International, *Sudan: 'The Tears of Orphans': No Future Without Human Rights* (London, 1995)

Gáspár Bíró, Special UN Rapporteur, *Situation of Human Rights in the Sudan*, submitted to the Commission on Human Rights, New York, on 30.1.95

Human Rights Watch/Africa, *Sudan: New Islamic Penal Code Violates Basic Human Rights* (New York, 1991)

US State Department, *Patterns of Global Terrorism* (Washington, August 1993)

Other documents:

Austrian government, *Die Vorfälle vom 21 und 22 Dezember 1975 (Überfall auf die Teilnehmer der OPEC-Konferenz)*, published in the wake of the Vienna raid

Brigade Criminelle, Commandant Hugues Saumet and Capitaine Claude Legros, *Procès-verbal* on testimony of Vladimir Ramírez Sánchez in questioning by investigating magistrates in Caracas, Venezuela, on 15.7.96, dated 1.8.96

Brigade Criminelle, Commandant Hugues Saumet and Capitaine Claude Legros, *Procès-verbal* on testimony of Elba Maria Sánchez in questioning by investigating magistrates in Caracas, Venezuela, on 18.7.96, dated 1.8.96

Correspondence of Ilich Ramírez Sánchez, including letters to François Genoud, Judge Yves Corneloup, his lawyers and the author

Ministerium für Staatssicherheit (Stasi), Section XXII, Files including letters and notes in handwriting of Ilich Ramírez Sánchez and Johannes Weinrich, from 1978 to 1989

New Scotland Yard, SO13 anti-terrorism branch, *Report by Detective Inspector David Cooper on case papers referring to attempted murder of Joseph Edward Sieff*, dated 29.8.96

Testimony of Ilich Ramírez Sánchez to Judge Jean-Louis Bruguière since 15.8.94. This includes *Procès-verbal d'interrogatoires de Curriculum Vitae*, dated 28.10.94, 15.11.94 and 19.12.94

Tobias Wunschik, *Die Hauptabteilung XXII: 'Terrorabwehr'*, Der Bundesbeauftragte für die Unterlagen des Staatssicherheitsdienstes der ehemaligen Deutschen Demokratischen Republik (Berlin, 1995)

BOOKS

Abu-Sharif, Bassam, and Mahnaimi, Uzi, *Tried by Fire: The Searing True Story of Two Men at the Heart of the Struggle between the Arabs and the Jews* (Warner Books, London, 1995)

Atlas mondial de l'Islam activiste (La Table Ronde, Paris, 1991)

Attali, Jacques, *Verbatim I 1981–1983* (Fayard, Paris, 1993)

Attali, Jacques, *Verbatim I Deuxième partie 1981–1983* (Fayard, Paris, 1993)

Attali, Jacques, *Verbatim II 1986–1988* (Fayard, Paris, 1995)

Attali, Jacques, *Verbatim III 1988–1991* (Fayard, Paris, 1995)

Barril, Paul, *Guerres secrètes à l'Elysée 1981–1995* (Albin Michel, Paris, 1996)

Barril, Paul, *Missions très spéciales* (Presses de la Cité, Paris, 1984)

Baud, Jacques, *Encyclopédie du renseignement et des services secrets* (Lavauzelle, Paris, 1997)

Boltanski, Christophe, and el-Tahri, Jihan, *Les sept vies de Yasser Arafat* (Bernard Grasset, Paris, 1997)

Boukovsky, Vladimir, *Jugement à Moscou: Un dissident dans les archives du Kremlin* (Laffont, Paris, 1995)

Bower, Tom, *Klaus Barbie: Butcher of Lyons* (Corgi, London, 1985)

Bresler, Fenton, *Interpol* (Presses de la Cité, Paris, 1993)

Brogan, Patrick, *Eastern Europe 1939–1989: The Fifty Years War* (Bloomsbury, London, 1990)

Broussard, Commissaire, *Mémoires* (Plon, Paris, 1997)

Burdan, Daniel, *DST: Neuf ans à la division antiterroriste* (Robert Laffont, Paris, 1990)

Carton, Daniel, *Pasqua* (Flammarion, Paris, 1995)

Chalet, Marcel, and Wolton, Thierry, *Les visiteurs de l'ombre* (Grasset, Paris, 1990)

Childs, David, and Popplewell, Richard, *The Stasi: The East German Intelligence and Security Service* (Macmillan, London, 1996)

Clarridge, Duane R., *A Spy for All Seasons: My Life in the CIA* (Scribner, New York, 1997)

Cobban, Helena, *The Making of Modern Lebanon* (Hutchinson, London, 1985)

Dobson, Christopher, and Payne, Ronald, *The Carlos Complex* (Coronet, London, 1978)

Dobson, Christopher, and Payne, Ronald, *The Dictionary of Espionage* (Harrap, London, 1984)

Etienne, Genovefa, and Moniquet, Claude, *Histoire de l'espionnage mondial: les services secrets de Ramsès II à nos jours* (Editions du Félin, Paris, 1997)

Faligot, Roger, and Krop, Pascal, *La piscine: Les services secrets français 1944–1984* (Seuil, Paris, 1985)

Faligot, Roger, and Kauffer, Rémi, *Histoire mondiale du renseignement* (Robert Laffont, Paris, 1994)

Favier, Pierre, and Martin-Roland, Michel, *La décennie Mitterrand 1. Les ruptures 1981–1984* (Seuil, Paris, 1990)

Favier, Pierre, and Martin-Roland, Michel, *La décennie Mitterrand 2. Les épreuves 1984–1988* (Seuil, Paris, 1991)

Favier, Pierre, and Martin-Roland, Michel, *La décennie Mitterrand 3. Les défis 1988–1991* (Seuil, Paris, 1996)

Foccart, Jacques, *Foccart parle: Entretiens avec Philippe Gaillard* (Fayard/Jeune Afrique, Paris, 1997)

Forsyth, Frederick, *The Day of the Jackal* (Viking, London, 1971)

Giscard d'Estaing, Valéry, *Le pouvoir et la vie* (Compagnie 12, Paris, 1988)

Gowers, Andrew, and Walker, Tony, *Behind the Myth: Yassar Arafat and the Palestinian Revolution* (Corgi, London, 1991)

Greilsamer, Laurent, *Interpol: Policiers sans frontières* (Fayard, Paris, 1997)

Greilsamer, Laurent, and Schneidermann, Daniel, *Les juges parlent* (Fayard, Paris, 1992)

Guisnel, Jean, *Les généraux: Enquête sur le pouvoir militaire en France* (La Découverte, Paris, 1990)

Guisnel, Jean, and Violet, Bernard, *Services secrets* (La Découverte, Paris, 1988)

Hamon, Alain, and Marchand, Jean-Charles, *P ... comme police* (Alain Moreau, Paris, 1983)

Hart, Alan, *Arafat: Terrorist or Peacemaker?* (Sidgwick and Jackson, London, 1987)

Hoy, Claire, and Ostrovsky, Victor, *By Way of Deception: A Devastating Insider's Portrait of the Mossad* (Stoddart, Toronto, 1990)

Jacquard, Roland, *Les Dossiers secrets du terrorisme: Tueurs sans frontières* (Albin Michel, Paris, 1985)

Jacquard, Roland, and Nasplèzes, Dominique, *Carlos: Le dossier secret* (Jean Picollec, Paris, 1993)

Klein, Hans-Joachim, *La mort mercenaire: Témoignage d'un ancien terroriste ouest-allemand* (Seuil, Paris, 1980)

Kostine, Sergueï, *Bonjour, Farewell: La vérité sur la taupe française du KGB* (Laffont, Paris, 1997)

Krop, Pascal, *Les secrets de l'espionnage français de 1870 à nos jours* (JC Lattès, Paris, 1993)

Laske, Karl, *Le banquier noir* (Seuil, Paris, 1996)

Laughland, John, *The Death of Politics: France under Mitterrand* (Penguin, London, 1995)
Levergeois, Pierre, *J'ai choisi la DST: Souvenirs d'un inspecteur* (Flammarion, Paris, 1978)
Lieuwen, Edwin, *Venezuela* (Oxford University Press, London, 1965)
Liszkai, László, *Carlos à l'abri du rideau de fer* (Seuil, Paris, 1992)
Madelin, Philippe, *La galaxie terroriste* (Plon, Paris, 1986)
de Marenches, Alexandre and Andelman, David A., *The Fourth World War: Diplomacy and Espionage in the Age of Terrorism* (Morrow, New York, 1992)
Marion, Pierre, *La mission impossible: A la tête des Services Secrets* (Calmann-Lévy, Paris, 1991)
Médecins Sans Frontières, *Face aux crises* . . . (Hachette, Paris, 1993)
Meier, Stephan Richard, *Carlos: Demaskierung eines Topterroristen* (Knaur, Munich, 1992)
Melman, Yossi, *The Master Terrorist: The True Story Behind Abu Nidal* (Sidgwick and Jackson, London, 1986)
Montagnon, Pierre, *42, rue de la Santé: Une prison politique 1867–1968* (Pygmalion/Gérard Watelet, Paris, 1996)
Niedergang, Marcel, *The 20 Latin Americas* (Penguin, London, 1971)
Observatoire international des prisons, *Le guide du prisonnier* (Editions de l'Atelier/Editions Ouvrières, Paris, 1996)
Ockrent, Christine, and de Marenches, Comte Alexandre, *Dans le secret des princes* (Stock, Paris, 1986)
Ó Maolàin, Ciarán, *Latin American Political Movements* (Longman, London, 1985)
Ottavioli, Pierre, *Echec au crime: 30 ans 'quai des Orfèvres'* (Grasset, Paris, 1985)
Pasqua, Charles, *Que demande le peuple* . . . (Albin Michel, Paris, 1992)
Péan, Pierre, *L'extrémiste: François Genoud, de Hitler à Carlos* (Fayard, Paris, 1996)

Péan, Pierre, *Vol UT 772: Contre-enquête sur un attentat attribué à Kadhafi* (Stock, Paris, 1992)

Phillips, David, *Skyjack: The Story of Air Piracy* (Harrap, London, 1973)

Poniatowski, Michel, *L'avenir n'est écrit nulle part* (Albin Michel, Paris, 1978)

Poniatowski, Michel, *Lettre ouverte au Président de la République* (Albin Michel, Paris, 1983)

Pontaut, Jean-Marie, *L'Attentat: Le juge Bruguière accuse la Libye* (Fayard, Paris, 1992)

Porch, Douglas, *The French Secret Services: From the Dreyfus Affair to the Gulf War* (Macmillan, London, 1996)

Quadruppani, Serge, *L'anti-terrorisme en France ou La terreur intégrée 1981–1989* (La Découverte, Paris, 1989)

Raufer, Xavier, *La Nébuleuse: Le terrorisme du Moyen-Orient* (Fayard, Paris, 1987)

Rondot, Philippe, 'Du bon usage des services spéciaux', in *Politique Internationale* (Politique Internationale, Paris, n° 29 – 1985)

Rondot, Philippe, *La Syrie* (Presses Universitaires de France, Paris, 1993)

Sablier, Edouard, *Le fil rouge: Histoire secrète du terrorisme international* (Plon, Paris, 1983)

Schmaldienst, Fritz, and Matschke, Klaus-Dieter, *Carlos-Komplize Weinrich: Die internationale Karriere eines deutschen Top-Terroristen* (Eichborn, 1995)

Silberzahn, Claude, and Guisnel, Jean, *Au coeur du secret: 1500 jours aux commandes de la DGSE 1989–1993* (Fayard, Paris, 1995)

Smith, Colin, *Carlos: Portrait of a Terrorist* (Mandarin, London, 1995)

Thyraud de Vosjoli, Philippe, *Lamia* (Little, Brown, London, 1970)

Tobon, Nydia, *Carlos: terrorista o guerrillero* (Grijalbo, Barcelona, 1978)

Védrine, Hubert, *Les mondes de François Mitterrand: A l'Elysée 1981–1995* (Fayard, Paris, 1996)

Vergès, Jacques, *Intelligence avec l'ennemi* (Michel Lafon, Paris, 1994)

Vergès, Jacques, *Le salaud lumineux* (Editions numéro 1/Michel Lafon, Paris, 1990)

Villeneuve, Charles, and Péret, Jean-Pierre, *Histoire secrète du terrorisme: Les juges de l'impossible* (Plon, Paris, 1987)

Violet, Bernard, *Carlos: Les réseaux du terrorisme international* (Seuil, Paris, 1996)

Wieviorka, Michel, *Face au terrorisme* (L.Levi, Paris, 1995)

Wolf, Markus, with McElvoy, Anne, *Man Without a Face: The Autobiography of Communism's Greatest Spymaster* (Jonathan Cape, London, 1997)

Yallop, David, *To the Ends of the Earth: The Hunt for the Jackal* (Jonathan Cape, London, 1993)

Index